NEOPLATONISM AND NATURE

NEOPLATONISM AND NATURE

Studies in Plotinus' *Enneads*

Michael F. Wagner, Editor

INTERNATIONAL SOCIETY FOR NEOPLATONIC STUDIES

Volume 8 in *Studies in Neoplatonism: Ancient and Modern*
R. Baine Harris, General Editor

STATE UNIVERSITY OF NEW YORK PRESS

Published by
State University of New York Press, Albany

Printed in the United States of America

For information, address State University of New York Press,
90 State Street, Suite 700, Albany, NY 12207

Production by Michael Haggett
Marketing by Fran Keneston

Library of Congress Cataloging-in-Publication Data

Neoplatonism and nature / studies in Plotinus' Enneads / Michael F. Wagner, editor.
p. cm. — (Studies in Neoplatonism; v. 8)
Includes bibliographical references and indexes.
ISBN 0-7914-5271-9 (alk. paper). — ISBN 0-7914-5272-7 (pbk. : alk. paper)
1. Neoplatonism. 2. Plotinus. Enneads. I. Wagner, Michael F., 1952–
II. Series.

B645.N465 2001
186'.4—dc21 2001049175

10 9 8 7 6 5 4 3 2 1

CONTENTS

PREFACE

R. Baine Harris

Those who dismiss Neoplatonism as only a form of religious mysticism are often not aware that Plotinus does have a fairly well defined philosophy of science. It is not a philosophy of science in the modern sense of an explicit treatment of the specific philosophical basis of each natural science and its problems, but he does have a systematic philosophyof nature. If we were to stretch the meaning of the term a bit, he could even be labeled a naturalist. He once said "All things there are here." His philosophy of nature is an effort to look at natural phenomena and imagine what sort of structure must be behind it. As such, it is not derived solely from thinking about our experiences of nature, but is rather a rational proposal of the hypothetical nature of that which is behind what we see in nature. It is a generic philosophy of science that is not limited to the limits of science and thus is not restricted to any particular conception of science or any particular scientific conceptions. Even though it is about the natural universe of science, it is philosophy, not science.

Plotinus was an unqualified monist. He was not really an idealist, at least not in the sense that Hegel and the German and British Post-Hegelian uses the term, even though he does affirm the immateriality of the One, the ultimate source of all nature and being. Only the One, however, is strictly immaterial. Principles of being have a certain materiality. Every living thing is a soul; and souls are mainly principles of material bodies. Nothing in his philosophy precludes an empirical consideration of natural phenomena, even though he cannot be called an empiricist.

The essays in this volume were specially commissioned by the general editor some twelve years ago and this book has been ten years in the making. Two of the writers, Ronald F. Hathaway and Reiner Schurmann have died in the meantime. All of the writers are recognized scholars of Neoplatonism with other publications in the field.

The purpose of the volume is to show that Plotinus does have a *de facto* philosophy of the nature and role of science embedded in what he has to say about the nature of the natural universe, albeit not a modern one. In contrast to those in the other volumes of this series, these essays were not presented at one of the international conferences of the International Society for Neoplatonic Studies. In the main they constitute an analysis of the Plotinian view of the nature of nature, rather than a consideration of the impact that the Neoplatonic conception of nature has had in the development of Western science and philosophy, a project that still very much needs to be done.

Old Dominion University
September, 1995

We wish especially to acknowledge and thank Vivian Holland and Monica Wagner in the College of Arts & Sciences' manuscript office at the University of San Diego for their expert work in preparing this volume for publication. [Ed.]

INTRODUCTION

Michael F. Wagner

The essays in this volume explicate main features of Plotinus' understanding of the natural universe set forth in his collected treatises, the *Enneads*, as they relate to his Neoplatonic approach to understanding existence and reality—as they relate, in other words, to his metaphysics. A recurring theme here pays special attention to features of Plotinus' philosophy of Nature which are also pertinent to the history and philosophy of science. Ronald Hathaway initiates this theme by examining several discussions in the Enneads of natural phenomena in terms of two notions commonly associated with natural science: that the material universe in uniform with respect to the results of natural science, whose methodology involves an interplay between observation and theoretic conjecture and innovation.

This latter notion also serves as one way to address whether Plotinus' Neoplatonic approach and metaphysics comports with science as an ongoing activity or discipline; in other words, whether Plotinus' own philosophy of Nature may legitimately be counted among those associated with the emergence and development of natural science. Jonathan Lee parses this variation on the theme in terms of the degree of independence and(or) dependence which Plotinus' Neoplatonism accords natural science *vis-a-vis* metaphysics and he especially examines relationships between certain of Plotinus' metaphysical (or 'dialectical') conceptions and his understanding of physical things and processes.

Inasmuch as a number of those conceptions have a vitalistic dimension and etymology, Anthony Preus next considers features of Plotinus' understanding of the natural universe which pertain specifically to biological science. In so doing, he examines similarities and differences between a properly Plotinian approach to understanding biological phenomena or processes and the Aristotelian approach, and ways in which Plotinian vitalism may be conceptually related to the evolutionary perspective commonly associated with the emergence of biology as a distinct science.

Scientific explanation and natural laws are fundamental topics in the philosophy of science. Natural essence and causality, in turn, are fundamental topics in the historical development of scientific conceptions of explanation and lawfulness. Accordingly, Lloyd Gerson examines Plotinus' (re)conception of the Platonic image-relation between natural existents and their metaphysical causes, or archetypes, especially *vis-a-vis* the notion associated with Aristotelianism known as *essentialism*; and, Sara Rappe considers more thematically various notions of causality in establishing the significance and meaning of Plotinus' related doctrine that the real existence of individual things or processes depends upon the metaphysically singular 'descent' of the natural universe from its archetype.

In the first of his two essays in this volume, Gary Gurtler explicates further key texts in the Enneads pertaining to Plotinian archetypal (or, archetypically lawful) causality, especially as it relates to the Platonic conceit that Nature is a moving image of eternity and to the Hellenistic notion of Providence, as this notion was introduced into scientific discourse by Stoic philosophers. The contrast between Plotinus' conception of Providence and the Stoics' is also highlighted by the fact that it was the latter conception which emerged in Early Modern philosopher-scientists' understanding of the natural universe as a deterministic system. Laura Westra thus discusses the place and meaning of freedom in Plotinus' philosophy, including its relation to his conception of Providence, and she also examines its significance for Plotinus' related understanding of human beings as persons and as moral agents.

In addition to notions of causality and lawfulness, the historical development of natural science owes much to at least three other features of classical Greek thought: its application, especially in the Pythagorean and Platonic traditions, of mathematical concepts to Nature; its notion of a minimal set of explanatory or causative principles and the possibility even of a single first-principle of all reality, including Nature; and its notion(s) of matter, or a material principle. Accordingly, Aphrodite Alexandrakis explores Plotinus' use (and modification) of certain Pythagorean conceptions in his own understanding of the natural universe; Reiner Schurmann explicates the nature and function of Plotinus' first-principle of reality (the One) in what he argues is more properly termed Plotinus' *henology*; and William Carroll examines the main texts in the *Enneads* where Plotinus discusses the notion of matter, its nature and(or) function and whether it is a real principle.

These (and previous) essays attest, moreover, to the subtlety and originality of Plotinus' Neoplatonism and his cognizance of previous philosophers and traditions. In this regard, two additional major features of Plotinus' understanding of Nature are his critique of Aristotelian categorial theory, explicated here by Christos Evangeliou; and his adaptation, examined next by Gary Gurtler, of the (Stoic) notion of *sympathy* as his primary conceptual nexus for relating natural phenomena and causal processes to his Neoplatonic understanding of existence and reality. In this volume's final essay, I offer additional historical considerations regarding the relationship between natural science and metaphysics; and I examine the special place in Plotinus' understanding of Nature of dynamic conceptions related to the classical Greek notion of *becoming* as well as Plotinus' special place in the history of responses to Skepticism, a history which also shaped and defined much of the history of scientific thought itself.

Of course, this thematic introduction hardly does justice to the wealth of issues, materials, ideas, and explicative details to be found in the essays comprising this volume.

PLOTINUS AND THE POSSIBILITY OF NATURAL SCIENCE

Ronald F. Hathaway

Is there room for natural science in the philosophy of Plotinus? The question has seldom, if ever, been raised.[1] There are two obvious general reasons for this. The first is the inferior role assigned to matter and the sensible realm by Plotinus, with obvious negative implications for any empirical science. The second is the general absence of natural science in those cultures in which Plotinian Platonism flourished. Some would argue that the question of natural science in Plotinus is pointless because Plotinus' metaphysics reduces to a form of mysticism, and mysticism and natural science are incompatible.[2] A view more worthy of our attention could be inferred from Duhem's claim that it is impossible to derive all the elements needed for the construction of a physical theory from a purely metaphysical system.[3] If Duhem's principle is correct, and if Plotinus' philosophy is in fact a purely metaphysical system, then no definite natural science could be derived from it. Duhem's principle can be regarded as a circumspect formulation of an old suspicion that all ancient philosophies are attempts to derive physical theories from metaphysical principles.[4]

This suspicion is not without substance; however, recent work in the philosophy of science compels us to reappraise the basis of the suspicion itself. The search for epistemological and metaphysical foundations of scientific theories is now seen as being so central in the history of philosophy that Frederick Suppe can say that the history of epistemology and metaphysics is the history of the philosophy of science.[5] It is challenging to extend the application of Suppe's opinion from the modern era which he clearly has in mind to the history of ancient philosophy. Recent research in ancient physical theory, on Plato's theory of elements, on Aristotle's embryology and animal kinesiology, and on Stoic physics has uncovered an interplay between ancient physical theory and ancient metaphysics that raises significant issues in the philosophy of science.[6]

Can one make an analogous claim by reconstructing Plotinus' theory of material body and the sensible realm, or does his metaphysics shut out the existence of natural science in any sense intelligible to us? The answer can be found only by a closer examination of Plotinus' physical theories, especially in *Ennead* II, and of Plotinus' occasional thoughts about natural theory as such; to which I shall turn in a moment.

The historical argument according to which Plotinus' metaphysics and the cultures with which it had an apparent affinity *caused* the stifling or neglect of natural science raises issues well beyond the scope of my present remarks. However, the historical argument raises one issue that is central to my purposes. It is an issue that surfaces when we ask the following counterfactually phrased question: If Plotinian Platonism had dominated modern European culture, would natural science as we know it not have emerged? Or would there have emerged a different natural science based on the organic and dialectical model of Plotinian Platonism? It is conceivable that the cultural substratum and Plotinian Platonism could have taken independent courses of development.[7] Clearly, the issue posed is what we mean by natural science. It is senseless to ask whether natural science is possible in Plotinus' philosophy until we assign definite content, however general, to the notion of natural science as we know it.

I

It would beg our question from the beginning if we either assigned a content to the notion of natural science that is inadequate or false for modern science, or if we wholly excluded resembling yet different models of science, for instance, models constructed with organic or holistic assumptions. For brevity's sake, I have reduced the notion of natural science as we know it to two broad truisms. The first is that natural science postulates that the material universe is uniform; whatever explains the properties and processes of matter in one part of the universe explains the same properties and processes in every other part of the universe. I will call this *The Galilean Thesis*.[8] The second truism is that natural science is a disciplined empirical inquiry consisting of a body of theoretical conjectures, as distinguished from rational speculations; changes in this body of conjectures are governed by definite practices and rules, in particular by a high level rule that makes all propositions of scientific theory subject to a test in which both observation and theoretical innovation play their parts.[9] This second truism I call *The Principle of Empirical Scientific Inquiry*.

To take the Galilean Thesis first, does Plotinus believe in the uniformity of matter and in a uniform explanation of material properties and processes? Plotinus accepts the Platonic dualism of sensible and intelligible realms; but this dualism does not answer our question, since it is conceivably compatible with various kinds of physical theory. The question is whether Plotinus is a dualist with regard to the sensible realm alone. I will call monism and dualism relative to the observable realm *physical monism* and *physical dualism* respectively. If Plotinus is a physical dualist, this would count as evidence against his holding the Galilean Thesis.

In some passages, Plotinus accepts a strong differentiation of sublunar and celestial phenomena (II.1.5). In Plotinus' cosmology, the inferior level of soul, the 'generative soul' in matter (II.3.17), does not as firmly hold and control the material constituents of bodies in the near-earth region as it does in the celestial sphere. In the near-earth region, "it is not the individual thing which lasts forever, but the unity of form" (II.1.9, 9–10).[10] Plotinus thinks that the sun and stars existed in the past always and will always exist in the future as individuals (II.1.8) because they are more directly controlled by the superior level of soul, although he is genuinely perplexed about how this can be true. He thinks that the circular motion of the celestial sphere[11] is constructed in imitation of the Intellect (II.2.1)—which implies an even stronger dividing line between motion governed by the superior soul, which receives forms directly from Intellect (II.3.17, 15–17), and motion governed by the inferior soul, whose rational forms (*logoi*) are not the originals (II.3.17, 19). This dualism leads Plotinus to question the relatively uniform distribution of matter in the cosmos. He asks whether fire is the only element in the celestial sphere, and whether it is in flux, like other bodies (II.1.6). At IV.1.6, 57–60, he bluntly claims that "to lift up earth into the celestial sphere is against nature and opposed to her regulations."

A clearer indication of physical dualism is found in Plotinus' theory of light (*phōs*). He interprets Plato's light "other than flame" (*heteron phlogos*: *Timaeus* 58C5–7) as being a body. This light distinguishes the sizes and colors of the stars (II.1.7, 43–46) and composes "the rest of the celestial sphere" (46–47). It is visible in the stars but invisible in the night sky because of its fineness, nonreflective transparency, and distance. From light of this kind there can be no outflow (*aporroē*). It is the purest body in the purest region, and a kind of fire. It is body "joined with soul" (*meta psychēs*), and a body with a higher status than body "alone by itself" (II.1.8, 6–7). This implies a dualism of types of body. Plotinus further distinguishes a second kind of light which "shines from [the first], having the same name, which [second kind] we say is bodiless" (*asōmaton*). Plotinus is evidently referring to radiant light coming from the sun. The first kind of light is a body, partly visible, partly invisible. Radiant light, the second kind, is bodiless and in this regard seems to resemble the intelligible realm (Cf. II.1.8, 27–28). The first kind of light has physical properties such as fineness, transparency, and distance, and by it one can distinguish sizes and colors. The second kind of light, which Plotinus could have detected as the glow surrounding the sun, is only problematically a physical thing at all if it is without body. Stellar fire of this radiant kind differs in some seemingly irreducible way from terrestrial fire. This radical discontinuity within the observable order suggests again that Plotinus is a physical dualist. This implies the denial of the Galilean Thesis.

I turn next to Plotinus' attitude toward physical theory as a form of inquiry governed by a method in which observation plays a role. For Plotinus, the highest form of theoretical inquiry requires us to "cut away everything" (V.3.17)—sensible substances, their properties, and our mental representations of these. But when Plotinus is thinking in this vein, he is not thinking of physical theory. Thinking of the physical universe, he grants that forms are embedded in sensible material bodies. Do our minds gain the kind of access to these forms that enables us to attain theoretical insight? What kind of theoretical enterprise is involved? The road to insight and knowledge is dialectic, which deals with real beings, forms or rational principles (Cf. II.4.16, 2–3), not with sensible things, which are objects of opinion (I.3.4, 9–12). In dialectic, theoretical statements (*theōrēmata*) and the things about which they are true are grasped at the same time (I.3.5, 12–13). Physical theory (*peri physeōs theōria*) is a different part of philosophy. It theorizes "about nature by borrowing help from dialectic, as other crafts make use of arithmetic; but it stands nearer to dialectic [than the other crafts stand to arithmetic]" (I.3.6, 2–5). What Plotinus means by the relation between the crafts and arithmetic is unclear. He might mean that arithmetic is only instrumental in the activities of the other crafts. Or, if we believe Porphyry's accounts of Plotinus as having thorough knowledge of geometry, mechanics, optics, and music (*Vita*, 14), he could mean that other crafts are theoretical skills that are parts of a more general theoretical system within which they draw certain of their 'theorems' from number theory—one possible meaning of *arithmētikē*. A third interpretation is also possible. If Plotinus knew Eratosthenes' works, or had read other reports of the Academy's work on the Delian Problem, he could be thinking of the way in which crafts like architecture seek help from branches of mathematics in the form of proofs of the possibility of certain physical constructions.[12]

I cannot pause to canvas separately these interpretations. What seems clear is that Plotinus' claim that physical theory is closer to dialectic than other crafts are to arithmetic implies that the former relation cannot be only technical and instrumental, but must involve some more integral and systematic relation, either in the field of inquiry or in methodology. If the affinity between dialectic and physical theory were this close, the test of the truth of physical theories would more likely be truths about forms embedded in matter yet apprehended as intelligible, not observable. Hence it seems doubtful that observation can play any direct role in testing physical theories for Plotinus. This implies the denial of the Principle of Empirical Scientific Inquiry.

Since Plotinus seems to reject both of our truisms about natural science, it seems to follow that natural science as we know it is impossible inside the framework of his philosophy. Until now, I have argued that a *prima facie* case can be made for this conclusion. Unfortunately, this *prima facie* case needs careful qualification, as we shall see. Plotinus remains honestly perplexed about both physical dualism and about the validity of observation as a test of the truth of physical theory.

II

The passage in which Plotinus distinguishes stellar fire as body joined with soul from body by itself alone (II.1.8, 6–7), which implies radically differing types of body, is misleading. Elsewhere he thinks of soul as extending to the lowest levels of sensible reality (Cf. II.3.18). Strictly speaking, there is no body alone by itself anywhere. The entire observable order has body (II.1.1, 2). Every body has shape or form (II.4.3, 14–16).[13] Form, or the traces of form, are imprinted in generative soul. Since Plotinus argues that there must exist something that underlies the sizes, shapes, and volumes of bodies to explain their intertransformability, viz. matter (II.4.6), the entire observable order for Plotinus is material body. Does Plotinus really reject a uniform explanation of the observable cosmos?

It is useful to consider the details of one of his arguments dealing with physical theory. His line of thought in his treatise 'On the Celestial Sphere' is not a dogmatic monologue, but an inquiry filled with doubts.[14] "We say"[15] that the universe exists eternally, but something more adequate than the will of God is needed to explain this (II.1.1). It is possible that God causes the cosmos to persist not as a particular, but as a form imposed on an endless succession of individuals, like living organisms. Why should terrestrial animals persist in form only while celestial bodies persist as particulars if the cosmos is itself an organic whole? Plotinus, as a matter of honest perplexity, is raising a question about a uniform cosmos. At first (II.1.2), he thinks tentatively: If we accept the opinion (*doxa*) that the celestial sphere and all bodily things in it last forever as particulars (*to tode*) and sublunar things last forever only in form, one then has to show how anything having body can persist forever as a particular, when body is always in flux.[16] Since Plotinus rejects Aristotle's fifth body as a special explanation of the eternity and continuous motion of the celestial sphere, and also rejects the Stoic theory of an immanent eternal fire, this problem is fundamental for him.

He starts his resolution of this problem by assuming with Plato that the cosmos is a "universal living thing" (*to pan zōion*)(II.1.3, 30). In a Platonic cosmobiology[17] this analogy entails that the cosmos, like any organism, has both body and soul. If, then, the celestial sphere is an eternal particular (II.1.2, 19), it is to both soul and body, to soul alone, or to body alone, that it must owe its eternity. But body is not indestructible, so it alone cannot furnish the explanation. Soul alone cannot furnish one either, since Plotinus thinks that the cosmobiological analogy requires an indissoluble connection between cosmic soul and cosmic body; the soul of the cosmos is an inseparable soul. It follows that "the matter and body of the totality" (II.1.3, 1) must contribute in a synergistic way to the eternity of the whole. How can this be explained? Plotinus at first tries a weak compromise by suggesting that body is in flux but not in total flux. He argues by appealing to observation of terrestrial instances: "One must observe" (*horan de dei* II.1.3, 5), he writes, that individual organisms and we too remain the same despite changes of constituents, just like the whole mass of the earth and water (II.1.3, 7–10). Sublunar particulars thus have two kinds of persistent identity: (a) sameness of kind or form, and (b) relative sameness as physical individuals. Plotinus infers from this observational generalization that stellar fire is (perhaps) not in the kind of flux that would undermine the synergism of cosmic body and soul that produces stability. Stellar fire is tractable (*euagōgos*: II.1.3, 18). But is stellar fire tractable enough to compose an eternally persistent particular? Let us note here, aside, that Plotinus' appeal to observation seems to commit him to argue from truths about the near-earth sensible region to truths about the celestial sphere. His problem is that the (b) type of persistent identity still falls short of the absolute eternal sameness demanded by partisans of an eternal celestial sphere.

Here Plotinus vacillates. In II.1.4 he contends that because celestial fire is immediately governed by soul, it at least is not in a "boiling state" (*zesis*) (Cf. Aristotle, *Meteorologia* 340b23). He appeals again to a fact of observation: "Even if [the elements of a thing] are continually changing [e.g. wearing out like pieces of wood], the whole remains." It is thus possible that stellar fire boils as a whole mass but remains as a mass or distinct body. Again he refers to soul concessively: "Even if it were possible for all body to perish, nothing would happen to alter soul" (II.1.4, 32–33). Obviously, he is unwilling to concede this much—that the bodily component of the cosmos could entirely perish—since it is a necessary synergistic condition of the identity through time of the cosmos. He thus retreats to a new position: The bodies that compose the cosmos, stellar fire, are "pure and in every way better" (II.1.4, 8), i.e. better than terrestrial bodies. In what sense does Plotinus ascribe higher value to stellar fire? To say that those bodies are better because eternal would reverse the order of explanation. Plotinus' ultimate reason is based on his cosmobiological analogy: In other organisms, "nature selects and places the better things in their most important parts" (II.1.4, 9–10). The celestial sphere is the most important part of the cosmos, the universal living organism; so, Nature has selected and placed stellar light there. Plotinus construes his Platonic analogy in the strongest sense, as entailing an organic internal organization analogous to terrestrial organisms. Again let us note that his argument depends on the observed nature of terrestrial organisms.

His view of the universe as organized and as persisting through time in the same way that organisms persist as individuals allows for a kind of uniformity in nature, namely an organizational uniformity. But, as he notices, it presents an even greater problem. Why does the cosmic organism not ultimately perish, like all other organisms? Plotinus' explanation depends on a double appeal to Plato's authority in the *Timaeus.* The first depends on the mythic aspect of the text, and I will not dwell on it here.[18] The second involves a serious attempt to reinterpret what Timaeus says about stars having been composed "mostly" (*tēn pleistēn*) though not entirely, from fire (cf. II.1.6, 10 with *Timaeus* 40A2–3).[19] Plotinus realizes that Plato seems committed to the view that stars are solids (II.1.6, 6), and that an element other than fire is probably required to explain this. This implies that Plato is one of those, to whom Plotinus referred earlier, who hold that the body of the celestial sphere is composed of the same elements of which organisms are made (II.1.2, 14–17). If Plato holds a version of this theory of the relatively uniform distribution of physical elements, there would be no need for a special kind of fire, like Plotinus' light. Anticipating his own theory of light, Plotinus appeals weakly to the fact that Plato distinguishes different kinds of a given element, e.g. different kinds of earth (II.1.7, 33–34), and even refers to gold as a kind of water (II.1.6, 51–53).[20] Yet Plotinus knows that Plato does not give stellar fire any *ad hoc* special status. The implied relatively uniform distribution view is troubling to Plotinus. The notion that organisms and stars are composed of the same matter is an anti-Aristotelian uniformity of elements position (and it is incidentally in striking agreement with the modern theory that the material of organisms is the residual product of stellar evolution). This uniformity of elements position troubles Plotinus because even though he rejects the Aristotelian fifth element theory, he continues to think of stellar fire as occupying a privileged place in the cosmos. His position thus looks like an uneasy truce with the Aristotelians, or an attempt to harmonize Plato and Aristotle.

Plotinus' final resolution of his own position is found at II.1.7. The stars are solids, but it is not the element earth that explains their solidity; but it is a quality ('resistance') normally associated with earth. Physical qualities such as resistance, density, hardness, and brightness can be gained or lost or intermixed independently of the elements with which they are normally associated. It is not physical elements but physical qualities that are relatively uniformly distributed through the cosmos. Plotinus refers to this general idea as "the community in the cosmos" (II.1.7, 15). By this he does not mean the Stoic notion of universal *sympathy*, which is explained by an immanent universal fire and entails physical monism. Plotinus' view amounts rather to the independence and associativity of qualities admitted as a universal high-level feature of the cosmos. Therefore, in two ways Plotinus' argument turns on high-level features: the ordering of parts of the cosmos according to the cosmobiological analogy, and a principle of independence and associativity of physical qualities.

This long detour through Plotinus' treatise on the celestial sphere enables us to assess more fully his position relative to the Galilean Thesis. The Galilean Thesis is both a doctrine of the relative uniformity of matter and a doctrine of the strict uniformity of physical explanations. Plotinus rejects a relatively uniform distribution of material elements, but he accepts a notion of uniform physical explanation. This is what his reference to 'the community' in the cosmos means: The kinds of the element fire are not uniformly distributed—stellar fire does not flow downward (II.1.8) and terrestrial fire is prevented from reaching beyond the near-earth region (II.1.7)—but they both have the quality that makes them solids. The community or association (*koinōnia*) in the cosmos is an association of common qualities. If physical explanations using the same physical qualities are the same kinds of explanations, then Plotinus' notion of the cosmic community of physical qualities entails uniformity of physical explanation. In this respect, he accepts the Galilean Thesis.

Plotinus' notion of explanation in terms of qualities or properties independent of material constituents or physical elements raises serious questions. What is the physics of complex properties compounded of other properties? How can Plotinus appeal to the authority of Plato's *Timaeus* when he avoids the Timaean theory of physical elements as intertransformable, geometrically defined components of the regular solids, in which the ultimate constituents and properties of fire supply a uniform and interconnected explanation? Plotinus follows his Middle Platonist predecessors in avoiding any detailed investigation of the Timaean theory.[21]

III

Turning once again to the Principle of Empirical Scientific Inquiry, can anything be added to our initial judgment of Plotinus' position? I have noted that Plotinus appeals to observation. To these cases one can add other, more telling cases of Plotinus' use of appeals to observation. For instance, in discussing the physical explanation of "complete coalescence" (II.7.1 & 2), his use of Alexander presupposes close attention to the phenomenon of the expansion of wetted papyrus pulp. Plotinus rejects atomism, since he holds that bodies are completely divisible (II.4.7, 20–22). The expansion of wetted pulp is for him a case of complete interpenetration without complete division.[22] His resolution of what he calls "these difficult questions" (II.7.2, 42–43) involves defining the quality of density (*pyknotēs*) as itself made up of other qualities (II.7.2, 35–37). The pulp expands because it is interpenetrable, and its interpenetrability is explained by its relative density. Interpenetration is explained by the mingling of the qualities of the water and the papyrus. The absence of division of the water and pulp by one another is explained by his theory that qualities "can go through bodies without cutting them"

(II.7.2, 28–29) because they are "bodiless" (II.7.2, 29). His notion of bodiless qualities may seem like a metaphysical speculation without any clear justification; yet the purpose of his reasoning is the attempt to make coherent sense out of the observed facts. For Plotinus, *interpenetration* is a theoretical term whose definition rests on an account of the nature of qualities, and his introduction of the theoretical meaning of the term is part of an attempt to determine which descriptions are to count as the facts in need of explanation, as well as part of an attempt to explain the facts. Admittedly, Plotinus does not clearly distinguish this kind of determination of a domain of facts from their explanation.

This intimate pairing of observation and theory may be found in many of Plotinus' discussions. The soul that regulates the celestial sphere also enters the realm subject to chance (*tychē*: II.3.10). The stars produce nonessential changes in terrestrial things. The higher and lower levels within the sensible realm interact, which suggests that they must share common general descriptions; there is a common repertoire of physical theoretical terms. In general, all sensible matter is formed in some way and is thus a proper object for physical theory (II.4.3, 16–17; II.2.1, 38–39). But does Plotinus imply the general view that physical theories must as such be open to a test of adequacy such that not reason alone but observable facts must be appealed to, even if indirectly?

A prior, more central question is this: Did Plotinus have even the idea of physical theory as only *partially* justified or contestable? In particular, we ought to ask what his attitude was towards the doctrine of physical theories as partially justified or 'probable' accounts that is the cornerstone of Plato's *Timaeus.* Plotinus refers to this doctrine indirectly in the passage already cited (II.1.6) in which he asks whether celestial bodies are made of fire only or of fire and other elements.[23] Contrary to his normal usage, there Plotinus does not cite Plato's text with "He says," but with the words: "For Timaeus... the stars contain not all fire but mostly fire, since the stars obviously have solidity" (Cf. II.1.6, 2–6, with *Timaeus* 40A2–3). He says that "perhaps" (*isōs*) Timaeus' view is correct, and in any case Plato "agrees" with Timaeus in judging that the view in question accords with what is 'probable' (*tōi eikoti*). The fact that Timaeus and Plato might not agree underscores the plurality of possible positions that are measured against the yardstick of 'probability.' Nowhere else does Plotinus treat Plato and Timaeus as holding potentially different positions. As if to excuse this distancing of Plato from Timaeus, Plotinus adds a twofold justification of Plato's position:

> From our sense perception, by sight and the exchange of contact [with starlight], it appears that they contain all or mostly all fire; but when we consider them rationally, we see that if there is no solid without earth, they must contain earth.[24]

Plato's position is supported either by sense perception or by reasoning, or by both. What sense perception reveals is unclear: either stars are composed of fire, or they are composed mostly of fire and partly of other elements. Reason argues that since stars are solids, then if there is no solid without elements other than fire, stars must contain elements other than fire.

Since Plotinus' own theory of stellar composition requires that stars be composed only of a special type of fire and contain no earth, he in effect rejects the argument from reason alone and accepts one of the two alternative testimonies of the senses—but in any case, he rejects Plato's position. He later explains that stellar fire is a solid in having resistance (*antereisis*) but not hardness (*sklērotēs*: II.1.6, 48–50). For my purposes, two things are worth noting. Plotinus appeals in a roundabout way to observation, not just to reason. Thus, for him the *Timaeus* account is in fact only partially justified, not only because it is a merely 'probable' account, but also because it is an account that is contested both by the evidence of perception and by Plotinus' countertheory. In this passage, Plotinus proves that he is capable of viewing physical theory as a group of competing theories, of which Plato's theory of stellar composition is only one, and not necessarily the correct one. It should also be added that Plotinus is exceedingly coy about this conflict with Plato. He wishes to appear not to disagree with Plato.

This rare passage placed Plotinus closer to the spirit of Plato's doctrine of partially justified accounts than all the passages in which Plotinus accepts Plato as an authority without reservation It leads Plotinus closer to the idea of physical theory as conjecture, and this is a fundamental step towards a grasp of natural science as a disciplined inquiry. Since it is possibly unclear what I mean in ascribing the idea of a physical conjecture to Plato, I will restate Plato's position and then, in conclusion, I will evaluate Plotinus' precise attitude. For Plato, physical theory deals with what "comes to be and is perceptible"; since the perceptible is "grasped by opinion together with sense perception" (28B4–C1), the sensible realm is also properly thought of as an object of changeable opinions (*doxaston*). Physical theories therefore are never 'exact' accounts, "in every way in agreement with themselves"(29C5–7). Physics is not an exact science like geometry; it is not an entirely consistent body of theory. The best one can hope to achieve is accounts that are "no less probable than others" (29C5–D1). Since physical theory is a matter of belief (29C4) and opinion, or at best a mixture of probability and necessity of the kind sought for in the Timaean theory of elements, the most we can hope to achieve is contestable belief.[25] The choice of a theoretical model at the core of the Timaean theory of elements is explicitly open to contest. "The prize of the contest goes in a friendly way to the one who refutes this, and discovers that it does not hold in this way" (54B1–2). It is arguable that refutability of a physical theory is a kind of falsifiability.[26] Given this doctrine of refutability together with Plato's strong epistemological distinction between belief and knowledge, the Timaean doctrine can be said to sever physical theory cleanly from dialectic. Physical theory for Plato is thus advanced as a species of conjecture rather than as a body of rational argument or speculation. In Platonic physics, it must be granted that more weight is given to the choice of theoretical models than to empirical confirmation or disconfirmation—for Plato 'the appearances' are treated as what need to be explained, not what tests theory—but it is not this that should be the important issue, but rather Plato's first fledgling conception of a physical conjecture.

Plato's reference to 'probability' in the passage about stellar composition may have loosened Plotinus' commitment to Plato's own authority—a salutary effect—but it did not serve as a springboard for a Plotinian investigation in the philosophy of science, for instance, in the epistemological or metaphysical foundations of natural theory as such. Plotinus' rare appeals to observation and sense perception, when seen in this light, are but vague pointers towards an empirical criterion; they do not even hint at the more important conception of a physical conjecture.[27]

Plotinus' view that physical theory is closer to dialectic than the crafts are to arithmetic implies that physical theory makes use of dialectic in some systematically close way that would leave little room for the idea of a partially justified or contestable theory. Plotinus does not reflect on the structure of physical theory as distinguished from dialectic.[28] On the other hand, the charge or suspicion that Plotinus is a philosopher who simply derives physical theory from his metaphysical system is not accurate. When compared with the Stoics, Plotinus' metaphysical system does not directly logically entail any consequences in physical theory, although it stands in a constant rapport with it. Plotinus' theories of physical coalescence, of stellar composition and causation, or of the nature of physical qualities are not derived from the metaphysical principles of unity, intellect, and soul—even though certain references to soul and the 'traces' of its *logoi* are presupposed by them. It is conceivable that the outlines of a Plotinian physics could be put together from Plotinus' accounts of density, interpenetrability, divisibility, transparency, resistance, and other material qualities. This is not to say that it was ever Plotinus' intention to do so.

In conclusion, I have argued that Plotinus' position relative to the Galilean Thesis is ambiguous. The sensible universe is bifurcated into two regions that differ materially because of the overall organization of the biocosm. The two regions share the same physical qualities. Plotinus is not a physical monist like the Stoics. The uniformity of the physical order is not due to an immanent unifying element nor to the relatively uniform distribution of a plurality of elements, but rather to the "community," i.e. the independence, associativity, and relatively uniform distribution of physical qualities. It is in this sense that Plotinus' cosmology rests on an organic and holistic basis. If, then, the Galilean Thesis entails the uniformity of matter, Plotinus' position rejects the Galilean Thesis. On the other hand, if the Galilean Thesis entails only the uniformity of physical explanation, Plotinus' position is at least compatible with the Thesis. As for the second of my truisms about natural science, it is clear that Plotinus has no well formulated idea of physics as an empirical inquiry or even as a body of physical conjectures. On balance, we might be able to speak sensibly of a 'Plotinian physics,' but this physics would lack certain of the key ingredients of physics as we know it.

Temple University

NOTES

1. Cf. B. Marién, *Bibliografia Critica degli Studi Plotiniani* (Bari, 1949), and, thereafter, *L'Année Philologique*. Of interest are Pierre Duhem, *Le Système du Monde: Histoire des Doctrines Cosmologiques de Platon a Copernic*, I–IV (Paris, 1954–1965) and A. Graeser, *Plotinus and the Stoics: A Preliminary Study*, Philosophia Antique 22 (Leiden, 1972). Possibly of interest is the unpublished work by M. I. de Santa Cruz de Prunes, *Le problème du monde sensible dans la philosophie de Plotin*, Annuaire de l'École pratique des Hautes Études (Paris). It is surprising that Duhem did not directly address the question of a Plotinian cosmology.
2. For a working scientist's expression of this view, Cf. Carl Sagan, *Cosmos*, Program 7 (Carl Sagan Productions and KCET, 1979). Kepler, Newton, and Einstein all held a mystical attitude toward the natural order.

3. Pierre Duhem, *The Aim and Structure of Physical Theory*, translated by P. Wiener (New York, 1962), 18.
4. Stoic physical theory offers perhaps the best case of something like such a 'derivation'; but Cf. Proclus, *Institutio Physica* ("Treatise on the Elements of Physics"), ed., A. Ritzenfeld (Leipzig, 1912) and, on Proclus' model of deductive knowledge, see R. Hathaway, "The Anatomy of a Neoplatonist Metaphysical Proof," *The Structure of Being: A Neoplatonic Approach*, ed. R. Baine Harris (SUNY Press, 1982), 122–136.
5. Frederick Suppe, *The Structure of Scientific Theories* (Chicago, 1977), 717.
6. Cf. Gregory Vlastos, *Plato's Universe* (Seattle, 1975); Aristotle, *De motu animalium*, edited and translated by Martha C. Nussbaum (Cambridge, MA.); Robert B. Todd, "Monism and Immanence: The Foundations of Stoic Physics," *The Stoics*, ed. John M. Rist (Berkeley, 1978), 136–160. Of special interest is Montgomery Furth's forthcoming work on the metaphysical foundations of Aristotle's biological theory. See also *Science and Speculation: Studies in Hellenistic Theory and Practice*, ed. Jonathan Barnes, Jacques Brunschwig, Myles Burnyeat, and Malcolm Schofield (Cambridge, 1982).
7. At the time that Ficino translated Plotinus into Latin (1485, published 1492; cf. P. Kristeller, *Suppl. Ficinianum*, lxvi), Italian science combined mechanical explanation with teleological, organic, and holistic explanations taken from a variety of Aristotelian and Neoplatonic sources; Italian culture and its physics could have branched in any of a number of directions. Plotinian modes of thinking had been embedded in Christian culture by the anonymous Pseudo-Dionysius. Critical reaction to the 'fraud' implied by Valla's suspicions about the provenance of the Dionysian Corpus (published in 1505 in the *Annotationes* by Erasmus) may be one significant reason for the loss of respectability of Plotinian Platonism among many scientists and intellectuals. Such adventitious events independent of scientific theory often play a role in the choice of models of scientific theories.
8. Because of Galileo's well known role in publicizing the view (not fully extended until Newton). Does the Galilean Thesis still hold for physical science? At the 1982 Cambridge Conference on Particle Physics, a new version of what has come to be called the 'inflationary [cosmological] model' was put forward by Steinhardt and Albrecht (and independently by Linde) which implies that the totality of the observed universe is merely a local universe cut off from very remote 'universes.' Moreover, the Steinhardt-Albrecht-Linde version allows different physical laws as a possibility for these remote universes, and thus implies both real space-time discontinuity and explanatory non-uniformity. However, their version is so conjectural that it would be false to say that physics has adopted anything like it. Most physicists continue to hold something like the Galilean Thesis.

9. Theoretical innovation enters the test of theories as background in determining a given domain of facts. I have merely tried to encapsulate accepted positions here, holding controversy at bay. In particular I omit any reference to the contents of a 'body of conjectures,' especially any reference to claims to knowledge. If Plotinus accepts Plato's cosmological epistemology, natural science would not be a body of claims to knowledge, a position that would challenge contemporary discussion and only raise a multitude of troublesome questions.
10. All citations are to the Henry-Schwyzer edition, *Plotini Opera* (Paris, 1951–1959). All translations are my own, though I have profited by consulting Armstrong's *Plotinus* (Cambridge, MA, 1966–1988.).
11. 'Celestial sphere' seems to me to be less misleading than 'heaven' as a synonym of *ouranos*. That what is meant is neither the ancient sphere of rotation nor the celestial sphere of the modern astronomer will be clear from context.
12. Eratosthenes, *Platonicus,* as cited by Theon by Smyrna, ed. Hiller (Leipzig, 1878), 2. For a discussion, Cf. B. L. Van der Waerden, *Science Awakening*, translated by Arnold Dresden (Oxford, 1961), 150, 160–161.
13. II.4.3 says that all sensible matter has shape, but it is clearly only as body occupying place that matter is shaped. Does Plotinus regard a proposition such as 'All body has shape' as true in virtue of sense experience or as a truth of reason, a 'dialectical' truth? For the role of observation in Plotinus, cf. below in this essay.
14. Against this, W. Theiler, "Plotin zwischen Plato und Stoa," *Les Sources de Plotin* (Vandoeuvres-Genèva, 1957), 68: "Plotin auch [hat] nicht Dialoge geschrieben. Fragen wurden gestellt in seiner Vorlesung (Vita 13), *aber die Antworten lagen schon fest*. Philosophie und Leben waren monologisch geworden." (My italics.) Theiler's general contention that Socratic elenchus is absent from Plotinus' view of Plato is correct, or so I have argued in "The Neoplatonist Interpretation of Plato: Remarks on its Decisive Characteristics," *Journal of the History of Philosophy* VII (1969), 19–26. On the importance of elenchus further, Cf. n27 below.
15. Literally, "in saying (*legontes*) that the cosmos has always existed before...if we refer (*anagoimen*) the explanation to the will of God..." (II.1.1, 1–3). It is grammatically correct to render *legontes* as "when we say," as Armstrong does, but it misses the tentative mood of this opening sentence. Armstrong's comment that the whole purpose of II.1 is "to defend the doctrine...of the incorruptibility of the heavens" exaggerates the dogmatic character of Plotinus' thought in II.1. MacKenna's "We hold that..." is too strong. The persons implicit in *anagoimen* are not necessarily restricted to Plotinus and his followers; note that the view in question is not easy to reconcile with Plato's position (Cf. II.1.2, 8–10, with Republic 530B2–3, but on *Timaeus* Cf. VI.7.3). For an instance in which Plotinus is making an apparently dogmatic

claim, Cf. the *phamen* at II.1.7, 27.

16. II.1.2, 1–6. The stars, sun, and planets are eternal particulars "in the strongest sense" (*epi tou autou kyriōs*). Plotinus' explanation of just what this means (*hōs to kath'hekaston kai to hōsautōs*: II.1.2, 5) is obscure. On different kinds of persistent identity in Plotinus, Cf. below in this essay. Stars are not changeless in *every* way (II.1.8, 27–28).
17. I borrow this term from Todd, "Monism and Immanence," 147.
18. The argument is that celestial things are derived from the Craftsman or Intellect, but terrestrial organisms derive from or are produced by gods produced by the Craftsman; since the celestial gods made by the Craftsman are instrumental in producing terrestrial organisms, they therefore cannot be instrumental in producing themselves.
19. On this passage, cf. below in this essay.
20. *Timaeus* 59A8–B4, viz. a dense, uniform, fusible kind of water (*hydōr*). Plato's use of *hydōr* in this and other passages suggests that he means by it any substance found in liquid form. The example seems irrelevant here, but may be important for Plotinus' later notion of separable qualities like density (*pyknotēs*).
21. John Dillon, *The Middle Platonists: A Study of Platonism 80 B.C. to A.D. 220* (London, 1977), 48–49: "I can discern no sign of philosophic questioning behind Albinus' summary of Platonic physical theory...If the Middle Platonists seem uninterested in questions of what we would term Physics, they are after all only reflecting the remarkably nonscientific bias of the age in which they lived." Dillon's comment furnishes a good example of what I referred to above as the historical argument. The bias of the culture and Middle Platonism are mutually affined; they reflect each other. One ought to note that 'the age' in question produced such outstanding scientists as Heron, Ptolemy, Theon and Galen, and that familiarity with Plato, Aristotle, Euclid, Archimedes and Apollonius should have been taken for granted. Why do we think that people like Albinus reflect a bias, like innocent and passive mirrors, rather than actively choosing to adopt a bias?
22. If there were complete division, the pulp and the water would completely destroy each other. Every volume of matter is a continuum (Cf. II.7.1, 32).
23. II.1.6, 8–12. II.1.7, 46–50, implies the denial that there is no solid without earth; it also implies that fire is a solid but is neither three dimensional nor hard. The implicit denial that fire is three dimensional seems to imply the rejection of Plato's Timaean polyhedral theory of the elements.
24. It is probably necessary to note here that the term *eikos* as it is used in these passages in the *Timaeus* (cf. note below re Kepler) has nothing to do with probability in the sense of frequency of occurrence. Burnyeat's comments about Aristotle's notion of *eikos* involving a subjective element—viz. what most or some people would grant as being convincing or acceptable—apply, at least in part, to Plato as well. Cf. M. F. Burnyeat, "Carneades was no

Probabilist," paper read at the Colloquium on Ancient Scepticism (Princeton University, 1982), 7–10.

25. *Timaeus* 53D5 & 56B4. At 59D1 the search for more adequate physical theories is said to involve a pleasure that imparts a kind of measured quality (*metrion*) to life, a measure characterized both by playfulness and shrewd thinking. Plato is thinking here, possibly, of the contest described at 54B1–2.
26. It is unclear what Plato's idea of the adequacy of a theory amounts to. It may involve questions about how well one's theoretical model captures certain features of its domain of facts, e.g. as the sharp vertices of his tetrahedra capture the 'cutting' quality of fire. If the only question for Plato is how 'admirable' (*kalon*) one's model is (54A6), adequacy would depend on standards of elegance or symmetry. I believe that Plato's yardstick for adequacy involves at least both of these questions. Had he developed his idea of refutability in the *Timaeus*, it would have reflected this complexity.
27. A better instance of physical conjecture, and perhaps of the influence of the Timaean doctrine, is found in the works of Kepler. The question about what spurred Kepler to move from the 1596 *Mysterium Cosmographicum*, based on the use of the Timaean regular polyhedra to determine planetary orbits, to the 1609 *Astronomia Nova*, which adopts the ellipse and revolutionizes astronomy, is normally answered by ascribing to Kepler an obsessive concern with matching Brahe's data. But this motive, to be credible, must have begun with a willingness to treat authoritative models in physical theory as falsifiable. Kepler's motives in this respect become fully intelligible if this, the crux of his method, was found in his greatest authority as the Timaean principle of partially justifiable accounts. Cf. not merely 54B1–2, but the pervasive insertions of it: *Timaeus* 28B4–C1, 29C4–D3, 29D2, 30B7, 48D–E, 53D5, 55D5, 56A1, 56B4, 68B7, 68D2, 72D7–8.
28. The serious questions here concern the relation between Socratic elenchus and the elenchus mentioned at *Timaeus* 54B1–2, which we might term Timaean elenchus. The consistency of a set of beliefs (or a single belief) is established by Socratic elenchus; the method is purely rational, but inductive appeals are often an intrinsic part of this (including the method of counterexample). Timaean elenchus establishes the 'probability' or 'likelihood' (adequacy?) of a general theory. The different uses of *eikos* in *Timaeus* need a careful examination. F. M. Cornford's criticisms of A. E. Taylor's views about this are as exaggerated as Taylor's own claims. Cf. *Plato's Cosmology* (New York, 1937), 30–31, with A. E. Taylor, *A Commentary of Plato's Timaeus* (Oxford, 1928). Cf. Vlastos, 93. Plotinus, of course, is not thematically concerned with either type of elenchus.

THE PRACTICE OF PLOTINIAN PHYSICS

Jonathan Scott Lee

The casual reader of the *Enneads* cannot help but be struck by a paradox in Plotinus' treatment of the sensible world. On the one hand, he has a great deal to say both about the beauty and the positive moral status of this world (particularly in his replies to the Gnostics in II.9 and III.2 & 3)[1] and about the moral and philosophical danger that attachment to this world poses for the soul (most notably in I.8). On the other hand, Plotinus offers rather little in the way of an account of the nature of the sensible world, and much of what he does provide concerns its metaphysical analysis as an image of the intelligible world of forms (*eidē*); for example, the treatise on the categories of the sensible world (VI.3) must be read in this light. Even in *Enneads* II and III, which Porphyry explicitly describe as concerned with physics and other subjects relating to the physical universe,[2] there are very few passages in which Plotinus explicitly deals with what might be called physical analysis of this universe or in which he offers any sort of detailed description of things or events in the sensible world. That this marks a striking departure from the concerns of Plato, Aristotle, and the early Stoa has often been noted,[3] but the deeper issue of determining the precise status of physics in Plotinus' conception of theoretical inquiry has received rather little attention.[4] The guiding assumption of the commentators seems to have been that the issues of genuine philosophical interest in Plotinus in particular and in Neoplatonism in general are largely metaphysical, ethical, psychological and theological.

In the following pages, my aim is to show that Plotinus does in fact have something of philosophical interest to say about the status of physics and about the actual practice of the physicist; to this end, I am perhaps more interested in raising issues and breaking new ground than I am in resolving the difficulties raised. In section 1, I argue for the legitimacy (on Plotinus' own view) of considering physics as a discipline relatively independent from metaphysics (understood in terms of Platonic dialectic). In sections 2 and 3, I consider Plotinus' actual practice of physics in two treatises of the second *Ennead* (II.7 and II.1), focusing particular attention on contrasting ways in which he treats the relation between physical investigation and metaphysical analysis. Finally, in section 4, I summarize the tentative results of my inquiry.

1. Physics and Dialectic

Plotinus' most explicit statement as to the character of natural philosophy in general is found at the beginning of the last chapter of his short treatise, 'On Dialectic' (I.3), where he briefly describes the relation of dialectic to natural philosophy: "So dialectic is the valuable part [of philosophy]. Philosophy has other parts; it also surveys the nature of the physical world with assistance from dialectic, as the other skills use arithmetic to help them; though natural philosophy stands closer to dialectic in its borrowing...." (I.3.6, 1–5). Rather than clarifying the nature of physics in itself, this statement maps the territory in which some such clarification must be sought: To understand the proper role of physics is to understand its relation to and specific difference from dialectic. Plotinus maintains that physics borrows from dialectic and is assisted by dialectic, but there are a number of ways in which such a relation might be construed. In describing physics' relation to dialectic as like the relation of certain other skills to arithmetic, Plotinus is apparently alluding to Plato's claim at *Republic* 522c1–9 that every sort of skill, understanding, and knowledge presupposes number and calculation. However, this reference back to Plato does little more than complicate the issue for Plotinus, since the *Republic* passage is most naturally taken to mean that all skills use mathematics as some sort of tool, while Plotinus has already denied (at I.3.5, 8–13) that dialectic is to be thought of as a tool (*organon*) for the use of the philosopher.

If dialectic cannot be taken to be a tool for the physicist (in roughly the way Aristotelian logic serves as a tool for the Aristotelian physicist), then it would seem that the relation between the two disciplines must be more intimate; indeed, it would seem that physics must borrow at least some of its content from dialectic, and this may be Plotinus' point when he remarks that physics "stands closer to dialectic in its borrowing" than do the other skills to arithmetic. At a rather schematic level of analysis, there are at least two ways in which it could be argued that Plotinian physics actually borrows all of its content from dialectic. (a) Given Plotinus' commitment to Platonism and to the fundamental Platonic claim that the intelligible forms are the true causes of the sensible world,[5] a Plotinian could maintain that the complete account of the sensible world—and thus all of physics—is simply implicit in the results of dialectic. From this perspective, physics would tell us nothing which dialectic (understood in terms of the method of collection and division: see I.3.4 & 5) does not reveal, and reveal in a more systematic (because methodologically rigorous) way.[6] (b) Given Plotinus' routine acceptance of the *Timaeus* and, in particular, its doctrine that the physical universe exists as an animal endowed with soul, a Plotinian could maintain that all of physics—as an account of the nature and action of the world's body—is implicit in the psychology of the world-soul.[7] On such an analysis, to understand the sensible world would be simply to understand the world-soul, and this latter understanding would directly involve in turn the dialectical understanding of the intelligible world, thus collapsing (b) into an elaborated form of (a). On either interpretation, it would seem that physics is reduced to a gratuitous pastime wholly dependent upon dialectic.[8]

Nevertheless, even on interpretations such as (a) and (b) which emphasize the extreme dependence of physics on dialectic, there is room (and even a necessity) for a conception of physics as a discipline at least relatively independent from dialectic. If dialectic is to provide the basis for an explanation of the sensible world in terms of reference to the forms, there is a place for the description of the sensible world in terms other than those of dialectic; that is, physics can be construed as a discipline dedicated to (roughly) the metaphysically neutral description of things and events in the sensible world, such description then providing the data that are to be explained by dialectic. Without some such description, it does not seem that a causal explanation of the sensible world by the forms—such as that required by (a)—would even be possible. To put the same point in another way, without the results of physics, dialectic could not be shown to be the genuine explanation of reality in all its dimensions that Plotinus clearly takes it to be (see I.3.4 & 5, especially I.3.5, 5–13). Precisely similar considerations apply to (b), but here we can perhaps go a bit further and maintain not only that physics can and must exist as a discipline devoted to the metaphysically neutral description of the sensible world but that such a physics can also describe sensible things and processes without explicit reference to the soul or souls that are ultimately causally responsible for such things and processes. Again, such a psychologically neutral description would provide precisely the data which world-soul psychology (taken in conjunction with dialectic) would then explain. That Plotinus is willing to countenance this sort of psychologically neutral physics is made clear in the final part of the treatise on the genera of being, where he insists that a study of the genera of the things that constitute the sensible world must exclude any direct reference to soul, since "the nature of the soul is in the intelligible" (see VI.3.1, 21–31).[9] Later in the same treatise he argues that sensible substance may be distinguished into two classes of bodies, material (*hylikōtera*) and organic (*organika*) (VI.3.9, 1–18), and that organic motion (*kinēsis empsychōn*) must be distinguished from inorganic motion (*kinēsis apsychōn*) (I.3.26, 4–5). From this it would seem to follow that both organic and inorganic bodies and motions can be studied without reference to any sort of psychology (either of the world-soul or of any other individual soul), and this would certainly provide at least one kind of domain for physics.

Two rather different conclusions come out of the preceding considerations. First, on general philosophical grounds, it appears that Plotinus must be willing to make room for a conception of physics as a (at least relatively-speaking) metaphysically and psychologically neutral description of the things and processes of the sensible world. Second, on specific textual grounds, it appears that Plotinus does in fact grant legitimacy to a description of things and events in the sensible world conducted in isolation from any sort of psychology (and from now on in this essay, I will take 'physics' in the narrower sense of this sort of extra-psychological inquiry). There is, thus, a reasonably clear domain for physics in Plotinus' conception of intellectual inquiry as a description (lacking ultimate explanatory power) of the sensible world. What remains unclear, however, is the precise character of this sort of physical description; in particular, what still needs to be examined is the extent of the borrowing that physics does from dialectic. In order to come to a better grasp of these issues, we need to go beyond the general arguments advanced thus far and to turn to some specific examples of physical description and analysis in the *Enneads*. As Émile Bréhier has pointed out, the question of Plotinian physics is "not one of a well-defined field of investigation, but of the way in which Plotinus deals with the questions included under this head by Aristotle and the Stoics, such as the questions concerning the nature of bodies, the elements, action and passion, mixture, the celestial movements, time, and the nature of living bodies."[10] While we have now seen that such a field of investigation can be somewhat carefully defined, such a definition remains essentially empty in the absence of some specific examples of the actual practice of Plotinian physics.

2. Total Mixture

Perhaps the single most straightforward example in the *Enneads* of Plotinus' actually practicing physics comes in the short treatise, 'On Total Mixture' (II.7), in which he offers a very direct critique of an unambiguously physical doctrine integral to Stoicism. The Stoic doctrine at issue is the claim that two or more material substances or material qualities[11] can so totally interpenetrate one another than "any volume of the mixture, down to the smallest parts, is jointly occupied by all the components in the same proportion, each component preserving its own properties under any circumstances, irrespective of the ratio of its share in the mixture."[12] Such a total mixture (*krasis di' holōn*), if it were possible, would make the totality of things mixed (in Plotinus' words) "a whole of like parts" (II.7.1, 6–8). Now, whether or not total mixture in this sense is possible would seem to be a clear case of a physical issue: that is, a decision about the truth or falsity of the Stoic doctrine will entail the truth or falsity of a variety of particular descriptions of things or processes in the sensible world (descriptions, for example, of alleged cases of total mixture). Thus, Plotinus' treatment of the doctrine should shed some clear light on the procedures of Plotinian physics, particularly since his analysis is heavily indebted to the arguments of both Stoic and Peripatetic predecessors (as has been particularly well shown by Bréhier[13]).

Oddly enough, commentators on Plotinus are rather divided about the actual results of Plotinus' critique. Thus, A. H. Armstrong emphasizes his basic acceptance of the Stoic view,[14] while H. J. Blumenthal claims that II.7 amounts to a refutation "in detail" of the view.[15] As we shall see, both interpretations can in fact be defended—Plotinus does refute the notion that *bodies* can mix totally, while he defends the claim that *qualities* might at least often so mix[16]—but to understand how this can be the case, we need to turn to the actual course of his argument, noting the points at which physics appears to 'borrow' from the results of metaphysics.

After an initial chapter reviewing in fairly elaborate detail a series of Peripatetic arguments against the doctrine of total mixture and a parallel series of Stoic responses to these arguments (for a marvelous analysis of these arguments and their sources, see Bréhier's 'Notice' to II.7), Plotinus turns in chapter 2 to develop his own position on the possibility of mixture (II.7.2, 4–6). He begins with the empirical example of water soaking through a piece of papyrus and asks, "how can we deny that the whole body of the water goes right through the papyrus?" (II.7.2, 8–9), going on to insist that this example seems to dictate the actual occurrence of total mixture: "For, the whole papyrus is wet and its matter is nowhere destitute of the quality [of wetness]. But if the matter is everywhere accompanied by the quality of wetness, the water is everywhere in the papyrus" (II.7.2, 13–15). However, this apparent vindication of the Stoic doctrine is immediately tempered by a dose of Plotinus' own version of Platonism, when he suggests that "perhaps it is not the water [that is everywhere in the papyrus] but the quality [*poiotēs*] of the water" (II.7.2, 15). The Platonic roots of such a claim are to be found at *Theaetetus* 182a8–b2, where Plato introduces the term 'quality' (*poiotēs*) as denoting sensible qualities such as hot or white (as opposed to hotness or whiteness) and at *Timaeus* 49d3–e7 & 51b4–6, where Plato insists that the elements such as water are "suches" rather than "thises" and, thus, that water is simply a region of the receptacle that has been moistened. What Plotinus is doing at line 15 is to introduce this Platonic analysis of sensible things as qualities into his discussion, thus shifting the focus of the doctrine of total mixture away from Stoic materialism. (For a clear statement of Plotinus' acceptance of this Platonic doctrine, see II.6.1, 44–49, as well as VI.3.8, 9–27, to be discussed below.)

That this is the import of line 15 is made clear in lines 16–20, where Plotinus sketches a materialistic response to the Platonic reduction of sensible things to qualities, a response which hinges on the equation of size, mass, and matter. This response (which itself is anti-Stoic) involves the claim that, because the papyrus is enlarged by the presence of water in it, it has taken on additional mass, which entails that "the matter of the water and the matter of the papyrus must be in two different places" (II.7.2, 19–20) and that this is not an example of total mixture after all. This materialistic view, in attributing mass to matter, is of course far-removed from the Plotinian doctrine of the incorporeality of matter (for which see, in particular, II.5.5, 3–7, 20–24 & 34–36, and III.6.7, particularly in the light of Plotinus' analysis of corporeality in chapter 3 of 'On Total Mixture'), a doctrine which will be affirmed in lines 29–32, but Plotinus chooses here to emphasize that the core of the objection has some merit. In lines 20–26 (which in large part repeats the Peripatetic argument of II.7.1, 38–48), he argues in effect that size is a special sort of quality (and, in VI.3.11–15, 23, he will defend the claim that quantity is a genus of sensible things which is distinct from quality): In the case of qualities other than size (e.g. colors), when two or more qualities are mixed together, each of the qualities loses its purity as the result of its mixture (so that yellow is no longer itself when it is mixed with blue to form green); in contrast, the mixing of one size with another does not result in the disappearance of size. It is this apparent truth that lies behind the materialist's singling out size as, in effect, constituting the matter of sensible things.

Plotinus does not go beyond this to refute the position of lines 16–20. Instead, he turns to another anti-Stoic, Peripatetic argument (first sketched at II.7.1, 8–15 & 31–32) to the effect that total mixture would require that the bodies which are completely interpenetrated in the mixture be actually divided into an infinite number of parts which is absurd (II.7.2, 26–27). However, Plotinus himself uses precisely the same argument in the very early treatise, 'On the Immortality of the Soul,' in order to show that the soul—because it is present in every part of the body and is, thus, totally mixed with the body—cannot itself be a body but must be incorporeal (IV.7.8², 7–22).[17] In the context of II.7, this earlier argument is implicitly recalled in order to move from the empirical fact that the papyrus is completely soaked with water (understood Platonically as wetness) to the new claim that qualities, such as wetness, can "go through bodies without cutting them" because these qualities are incorporeal (II.7.2, 27–29). In other words, Plotinus uses the empirically confirmed fact of total mixture in the case of the wet papyrus, a fact understood in terms of the Platonic analysis of sensible things as qualities, in order to show that sensible qualities are incorporeal (just as he had used in IV.7 the fact of soul's omnipresence in or total mixture with the body in order to show that the soul is incorporeal). It follows that he is willing to allow the possibility of the total mixture of *qualities*, while he denies the possibility of the total mixture of *bodies*.

The remainder of chapter 2 of II.7 provides a general analysis of the constraints on total mixture. It might seem that, given the incorporeality both of matter and now of sensible qualities, there would be no limits to the possibility of total mixture (II.7.2, 29–32). Nevertheless, Plotinus suggests (and here again it seems that the evidence for his claim is largely empirical, although no examples are cited) that certain qualities at least cannot completely interpenetrate solids (*ta sterea*), because solids "have qualities of such a kind as to prevent their penetration" (II.7.2, 33–34). He elaborates this claim by maintaining that the failure of solids to enter into total mixture may stem either from their being constituted by a large number of qualities—density (*pyknotēs*) being understood as a multiplicity of qualities—or from solids possessing the particular quality of density (II.7.2, 34–38). In either case, it follows that "it is not in so far as they are qualities that they will blend but in so far as they are qualities of a certain kind" (II.7.2, 38–39). The final, very difficult lines of the chapter suggest that qualities essentially connected with size may not admit of total mixture (thereby picking up the thought of lines 20–26?), but it is not at all clear just how this suggestion may be developed (II.7.2, 39–42).

With the end of chapter 2, the *physics* of II.7 comes to an end. We are now in a position to try to say something about the actual practice of physics that is exemplified in the treatise we have been considering. The first thing to be noted is that Plotinus does in fact offer (at a general level, to be sure) a description of the sensible world when he claims that total mixture is possible in certain situations. The further claim that these situations depend upon the nature of the sensible qualities to be mixed is, again, a claim that ultimately will shape detailed descriptions of the sensible world. To this extent, then, the treatise does conform to the conception of physics as a more-or-less metaphysically neutral description of the sensible world defended in section 1 of this essay. The second thing to be noted is that these general physical propositions descriptive of the physical world are defended by an argument which essentially involves the metaphysical claim that sensible things are to be analyzed as qualities (or sets of qualities). That this claim is simply borrowed from Plato makes it no less a result of dialectic (in the broad sense of dialectic as the discipline that develops the most general accounts of reality: see I.3.4 & 5, especially I.3.4, 1–9), and thus what we have here is a fairly clear case of a physical assertion which ultimately rests on an argument which makes essential use of a metaphysical assertion. This would appear to be a striking example of one way in which physics can 'borrow' from dialectic and borrow from dialectic in such a close way that the argument for the physical claim presupposes the truth of certain dialectical results. In this sense dialectic would serve Plotinian physics not as a tool (Cf. I.3.5, 8–13) but as a source of premises essential to the defense of physical claims. Moreover, the relative independence of physics from dialectic would be preserved in the distinction between the propositions of physics (which issue directly in statements descriptive of the sensible world) and the propositions of dialectic (which lead to statements descriptive of the sensible world only in conjunction with other, apparently non-dialectical propositions, such as descriptions of empirical fact).

The dialectical—or metaphysical—step in Plotinus' analysis of total mixture in chapter 2 of II.7 is elaborated in the brief third chapter of the treatise, which offers by way of an appendix to the argument of chapters 1 and 2 a metaphysical analysis of 'corporeity' (*sōmatotēs*). Corporeity is simply "a certain form [*eidos*] and a certain *logos* which enters matter and makes it body. If, then, this is what body is, that which is composed of all the qualities with matter, this is what corporeity would be" (II.7.3, 3–5). In other words, the term corporeity denotes the particular group of qualities that makes a body a body, a group which is itself an incorporeal thing (or quality) made up of incorporeal qualities (hence, Plotinus' insistence that corporeity is a *logos*). Implicit in this analysis of corporeity is Plotinus' basic metaphysical claim about the things that make up the sensible world, namely that they are nothing more than clusters of qualities in matter (matter understood here as the formless receptacle of the *Timaeus*).[18] The clearest expression of this view comes in the third treatise on the genera of Being (VI.3), where Plotinus writes:

> But then sensible substance will be a certain conglomeration [*symphorēsis*] of qualities [*poiotētōn*] and matter, and all these qualities compounded together in one matter will be substance, while each taken separately will be either a quality [*poion*] or a quantum or many qualities. (VI.3.8, 19–23)

A few lines later Plotinus describes the "so-called substance" of each sensible thing as a mixture (*migma*) of these qualities (lines 25–27), and—as J. M. Rist has pointed out—this term calls to mind the Stoic notion of total mixture (*krasis*). Rist maintains that Plotinus probably uses 'mixture' here "because 'collection' might be held to imply that the particulars were in some way physically divisible or reducible to their qualitative parts—which would be absurd."[19] While this is a reasonable interpretation, what is most striking about this passage in the context of our discussion is that Plotinus uses a notion of mixture both in physical description of the sensible world (where the term used is '*krasis*') and in metaphysical analysis of the substances that make up the sensible world (where the term used is '*migma*').[20] Moreover, in both cases the mixture at issue is a mixture of sensible qualities, which qualities are inherently incorporeal. What we see here, then, is that Plotinian physics shares with Plotinian metaphysical analysis of the sensible world a key concept—that of mixture—and it is by no means inconceivable that dialectic has borrowed the concept from Stoic physics. Later in the treatise on the genera of the sensible world, Plotinus again has recourse to the concept of mixture in his discussion of integration and disintegration as species of motion in chapter 25. Here he refers to the coming into being of new unities in the sensible world by means of *synknesis*, *mixis*, and *krasis* at lines 9–12, and later he sketches a rather Anaxagorean analysis of sensible alteration in general in terms of integration and disintegration (understood along the suggested lines of mixture)[21] and illustrates this with the example of the mixing (*mignuein*) of wine and water to produce something different from either of its constituents (VI.3.25, 24–29). What makes this sort of analysis dialectical (as opposed to physical) would seem to be the level of its generality more than anything else. An account of sensible change in general as a mixing and remixing of sensible qualities is compatible with almost any more particular description of the actual sorts of sensible changes (or quality mixtures) which are found to occur; in contrast, the Plotinian claim that total mixture is possible in the case of certain mixtures of qualities and impossible in the case of other mixtures of qualities (once this claim is made suitably specific, along the lines sketched in II.7.2.29–42) clearly dictates precise features of detailed descriptions of sensible things and processes.

Thus, our discussion of 'On Total Mixture' yields two results of importance to the understanding of Plotinian physics. First, while physics may issue in descriptions of the sensible world which are relatively independent of the ultimate metaphysical explanations of this world, the practice of physics may legitimately borrow premises from dialectic in order to justify or even to derive its descriptions. While Plotinus' practice in II.7 in no way suggests that such borrowing would be a necessary feature of physical argument, the alleged independence of physics from dialectic remains rather unclear. Second, the still puzzling difference between dialectic and physics seems (at least in the case of the contrasting uses of the concept of mixture) to come down ultimately to a difference in the degree of generality or universality of the claims of the respective disciplines, with dialectic offering exceedingly general characterizations of conceptual and ontological relations which find concrete and more specific exemplification in the propositions of physics. This analysis finds some confirmation in the treatise, 'On Dialectic,' where after making the rough distinction between dialectic and physics which we discussed in section 1 of this essay, Plotinus goes on to distinguish dialectic from moral philosophy, as well as to distinguish practical wisdom from the other virtues, primarily in terms of degree of generality, emphasizing for example that practical wisdom (*phronēsis*) is more concerned with the universal than are the other virtues (I.3.6, 5–14). The immediate proximity of this analysis to the distinction between dialectic and physics at least suggests that degree of generality may be relevant to the earlier distinction as well. With these issues in mind, let us turn to another example of Plotinian physics.

3. The Composition of the Stars

The treatise, 'On Heaven' (II.1), written apparently in the same period as 'On Total Mixture' (in Porphyry's chronological ordering of Plotinus' treatises), is devoted to a defense of the Platonic doctrine of the incorruptibility of the heavens against the objections of Stoics and Stoicizing Platonists. As Bréhier has shown,[22] the treatise falls into two fairly distinct parts: Chapters 1–5 defend the general position, insisting that the heaven as a whole and all its parts are equally incorruptible, everlasting and immutable, and attempt to show how such a view is compatible both with much of Aristotelian doctrine and with the *Timaeus*, as well as with certain tenets of common sense; chapters 6–8 strengthen this position by developing an interpretation of the *Timaeus* which shows that the heavenly bodies are not made up of any mixture of the terrestrial (or sublunary) elements, but are composed of a pure variety of fire, thus undermining any argument for the corruptibility of the heavens by appeal to the instability of the elements (and also undermining the curious Stoic notion that the heavenly bodies need nourishment). This discussion of the composition of the stars is forced upon Plotinus by his earlier denial of Aristotle's doctrine of the quintessence (II.1.2, 12–16). It is with the second part of the treatise that we shall be concerned here, because it is in chapters 6 and 7 particularly that an unambiguously physical doctrine is defended. The claim that the heavenly bodies are made of a pure variety of fire is surely a clear case of a description of the sensible world, and it is thus a particularly striking feature of Plotinus' argument for this claim that it proceeds in large part by way of textual exegesis, with the *Timaeus* as the text at issue.

Two passages from the *Timaeus* set the argument in motion in chapter 6: At 31b4–8 Plato maintains that the universe must be made up of fire (on the grounds that it is a visible thing, and nothing is visible without fire) and of earth (on the grounds that it is a solid thing, and nothing is solid without earth); at 40a2–3 Plato suggests that the bodies of the gods—i.e. the stars—must be made primarily of fire, given their brilliant sensible appearance (see II.1.6, 2–12). The apparently clear view developed here is, however, complicated by a third passage—*Timaeus* 31b8–32c4—where Plato, arguing that two distinct things can only be unified by a third, claims that air and water provide the necessary intermediates for the proportionate uniting of fire and earth. This would appear to require that the heavenly bodies—like all other bodies in the sensible world—be made of some ratio of all four elements.

Now, while such a view seems to be perfectly consistent with the passages from the *Timaeus* at issue here, Plotinus is uneasy with it, in part for apparently empirical reasons—it certainly appears that water and earth can be mixed together, for example, without the presence of fire or air (II.1.6, 14–17)—and in part because it seems to compromise the very identity of the elements. Indeed, the remaining portion of chapter 6 brings up a series of arguments—arguments of a curiously hybrid character, making conceptual points on the basis of empirical observation—each of which is meant to cast doubt on the (again Anaxagorean[23]) claim that "no element would ever have its own essential nature by itself, but all are mixed and take their names from the dominant element in each" (II.1.6, 22–24).[24] A representative example of these arguments is that concerned with the essential presence of water in earth:

> They say that earth cannot have concrete existence without moisture; the moisture of water is earth's adhesive. But even if we grant that this is so, it is absurd to say that each element is a separate something and not give it any concrete existence but only an existence along with the others, without anything being separate. How could there be a nature and substantial reality of earth if there is no particle of earth which is earth unless water is present in it to stick it together? What could the water stick if there was no bulk of earth at all which it could join to another contiguous particle? And if there is any bulk of absolute earth at all, then earth can exist by nature without water; and if it is not so, there will be nothing to be stuck together by the water. (II.1.6, 24–35)

We see Plotinus here moving rapidly from what seems to be a conceptual point about the need for the terms of a relation to have some existence separate from that relation to a series of rather oddly materialistic claims about the need for 'natures' and 'substantial realities' (the Aristotelian term *to ti ēn einai* is used at lines 29–30) to be exemplified in a relatively pure form in the sensible world. Curiously enough, both the conceptual point and these materialistic claims are at odds with Plotinus' assertions in the treatise 'Against the Gnostics,' that the coming-to-be of the sensible world does not proceed one element at a time (beginning with fire, according to certain Gnostics) and that this coming-to-be follows a sort of mathematical blueprint or outline which already contains all the elements in their mutual relations (II.9.12, 12–23 & II.9.17, 4–10). Thus, it comes as no surprise that Plotinus eventually grants the claim that at least many sensible things (those "on earth") are composed of all the elements (II.1.6, 54–60); indeed, in the treatise on the genera of Being, he even grants the truth of the *Epinomis* principle of naming by predominance (VI.3.9, 15–18). What he is not willing to grant is that these claims hold true of the celestial bodies, and his apparent argument for this restriction is simply that "to lift up earth into heaven is against nature and opposed to her laws" (II.1.6, 56–57).

In chapter 7, Plotinus' doubts about the omni-elemental composition of sensible things find a deeper analysis in his reinterpretation of *Timaeus* 31b4–8, where Plato appears to maintain that the stars must be made up of both fire and earth. Here he draws a distinction between the nature or substance of an element and certain qualities that belong to that element, suggesting that it is these latter qualities that may mix together to make sensible things appear to be constituted by all the elements. At lines 10–19 he writes:

> Earth is mingled with the upper fire, not in the constitution of the stars but because, since they are both in the universal order, fire gains something from earth as earth does from fire and each element from each of the others; not in the sense that the element which gains something is composed of both, itself and that of which it has a share; but, through the community of the universe, while remaining itself it takes, not the actual other element but something which belongs to it, not air, for instance, but the yielding softness of air, and earth the brightness of fire: the mixture gives all qualities and consequently produces the compound thing, not supplying earth only and the nature of fire but this solidity and density of earth.

Given this distinction, Plotinus seems to believe that he can maintain that the pure fire of the stars need not be mixed with earth itself in order to share in earth's quality of solidity, and this neatly solves the problem of *Timaeus* 31b4–8. Thus, he concludes (and the rest of the treatise pursues the implications of this conclusion) that the stars are composed of this pure variety of fire, without any admixture of other elements (or even of other species of fire).[25]

I have quoted extensively from Plotinus' argument in chapter 7 so that the striking language of the passage may be apparent. From the mingling (*memichthai*) of earth and fire Plotinus moves on to the mixture (*mixis*) which bestows all qualities, and the link between these two sorts of mixing appears to be the community (*koinōnia*) of the universe as an ordered system (*kosmos*). The language of Stoicism is pervasive here in the reference to mixture and in the suggestion of the doctrine of cosmic sympathy; at the same time, the language of Plotinus' analysis of sensible substances as conglomerations or mixtures of sensible qualities is recalled.

Here, however, and in contrast to other discussions, Plotinus suggests that there is a legitimate distinction to be made between sensible elements and their qualities, which in turn suggests that the elements—which surely are examples of sensible substances—cannot simply be groupings of sensible qualities. The attempt to make a sharp distinction between, for example, earth and its solidity threatens the analysis of cases of total mixture in II.7 (where, it will be remembered, Plotinus identifies water with its wetness: see II.7.2, 15). The key to the resolution of this problem would seem to lie in Plotinus' endorsement of the Aristotelian distinction between qualities and essence in his account of the sensible world (VI.3.16, 1–5) and in his tendency to conflate the notion of sensible essence with the notion of the intelligible *logos* which comes to be present in matter (for a striking example of this, see II.6.2, 6–34). This would allow him to maintain that the stars are essentially composed solely of fire—implicitly making reference to the *logos* of fire manifested in the bodies of the stars—while granting that they possess incidentally such earthy qualities as solidity—here referring to the mixture of sensible qualities which is, strictly speaking, the sensible substance. Such an analysis would leave Plotinus denying the Aristotelian identity of substance and essence (at least for sensible things), but this is not at all unreasonable for a serious Platonist who would maintain that the real essences of sensible things are to be found outside the sensible world in the intelligible world of forms.[26]

Looking back over the argument of II.1.6 & 7, we can see that Plotinus has once again had recourse to the dialectical analysis of the sensible world in order to establish a proposition descriptive of that world, in this case the proposition that the stars' bodies are composed solely of a pure species of fire and not of a mixture of all the elements. The dialectical results employed here are in fact two: First, he endorses the analysis of sensible substances as mixtures of qualities (which analysis had paved the way for his views on the possibility of total mixture); second, he introduces the distinction between the essence and the (nonessential, incidental) qualities of sensible substances. Both of these points are clearly dialectical in their origins—having to do with those most general characterizations of reality which are the special province of dialectic, as described at I.3.4, 1–9—and in themselves seem compatible with a variety of (physical) descriptions of the sensible world. However, in the course of his exegesis of *Timaeus* 31b4–8, Plotinus manages to use these dialectical results to lend support for a claim about the composition of the stars which clearly is a matter of physical description. It should be noted that chapters 6 and 7 of 'On Heaven' in no way constitute a proof of or even an argument for Plotinus' physical description; at best, the chapters shows that such a description is both coherent and compatible with Plato's text. This is in clear contrast to Plotinus' procedure in 'On Total Mixture,' where the physical claims about the possibility of total mixture were quite clearly defended by an argument making explicit use of dialectical results. Our study of II.1 also suggests that we were on the right track at the end of section 2 of this essay in suggesting that dialectic is to be distinguished from physics (at least partially) by reference to the greater generality or universality of its claims. Here, we see that dialectic yields the distinction between essence and qualities, while allowing an elaboration of sensible substance in terms of mixtures of qualities, but it is left for physics to offer the highly specific claim that the bodies of the stars are composed of fire alone.

4. Tentative Conclusions

In the preceding pages I have attempted to uncover the nature of Plotinian physics in part by considering the implications of Plotinus' Neoplatonism in general (in section 1) and in larger part by considering two specific cases of his actual practice of developing and defending what are clearly propositions descriptive of the physical world (in sections 2 and 3). Several things have emerged from the discussion. (1) There does seem to be room within Plotinus' conception of philosophy for a (perhaps relatively unimportant) discipline of describing the sensible world, a discipline which would in effect find its ultimate justification in providing the data to be explained metaphysically by appeal to the intelligible world of forms. (2) Plotinus at times develops the claims of such a descriptive physics by appeal to empirical observation: In 'On Total Mixture,' the observation of water soaking through papyrus was suggested by the Stoic doctrine under review in the treatise, but what Plotinus emphasizes is the apparent empirical support for the doctrine. (3) Plotinus at times finds his physical doctrine in the texts of earlier thinkers, most notably in the *Timaeus*; and even when he cannot quite find the doctrine he wants (as in 'On Heaven') he is concerned to show how the doctrine is at least consistent with the claims of Plato. (4) In the arguments in support of his physical claims, Plotinus is willing to countenance the borrowing of indispensable premises from dialectic: In II.7, for example, the defense of the possibility of total mixture is dependent upon the metaphysical analysis of sensible things as collections—in fact, mixtures—of sensible qualities.

Here we find that an empirically plausible view is made compelling by means of metaphysical analysis. (5) Plotinus' attempts to derive physical doctrines from other texts—what might be called *exegetical physics*—at times make use of distinctions or analyses which are properly dialectical in their origins: In II.1 we find that he makes use of both the mixture analysis of sensible substance and the Aristotelian distinction between essence and quality not so as to prove that the stars are composed solely of fire but to show how such a physical claim could be consistent with Plato's text in the *Timaeus*.

Each of these five points helps to clarify Plotinus' remarks in 'On Dialectic' about the relation between dialectic and natural philosophy, and I believe that our discussion at least allows us to rule out one plausible analysis of the practice of Plotinian physics. Bréhier, for one, argues that the method of Plotinus' physics is "always the same," something that we have seen is quite clearly not the case, based on our study of II.7 and II.1. He goes on to explain the character of this method:

> It is a method of conversion which consists in excluding from matter and bodies all positive reality that one might be tempted to attribute to them, and in ascribing it to an action from above....[Physical explanation] consists in first stripping matter and then bodies of all positive realities which experience reveals to us as existing in them, inasmuch as, at each level, these realities are traces of the Soul. One will be a good natural philosopher to the extent that one knows how to convert the sensible world into spirit...[27]

While it is clear that Plotinus will insist that appeals to soul and the forms are necessary for the ultimate explanation of things and events in the sensible world, our study of the actual practice of his physics shows that there is a properly physical describing of the sensible world which can proceed without any overt such appeals to soul or the intelligible. Indeed, the metaphysical claims that play such an important role in the treatises we have been considering concern precisely the analysis of sensible substances taken in themselves (and not in their relation to the intelligible). Moreover, it is simply not the case that Plotinus attempts to eliminate empirical observation and its results from his physical descriptions of the sensible world, as Bréhier suggests. He uses dialectic to reinterpret or to reanalyze the results of observation, but he does not substitute metaphysical analysis for empirical description.

Nevertheless, it does appear that Plotinus' willingness to allow physics to borrow from dialectic raises some problems for the interpretation of Plotinian physics that may prove quite difficult to resolve.

In the passage quoted earlier from chapter 7 of 'On Heaven,' we saw that Plotinus maintains that each of the elements possesses the qualities of the other elements, and he attributes this to the community (*koinōnia*) of the universe, which is in turn apparently described as a mixture (*mixis*) (lines 10–19). One plausible interpretation of this admittedly obscure passage would be that the community of the universe is in fact the total mixture of all things in all things; corresponding to the Stoic doctrine of cosmic sympathy that Plotinus attributes to the fact that the universe is a single living organism,[28] this theory of community would provide an analysis of the unity of the world's body in terms of the omnipresence of all sensible things in all sensible things. The principle that 'all things are in all things' has a long history, beginning as early as Anaxagoras[29] and continuing through the later Neoplatonists (where it provides among other things a crucial premise in the analysis of the functioning of magic).[30] What is striking here is that the logic of Plotinus' position in II.1.7 appears to force him into accepting this principle at a very general level as describing the relation of the elements to one another,[31] and there is no clear reason why the principle could not and should not be extended to cover the relation of all sensible substances to one another. However, if the principle is so extended, it appears to run into conflict with Plotinus' treatment of total mixture in II.7. As we saw in section 2, Plotinus argues at some length that total mixture (of which 'all things are in all things' would be the extreme case) is possible in certain mixtures of sensible qualities; however, he also clearly indicates that certain qualities (apparently constituting density) may not allow of such total mixture. The suggested reading of II.1.7 dictates that total mixture must, on the contrary, be characteristic of the entire sensible world, and this is difficult to reconcile with Plotinus' earlier willingness to grant that not all qualities completely intermix.

One way out of this puzzle would be to insist that the principle that 'all things are in all things' commits Plotinus to a general acceptance of total mixture at the level of a dialectical analysis of sensible things but not at the level of physical description. This, of course, would serve to confuse further the still problematic distinction between dialectic and physics, although perhaps the distinction could be salvaged once again by appeal to varying degrees of generality. However, such an analysis would still require the Plotinian physicist to explain how it is that not all sensible qualities appear to mix totally in the sensible world (it being understood that they are all *really* mixed totally, when considered dialectically). Part of the difficulty here is that physics and dialectic seem to be competing with one another in describing the sensible world, the greater generality of dialectic nevertheless dictating rather specific physical claims; and it is not immediately clear how the Plotinian is to show that sensible qualities can both be and not be mixed totally at the same time.

In the final analysis, the difficulties and obscurities of Plotinian physics may simply be the inevitable consequences of a general philosophical *Weltanschauung* which stresses the comparative unimportance and even moral danger of preoccupation with the sensible world. Indeed, in his dialectical examination of the genera of the sensible world (VI.3), Plotinus often emphasizes the possibility that there are competing views of more-or-less equal plausibility, although he usually does attempt to resolve the lingering uncertainty by arguing for one analysis rather than for another. At the end of the treatise, arguing about the role of stability (*stasis*) as a possible genus of sensible things, Plotinus finally betrays a certain impatience with his discussion: "But about these questions let it be decided in whatever way seems best to each individual" (VI.3.27, 44). If the dialectical analysis of the sensible world's genera is thus relatively unimportant to Plotinus, it would come as no surprise to see him dismiss worries about the proper (physical) description of the sensible world. In his discussion of matter's impassibility in III.6, he in fact comes very close to this, suggesting that the presence of form in matter may be described almost any way one likes—since matter (i.e. Plato's receptacle) is utterly without form—and quoting Democritus' strikingly relativistic saying, "Color by convention and other things by convention,"[32] as illustrative of this point (III.6.12, 19–24). What these passages suggest is that it may be asking too much of Plotinus to expect a firm, clear, and consistent account of the sensible world to be found in the *Enneads*. Nevertheless, I have tried to show that there a number of hints in Plotinus' own analyses of physical issues as to how the project of the physical description of the sensible world might be carried out along Plotinian lines. That there remain unresolved problems in working out the details of the Plotinian conception of physics as a branch of philosophy distinct from dialectic will not, I hope, discourage further examination of these issues.

The Colorado College

NOTES

1. All references to Plotinus are to the critical edition of Paul Henry and Hans-Rudolf Schwyzer (Paris and Brussels: Desclée de Brouwer, 1951–1973). All translations from *Enneads* I–III are essentially those of A. H. Armstrong in *Plotinus*. (Cambridge, MA: Harvard University Press, 1966-1988). All other translations are those of the author.

2. For Porphyry's descriptions of these treatises, see his *Vita Plotini* 24, 37–39, 59–60, & 25, 1–11.
3. For a recent example, see John P. Anton, "Plotinus' Approach to Categorical Theory" in *The Significance of Neoplatonism*, ed. R. Baine Harris, (Norfolk, VA: International Society for Neoplatonic Studies, 1976), 89 & 94–95.
4. The major exception to this is Émile Bréhier, whose explicit treatment of Plotinian physics is discussed below.
5. On this dimension of Plotinus' Neoplatonism, see my "Omnipresence, Participation, and Eidetic Causation in Plotinus" in *The Structure of Being: A Neoplatonic Approach*, ed. R. Baine Harris, (Norfolk, VA: International Society for Neoplatonic Studies, 1982), 90–103.
6. Such a claim may be presupposed by Plotinus himself at VI.3.10, 7–20.
7. On the role of the soul in the structuring and maintenance of the sensible world, see IV.3, 9–16, III.2 & 3 & II.3, 16 & 17, as well as such curious shorter passages as II.2.1, 37–39 & II.1.3, 13–23.
8. Compare Plato's rather different emphasis at *Timaeus* 59c5–d3.
9. Compare Émile Bréhier, *The Philosophy of Plotinus*, translated by Joseph Thomas (Chicago: The University of Chicago Press, 1958), 171.
10. Bréhier, *Philosophy of Plotinus*, 175.
11. Rist points out that even as early as Zeno the doctrine is held to be true of both substances and qualities; see J. M. Rist, *Stoic Philosophy* (Cambridge: University Press, 1969), 158.
12. S. Sambursky, *Physics of the Stoics* (London: Routledge and Kegan Paul, 1959), 13.
13. See his "Notice" to II.7 in Plotin, *Ennéades*, texte établi et traduit par Émile Bréhier (Paris: Société d'édition *Les Belles Lettres*, 1924–1938), II:89–90[sic].
14. A. H. Armstrong, *The Architecture of the Intelligible Universe in the Philosophy of Plotinus: An Analytical and Historical Study* (Cambridge: Cambridge University Press, 1940), 37. Reprinted, Amsterdam: Adolf M. Hakkert, 1967.
15. H. J. Blumenthal, *Plotinus' Psychology: His Doctrines of the Embodied Soul* (The Hague: Martinus Nijhoff, 1971), 3 and 10.
16. Bréhier is clear about this implication of the treatise; see his "Notice" to II.7 and *Philosophy of Plotinus*, 177. This also appears to be Rist's view; see J. M. Rist, *Plotinus: The Road to Reality* (Cambridge: University Press, 1967), 173.
17. Armstrong notes that there thus appears to be some connection between the doctrine of total mixture and Plotinus' doctrine of omnipresence: see *Architecture*, 37. Compare Blumenthal's very different reading of IV.7: see *Plotinus' Psychology*, 10.
18. Plotinus' metaphysical analysis of sensible particulars has been carefully discussed by A. C. Lloyd, "Neoplatonic Logic and Aristotelian Logic," *Phronesis* I (1955–1956), 158–159; Rist, *Plotinus*, 107–108; and Kevin

Corrigan, "The Internal Dimensions of the Sensible Object in the Thought of Plotinus and Aristotle," *Dionysius* V (1981), 98–99. All of these stress the essentially Platonic origins of this analysis.

19. Rist, *Plotinus*, 108.
20. Sambursky points out that *krasis* refers to the mixture of liquids, while *mixis* refers to the mixture of non-liquids in Stoic texts, but I see no reason to think Plotinus' use of '*migma*' in VI.3.8 is influenced by this distinction: see Sambursky, *Physics*, 12–13.
21. The roots of this analysis of sensible change are to be found in Anaxagoras, *fragment* B 17.
22. See his "Notice" to II.1, *Ennéades*, II:3–5.
23. For Anaxagoras' version of this position, see Aristotle, *Physics* 187a23–b7.
24. Armstrong emphasizes that this view is developed in the pseudo-Platonic *Epinomis* 981c8–982a3: see his translation, II:24, n1. It is worth noting that this view is itself again perfectly compatible with the passages from the *Timaeus* at issue here.
25. This pure species of fire which "is other than flame and only gently warm" (Cf. *Timaeus* 58c5–7) is nevertheless a body and is not to be confused with incorporeal light: see II.1.7, 25–30.
26. Aristotle's complex analysis of the relation between substance and essence is the central topic of *Metaphysics* Z, especially chapters 4 & 6.
27. Bréhier, *Philosophy of Plotinus*, 175 & 178.
28. On Plotinus' account of cosmic sympathy, see R. T. Wallis, *Neoplatonism* (London: Duckworth, 1972), 70–72.
29. See the passage from the *Physics* (187a23–67) cited above.
30. On the principle in general, see Wallis, *Neoplatonism*, 107 and 123–124, and Dodds' note in Proclus, *The Elements of Theology*, revised text with translation by E. R. Dodds (Oxford: Clarendon Press, 1963), 254.
31. Dodds notes that Proclus accepts the principle at precisely this level in his *Timaeus* commentary, II.26, 23–27, 7: see *Elements*, 254.
32. See Democritus, *fragments* B 9 & B 125.

PLOTINUS AND BIOLOGY[1]

Anthony Preus

A reader might find the subject of this essay somewhat surprising, since Plotinus is not generally credited with having contributed to biology. In fact, Plotinus says very little about what we would call the science of biology. It would have been surprising had he done so, for the earlier Neoplatonists as a group developed a philosophical position which seems in its broad outlines independent of biological investigations. The classic interpretation of Plotinus and his associates would lead us to believe that few philosophies have turned so completely away from empirical studies of nature; Plotinus especially is taken to have pursued the formal, eschewing the multiplicities of the material world. However, in this essay I argue that Plotinus did, after all, make some very important contributions to the development of later biological thought, and in particular to the development of biological concepts which broke away from the dominance of Aristotelianism. The common notion of historians of biology is that Aristotle's philosophy, augmented by the Alexandrians and Galen, reigned supreme throughout antiquity and the middle ages, and continued to dominate Renaissance and early modern biological thought. In this connection, such people as Harvey and Cisalpino come to mind. My objective in this essay is to indicate one way in which that Aristotelian synthesis was seriously modified by a philosophical position which opened the way to a quite different way of understanding the living world.

A survey of the literature on Neoplatonism supports the impression that biological concerns are not easy to tease out of their texts. Many pages have been written about the theory of the soul in Plotinus and others of his school, but until Emilsson published *Plotinus on Sense-Perception* (1988) only a few pages dealt with the physiological consequences of the embodiment of soul, and still today very few pages indeed discuss the non-psychological parts of biological theory in Plotinus.[2] H. J. Blumenthal explains that for Plotinus, all soul is derived from Nous (Intellect), and from the World Soul, and consequently the particulars of embodiment are not so worthy of investigation as the bare fact of embodiment; the entelechy theory of the soul, so fruitful for Aristotle's biological investigations, is explicitly rejected.[3] Perhaps there exists somewhere an extensive study of Plotinus and biology, but I have found only one short essay and a part of a book chapter explicitly with any early Neoplatonist's approaches to biology as such: The article is Pierre-Maxime Schuhl, 'Plotin et la Biology' (CNRS, 1971), 110; and it is barely half a page long. Schuhl's summary is suggestive, however; my comments owe much to his. The section in a book is Grigorios Kostaras, *Der Begriff des Lebens bei Plotin* (1969), 27–37. I found Kostaras' book only after I had completed this essay, but was pleased to find that he anticipated several of my interpretations.

There are several reasons for thinking that Plotinus *ought* to have something to say about biology. In the first place, Plotinus, like all Neoplatonists, takes Plato's *Timaeus* almost as a sacred text—and the last forty pages of that dialogue are full of suggestions for directions which could be taken in biological investigation. Those suggestions were not lost on the *middle* Platonists. Secondly, the interests and pursuits of several of the middle Platonists would lead us to expect comments on biology from the Neoplatonists as well. It is well-known that Galen thought of himself as a Platonist, and that he tried to synthesize the *Timaeus* with the Hippocratic medical tradition in the *Doctrines of Plato and Hippocrates* and elsewhere.[4] But it is also true that several of the essays in Plutarch's *Moralia* rely upon biological knowledge, and show an interest in the character, if not the structure or physiology, of various species of animals; such essays include 'On the Cleverness of Animals,' 'Beasts are Rational,' 'The Eating of Flesh,' and 'The Causes of Natural Phenomena,' which last also shows some interest in plants, along with much else. Another middle Platonist treatise, the *Epitome of Plato's Doctrines* attributed to Alcinous in the manuscripts and to Albinus by most modern scholars, synthesizes Platonic and Aristotelian attitudes toward biological investigation, finding particularly significant the physiological implications of the embodiment of the soul. Chapters 17–22 explicitly summarize the later pages of the *Timaeus*. Another middle Platonist who interested himself in biomedical matters was Apuleius; probably some degree of interest was rather widespread in that period among those who considered themselves Platonists.[5]

Nevertheless none of the earlier Neoplatonists (Plotinus, Proclus, Porphyry, Iamblichus) seems to have paid significant attention to the later pages of the *Timaeus*. I have found nothing in Plotinus which refers unambiguously to those pages, and that impression is supported by

Charrue's reading (*op. cit.*) The great commentary by Proclus stops well before the biological material begins, and my survey of the other early Neoplatonists has turned up only vague secondhand echoes of Plato's biomedical interests. Of course *later* Neoplatonists knew the entire *Timaeus* quite well, and some of them were guided in their reading by Galen and other middle Platonists.

P.–M. Schuhl calls attention to several more sophisticated reasons for thinking that Plotinus and the Neoplatonists should be interested in biology. His brief summary claims that no one has studied the specifically biological aspects of the thought of Plotinus, but that several passages of the *Enneads* touch upon biological issues of interest even today. He calls attention to Plotinus' rejection of mechanistic explanations (III.8), although there is much more to be said about that tractate; he notices also some comments in passing (II.4.8 on specific size, IV.4.7 on the continuity of biological movement) which he thinks bring Plotinus close to the biologically motivated thought of Andre Meyer and Henri Bergson; finally, he notes the chapter (IV.9.6) in which Plotinus most clearly tries to explain how *logoi* are present in the seed in sexual generation. The references to Meyer and Bergson might seem hyperbolic, but they are not; Bergson lectured in 1897–1898 on *Enneads* IV, which includes the passage Schuhl compares with Bergson's thought.[6]

1. *Enneads* II.4.8.

Looking more closely at the passages cited by Schuhl, we find that one of them states the notoriously Neoplatonistic doctrine of the negativity of matter:

> All that ever appears upon matter is brought in by the *eidos* [form]; the *eidos* alone possesses: to it belongs the magnitude and all else that goes with the *logos* or follows upon it. Quantity is given with the *eidos* in all the particular genera—man, bird, and particular kind of bird. The imaging of quantity upon matter by an outside power is not more surprising than the imaging of quality; quality is no doubt a *logos*, but quantity also is, being measure and number.[7]

If explanation is so completely dependent upon form, we may readily suppose that Plotinus does not have available the sorts of explanations of defects, errors and oddities to which Aristotle has recourse; even Plato appeals to irregularities of matter more readily than can Plotinus. For Aristotle, inadequacies of material entities may be ascribed to the failure of form to master the matter; for Plotinus there is ultimately nothing to be mastered, so must not the inadequacies be ascribed to the form or to the *logos* itself? Probably there is a Plotinian answer, but it must be different from the Aristotelian. Another point worth noticing in this passage is that Plotinus does not distinguish between '*eidos*' and '*genos*' is such a way that we would be tempted to translate those words into the modern concepts of 'species' and 'genus'; in this passage *eidos* and *logos* are adventitious forms, while the word '*genos*' refers indiscriminately to two classificatory levels of animal. This is not actually as much a break with the Aristotelian tradition as one might think, since it is not correct to translate even Aristotle's uses of the words '*eidos*' and '*genos*' as 'species' and 'genus.'

2. *Enneads* V.9.6

Plotinus comments several times on how form is present in sexual generation. It seems to me that he was worried about how his general philosophical position could handle the ontological problems involved in sexual generation; at least he suggests ways in which defects and errors may occur, even if he does not answer questions we may have about the ontological status of new members of a species. A positive theory of the transmission of form might be derived from V.9.6, where the containment of powers in seeds (*spermata*) is used as an image to explain how the mind includes the contents of intellection:

> The entire mind includes as a genus includes species and a whole includes parts. The powers of seeds provide an image of what I'm saying; for all are undistinguished in the whole, and the *logoi* are as it were in one center; there is one *logos* of the eye, another of the hands, known to be other from the visible thing generated from it. The powers in the seeds are each of them one whole *logos* with the parts wrapped up in it; the bodily has a matter, for example some fluid, but the *eidos* itself is the whole and a *logos*, being the same in *eidos* as the soul in the generator, which is an image (*indalma*) of another better soul. Some call this power in the seeds 'nature,' which was driven thence from those prior to it, as light from fire, and it turns and enforms the matter, not relying on the help of those much—discussed mechanisms (levers), but by imparting the *logoi*. (V.9.6: my translation)

In the context, Plotinus is trying to explain how the mind contains many different sorts of knowledge simultaneously, how the mind can, as Aristotle put it, think all things. The 'seed image' argues that the mind thinks all things in a way analogous to that in which semen contains all the parts of the body which it generates. Brèhier, in his note to this passage, supposes that Plotinus commits himself here to preformationism, the theory that the parts are already present in the semen determinately. It seems to me more likely that Plotinus is aiming at something closer to what we would call an epigenetic position, not so very dissimilar from Aristotle's, since what is present in the seed is not the parts, but the *dynameis* (powers) for bringing the parts into being. Plotinus actually paraphrases some of Aristotle's account of sexual generation—his use of the word '*emperiechomenon*' ('wrapped up in') echoes Aristotle's use of the word '*emperilambamenon*' at *De Generatione Animalium* II.3, 736b36.[8] Further, Plotinus says explicitly that the *logos* as *dynamis* enforms nothing more than something fluid when it is in the seed, that it is the power to bring about the development of the organ, and not the organ itself. Plotinus, as I understand this passage, accepts the Aristotelian doctrine that there are active powers present in the seed, and calls them *logoi* as does Aristotle himself. But Plotinus cannot have the *entire* Aristotelian theory of sexual generation, since he does not have the passive powers, the capacities of materials to be acted upon by those active powers or *logoi*.

We may discern some other unAristotelian ideas in the passage. The notion that the generative soul is an image of another better soul would be puzzling from an Aristotelian point of view—plants have only generative soul, yet are perfect of their kind. Certainly mind and entities that have minds are regarded by Aristotle as much as by the Neoplatonist as the 'best' entities that exist, but the structuring of the continuum between the various psychic functions by means of the image-relation (*mimēsis*) would be alien to Aristotle, and not readily explicable in terms of the physiological structure of plants in comparison with animals and human beings.

Another peculiarly Plotinian touch is the suggestion that the nature present in generation is caused to act by something else not present, "as light from fire"—in other words, as an action ('emanation'?) from some higher power. For Aristotle, the nature present in generation is a tool, (*organon*), of the male parent, and even perhaps of the male line going back to some distant progenitor, but the moving cause in generation is not traced to a transcendent origin. To be sure, Aristotle does say in

Metaphysics Λ.5 that the causes of a person are the elements, the father, and "besides these the sun and its oblique course" (1071b15) but that means little more than that the climate, the existence of a biosphere, and perhaps a propitious season of the month or year, are necessary conditions for individual acts of procreation.

Plotinus seems to take a slap at Aristotle's account of sexual generation when he attacks the appeal to mechanisms, since it is at just this point in his argument that Aristotle appeals to the marvelous automatic puppets (*De Generatione Animalium* II.5, 741b8). It is as if Plotinus were saying that his version of the theory of sexual generation is more purely Aristotelian, more purely antireductionist, because it explicitly refuses *any* appeal to mechanical explanation, relying *only* on the image of the propagation of the *logos*. The refusal to accept Aristotle's mechanical analogy is symptomatic of what I take to be the central problem with Plotinus' implicit explanation of sexual generation: For Aristotle, the mechanical image is introduced to show how active and passive powers can work upon each other in series, until a final result is obtained. For Aristotle, the seed has the power of making, and in a way becoming, the source (*archē*) of the body, which in turn makes the rest of the body. The male and female seeds have in them all the parts *as powers*, but not as actualities; Plotinus appears to agree. But Plotinus does not seem willing to distinguish active and passive powers, and thus cannot easily explain why the actual presence of the *logos* does not also mean the actual presence of the part. It is because of this embarrassment, as I would call it, that Bréhier concludes that Plotinus must have meant to assert preformationism in this passage. It makes more sense to put Plotinus in the epigenetic camp; after all, the mind is not simultaneously conscious of all the thoughts of which it can be conscious. Thoughts which are not currently conscious are present in the mind as *logoi*, as *dynameis (passive powers)*, according to this passage. A preformationist image of thought would have all thoughts actually present consciously simultaneously—that certainly won't work!

Although we may discern some distinctions between Aristotle's theory of sexual generation and its altered form in Plotinus, ultimately neither version is especially convincing. Neither Aristotle nor Plotinus imagines anything remotely ancestral to our DNA and so on, nor do they observe the patterns of heredity which we associate with Gregor Mendel. Both Aristotle and Plotinus knew that information, *logoi*, has to be transferred from parent to child through the generative materials, but neither had any real notion of how. The theory expressed in this passage of Plotinus is largely derivative from Aristotle, but it is less successful, vaguer, less argued, less developed.

3. *Enneads* III.8

In III.8, Plotinus takes up the theme of sexual generation again, and clarifies the place of generation in his system. In this important tractate Plotinus argues that generation is the actualization of *theoria* (contemplation). He admits the paradoxical look of that notion, since the first word of the tractate is 'playing' (*paizontes*); but he becomes quite serious in his defense of the thesis that all nature both stems from *theoria* and aims in all natural processes toward an actualization of *theoria.* This thesis he believes to be true of the universe as a whole, of humankind including children, of animals, plants, and the changing character of the inanimate world.

The interpretation of *all* natural change as an urge toward *theoria* is, I suppose, a radical interpretation or application of Plato's doctrine of *eros* (love).[9] Plato had suggested the possibility of the general application of the doctrine of *eros*, first in the *Symposium*; one might want to take it as Plato's solution of the problem of explaining goal-directed change. But we may remember that Aristotle, in *Metaphysics* A, charges that Plato *fails* to explain goal-directed change, despite the well-known criticism which Socrates in the *Phaedo* directs at Anaxagoras for the same failure. In the *Timaeus*, the most 'scientific' of the dialogues, Plato uses neither *eros* nor *theoria* in biological explanation. It was left to Plotinus, among others, to make the connection.

Rejecting all mechanistic explanations of life, Plotinus asks rhetorically: "What jostling, what levers could bring about all those colors and forms?" (III.8.2) The reference to jostling (*ōthismos*) sounds very like an explicit rejection of Epicurean atomism. As if the rejection of mechanistic explanations were to imply idealism directly, Plotinus immediately claims that nature is an 'unmoved form,' a *logos* which produces another *logos* in animals and plants (III.8.2). Since nature itself is not identical to the *logos* which is in the entity produced, and it is not an action, it must be a *logos* which is simultaneously a *theoria* (III.8.3); this means to me that Plotinus believes that a *logos* which is separable from a particular physical entity, yet identifiable in some sense as the *logos of* that entity, must be 'theoretical' in this special sense. The idea that nature is an unmoved mover in that to which it belongs primarily is not, of course, an unAristotelian notion, but the separation of the nature from the generated entity *is* unAristotelian, and makes a purely biological analysis impossible. Indeed, it tends toward a personification of nature, and Plotinus succumbs to that temptation with poetic enthusiasm.

Personified nature is represented as telling us that the generated entity is the *theama*—the visually produced presentation—and the *theorema*—the object of contemplation and so on—of nature; that nature is generated by the *theoria* of higher entities, and reflects that activity in natural generation. Plotinus has nature saying (I paraphrase): "As the lines drawn by the geometer are the *theoria* of the geometer, so when I theorize, the limits of body come into being, as if from me" (III.8.4). This literally 'theoretical' understanding of the activity of nature is applied directly to sexual generation at the end of III.8.7:

> When an animal generates, the *logoi* within move, and this is an activity of *theoria*, and a labor of giving birth to many forms and many objects of *theoria*, to fill everything with *logoi* and thus always to theorize; for to make something is to make an *eidos*, but this is to fill things with *theoria*.

This is obviously meant to answer the question, why do kinds of animals continue to generate offspring? It might help to compare the answer given by Aristotle, that sexual generation occurs so that each *eidos* may be everlasting in the way open to it; Aristotle does not argue, at least not in *De Generatione Animalium* II.1 where this question is discussed, for a principle of plenitude. He seems to imagine that all the natural kinds which exist today have always existed and always will exist, if only contingently. Plotinus, in contrast, tells us that the *logoi* actualize themselves in the generation of forms, and the actualization of a plenitude of forms is the theoretical activity of nature.

It would be difficult, but not impossible, to develop an Aristotelian theory of the evolution of different kinds of animals. An Aristotelian *genos* is a *lineage*, a hereditary line, and an Aristotelian *eidos* is an appearance as much as anything else; nothing prevents individuals in a *genos* from being different in *eidos* from other individuals of that *genos*, so a failure of the male seed to dominate, or the recalcitrance of the material presented, could well result in an offspring which was not of the same *eidos* as its parents (Cf. *De Generatione Animalium* IV.4, 770b3ff). The most likely case is that the offspring is *defective* in some way, but what if the offspring were in some respect 'better' than its parents? What would Aristotle say then? Certainly *not* that the improvement could be ascribed to *chance*; that is one consequence of the criticism which he levels (more than once) at Empedocles, for example (Cf. *De Partibus Animalium* I.1, 640a19ff). If there *were* an improvement from parent to offspring, the cause would have to be found in something superior to the parent, implicitly containing the form which appears explicitly in the offspring. Aristotle never suggests that he considers the possibility of such an explanation within a biological realm, to the best of my knowledge, but he does suggest a comparable explanation of the 'evolution' of the *genos* 'tragedy' in the first part of his *Poetics*. There, obviously the higher source of form is human experience, which tragedy partly imitates.

In contrast, it would be a delightful exercise to construct a Plotinian evolutionary theory. Genetic lines could be seen as generating variations in much the same way as a rational being generates hypotheses; stable species might be compared to theories with a high degree of confirmation, the forces which limit the reproduction of some of the variant forms might be compared to the rebuttals and refutations to which hypotheses are subject. If Plotinus had been acquainted with paleontology, how pleased he could have been with *that* spectacle of concrete dialectic!

But Plotinus has a difficult time explaining those productions which seem best understood as failures of generative processes; in III.8.7 his reasoning is brief and unsatisfactory:

> Errors occur in things generated and things done when the theorizing gets carried away from the object of theory. The bad workman is the one who makes ugly forms. Lovers see and strive toward the form.

The explanation may be traced to Plato's *Republic* (X, 601c–602a: the maker has only belief about how things should be made; the user knows) and to the charioteer of the *Phaedrus*, led astray by the mistaken theorizing of the ignoble horse (248b: feeding on the food of semblance). The trouble with this sort of explanation of biological 'error' is that it always places the blame on the formal, what Plotinus calls the theoretical, and thus on the active cause, and never on the matter. It would lead to some rather strange explanations of birth defects, as if they were always caused by defective genetic structure, and never by environmental or nutritional defects.

The extension of *theoria* throughout living processes is explained, to some degree, by a distinction made most clearly at III.8.8: all life is thought (*noēsis*), but there are at least three levels of thought: vegetative thought, sensitive thought, and ultimately psychic thought. Probably we would not be wrong to add 'mineral' thought at one end of the scale, and 'divine' thought at the other. That is a direction of investigation taken up later by several philosophers, notably Leibniz.

A more clearly biological direction is taken at III.8.10, where life is compared first to an inexhaustible spring, from which flows or emanates all things. More to our point, life is then compared to a tree:

> The life of a great tree goes out to all parts, yet remains a source (*archē*) and is not dissipated in the whole as it rests in the roots. This source furnishes the whole life to the tree, but it remains itself, the source of the whole, and not many things.

This 'Yggdrasil' (so to speak) is for Plotinus an image of the unity of life, the unity of the soul, the unity of the universe. This tree motif also appears in III.3.7, where (I am paraphrasing now) the source (*archē*) is said to be all in one, immobile as a root; the parts which grow out from it carry an image of the source; the parts closest to the roots contain the others, which going out split ultimately into twigs, leaves, and fruit. Some parts live for a season and die; others persist, generating again new leaves and fruits, and having in them the seeds of the prior parts, as if they wanted to become in their turn small plants. Although each growth seems to come only from the neighboring branch, in fact it comes from the source, which in turn depends upon another source. According to Brèhier, this image had already appeared in Philo of Alexandria's *De Plantatione* #4ff; certainly it expresses a view of life which draws upon biological understanding, and in turn contributes to a biological interpretation of the world. The concept of the universe as one living organism, familiar from the beginning of the *Timaeus* (and Cf. *Ennead* III.2.7), requires an examination of the characteristics of organisms as its basis, and as a part of its heuristic program.[10]

4. Excursus

Nevertheless, Plotinus did not actually *do* any biology, and he took little interest in the biological investigations carried out by his predecessors, even by his Platonistic predecessors. Despite that abstention, his contributions to the history of biological thought are neither negative nor neutral. The philosophy of Plotinus is a most energetic defense of the thesis that we should investigate form rather than matter, principles of unity rather than principles of disunity; that one should expect to find universal laws of nature, and unified sources of life, rather than special principles, separate causes, accidents, multiplicities.

No one among the immediate followers of Plotinus was prepared to follow this vision as a scientific goal, and probably nothing Plotinus said or did would encourage scientific investigation as a way of life, but it is not unreasonable to suppose that the indirect influence of Plotinus has been one of the many sources of the modern synthetic theory of living nature. We have indicated some of the ways in which his thought leads toward an evolutionary theory, a theory perhaps more like that of Lamarck than that of Darwin, but closer to modern viewpoints that the apparent immutability characteristic of Aristotle's biology. In addition, Plotinus contributed heavily to the sources of the vitalistic theory of life, and vitalism has certainly played a large role in the turn toward biological science, and away from the radical reductionism of modern physics, during the past hundred years or so. Sometimes the role of vitalism has been more dialectical than constitutive, but it continues to be an important theoretical force. Schuhl's reference to Bergson is not amiss, not only in that Bergson read and lectured upon Plotinus, but also because Bergson and others philosophically akin to him have forced twentieth-century biologists to define clearly the ways in which living beings are based upon nonliving structures, and in what ways living beings differ from nonliving systems.

Nothing could contribute more, in the long run, to biological thought than a thoroughgoing love of the natural world, in all its complexities and flourishing variations. I believe that Plotinus laid the groundwork for that love, without doing much about it himself; of his immediate successors, only Porphyry pursues any biological interest so far as I can see, and that seems to be limited to his spirited defense of vegetarianism in the *On Abstinence from Animal Food*.[11] But later Neoplatonists *did* take up the challenge; more about that on another occasion.

The State University of New York at Binghamton

NOTES

1. This paper was originally presented at a conference on "Neoplatonism and Islamic Philosophy" sponsored by the Society for the Study of Islamic Philosophy and Science, and the Society for Ancient Greek Philosophy. I thank several of the participants, especially John P. Anton, for their

helpful comments. Other parts of the same larger study are my "Animal and Human Souls in the Peripatetic School," *Skepsis* I (1909), 67–99, and "Biological Theory in Porphyry's *de Abstinentia*," *Ancient Philosophy* III (1983), 149–159.

2. Literature research has included *L'annè philologique* and bibliographies in:
A. H. Armstrong, *The Architecture of the Intelligible Universe in the Philosophy of Plotinus* (Amsterdam: Hakkert, 1967);
H. J. Blumenthal, *Plotinus' Psychology: His Doctrines of the Embodied Soul* (The Hague: Nijhoff, 1971), referred to as "Blumenthal" below;
Emile Brèhier, *The Philosophy of Plotinus*, translated by J. Thomas (Chicago: University of Chicago Press, 1958);
J.–M. Charrue, *Plotin Lecteur de Platon* (Paris: Belles Lettres, 1978);
CNRS (P. Hodot), *Le Ne'oplatonisme* (Paris: CNRS, 1971);
Eyjdfur K. Emilsson, *Plotinus on Sense—Perception* (Cambridge: Cambridge University Press, 1988);
Grigorios Kostaras, Ph., *Der Begriff des Lebens bei Plotin* (Hamburg: Felix Meiner Verlag, 1969);
John, Rist, *Eros and Psyche* (Toronto: University of Toronto Press, 1964);
John, Rist, *Plotinus, The Road to Reality* (Cambridge: Cambridge University Press, 1967);
A. Smith, *Porphyry's Place in the Neoplatonic Tradition* (The Hague: Nijhoff, 1974);
R. T. Wallis, *Neoplatonism* (London: Duckworth, 1972);
T. Whittaker, *The Neo-Platonists* (Cambridge: Cambridge University Press, 1901; reprinted 1928).
3. Blumenthal, 12 (commenting on *Ennead* IV.17.8@fl[5]).
4. P. DeLacy, "Galen's Platonism," *American Journal of Philology* 93 (1972), 27–39; W. D. Smith, *The Hippocratic Tradition* (Ithaca: Cornell UP, 1979), 86 ff.
5. Albinus, *Epitome*, ed. Pierre Louis (Paris: Budè, 1945); John Dillon, *The Middle Platonists* (Ithaca: Cornell UP, 1977), for Apuleius see 315 ff.
6. R. T. Wallis, *Neoplatonism*, 173–4; I have not seen R. M. Mossé-Bastide, *Bergson et Plotin* (Paris, 1959), cited in Charrue's bibliography.
7. II.4.8. The translation is radically reworked from Stephen MacKenna's translation of the *Enneads*, (London: Faber, 1956, revised edition). Since I find that MacKenna's English does not correspond with my understanding of the Greek text, subsequent translations owe more to the French of Brèhier, *Plotin: Ennèades* (Paris: Belles Lettres Budè, 1960–1963).
8. See also *De Generatione Animalium* IV.10 and Peck's "Appendix A" in the Loeb edition of *GA*.
9. See J. M. Rist, *Eros and Psyche*, for an exploration of the development of this theme.

10. It is this aspect of Plotinus' 'biological' comments which most interests G. P. Kostaras, as well it might, since it is fundamental for Plotinus' concept of Life. Kostaras talks of Plotinus describing the "biologischen Bewegung der Seele nach dem Sinnlichen," and in his summary, at the end of his book, notes that for Plotinus, "Das Leben ist ein Baum, ein Organismus, d.h. ein einheitliches Canzes von angeborenen Kräften, Tendenzen und Spannungen. Dieser Lebensbaum hat die Fähigheit sich zu entwickeln und zugleich die Möglichkeit sich zu teilen, ohne seine eigene Form zu verlieren und ohne dass seine Einheit zerstückelt wird" (135).
11. See my discussion of this treatise in *Ancient Philosophy* 1983. The research upon which this paper depends has been supported by the National Science Foundation, the National Endowment for the Humanities, and the SUNY Foundation.

PLOTINUS AGAINST ARISTOTLE'S ESSENTIALISM

Lloyd P. Gerson

Aristotle's criticisms of Platonism frequently appear in a simple logical form: if P, then Q. But Q is absurd, therefore P is false. For example, if Forms exist, then the reality (*ousia*) of something will be separate from that thing.[1] But it is absurd that the reality of, say, a man should be separate from the man. Therefore, Forms do not exist. Why exactly is it absurd for the reality to be separate? Aristotle is not very explicit on this point. The central books of the *Metaphysics*, however, make it sufficiently clear that since reality (*ousia*) accounts for the being and unity of a substance, to separate it is to make unaccountable a substance's identity.[2] This claim might be formulated as follows. For any sensible substance S, there must be a true statement of the form 'S is P' where 'is P' indicates some sort of identity with a natural kind P. If the reality of S were separate, then there would be no such true statement. This I take it is just an explication of what it means to claim that a substance is a particular or 'this-such' (*tode ti*). Thus, for Aristotle, if the Form of Man is separate from Socrates, then it is false that Socrates is really, that is, essentially, a man. Perhaps he could turn into a cat. But this is thought to be absurd because Socrates' identity is determined by his being a man.

Some modern defenders of Plato are inclined to respond to Aristotle's attacks by denying that Plato's doctrines entail the absurdities indicated by Aristotle. For example, Harold Cherniss seems to argue that the separation of Forms does not entail that 'the reality of a particular' is thus separated from it. For the Forms are not intended to account for this reality.[3] So presumably, for Cherniss it does not follow that Socrates cannot have an essential identity as a man if the Form of Man is separate from him. Socrates is a man because he participates in the Form of Man. I think that Cherniss in his zeal to show Aristotle's lack of understanding of Plato's position has in fact himself misunderstood Aristotle's point. I take it that the point is that if the Form of Man is separate, then there is no way that the *identity* of Socrates if fixed by that Form. It is, thinks Aristotle, absurd that the reality of a man should be separate from him because the reality of a man in just his identity. His identity is determined by the essence predicated of him.

In contrast to Cherniss's continual refusal to accept the implications that Aristotle draws from his interpretation of Plato's claims, Plotinus embraces the other extreme. He simply accepts it that if Aristotle says that if Plato says P, then Q follows, then this is indeed so. It is evident, though, that he does not accept Aristotle's interpretations and their implications because he believes that Platonism is absurd. Rather, his approach is to embrace the putative absurdity and to show that in fact it is true largely because the (Aristotelian) alternative is itself absurd. I think that in the above example Plotinus understands Aristotle's point better than Cherniss does. If the Form of Man is separate from Socrates, then the identity of Socrates is not determined by that Form. 'Socrates is a man' is not in any sense an identity statement. Hence, essentialism and the substance metaphysics from which it is inseparable, are false. Plotinus, unlike Cherniss I suspect, thinks that this is what Plato holds and that Plato is right to do so. In the remainder of this paper I will try to show why Plotinus thinks that Aristotle's criticism of Plato turns upon itself and serves to vindicate a rejection of essentialism in the sensible world.

Plotinus' analysis of 'Socrates is a man' is definitely peculiar.

> For when I predicate 'man' of Socrates, I mean it not in the sense in which the wood is white, but in the sense that the white thing is white; for in saying that Socrates is a man, I am saying that a particular man is man, predicating man of the man in Socrates; but this is the same as calling Socrates Socrates, and again as predicating 'living being' of this rational living being.[4]

It is clear that in this passage Plotinus is interpreting what Aristotle would call the 'said of relation' between secondary and primary substance (*ousia*) and which is expressed grammatically as 'Socrates is a man' in terms of Platonic participation. For Aristotle, 'Socrates is a man' is based on an analysis which yields the priority of the individual over the form along with their real distinction. For Plotinus, 'Socrates is a man' means that Socrates partakes of the Form of Man. But what is Socrates? A man, of course. There does, however, seem to be a good deal of difference between saying that this man partakes of the Form of Man and that Socrates is Socrates, counter to what Plotinus says. For in the former case there is a distinction between the instance of the Form and the Form; in the latter case there is a identity statement. Or perhaps it is not quite so straightforward. It is true that Plotinus wishes to insist on a distinction between an instance of a Form and the Form itself. But he also must insist on their identity, otherwise instantiation would be entirely opaque.[5] So, the man that Socrates is, is and is not identical with the Form of Man.[6]

I think we can better understand these obscure claims as intended to be directly inferable from a denial of what Aristotle says. Assume that the essence of man is the Form of Man and that this is separate. Nevertheless, Socrates is a man because there is humanity in him just as Helen is beautiful because there is beauty in her and a building is tall because there is tallness in it. Why cannot we say then that if humanity is in Socrates, then the essence of humanity is in Socrates and that therefore Socrates is essentially a man? The simple response to this question is that the essence of humanity is identical with the Form of Man and this is separate. But why we might ask is it not enough that there be humanity in Socrates in order for us to say that the essence of humanity is in him and that he is essentially a man? It is not enough because unless Socrates is identical with that essence, its presence does not make Socrates essentially a man anymore than, say, having the essence of baldness in him makes him essentially bald.

Then why not take the next obvious step and just say that Socrates *is* identical with his essence? From Plotinus' perspective, the answer to this question is that we must refrain from doing so because it is false, and furthermore, Aristotle himself must admit this. In chapter 6 of *Metaphysics* Z Aristotle raises the question of whether each thing and its essence (*to ti ēn einai*) are the same or not. Answering this question, says Aristotle, is useful for the investigation of substance because each thing is thought to be nothing else than its own substance, and this substance is said to be to essence.[7] The answer given to the question at the end of the chapter is that "of things which are primary and are stated by themselves [*kath' auta legomenōn*], then, it is clear that each of them and its essence are one and the same."[8] But for us and no doubt for Plotinus the obvious puzzle is just what these things 'which are primary and are stated by themselves' are supposed to be. A passage a bit further on in chapter 11 supplies the answer: "And we have stated that in some cases the essence of a thing and the thing are the same, as in first substances; for example, curvature and its essence are the same, if curvature is a first substance. (By 'first substance' I mean one which is not stated as being in something else in an underlying subject as in matter.) But things which exist as matter, or which include matter, are not the same as their essence; nor are those things which are one by accident, such as Socrates and the musical, since these are the same by accident."[9] It seems plain that 'first substance' is equivalent to 'things which are primary and are stated by themselves' and equally clear that Aristotle excludes sensible composites from this class. The reason given is that the composite is in an underlying subject, its matter. Thus, in the next book Aristotle says: "For a soul and the essence of a soul are the same, but the essence of a man is not the same as the man, unless also the soul is called 'a man'; accordingly, in some cases a thing and its essence are the same, in others this is not so."[10]

According to Aristotle's own analysis, a sensible substance does not seem to be identical with its essence because that substance includes matter. Therefore, the putative absurdity of separating the essence of humanity from Socrates cannot consist in the non-identity of Socrates and his essence. This much Aristotle admits. How then can Aristotle infer from the Platonic proposition that Socrates is a man because there is humanity in him to the anti-Platonic conclusion that Socrates is essentially a man? For it is evident that this is just the inference that Plotinus refuses to make. The answer is roughly that the sensible composite, Socrates, is qualifiedly identical with his essence according to the order of act and potency. This man and 'what it is to be a man' are thus related.

It cannot be stressed too strongly that Plotinus' reasons for denying this claim are not based on his rejection of the basic distinction between act and potency. Quite the contrary. Plotinus makes abundant and fruitful use of the distinction when addressing numerous metaphysical and epistemological problems. Indeed, despite his rigorous negative theology, he will insist that the source (*archē*) of all, the One, is properly identified as perfect actuality (*energeia*).[11] So it is somewhat puzzling why Plotinus wants to maintain an extreme position that might reasonably be thought to be defeated by employing the distinction between act and potency.

Against Aristotle's assertion that 'man and what it is to be a man are not identical'. Plotinus says 'the Form of Man and man are identical,' holding that the 'what it is to be' of anything is in fact a Platonic Form.[12] Aristotle can say that 'Socrates is a man' is an identitative use of 'is' and not predicative without holding that 'man and what it is to be a man are identical' just because there is a real distinction *within* Socrates between the composite individual and the form of man.

Plotinus sees a contradiction latent in Aristotle's position. On the one hand, Aristotle wants to say that sensible composite is related to essence as act to potency. But Aristotle also want to hold that the sensible composite is *posterior* to the form because it is not perfectly actual.[13]

The crux of the dispute between Plotinus and Aristotle comes down to this. Grant that 'S is P' but that whatever is P's nature is not unqualifiedly identical with S. It would seem that all anti-nominalists, Plato, Aristotle, Plotinus, *et al.* must grant this much. Let us grant further that form and actuality are identical.[14] Then, how is S related to that nature of P in terms of priority and posteriority in reality? For Plotinus, the correct answer is unavoidably Platonic. Somewhat less tendentiously, the position which at once maintains that act is prior to potency, that form is act, and that the composite is posterior to form, cannot consistently also maintain that the composite is prior to the form which is not identical with it.

An Aristotelian will no doubt want to object that this argument depends on an equivocation. For the sense in which a sensible composite is prior in actuality to essence is different from the sense in which form is prior to sensible composite. The priority of form to sensible composite refers only to the priority of non-sensible form which is substance. A sensible form such as the form of man, which never exists separately, is always posterior in actuality to the composite. Form and essence are identical only in the former case, never in the latter. If the form of man could exist separately, then it would indeed be incoherent to hold that there is one actuality, this man, and another actuality, the separate form.

This objection, however, is circular. It depends on saying that the form of man does not exist separately because it is a sensible form. What is the proof of this? Just that man and 'what it is to be a man' are not identical. And this is so because the reality of man is the man and not 'what it is to be a man'. But this is precisely what Plotinus denies when he asserts that the true man is the Form of Man.[15] Plotinus does not deny that there is a distinction between the sensible form and the Platonic Form. Rather, he holds that the former is posterior to the latter. The instance of the Form is an image of it.[16] Let us consider both claims in turn.

Plotinus wants to hold that if a sensible form is posterior to a Platonic Form, then they cannot be related according to the order of act and potency.

> For literary skill [*hē grammatikē*] is not posterior to the particular literary skill but rather it is because literary skill exists that that in you exists; since that in you is particular by being in you, but in itself is the same as the universal. And Socrates did not in his own person give being human to the non-human but humanity gave being human to Socrates: the particular human is so by participation in humanity. Since what could Socrates be except 'a man of a particular kind' and what could the 'of a particular kind' do towards being more of a substance?[17]

I believe the following argument underlines this passage. The relation between humanity, i.e., the Form of Man, and particular instances of this Form is a one-many relation. So too for the Form of Grammaticality or Literary Skill and its instances. In such a relation, the one is prior to the many, because it is the source (*archē*) of the many. And this priority is not that of potentiality to actuality. This is so because if a subject has a property that *could be* instantiated in another subject, the explanation of this is that they are instances of the same thing. But a potentiality as such does not explain anything because potentialities as such are not actual. No one would, say, accept the potentiality for death as an explanation of death or the potentiality for learning as an explanation for learning. These are at best conditions for their actualization. But the conditions are dependent on actualities. Thus, having the potentiality for death is a condition of an actual body.

To say that a Form is the source (*archē*) of its instances is in part to say that it is the explanation of instantiation or of identity in difference. If more than one thing has the same property, then the explanation of this must at least start with the existence of the property as distinct from the instances. It is of course not to the present point that a nominalist would deny the antecedent of this claim. Aristotle must allow that there is such a datum to be explained, but there is no question of a property serving an explanatory function by being potentially its instances. It is not even coherent to say that the explanation of Socrates possessing an instance of the Form of Man is the (his?) potentiality for being a man.

Recall that the question of the priority and posteriority of man and 'what it is to be a man' is occasioned by Aristotle's own conclusion that only in primary substance are they the same and that sensible substances are not primary. Aristotle thinks that it is absurd that man and 'what it is to be a man' should be the same because then 'what it is to be a man' will be a man. But this only follows if one *assumes* that 'man' must refer primarily to Socrates. Such an assumption is a stellar example of being misled by language. There is no substantial dispute between Aristotle and Plotinus regarding the possibility of designating a sensible particular such that no non-sensible particular can be named univocally with it. Let 'man' stand for 'image of the Form of Man' and 'what it is to be a man' stand for 'Form of Man'. Then Plotinus would agree that it is absurd that 'what it is to be a man' should be a man. The issue is not the irreducibility of instance and universal, but their relative priority. When Plotinus asserts that the true man is the Form of Man it is the issue of relative priority that he is addressing.

The priority of Form to instance is characterized by Plotinus in the much maligned language of imagery. Plotinus' position is that substance is said homonymously (*homōnymōs*) of intelligible being and sensible bodies.[18] There are many passages in which Plotinus stresses the homonymy of the sensible world in general.[19] Aristotle clearly distinguishes between a term said homonymously of two things and a term that is relational (*pros hen*).[20] So, it would seem that Plotinus is denying a relational connection between the substance of the Forms and substance when said of sensibles. On the other hand, he also seems to connect them as 'prior' and 'posterior', which is not the way that things merely with a name in common are usually described.[21] This is in fact to be expected where sensibles are images of Forms. As we saw in the passage quoted above, an instance of a Form 'is the same as the universal', though 'posterior' to the Form. For example, a drawing of a house is, as image, posterior to the real house, though its proportions may be the same as those of the house. But its proportions are not equivocally those of the house; they are the same, though posterior. Another example would be a film which is homonymously that which it images, but which also contains synonymous images as well, such as the words spoken by the actors.

In general, synonymous images are univocally named with their models, even though they are posterior. In this matter, Plotinus is actually following Aristotle's principle. For in the *Metaphysics* Aristotle asserts, "of things to which the same predicate belongs [*hyparchei to synōnymon*] in the highest degree is that in virtue of which it belongs also to the others. For example, fire is the hottest of whatever is truly called 'hot', for fire is the cause of hotness in the others."[22] In the *Organon* there is a precise and consistent meaning for synonymy (*synōnymon*): when things have a name in common and also the definition corresponding to the name, they are synonymous.[23] Synonymy implies univocal predication. Thus, fire and water can be said to be hot univocally, even though fire is the cause of hotness in the water and so is prior. I have elsewhere argued for the Platonic nature of such a claim and Aristotle's reasons for ultimately abandoning it.[24] The point here is that a Platonist is committed to such priority and univocity for Forms and instances. The priority follows from the argument discussed above. The univocity follows from the kind of explanatory entity that a Form is. The Form of Humanity explains the identity in difference of many men in the sense that it is just what is identical in all the many.

This point is misunderstood by many, including many modern defenders of Plato, because it is thought that synonymy excludes homonymy and hence the diminished reality of the sensible world. Thus, a false dichotomy is set up, one which perhaps leads Aristotle to suppose the obvious reasonableness of his own position and the absurdity of the Platonic alternative. If synonymy obtains between Form and instance, then priority of Form to instance is gainsaid. If homonymy obtains, then priority and posteriority can be claimed, but we are saddled with the quaint conceit that the real man is the Form of Man, not Socrates. We have, as Aristotle would put it, just copied the real world onto a notional world and arbitrarily transferred the appellation 'real' to the latter. But Aristotle himself testifies that priority and posteriority can coexist with synonymy, albeit his later conclusion that this is false for 'being'.

In effect, Plotinus wishes to hold that when their is priority and posteriority along with synonymy, as is the case with Forms and their instances, the priority and posteriority is to be analyzed as homonymy in being. The diminished reality of the sensible world, occasioned by the separation of Forms in the first place, is explicated as synonymy in nature and homonymy in being. Thus, there is humanity in Socrates, but this nature or form is present in a mode of being different from its primary mode. For one thing, the Form of Man is eternal, and the humanity in Socrates is temporalized. For another, the Form of Man is thoroughly transparent or intelligible, while the humanity in Socrates is infected with matter.

Perhaps the most illuminating and relevant example of homonymy combined with synonymy in representations is from Aristotle's realist epistemology. According to Aristotle's account, knowledge is the identification of knower with the form of a knowable object. The form in the intellect is synonymous with the form in that which is known, but cognitive being is homonymous with the being of the knowable. The concept of humanity is not a man. That is what homonymy indicates. But the form of humanity in the intellect really is that form. It is not an approximation or arbitrary symbol of it. That is what synonymy indicates. The real and the cognitional are ordered as prior to posterior.

Plotinus' point is that the Form of Man is related to the individual man analogous to the way the individual man is related to the form of man in the intellect. His reasons for holding against Aristotle that the being that is prior to cognitive being is itself posterior to a Form are twofold. The first reason is as we have seen that actual Forms are needed to explain the phenomenon of identity in difference. The second reason is Aristotle's own admission that the sensible composite is not substance in the primary sense. It is quite outside the scope of this paper to argue the case that

Aristotle's account of the relation of the absolutely prior unmoved mover to sensible substance is inadequate. It is appropriate to stress, however, that given Aristotle's hypothesis that being is substance, the posteriority of the sensible substance provides the groundwork for at least the homonymy in Plotinus' analysis.

From Plotinus' perspective, Aristotle has practically conceded the posteriority in being of the sensible composite. Furthermore, in the implication of his argument that primary being is to be identified with separate form, Aristotle has taken the next important step.[25] The last crucial concession that Aristotle refuses to make to the Platonic position is the recognition of the priority of separate form to the form of sensibles analogous to the priority of the form of sensibles to cognitive form. Aristotle seems to believe that the form of sensible composites, unlike the form that is primary being, could not exist separately. There is no reason actually given for this claim in the *Metaphysics* so far as I can tell. Perhaps his reason is that in a sensible composite there is one actuality, the composite itself. The form could not exist separately because for it to do so it would have to have its won actuality. But that would mean that in the sensible composite there are so to speak *two* actualities, that of the form and that of the composite. So, the unity of the sensible composite can only be preserved if the form is not an actuality apart from the composite.

Plotinus would find this line of reasoning unpersuasive for at least two reasons. First, the preservation of the unity of the sensible composite is only a desideratum if one is committed to holding that sensible being is primary being, as Plotinus and presumably Aristotle are not. By contrast, the unity that a dependent being has can be compromised. Second, Aristotle identifies form and actuality. It is unclear why this should be so for the separate form but not for the form of the sensible composite. If it is true for the latter as well, then there is no reason why that form cannot exist separately except that its actuality in the sensible composite would undermine its unity.

What Aristotle finds incomprehensible in the Platonic position and what Plotinus take pains to defend is the claim that 'what it is to be P' and 'P' are the same. This might be understood to mean that either now there are two men or there are none, because the essence has been separated from what it is the essence of. But once homonymy is combined with synonymy, one is not obliged to say either that the Form of Man is a man or that Socrates is not a man because the essence of man is separate from him. He participates in the essence and so he is a man, but he is not identical with the essence.

Plotinus' alternative to essentialism is to say that the sensible composites is a 'conglomeration' (*symphorēsis*) of qualities and matter, or bodies.[26] The qualities are just the instances of Forms, or what Aristotle would call sensible forms. Since the only subject in these conglomerations is matter, Aristotle's claim that essence is what a thing is in virtue of itself is rejected.[27] Thus, Socrates is not essentially a man. He is the actual composite of qualities in matter. These qualities in matter, like the visible qualities 'tall' and 'white' are images of Forms. These images bear their names univocally with Forms. But their *logoi* necessarily include matter. Thus the tallness in Socrates is self-identically tallness, like the Form. But the tallness in Socrates is necessarily the particular tallness of a body. So, the composite Socrates, who is just these qualities in matter, is an homonymous image of the Form of Man, 'containing' a synonymous image, namely, an instance of the nature of man.

It might be objected, however, that if qualities A, B, and C together in matter represent the Form of Man, then the essence of man is in the individual man just if the essential qualities are present. For the presence of the essence is just the presence of the representation of the Form. But unless the essence identifies Socrates, then Socrates is not essentially a man any more than he is essentially any other quality that he may have. In one sense, Socrates is indeed identified by all his qualities. Plotinus is not denying this. But the essentialist needs a special identifying sense for the essential qualities. And so long as Socrates is not identified with these, he is no more essentially a man than his body is essentially seated at any one moment or essentially bearded. So, we have to say that Socrates is a man if there is manness in him, but he is not essentially a man.[28]

Should we then allow that Socrates could become, say, a sparrow? One might suppose judging from what Plotinus says about reincarnation that the answer is yes. I think that would be too hasty an answer. For the Socrates now at issue is the sensible composite and it is false that the sensible composite is reincarnated as anything. It is the soul of Socrates that may enter the body of another animal. This suggests that the identity of Socrates is not the identity of a sensible substance (*ousia*) but that of a soul which exists apart from the body. This of course is what Aristotle explicitly denies. The identity of the individual sensible composite, however, severed from essence, is not non-arbitrarily determinable.

The abandonment of Aristotelian sensible substance as determined by essence is complete in Plotinus' embrace of what Aristotle regards as an absurdity: that we make substances out of non-substances.[29] Plotinus here of course means putative sensible substances. They are constructed out of qualities and matter. This apparently means both that we designate various 'conglomerations' as substance and that the elements of these conglomerations are matter and qualities. This naturally invites the question of whether matter then becomes substance, a result that Aristotle declares is impossible.[30] It does not become so for Plotinus any more than for Aristotle, because matter is not a 'this something'.[31] Its identity is not determined by essence.

Owing to the fact that qualities or instances of Forms are univocally bearers of the Forms' natures, pragmatic categorizations of sensible composites are possible.

> But what species of it [sensible substance] should one posit, and how should one divide them? Now the whole must be classed as body, and of bodies some are matterish and some organic; the matterish are fire, earth, water, air; the organic the bodies of plants and animals, which have their differences according to their shapes [*morphas*]. Then one should take the species of earth and of the other elements, and in the case of organic bodies one should divide the plants, and the bodies of animals, according to their shapes; or by the fact that some are on and in the earth, and, element by element [one should class separately] the bodies in each; or [one could class them on the ground that' some are light, some are heavy, and some in between, and that some stand in the middle, some surround them above, and some are in between; and in each of these the bodies are already differentiated by their outlines, so as to be some of them bodies of celestial living beings and other appropriate to the other elements; or one should divide the four according to their species and afterwards proceed in another way to weave them together by blending their differences according to places and shapes and mixtures, classing them as fiery or earthly, called so according to the largest and predominant element [in the mixture].[32]

It is important to grasp what is and what is not being suggested here. Plotinus wants to maintain that, say, the Form of Man is present in the sensible composite that is called 'Socrates'. The Form of Man is eternally self-identical and distinct from the Form of Horse. But since so-called sensible substances are not identical with the natures of Forms, the classifications of these composites must occur through perception.[33] Knowing what the Form of Man is does not provide the criterion for classifying a conglomeration of qualities and matter. We can call one organic composite a man and one a horse owing to their shapes (a quality plus a mass of extended matter), but this does not imply that things with these shapes are essentially human or horse. It is appropriate in this context to recall Plato's argument that Forms are manifested in sensible instances *via* material that can also instantiate opposite Forms. Thus in the first book of the *Republic* returning someone's possession can be an instance of justice, but it can also be an instance of injustice. And in the *Symposium*, Beauty can be manifested in a body, but bodily qualities are not essential to the manifestation of Beauty, for Beauty can be manifested in non-bodily souls.

A classification of conglomerates is a classification of homonymous images. Take a drawing of a conical shape. Is it a tepee or an ice-cream cone? The answer is purely contextual or pragmatic because what the drawing is of is not entailed by the shape.[34] The conical shape, however, is or contains a synonymous image of the Form. The classification of homonymous images, like sensible composites, in terms of synonymous images, like the instance of Forms, is interdicted because sensible composites are bodies that contain matter. There is no more of a necessary connection between these two types of images than there is between the proportions of a drawing and the medium in which the drawing is rendered.

The statement 'Socrates is necessarily a man' can be understood in two ways. In one way, Socrates is necessarily a man because 'Socrates' stands for a man, as Plotinus says. So necessarily, this man (the sensible composite) is a man. But this *de dicto* necessity will of course not do as an interpretation of Aristotelian essentialism. In another way, Socrates is not necessarily a man because there is no necessary identity between the subject, matter, and the sensible qualities that together make up the conglomerate. The matter in this composite could have and might yet participate in the Form of something other than Man. Therefore, there is no *de re* necessity in the connection of subject and essence. For Plotinus, the common sense plausibility of Aristotle's position actually trades on the ambiguity of these two types of necessity.

St. Michael's College
The University of Toronto

NOTES

1. Cf. *Metaphysics* 1.9, 991b1–2.
2. Cf. *Metaphysics* 7.13, 1038b14–15 & 7.17, 1041b7–9.
3. Harold Cherniss, *Aristotle's Criticism of Plato and the Academy* (New York, 1962), 373. Cherniss states: "Now the 'reality of a particular' which is peculiar and cannot be separate is just what the particular is as *this* particular, i.e. The particularity itself. That, however, is not the sense in which the immaterial essence is the 'reality of a particular,' i.e. the cause of the

particular's being..."

4. VI.3.5, 18–23. Cf. *Metaphysics* 7.17, 104la17–22, which is perhaps the passage Plotinus has in mind. There Aristotle tries to show that to inquire into why something is itself is to inquire into nothing.
5. The instrumental causality of Forms, as in Helen is beautiful because of Beauty is only explained by such identity as is the parallel self-identity of Form and instance in 'neither is Tallness short nor is the tallness in us short'. Cf. VI.5.8, 22–6: *ei gar mē en tēi hylēi estin hoion pyros hē idea...auto dē pyr tēi hylēi ouk eggenomenon auto morphēn pyros kata pasan tēn pyrōtheisan hylēn parexetai.*
6. One may perhaps compare Magrite's famous hyper-real painting of a pipe with the legend 'this is not a pipe'. Or we might think of a drawn circle which is and is not a circle. If we think it is wrong to call the drawn circle a circle, is it equally wrong to call it a square?
7. *Metaphysics* 7.6, 103la15–18.
8. *Metaphysics* 7.6, 1032a5–6.
9. *Metaphysics* 7.11, 1037a33–b7.
10. *Metaphysics* 8.3, 1043b2–4. Cf. A. Code, "On the Origins of Some Aristotelian Theses About Predication," *How Things Are: Studies in Predication and the History of Philosophy and Science*, ed. J. Bogen and J. E. McGuire (Dordrecht; 1985), 102: "...a particular like Socrates is not, according to the hylomorphic analysis of *Metaphysics* Z, a primary substance, and he is not identical with his essence."
11. VI.8.20, 9–15. Cf. V.4.2, 35; VI.8.7, 46–48; VI.8.12, 22–23; VI.8.13, 6–8; VI.8.16, 15, 25, 30, 31, 35.
12. VI.3.4, 17: *to de tou anthrōpou eidos kai ho anthrōpos tauton.* I take it that this is a direct denial of Aristotle's conclusion at *Metaphysics* 8.3, 1043b3: *anthrōpōi de kai anthrōpos ou tauton, ei mē kai hē psychē anthrōpos lechthēsetai.* Note that Plotinus embraces the counterfactual condition. In VI.3.5, 12–14, Plotinus adds: *hōste mēte to eidos en tēi hylēi einai hōs en hypokeimenōi mēte ton anthrōpon en tōi Sōkratei meros onta Sōkratous*—where the last clause must be intended to distinguish the sensible composite which is Socrates from his form.
13. *Metaphysics* 7.3, 1029a5–7 & 30–31.
14. Aristotle, at *Metaphysics* 9.8, 1050b2–4, affirms both the identity of *eidos* and *energeia* and the priority of *energeia* to *dynamis* in *ousia.*
15. Cf. VI.3.15, 24–38.
16. V.9.5, 17–19: *to gar en autois eidos epi hylēi eidōlon ontos, pan te eidos en allōi par' allou eis ekeino erchetai kai estin eikōn ekeinou.*
17. VI.3.9, 23–30.
18. VI.3.2, 1–4.
19. VI.3.1, 21; III.7.11, 27–29. Cf. I.2.2; II.3.18, 17; II.8.5, 6; II.9.8, 19–26; III.2.1, 25; III.2.14, 26; III.6.13; III.8.11, 29; IV.4.36, 7ff; V.3.7, 33; V.3.16, 8ff; V.8.12, 11ff; V.9.13, 10; VI.2.7, 11; VI.2.22, 38; VI.3.1, 20–21; VI.3.8,

32; VI.6.15, 4; VI.7.6, 6; VI.7.7, 21; VI.7.12, 2.

20. *Metaphysics* 4.2, 1003a33–34 & 7.4, 1030b1.
21. VI.1.1, 25–28.
22. *Metaphysics* 2.1, 993b23–26.
23. Cf. *Categories* 1.1a6, 5.3b7; *Topics* 4.3, 123a28–29; *Topics* 6.10, 148a24–25; *Topics* 7.4, 154a16–18.
24. Cf. "Causality, Univocity, and First Philosophy in *Metaphysics* ii," *Ancient Philosophy* 11 (1991), 331–349.
25. For form as *tode ti* see *Metaphysics* 5.7, 1017b24–26; 8.1, 1042a29; 9.7, 1049a35; 12.3, 1070a9–15. For form as *ousia* see 7.7, 1032b1–2; 11.1037a27–30, b3–4; 8.3, 1043b2–4.
26. VI.3.8, 20. Cf. VI.3.15, 24–38; II.7.3, 4–5 where *sōma* is defined as 'qualities with matter'. At VI.3.10, 12–17, we read: *epei gar peri aisthētēs ousias ho logos, ouk atopos an eiē, diaphorais ei lambanoito pais pros tēn aisthēsis. Oude gar on haplōs all' aisthēton on to holon touto. Epei tēn dokousan hypostasin autēs* [sensible *ousia*] *synodon tōn pros aisthēsin ephamen einai kai hē pistis tou einai para tēs aisthēseōs autois.*
27. *Metaphysics* 7.4, 1029b13–14.
28. Cf. Code, *art.cit.*, 105: "The separability of Forms goes hand in hand with the idea that Forms are participated in *accidentally*. If the Form of Man is separable, then particular men are accidentally, not essentially, men. Aristotle finds this unacceptable." But once Aristotle concedes that a sensible substance is not unqualifiedly identical with its essence, he no longer has the tools to defend the alternative.
29. VI.3.8, 30–31: *kai ou dyscheranteon, ei tēn ousian tēn aisthētēn ex ouk ousiōn poioumen.* Cf. II.6.1, 48–52. Cf. *Physics* 1.6, 189a33: *pōs oun ek mē ousiōn ousia an eiē.* Cf. *Metaphysics* 14.1, 1087a29–b4. The absurdity is said to arise from the fact that substances do not have contraries, but if a substance is in a subject, that out of which it is made, it will have a contrary. Further, if non-substances are prior, what is the subject they are in?
30. *Metaphysics* 7.3, 1029a26–27.
31. Cf. II.6.2, 14; VI.1.2, 11–12.
32. VI.3.9, 2–18. Cf. VI.3.17, 4; VI.3.18, 9–11.
33. VI3.8, 2–3. Cf. VI.3.10, 12–14: *epei gar peri aisthētēs ousias ho logos, ouk atopos an eiē, diaphorais ei lambanoito tais pros tēn aisthēsin.*
34. I take it that at VI.3.1, 13–16, when Plotinus proposes to order sensibles in terms of species and genera, he is doing this solely on pragmatic grounds.

EXPLANATION AND NATURE IN *ENNEADS* VI.7.1-15

Sara L. Rappe

Ennead VI.7, 'How the Multitude of Forms Came into Being and On the Good,' opens with a criticism of Plato's account of Demiurgic creation in the *Timaeus*. Under direct fire is language that describes the Craftsman as calculating, planning, or entertaining reasons for his act of production.[1] What is the philosophical context[2] for this exegesis? Our treatise's structure is guided by a series of six *aporiae*, each concerned with a Platonic text frequently adverted to within the tradition.[3] Yet the same denial of discursive thought to God is found in several other treatises, viz. 'On Providence,' 'On Problems Concerning the Soul,' and in the *Großschrift*,[4] all of which are non-Platonic contexts.

Because of the very similar language employed in a parallel passage in II.9, 'Against the Gnostics,'[5] most scholars agree that our passage alludes to the gnostic interpretation of Plato's Demiurge as the planning mind[6] (*nous dianoumenos*[7]) and to the Gnostic idea that Thought, unaccountably hypostatized, planned and carried out the work of creation—*albeit* faultily. More recent scholarship views the denial of discursive thought to the Demiurge as an attack upon the Stoic view of deity which identified human reason and divine intelligence, and holds that in this Plotinus was informed by earlier Academic criticisms of such anthropomorphism. Here III.2 is adduced.[8] To be sure, there continued a longstanding debate in the annals of Ancient Greek philosophy over the question as to whether God thinks the way we think, and Aristotle's negative answer[9] was definitive for the later Platonists.[10] However, in VI.7 itself, within the chapters that immediately follow the criticism of *Timaeus*, Plotinus refers neither to the Gnostics nor to the Stoics, but rather to Aristotelian teleological explanations of the kind adumbrated at *Physics* II, 199b34, and *Partibus animalum* 1641b25, as well as to the Aristotelian account of definition in *Metaphysics* Z.3.

In this paper I want to discuss the doctrine in terms of Plotinus' own philosophical methodology,[11] since source criticism has yielded such a plethora of interpretations. Within our treatise, this doctrine is tied to a discussion of the limits of philosophical explanation: Even though we may *describe* it by means of discursive thought, there is no such thing as a unique explanation for the structure of the world. A good statement of this position may be found in V.8, 'On the Intelligible Beauty.' The explanations by which we humans try to account for world, using discursive thought as we must, are always underdetermined by the available evidence:

> You can explain the reason why the earth is in the middle and round, but it is not because you can do this that things are so There; they were not planned like this because it was *necessary* for them to be like this, but because all things There are disposed as they are, the things here are well disposed, as if the conclusion was there before the syllogism which showed the cause, and the conclusion did not follow from the premises. (V.8.7: Armstrong translation)

The word that Armstrong translates as 'reason' is *aitia.* In Aristotle's *Posterior Analytics* it bears the meaning of 'explanation.' According to Aristotle,[12] if we come to know the 'reason,' we know both the reason for a given state of affairs and that, on account of the reason, it is not possible for the state of affairs to be otherwise. Such knowledge is said to constitute knowledge in its most proper sense. But things could not be more different with Plotinus. For him, the condition *sine qua non* for knowledge is the unity of the knower and the object of knowledge, a condition which discursive thought of any kind necessarily precludes.[13]

Our blue-prints for the world don't correspond to the architect's, because there simply is no discursive thought in intellect. Plotinus offers this critique in keeping with the caveat that Plato himself issues concerning the limits of philosophical explanation:

> One should distinguish between an image and its model in terms of the accounts given of them, since the account must resemble its subject matter: The account which describes something stable and evident to the intellect is itself reliable—insofar as words can be not subject to refutation, one must add this qualification—but the account of that which imitates the latter is analogously [deficient].[14]

By invoking the Platonic being/becoming dichotomy, Plotinus underscores the radical deficiencies of our cognitive powers when we try to look at phenomena apart from their source in the intelligible. Perhaps the modern concept of *metaphysical realism* can help us to get a handle on just where the difficulty lies with such explanations:

> What makes the metaphysical realist a metaphysical realist is his belief that there is somewhere 'one true theory'. In company with a correspondence theory of truth, this belief in one true theory requires a ready-made world: the world itself has to have a 'built-in' structure since otherwise theories with different structures might correctly 'copy' the world (from different perspectives) and truth would lose its absolute (non-perspectival) character.[15]

If by 'world' we mean, in keeping with the Platonic distinction just cited, the totality of phenomenal appearances as opposed to intelligible objects, then this can hardly be something which comes to us 'ready-made'.[16] Now causal relations are a prime instance of what is meant by a 'ready-made structure'. And Plotinus declines to discuss the structure of nature in terms of standard causal explanations, including teleology, one-directional causal connection, essentialism, and metaphysical dualism, all of which are characterized in various ways by the limitations of discursive thought. When Plotinus refuses to subscribe to such explanations, it is because he denies that discursive thought can ever be absolute.

To put it another way, Plotinus' degrees of reality theory has consequences for the way in which causation is understood within different levels of reality. His understanding of the relationship that exists between effect and cause is expressed differently for the physical order than for the intelligible, and again for the first hypostasis. Rather than either the metaphysical realism defined above or the perspectivism that it seeks to combat, Plotinus' view of causation as it relates to the multiple levels of Being could better be described as non-dualism. He sees all of the multiple states of existence as belonging to an integral but unique principle (the One).

We turn now to the critique of causal explanations offered in treatise VI.7. His arguments seem to cut in two directions. Plotinus corrects Platonic teleology with a healthy dose of what is ostensibly Aristotelian essentialism. But this essentialism is in turn modified beyond anything recognizably Aristotelian when Plotinus insists upon the unity of substance (*ousia*) with the second hypostasis, Intellect (*nous*). Aristotle's theory of explanation according to which 'what a thing is' (*to ti ēn einai*) is identical to the reason for its existence (*to dia ti*)[17] shows up in chapter 2 as a corrective to the idea that the teleological disposition of the world is imposed from outside.[18] In fact there really is no teleological disposition of the universe, since the world is well-disposed simply because it subsists together with its intelligible cause.[19] The identity of substance with its essence means for Plotinus that substances, once we understand them in terms of their essence, are self-explanatory, and do not have any external reasons for their being. At the same time, this Aristotelian account of substance (*ousia*) in terms of essence is stretched beyond its original metaphysical framework, because each of these same substances or forms is the whole of the second hypostasis, Intellect. So we cannot explain the world by appealing to the discrete essences of hylomorphic compounds anymore than we can be appealing to the demiurgic imitation of the Forms. It is not the case that the intelligible is only to be discovered in the sensible particular, or that the sensible particular is the teleological goal of the intelligible. Rather, we must go to the intelligible and see how the particular looks from that point of view.

Plotinus replaces or enhances these causal theories with the concept of *coordinate arising*. This doctrine presents a two-fold analysis of the phenomenal world, both parts of which are intended to break up any belief in an independently real or self-subsistent external world. The first theme is a description of the world as an *interdependent nexus of beings*. Under this description, the familiar Stoic idea of *cosmic harmony*[20] receives a more profound philosophical interpretation as a system of relationships which can be described as mutually reflective points of view. The second theme treats the multiplicity of individuals more on the analogy of thoughts arising in the mind, each expressing the nature of the thinker who has them.

Under the first theme, Plotinus uses the concept of *coordinate origination* in order to analyze individuals. Individuals are interrelated to each other with respect to their mutual subsistence within the world and with respect to the kinds of beings that they are. What it means to be an individual is to be an entity that is entirely relational, or to put it negatively, there is no what-it-is-to-be for an individual,[21] apart from the fact that it is interrelated to all other beings and that it represents this reciprocal origination from a certain point of view. Moreover, it is just this inherently relative nature which effectively blocks any adequate discursive account of the sensible world.

The second part of the analysis views individuation as a function of intellect together with soul, whose discursive thinking results in the differentiated world of discrete essences. Therefore Plotinus does not exactly revert to a Platonic model of formal causation, where the form is considered as an entirely separate entity which somehow causes the particulars. Rather he reframes the whole image-archetype dynamic and emphasizes the nature of image as a function of the archetype.[22] Thus the separation of cause (form) and effect (particular) is subject to criticism, and the whole of the phenomenal world is examined as a function of the intelligible.[23]

1. Theories of Explanation in VI.7.1&2.

The treatise begins with an attempt to understand why the individual has been endowed with the faculties of sensation: "God or a god send souls into genesis, endowed with sense organs." But why was this provision made? Answer: for the sake of preservation, which is to be accomplished by the activities of pursuit and avoidance (of sense objects). Plotinus follows a strictly teleological model of explanation to what he considers an absurd conclusion:

God endowed living beings with sense organs out of foreknowledge, that this would tend toward their bodily preservation. Since perception is a function of the soul and not the body, souls must possess some faculty for sense perception even before entering the world of genesis. Otherwise they would lack psychic faculties which constitute part of the definition of soul. Hence the conclusion must be that souls are endowed with the sense capacities by nature. The purely noetic or intellectual condition of the soul would therefore be unnatural for the soul. So the nature of the soul is to exist in a state wherein the sense faculties may be used, and so it must live in the sense world. The soul is designed by nature, then, to exist in a state of embodiment, multiplicity, and in general evil. But if the same intelligence responsible for the creation of the soul could be responsible for its being endowed with the ability for self-preservation, we would have contradictory purposes in the very creation of the soul: "The exercise of providence would amount to no more than the purpose, that the soul be preserved in evil."

The absurdity involves the fact that the Intellect could propose the sensible as an end for its own action. If Intellect is the starting point of deliberation, surely the conclusion will also be intellectual, not perceptible. Hence if deliberation were the mode of thought applicable to the Intellect, then it would not arrive at the sensible as the outcome of the reasoning process. And yet the sensible exists; its cause can only be the intelligible. So the intelligible brings about the sensible in a way that does not involve the production of something outside of itself. The conclusion is that the sensible already exists within the intelligible. At this stage of the argument, Plotinus does not yet tell us how the sensible exists within the intelligible. He seems to content to exploit a rhetorical trope suggesting the reversal of inner and outer, and to leave the language of the sensible intact as a kind of metaphorical or extended usage.[24]

Thus, after proscribing teleological views, Plotinus proceeds with his own account of the relation between the intelligible and the sensible. The immediate and glaring difference between the type of banned account and the kind of account found at the end of chapter 1 is the manner of reference to time. In the *Timaeus* narrative, events unfold temporally and causation is a developmental sequence that ends in the individual realization (*hekastēn energeian*) of a form within matter. But this kind of analysis is false because of the view that it adopts. It looks at reality as if it were a succession of temporal segments that somehow have to be linked to each other through the explanations we give. Instead of trying to explain things in this way, we should start with the realization that "no 'later' exists in the Intellect" (VI.7.1.40). So when we try to understand reality we should start with a perspective that sees things as simultaneously present.

Several recent studies have called our attention to the Neoplatonists' interest in theories of causation.[25] Of interest to moderns is the outright denial of horizontal or one-directional causal sequence among sensible particulars, or the denial that bodies are causally efficient.[26] Conversely only incorporeal beings such as form, intellect, and soul are agents. The Neoplatonists regularly accounted for the emergence of substances as well as the processes of the natural world by appealing to the idea of *immanent causation*, the doctrine that effects are contained within their causes. Therefore the sensible particular, inasmuch as it is not incorporeal, cannot be designated or isolated as the cause of a given individual or event. In the following passage, we see the denial of something that could be likened to a modern notion of causal relationships, which are very often thought to be capable of expression by means of counterfactual conditions. If event A precedes another event B, such that B would not have come about without the presence of A, then A is said to be the cause of B. In the following passage it appears that, although this counterfactual condition obtains, nevertheless the two events are said not to be causally linked.

> Fire does not arise without a cause—What is its cause? Not friction, as one might assume, since fire already exists in the universe and friction takes place with the bodies undergoing friction [already] containing [fire].[27]

Here event A, the friction, is not the cause of event B, the conflagration. Rather, the cause of the conflagration is just the fact that the element fire exists, and presumably, does so in dependence upon the form. This appears to be a denial of horizontal causation. Yet in other places, Plotinus seems more concerned not to deny horizontal causal sequences but rather to illustrate the difficulties involved in trying to specify just how events are supposed to be related to each other if one is to say that they are causally related.[28] One very basic issue involves the difficulty of picking out just what a cause is, such that it is both necessary and sufficient for the bringing about of a given effect. The problem has to do with being able to distinguish such a unique cause from what might be called the total causal field—in being able to distinguish a background condition from a cause. Hillary Putnam for instance illustrates the problem in this way

> Imagine that Venusians land on earth and observe a forest fire. One of them says, 'I know what caused that—the atmosphere of the darned planet is saturated with oxygen'... What is and what is not a 'cause' or 'explanation' depends on background knowledge and our reason for asking the question.[29]

The problem here arises from the ambivalent context in which the explanation is given, but we can generalize from this example. If for any given query we find that a complete answer will have to specify all of the relevant background conditions, then it seems that our answer will be reduced to something that does not look like an explanation for the event at all. Plotinus has this in mind when he asserts that the only real explanation for an event is to say that it belongs to a totality.[30] The theoretical background for this kind of problem is sketched at VI.7.2.35, in what I will refer to as Plotinus' doctrine of simultaneous arising:

> In fact just as in our universe which subsists from a multiplicity of elements all things are linked with each other, and the explanation for the individual consists in its being a member of the totality (that is, just as the part in the case of every individual is perceived in terms of its relation to the whole), it is not the case that first one thing arises, and then after that, this, but rather things subsist in relation to each other, both the cause and the effect.[31]

We can break this passage into three supporting theses and a conclusion: (1) *All things co-originate with one another*. This thesis does not simply mean that each thing co-originates with at least some other thing; it is more likely to mean that all things co-originate with all other things. This universal reciprocal dependence is suggested by the preposition *syn* as well as the reflexive pronoun. (2) *The reason for the existence of each thing consists in its membership within a totality.* And (3) *In the case of each individual, the part is seen to exist in relation to the whole.* This phrase should not simply be translated as 'the part is related to the whole,' since here *echon* is equivalent to the copula and denotes a state of being. Thus the idea is 'a part is within the category of relation to'—i.e. individuals are not substances, but relative entities that do not exist in themselves. Hence, (4a) (Conclusion) *It is not the case that first one thing comes to be, and next another comes into existence after this* [and dependent upon it?].

The first part of the conclusion seems to sketch and then to deny a theory of causation which could easily be compared to the Humean account of cause as:

> An object precedent and contiguous to another, and so united with it in the imagination, that the idea of the one determines the mind to form the idea of the other.[32]

Obviously things do arise one after the next. What this phrase (4a) in the text must mean then, is that although there may be sequences of events, these sequences are not causal sequences. The next part of the sentence presents an alternative causal theory: (4b) *The cause and the effect come to be simultaneously in relation to each other.* This alternative, non-teleological method of explanation, in which the relationship between cause and effect is one of co-arising, shows up in the subsequent puzzles of VI.7.1–15: In VI.7.1 it appears to be the inspiration behind the constant refrain in which the logic of temporal succession—*tode meta tode*[33]—is denied. Rather, the sensible arises as an immediate and necessary expression of the intelligible. In chapter 2 this conclusion is generalized as a corollary of the theory of explanation present in lines 32–35, examined above: The cause must include its effects within itself. Chapter 3 applies this theory to an analysis of soul and concludes that soul must arise simultaneously with its sense faculties. Chapters 8 and 9 show that the objects of sense, and so the whole realm of sentient beings must arise simultaneously from the intelligible world. In chapter 10 all sentient beings must arise simultaneously, as must the gross elements together with their inhabitants (chapter 12).

2. Simultaneous Arising within the Larger Scope of Plotinus' Metaphysics

In order to assess the significance of this causal theory, we have to ask whether it is an *ad hoc* solution to the problems of interpretation that beset Plotinus in VI.7, or whether it is a consistent statement of his philosophical orientation. I believe that Plotinus included the doctrine of simultaneous arising as a key concept within the larger framework of his metaphysical system, and that he presented this doctrine as such. The most explicit statement concerning its centrality is found in VI.4, to which we now briefly turn.

Plotinus frequently employs an image consisting in the simple model of a center surrounded by one or more concentric circles, with radii projecting from the center to the circumference of these circles. The terminal points of the radii form the circumference of the circles and the lines described by the radii fill up the surface of the circles surrounding the center. The diagram serves to represent the hypostatic view of reality, with the One symbolized by the center, and each of the circles standing respectively for Intellect and Soul

> For the sake of clarity, often the argument wishes to lead to a conception of the multiplicity which has come to be, by positing many lines from one center.[34]

Moreover, he uses the diagram in order to illustrate the causal structure of his entire metaphysical system. Briefly the parts of the diagram refer to a transcendent source (the center in isolation), an immanent source (the center to which the radii are connected) which unifies a multiplicity with which it is identical (the circle considered as the terminus points of the radii), and the individuals which arise simultaneously as members of this unified multiplicity (the radii which fill up the surface area of the circle).

This ontological schema,[35] the interrelationship of all three hypostases, demonstrates the interdependence of all of the aspects of reality upon all of the other parts. Each aspect of the diagram is necessary for and implies the existence of all of the other parts. It is this simultaneous co-presence of the three hypostases of being within the real which fully captures Plotinus' vision, in which the hypostases of soul, intellect, and pure unity, are necessary moments within the integral but unique reality.

The introductory line in chapter 5 gives us an important piece of information about the significance of this model. The model is designed to illustrate the Platonic doctrine of exemplarism or the theory of forms. Plotinus is using a geometric schema in order to illustrate the relationship existing between a form and its phenomenal expression. He states explicitly that this model serves as an illustration for the relationship between intelligible and particular in lines 21–23 of this chapter:

> The lines provide us, in this instance, with an analogy for those elements through which the intelligible nature, coming into contact with them, appears to be present to a multiplicity, as a multiplicity.[36]

Considering the diagram as a whole, Plotinus tells us to envision the lines, not as distinct rays, but rather as one surface: All the lines entirely fill up the space delimited by the circle. The unified comprehension of these distinct rays illustrates the relationship of phenomenal particulars, whose individuation is the condition of their multiplicity, with the unity of their own order. The lines arise simultaneously and comprise one totality, they cannot really subsist as realities distinct from each other.

> But one must bear in mind when one says this that the things which are said to become many are all together at once, just as there in the example of the circle one cannot take the lines as being separated: for it is one surface.[37]

It is because the individual arises as an integral condition of the totality that the order of individuals must be comprehended as a whole: no amount of discursive thought could succeed in tracing the innumerable relationships that the individual has with other things.[38] Thus we are told that individuals are not self-standing, but exist in ontological dependence within a community of finite entities: "All other things [apart from the One] when isolated are not self-subsistent."[39]

Among later Neoplatonists this analysis of the individual, in which paradigmatic causation by one form, *pace* Aristotle, is replaced by the concept of mutual coproduction[40] became standard. A. C. Lloyd[41] quotes Proclus' *Commentary on Parmenides* as an illustration:

> If one is to name one cause, then the order of the universe; or if one is to name several, the movement of heavens, particular types of nature, the properties of the seasons, climates, as well as those who superintend all these. (825, 13–17: Lloyd translation)

One way of comprehending the universe is to look at the entire network of individual components at any given time within the course of its development. This community of individuals, each producing an effect as a result of its interaction with others, is just the world of space and time, the place "from whence what is done is already an effect." Plotinus describes this interconnected community of action in III.2.6 as follows:

> Everything does not produce an identical effect when it interacts with everything, but is produces a different effect in relation to a different thing.[42]

Here the individual events take their rise in relationship to other things; they have no fixed character in themselves, but are entirely determined as relative entities.

Plotinus elaborates upon the relative character of the individual viewpoint by means of spatial symbolism, in treatise III.2.7, the end of his work 'On Providence,' in an image which encapsulates the entire teaching on this subject. The outer circumference of our circle is shown in this image as the extremities of branches stemming from a trunk, itself a projection of the central root. Here is what Plotinus has to say about the twigs:

> The empty spaces between the branches are filled from the [parts] that [stem] from the root which grow in a different manner, from whence the twigs on the branches are affected as well, as though imagining that the experience comes only from the immediate environment [sc. and not ultimately from the root].[43]

The individual viewpoint is shown as relative here in several ways: The twig, as an extremity of a branch connecting it to the root, really is not an individual at all, but belongs to one organism, and has no existence of its own apart from that organism. Secondly, what it experiences as another organism interacting with it or affecting it, is in fact not another organism at all.

3. Individuals and Explanation in VI.7

In chapter 3, Plotinus applies his theory of interdependent causation to the analysis of the human form: If we ask, why does man have eyes or eyebrows, the only answer can be in order that all things might come to be (*hina panta*). Why should this kind of answer constitute any kind of an explanation at all? Taking the example of eyes first, we can see that Aristotle would certainly find this answer unsatisfactory. Since it is a part of human nature to be a sighted being, we have eyes because they are components without which the human form would be incomplete. Aristotle describes this preferred type of explanation as follows:

> This is why we should for preference say (a) that man has these parts because this is what it is for a man to be. For without these parts he cannot be. Failing that, the next nearest thing: that is either (a') that it is altogether impossible otherwise, or at any rate (b) that it is good this way.[44]

At this point we can see difficulty emerging in the view which is explored in chapter 2 of VI.7. There, we read that each being has its reason why within itself, and that on a secondary level (in the order of individuals) the form is the cause of each individual's coming to be. Such a concession would seem to be completely in agreement with what Aristotle says here about the preferred form of natural explanation. Yet in this treatise Plotinus asserts that the reason why human beings have eyes is in order that everything may come to be (*dia ti oun ophthalmoi; hina panta*). Plotinus has not merely substituted the externally imposed teleology of the *Timaeus* which analyzes the constituent parts of the human form as in some sense instrumental to its good, with the Aristotelian teleology of natural kinds in which parts are described as directed toward the functioning of the mature organism. Rather, he seems to be assuming that the world order will tend toward a maximally rich and heterogeneous composition from among its members.[45]

The use of the word *panta* is a bit confusing in our passage. In chapter 2 it refers to the completion of the form as self-explanatory; in chapter 3 it is also used for the complete realization of a given form within matter. Completion in this sense can be applied to an individual that lacks no part contained within the formal definition of its nature. But he also uses the word 'complete' as part of his denial of teleology, as when he says that the "form means possessing everything"—meaning that the intelligible must contain the sensible within itself. In keeping with this latter usage, if the form (e.g.) of human beings is complete then this completion entails the capacity for sensation (line 27). The simultaneous origination of the physical from the intelligible goes against the strict dualism of Platonic two-worlds metaphysics[46] without embracing Aristotelian hylomorphism. It is within this context that Plotinus says:

"These perceptions here are dim intellections, but the intellections there are clear sense-perceptions."[47]

It becomes clear that a specifically Aristotelian doctrine of nature as principle of change is what is rejected by Plotinus.[48] That natural processes are directed toward the realization of form in matter and toward the most complete development of an individual substance is, according to the doctrine of the pre-existence of the sensible within the intelligible, an inadequate explanation of genesis as a whole. The actualization of form in matter cannot be the goal by which we can account for the specific structure of an organism, because form cannot in fact be actualized in matter. When the form comes to be in a material substrate, it exists in an incomplete state. The specific differentia are compensatory accretions due to the inherent deficiency of embodied individuality:

> For, as the powers [of the intelligible world] unfold themselves, they constantly leave behind [something of themselves] above. They proceed by losing something and in the various losses each power finds something else to add on as a result of the deficiency of the living being that appeared as a result of the loss.[49]

In fact, Plotinus goes on to suggest in this treatise that not only is the essence/accident distinction invalid, but it is so because the very differentia which are said in Aristotelian parlance to constitute the definition of something, and so to constitute its essence, are in fact inessential, or strictly accidental for that substance. In this section, Plotinus pursues his attack upon essentialism by means of a favorite strategy. He attempts to pry apart the essence/accident distinction by showing that it has no explanatory power, and thus that the individual substance lacks essential properties.

Aristotle seems to have thought that the concept of hypothetical necessity could be applied to the parts of an organism,[50] so that there were "features of a kind that explain other features of that kind without themselves being explained by features of that kind."[51] If we say that it is part of the human essence to be a sighted being, then eyebrows will be necessitated given this essential structure. So in this case we should be able to designate the eyebrows as 'protective' (*phylaktikon*) and so as something which contributes to the end but is in fact not the end. But then the reason for the eyebrows, the form of man, must exist before—although clearly not temporally since Intellect lives an atemporal life—the safeguard, since it determines that there be a safeguard. Plotinus concludes that the safeguard is not after all contributory to the essence, but is a part of the essence.

One part of an individual cannot explain another part; parts must arise simultaneously. Thus it is extremely difficult to come up with a functional analysis of the parts of an individual in such a way that one could specify which elements function for the sake of others: "One could say that all that belongs to an individual is its reason why."[52] The collapse of the concept of definitional necessity is based upon the rejection of the distinction between the parts of an individual which are components of the essence, and the parts of the individual which are contributory toward the essence.

This is not to say that the Neoplatonists rejected Aristotelian logic as incapable of yielding valid results for the reasoning process. Rather, the results obtained by this process will not yield necessary propositions about he reality which they describe.[53] As Lloyd points out in his well-known article, the Neoplatonists "are, as it were, assuming that all syllogisms are [only] dialectical [not demonstrative]." In V.8.7, 41 we read:

> As if the conclusion was there before the syllogism which showed the cause, and the conclusion did not follow from the premises; [the world order] is not the result of following out a train of logical consequences and purposive thought; it is before consequential and discursive thinking.

The doctrine of dependent origination coincides with Plotinus' assessment of the individual not only as lacking an essence, but as a construction of the discursive reasoning process trying to grasp the intelligible object. Plotinus explicitly tells us that individuation is due to the way that the discursive thought encounters the intelligible object:

> When the process of rational thinking separates the distinctive individuality in these realities, not taking it away from the intelligible world but rather grasping it and producing something else, it produces the qualitative as a kind of part of substance, grasping what appears on the surface of reality.[54]

This passage tells us that the individual is not something that exists in the intelligible order (*ouk ekeithen*), but is the creation of discursive thought when it simply grasps the surface presentation of the reality (*labōn to epipolēs phanen*). The individual viewpoint, while adequate for ordinary discourse, is only the mental reflection of the sensible world, and is not adequate for the practice of philosophical understanding or training. In fact, the individual is not a real being, but only what Plotinus calls a pseudo-substance, an appearance that lacks any self-subsistence. Thus in terms of discourse, as the subject of statements, the world of individuals is a system of place holders, or representations, which exist and are defined only as predicated by other such place holders, having entirely relative meaning and reference.[55]

4. Intellect and Explanation in VI.7

Plotinus in VI.7.2 describes the physical world as a mutually conditioning and conditioned causal nexus, which contrasts with his understanding of the intelligible world. In the physical domain, cause and caused are simply correlatives, so that any given thing, having an infinite number of relationships with other things, is an entirely relative entity. However, an idea, far from being related to an infinite plurality of individuals, has its cause within itself. It is causally independent, to the extent that Plotinus can say about the intelligibles at VI.7.2, 40 that each "contains the cause within itself" (*anaitiōs tēn aitian echein*).

By itself, this formula 'containing the cause within itself' specifically recalls *Posterior Analytics* b2, 90a15—to which Plotinus alludes at line 13[56]—but also more generally the identity of substance and essence at *Metaphysics* Z.7. Indeed, Plotinus makes this doctrine the starting point of his discussion of the formula at VI.7.2, 17. The discussion begins with the familiar notion of the convergence of formal and final causes: "What each thing is, is the reason why it comes to be" (VI.7.2, 16). But Plotinus does not confine himself to the case of an individual substance and its essential form: Not only is it true that for each substance, the form (*eidos*) is the cause (*aition*); he means that for each form there is a 'reason why' inherent in it:

> Not that the form is the reason for the individual's being—although this is certainly true—but rather if you unfold each form back on itself, you will discover its reason why within it.[57]

'Unfolding the form back upon itself' involves referring each form to the second hypostasis as a whole. Since Intellect (*nous*) is all of the things in it, each of the forms contains the cause of existence in itself, and Intellect, consequently, contains the reason why of all of the ideas in it.

Plotinus clearly uses the formula 'having its cause in itself' to suggest not that each of the forms fits into a system of which it is an essential member,[58] but rather that each form is the whole of Intellect due to the unity of knower and known at the level of the second hypostasis. So Plotinus contrasts the relationship of form to Intellect with that of part to whole in order to demonstrate that the structure of intellect is not fully comprehended through the discursive analysis which depends solely on the logic of essences.

At VI.7.9 we can see directly how the unity of subject and object are at the heart of Plotinus' views on the nature of essence and necessity. Chapter 9 takes up the problem of how the *logoi* of irrational animals can be present in the Intellectual cosmos (*kosmos noētos*). Here we have only what Plotinus reveals to be a pseudo-problem, since there can be nothing unintelligent in intellect itself, which is the source of the *logoi* for irrational animals. The unintelligent within intellect turns out to be intelligent, since both the thinker of the irrational form is intellect, and its thought is intellect. The consequence of this unity is not the improbable one that irrational beings are rational within intellect, but that the rational/irrational distinction simply is not applicable at all. Rational thought does not exist in intellect, so how could it belong to any of the beings in intellect? Now if thought could be different from its object, then the object could be thoughtless. But in intellect, the thinker will be the same as the that of which the thinker thinks. But since thought and object are one, thought can only be a thought of that which is itself intelligent.

In the case of the human self, it will turn out that Plotinus' critique of essentialism extends to the Aristotelian identification of substance (*ousia*) with the soul. In fact, the human soul, containing the *logoi* of all sentient beings, is potentially any one of them: "It exchanges [its body] for the body of an animal. Thus it is incredible that the soul could be the definition of the human being."[59] Since every soul contains the ideas of all living beings, it actually is accidental as to which *logos* a particular soul will exhibit as its essential type in an embodied state. Plotinus objects to defining substances by means of differentiae which are only applicable to embodied beings.

Plotinus elsewhere discusses the question of whether we can define the soul *per genus et differentiam*, as living being, where soul belongs to the genus 'living' and is defined by the differentia 'living'.

> Is then being one thing, and the rest something else, which contributes to the completion of the substance of the soul, and is there being [as such] and an essential difference makes the soul?[60]

Lloyd discusses the strategy for Plotinus' criticism of the definition of soul *per genus et differentiam* as living being:

> Soul is an ousia [substance], but its being is distinct from generic being. It cannot be being plus a differentia added to it from outside this generic being; otherwise it would be an essence or substance in respect of only half of its essence, viz. the generic half of its definition.[61]

The point is that for the Aristotelian definition, we must find a differentia outside of the category of the genus. But in this case the genus is Being, so to find a differentia outside of Being, would, according to Plotinus, necessitate that soul be less than substance in half (the differentia) of its definition. Lloyd gives this example in an attempt to show that the Neoplatonists deny the validity of Aristotelian essentialism by showing that there can be no necessary connection between the two parts of a definition, a problem about which Aristotle himself was certainly exercised. But if there is no necessary connection between the two parts of a definition, it is no longer possible to draw the distinction between accidental and essential.

This argument is an example of an across the board rejection of this kind of definition for any species: Since any species form is a *substance*, to say that the specific differentia falls into a different category, is to say that only one half of its definition is in fact substantial; the differentia would be by definition accidental. Plotinus goes on to tell us that the soul, if it is substance and not accident, must not obtain its differentia from outside of the category of substance (VI.2.5, 26).

To what does the definition of man refer? Not to the embodied individual, since its matter does not enter into the definition, but not to the idea either: The intelligible form is not susceptible say, to being defined as rational as opposed to irrational, since intellect is pre-rational. Intellect is universal; it cannot belong to any individual. But if there is to be any knowledge of the individual then an appeal must be made to its definition, or to that about it which is universal. We have to refer the sensible back to the intelligible, but in the intelligible, each form is Intellect, and Intellect is all forms. Therefore, in order to have knowledge of the individual, we must have knowledge of the intelligible, but to have this knowledge is to understand the unity of Being. We must therefore rethink the nature of the individual, and see that individuals are not separate substances, but aspects of the one universal being.

5. Explanation and Contemplation in VI.7

In order to show the connection between theoretical underpinnings and contemplative praxis, let us briefly glance at the two meditations that follow upon the exploration of teleology and paradeigmatism in chapters VI.7.1–11. One is macrocosmic, the other microcosmic. In the first vision, Plotinus contrasts the universal living being of the *Timaeus*, exemplar of the world of particulars, with this universe ("this all exists in relation to the paradigm of that intelligible world"— VI.7.12, 1):

> Since we maintain that this all exists after the pattern (so to call it) of that, *the universal living being must exist there too first, and, if its existence is to be complete, must be all living beings.* And certainly the sky there must be a living being, and so a sky not bare of stars, as we call them here below, and this is what being sky is. But obviously there is earth there also, not barren, but much more full of life, and all animals are in it, all that walk on and belong to the land here below, and obviously, plants rooted in life; and sea is there and all water in abiding flow and life, and all the living beings in water, and the nature of air is part of the universe there, and aerial living things are there just as air itself is...*For as each of the great parts of the universe is there, so is of necessity the nature of the living beings in them.* (Armstrong translation)[62]

This passage reflects the two-fold analysis of individuation, that of reciprocal origination, and that of the direct expression of the intelligible source in the individual. These two aspects of the meditation are explained by the fact that one facet, the interconnection of all beings, is used as a support for the more direct experience of unity which follows. On the one hand, the vision consists in perceiving the relationship between part and whole, as flowing reciprocally between the two terms of the hierarchy; but it ends, on the other hand, in a complete fusion between the sensible and intelligible, as well as a detachment from individuality, an experience of the unification of the phenomenal world in which the distinction between essence and accident, between body and mind, between any individuals, is no longer present.

This meditation is an introduction to the experience of intellect as the unifying ground of all individuated existence. By shifting the focus from a teleological account of discrete essences to a systematic account of individuals as interrelated, Plotinus hopes to effect a change in the kind of analysis we give of individuals. What counts as an adequate understanding of individuals? The physical aspect of living beings, by means of which they express their individuality, must be seen as a unity, objectively, as constituting one world body, and subjectively, as constituting one phenomenal presentation. What happens in the next step of the meditation is that the qualities that are known to comprise, on the Neoplatonist's account, the sum reality of the individual,[63] are no longer capable of doing the work of presenting attributes by which an individual might be discriminated from another individual. Instead, the qualities are apprehended in the most general form as one unified field of sense presentations, and it is the consciousness of the apprehender to which these presentations belong:

> They all flow, in a way, from a single spring, not like one particular breath or one warmth, but as if there was one quality which held and kept intact all the qualities in itself, of sweetness along with fragrance, and was at once the quality of wine and the characters of all tastes, the sights of colours and all the awarenesses of touch. (Armstrong translation)[64]

Thus the progress of the passage is from the objective description of the quality, as sweetness or smell, to its fundamental nature as a kind of awareness on the part of the perceiver.

In chapter 15 we have another vision in which Plotinus seems to be describing an experience which he may have had of the unity of intellect:

> So that if one were to compare it to a living, variegated sphere, imagining it either as an entity that consisted entirely in aspect, illuminating by means of its living aspects, or as all detached souls running together into identity, one would not be amiss.[65]

Each individual is no more nor less than a point of view, an aspect, an act of vision. Individuals, as part of the objective order, are intrinsically without their own nature. Thus the sphere is described as consisting entirely of aspect, being mere appearance. At the same time, when the knower succeeds in becoming detached from the objective order of reality—from its *procession* (*prosopon*), as it were—then these same appearances are seen within the context of a unity which is very difficult to define or communicate, without implicitly severing the unity which is the foundation of the vision. Therefore the meditation ends with an exhortation to 'make oneself the vision.' The reversal in cognition occurs together with the reversal in self-identity. This unity is only apprehended when discursive thought, responsible for the whole order of individuation, is set aside.

Plotinus finishes his study of nature in treatise VI.7 by offering a contemplative vision rooted in the theoretical position he has outline in the preceding first chapters. Does the doctrine of dependent origination express Plotinus' philosophical originality and does it differ in any significant way from the well-developed Stoic conception of world harmony that obviously informs it? The fact that Plotinus so carefully distances his own position from that of the Stoics by denying discursive thought to the Demiurge should at least invite the above questions.

It seems that Poseidonius attributes the intelligibility of the world's structure to the fact that the designing intelligence, God, and human intelligence share the same thought processes, since human souls are *apospasmata* of God.[66] Therefore the Stoics hold that a teleological description of the world is a factual description of a state of affairs that inheres within the cosmic structure. But this very structure, the systemic cohesion of individuals within their order of being, is understood by Plotinus as a reflection of the inherence of our world within its intelligible cause. And this latter, the Intellectual cosmos, is not systematic in the way that the physical cosmos is.

In chapter 13 the 'highest kinds' (*megistē genē*) of Plato's *Sophist* appear as a counterpoint to the Stoicizing conception developed in chapter 12. Here the reader encounters an extremely paradoxical aetiology for the complexity of the intelligible world:

> All things are varied to the extent that they are simple, and this means to the extent that they are not composites and are activities.[67]

And again in line 55:

> There is nothing in it which is not other, so that in its otherness it may contribute this too.[68]

Plotinus is describing the dynamic life of intellect in which the interplay between subject and object creates a proliferation of points of view, the subject discovering itself in the object and the object being discovered within the subject. The life of intellect, constantly projecting itself as object of its own realization is actually the very life that comprises the world of sentient beings.

World and soul, knower and known, must arise together. Plotinus finishes his examination of the sensible and the intelligible by showing that they are more like two sides of the same coin than two separate realities. The world of action, that world in which production occurs and things come to be, is implied by the very nature of the intelligible world. In much the same way one could say that when someone acts, there exists a relationship between his/her internal state and his/her action, for the latter reveals that internal state. The act, seen mentally in terms of one's intention, could not be intended without the awareness of the possibility of carrying it out, nor could we speak of an actor, apart from his/her intention.[69]

By analogy to the relationship between thinker and act, we can say that the life of the cosmos expresses the content of Intellect. Plotinus is emphatic in his assertion, however, that the cosmos has come to be, exactly as if its author had flawlessly calculated the optimum conditions for its existence. Nevertheless, this way of viewing the rational order inherent within the universal is purely metaphor. The divine intellect does not purposively determine any of the states of the cosmos. All things are at once implied by, as well as realized in, their conception, but what is intended, we might say, is the very conception itself. Hence the universe arises as a simultaneous expression of Being, and all phenomena are mutually interdependent within their respective orders.[70]

The University of Michigan

NOTES

1. The first lines quote *Timaeus* 45b3, directly alluding to the younger gods' dispatch of the souls into the world of space and time, but the general issue is the language of deliberation that Plato uses in the narrative. Cf. *Timaeus* 30b1, *logisamenos*; 29cl, *pronoian*; 34a9, *logismos*, etc.
2. For general discussions of VI.7. 1-15 in light of Plotinus' philosophical treatment of the idea of *Pronoia*, see Leroux 1990, 31–32; Theiler 1966; Schubert 1968; Hadot 1988, 31–36; Schroeder 1992, 16–20.
3. On the overall structure of VI.7, see Hadot 1987; Hadot 1988.
4. See Harder 3b; Schubert 1968; Leroux 1990; and Wallis 1987.
5. II.9.8, 20. In chapters 5 and 6 Plotinus censures the opponents' falsification of Plato's account of creation: "Often they have soul as the maker instead of the planning mind and they think that this is the maker according to Plato,

being a long way from knowing who the maker is. And in general they falsify Plato's account of the manner of the making" (II.9.6, 23–26). For a discussion of whose views precisely are being criticized, see Peuch 1960; Roloff 1970, 169–179; and Elsas 1975, in the appendix on Roloff's monograph. II.9 and VI.7 both oppose a literal reading of the *Timaeus* creation account not only because of Gnostic renderings which hypostasize the planning mind, but also because a literal rendering assumes that the world had a beginning in time.

6. The conception of a Demiurge or Creator God who uses the forms as a blueprint for the world is of course central to most Middle Platonic discussions that try to explain how God interacts with the world. See Witt 1930, 199; Dillon 1977, 46–49 & *passim*.
7. II.9.7
8. See Wallis 1987, 942–952.
9. *Metaphysics* Λ.9 and *De Anima* II. For the Aristotelianized Platonism of the Imperial period, see Blumenthal 1987.
10. It could be said that Plotinus reversed the terms of the debate and asked whether the human soul could ever think like the Divine mind. For his positive answer to this question in the form of the concept of the undescended soul and its heterodoxy within the Platonist tradition, see Blumenthal 1987.
11. Throughout the *Enneads* we find the insistence that the world is not an artifact whose genesis is owed to someone's intentions, associated with the 'two acts' theory of causation, wherein every level of reality must of necessity produce an image of itself in the form of a 'lower' existent. However what follows is a methodological interpretation rather than a strictly metaphysical one. For caution against a purely source-critical approach to Plotinus, see Leroux 1990, 23–26.
12. *Posterior Analytics* I, 71a16: *Epistametha de oiometh'hekaston haplōs, alla mē ton sophistikon tropon ton kata symbebēkos, hotan tēn aitian oiōmetha ginōskein di' hēn to pragma estin, hoti ekeinou aitia esti, kai mē endechesthai tout' allōs echein.*
13. See Lloyd 1986; Alfonso 1990.
14. *Timaeus* 29b3: *hōde oun peri te eikonos kai peri tou paradeigmatos autēs dioisteon, hōs ara tous logous, hōnper eisin exēgētai, toutōn autōn kai syggeneis ontas; tou men oun monimou kai bebaiou kai meta noun kataphanous monimous kai ametaptōtous—kath' hoson hoion te kai anelegtois prosēkei logois einai kai anikētois, toutou dei mēden elleipein—tous de tou pros ekeino apeikasthentos, ontos de eikonos eikotas ana logon te ekeinōn ontas.*
15. Putnam, 211.
16. Limitations of space prohibit a detailed discussion of this topic, but readers should refer to Wagner 1982 & Lee 1984.
17. *Physics* 197a32. Cf. *De Generatione Animalium* II, 742b23–36.

18. On Aristotle as a corrector of Platonic notions of teleology, see Balme 1987, 275.
19. Cf. VI.7.3, 9.
20. On Stoic cosmic *harmonia*, see Cicero *De Finibus* III, sections 38 ff; Edelstein-Kidd 1990, fragments 104 and 106. For Plotinus' familiarity with this Stoic tenet, and the probable influence of Poseidonius, see Reinhardt 1924, Graeser 1976, Witt 1930, Theiler 1966.
21. For Platonists of any century, of course, it is simply not true that the individual (the sensible particular, that is) will have an essence at all. As Code (1985) has shown, if x is a particular, then there is no y such that y=x and y is essentially predicable of x. The sensible cannot have an essence because it simply has no substance, hence it is neither defineable nor knowable. Whereas for Aristotle, although individuals do not have definitions (*Metaphysics* Z.12, 1039a) the essence of the individual is simply the essence of the kind under which it falls.
22. The relationship that Plotinus tends to find most expressive of this kind of causality is the relationship between thinker and thought, or mind and object of consciousness. Since thought and thinker are not two distinct entities, Plotinus treats the individual, not as a separate reality from the intelligible, but rather as an expression of the intelligible. As A. C. Lloyd puts the matter: "In the last analysis, substance and attribute coincide either as substances and their activities or as imperfect projections of such activities" (Lloyd 1990, 91).
23. See Schroeder 1980, 50: "The intelligible world is not merely represented by the things in the world of sense. It is truly present in them." And again on page 52: "In 6.3.15...the entire content of the world of sense is to be conceived as a quality, in the sense that it bears an adjectival relation to the intelligible world..."
24. Thus we find him talking about "the perceptibles that exist there" (VI.7.6, 2); "the eyes they have there" (V.8.4, 26); "*einai tas aisthēseis tautas amydras noēseis, tas de ekei noēseis enargeis aisthēseis*" (VI.7.7, 31: 'Our sensations are dim intellections; intellections are clear sensations').
25. Barnes 1983; Sorabji 1987; Wagner 1982.
26. Barnes 1983, 175, concisely summarizes Proclus' presentation of this view (*Elements of Theology* 80): (1) all bodies are passive; (2) everything incorporeal is active; (3) no body is active; (4) no incorporeal thing is passive. Barnes supplies the conclusion to the argument: Only incorporeal things are active.
27. VI.7.10, 40 (Armstrong's translation modified, reading *echontōn* as a temporal, not causal participle): *ouk ek tou automatou pyr—pothen gar; ou gar paratripseōs, hōs an tis oiēthein; ēdē gar ontos en tōi panti pyros hē paratripsis echontōn tōn paratribomenōn sōmatōn.*
28. On the difficulties of specifying the nature of causal connection between events, see Davidson 1980.

29. Putnam 1983, 214.
30. Cf. VI.7.2, 35, discussed in the next paragraph.
31. (1) *kai mēn, hōsper en tōide tōi panti ek pollōn synestēkoti syneirētai pros allēla ta panta*, (2) *kai en tōi panta einai esti kai to dioti hekaston*— (3) *hōsper kai eph' hekastou to meros pros to holon echon horatai*—(4α) *ou toutou genomenou, eita toutou meta tode*, (4*b*) *alla pros allēla homou tēn aitian kai to aitiaton synistantōn.*
32. Hume, *A Treatise of Human Nature*, Book I, Part 3 (as quoted by Mackie 1974, 3).
33. Cf. VI.7.1,37: *ho logismos touto anti touto*; VI.7.1,40: *touto, hina mē touto*; VI.7.1, 56: *tode meta tode.*
34. VI.5.5, 1 (Armstrong translation): *kai saphēneias men heneka ho logos pollakis hoion ek kentrou henos pollas grammas poiēsas eis ennoian tou plēthous tou genomenou ethelei agein.* See Ferwerda 1965, 30–34.
35. On the concept of a two-tiered unity (transcendent and immanent), see Gurtler 1989 *passim.* Gurtler acknowledges (page 5) that this structure was pointed out by Blumenthal 1971, 55–63.
36. *Hai grammai parechetōsan hēmin chreian en tōi paronti anailogon einai hōn ephaptomenē hē noētē physis polla kai pollachēi phainetai pareinai.*
37. VI.5.5, 3: *dei de tērountas homou panta ta legomena polla gegonenai legein. Hōs kakei epi tou kyklou ouk ousas grammas aphōrismenas esti lambanein. Epipedon gar hen.*
38. Cf. *Enneads* VI.8.14, 26: *kai holōs hē pros allēla pantōn symphōnia allēlois aitia.*
39. VI.8.15, 25: *ta men oun alla monoumena ouk estin hautois autarkē einai eis to einai.*
40. Cf. Hadot 1988, 203: "C'est dans leur production par l'Espirit, c'est à dire dans leur coproduction mutuelle (6.7.2.37) qu'elles ont leur pourquoi (6.7.2.26–27)."
41. Lloyd 1990, 163.
42. *Ou gar to auto poiei pan proselthon panti, alla to auto pros allo kai allo pros allo.*
43. *ta de diakena hoion tōn kladōn eplērounto ek tōn au ek tēs hrizēs kai autōn allon tropon pephykotōn, ex hōn kai epasche ta akpa tōn kladōn, hōs ek tou plēsion oiesthai to pathos ienai monon.*
44. *De partibus animalium* 1, 640 a33–b4.
45. Aristotle does not defend his assumption of the permanence of the world order by means of such a theory (Cooper 1987, 248). But Poseidonius evidently used the same description of the world order (poikilon zōon) that Plotinus uses in VI.7.12. See Witt 1930 & Graeser 1972. In this treatise, we find the concept of maximal diversity expressed in the word poikilon. This idea is elaborated upon at line 9 in chapter 13 of our treatise: *sōma homoiomeres ti kai apoikilon; alla gar ti to semnon* ("What is there worthy of adoration in a homeomerous body, one that lacks variation?"); and again

at line 25: *physin ara echei epi pan heterousthai* ("It [the living cosmos] tends toward maximal diversity"). See below, section 4, for the relationship of this idea to the Stoics and for its justification in Plotinus.

46. Once more, limitations of space prohibit extended discussion of this non-dual tendency within Plotinus' metaphysics, but readers should consult Wagner (1982) for a detailed discussion on the relationship between Plotinus' philosophy of perception and his two-worlds metaphysics.
47. VI.7.7, 31: *hōste einai tas aisthēseis tautas amydras noēseis, tas de ekei noēseis enargeis aisthēseis.*
48. Cf. the discussion in chapter 2 on the deficiencies of the sensible human particular as opposed to the form of the human being. Plotinus' point here is the denial of *Aristotelian* teleology, in which the goal of change is the realization of the form in matter, or the coming-to-be of the hylomorphic compound.
49. VI.7.9, 40–41: *echelittomenai gar hai dynameis kataleipousin aei eis to anō. Proiasi de ti aphienai d' alla allai dia to endees tou zōiou tou phanentos ek tou elleipontos heteron exereusai prostheinai.* It is true that Plotinus accepts an Aristotelian hylomorphic description of sensible particulars in the treatises concerned with matter, II.4 and II.5, in the limited sense that he accepts the necessity of a substrate for the sensible which in itself utterly lacks quality or is essentially a deprivation of form (see *Physics* Ia.192a2). "Matter is an outcast of reality and is separated from the perfection of being. As a result it can never unite with form, for how can the unreal add anything to the real? Plotinus' theory of matter reflects a dualism between matter and form and is alien to Aristotelian hylomorphism" (Hancock 1985, 139). For a more reconciliatory account of hylomorphism in II.4, see Corrigan 1981.
50. For a list of Aristotelian passages which apply a teleological analysis to the parts of an individual organism, see Gotthelf 1987, 190–191.
51. Gotthelf 1987, 189.
52. VI.7.2, 44: *panta hosa echei echois an eipein dioti hekaston.*
53. A great deal of scholarly work has been devoted over the course of the last decade to the exposition of Plotinus' notorious critique of Aristotle's categories, presented in *Enneads* VI.1–3. To name but a few of the major works appearing recently: Lloyd 1955–1956; Lloyd 1990; Wurm 1973; Strange 1981; Rist 1967, chapter 8; Corrigan 1981, 98–121.
54. *Hotan de chōrisēi ho logos to ep' autois idion ouk ekeithen aphelōn, alla mallon labōn kai gennēsas allo, egennēse poion hoion meros ousias labōn to epipolēs phanen aut'.*
55. The bundle theory of sensible particulars as encountered in Plotinus has been the subject of thorough discussion in the context of Neoplatonic scholarship. Strange (1981) relates the *migma* ('mixture') conception of sensible substance to the analysis of sensible substance into "nothing more than the conjunction of the sensible differentiae" (196). Strange is careful to distinguish this position from a nominalistic account of definition, in which

there is simply a list of attributes that in fact belong to a given class of objects. However, Plotinus does not lose touch with his Platonist roots, nor with the entailment relations that in fact govern which attributes are realized in a given class of objects. One feature of Strange's account with which I disagree, with all respect to his very carefully documented claims concerning treatises VI.1–3, is his conclusion that the intellect must be "a logical structure which somehow contains and makes possible the relationship between the terms of all necessary propositions"(199). Since Plotinus denies that discursive thought exists in the intelligible world, it cannot be a logical system which corresponds to discursive predicates. Since writing this dissertation, Strange seems to have changed his views (see Strange 1987).

56. See also the discussion of the coincidence of formal and final causes at *Physics* II.7, 198a.
57. *Ouch hoti to eidos hekastōi aition tou einai—touto men gar alēthes—all' hoti, ei kai auto to eidos hekaston pros auto aavaptyttas, heurēseis en autōi to dia ti.*
58. This is not to deny that there could be a sense in which the Forms are systematically related. But my point is simply that Plotinus is not concerned to specify what such a system might be, or even that this system exists.
59. VI.7.6, 22: *metalabouusēs de thērion sōma thaumazetai de, pōs logos ousa anthrōpou.*
60. VI.2.5, 22: *ar' oun to einai allo de to loipon ho symplēroi tēn tēs psychēs ousian kai to men on diaphora de poiei tēn psychēn.*
61. Lloyd 1955–1956.
62. VI.7.12. 1: *epei gar phamen pros hoion paradeigma ekeinou tode to pan einai, dei kakei proteron to pan zōion einai kai, ei panteles to einai autōi, panta einai. Kai ouranon dē ekei zōion einai, kai ouk erēmon toinun astrōn tōn entautha touto legomenōn ouranon, kai to ouranōi einai touto. Esti d' ekei dēlonoti kai gē ouk erēmos, alla polu mallon ezōōmena, kai estin en autēi zōia xympanta, hosa peza kai chersaia legetai entautha, kai phyta dēlonoti en tōi zēn hidrymena. Kai thalassa de estin ekei, kai pan zōion en hroēi kai zōēi menousēi, kai ta en hydati zōia panta, aeros te physis tou ekei pantos moira, kai aeria en autōi analogon autōi tōi aeri...hōs gar hekaston tōn megalōn merōn estin, ex anangkēs houtōs echei kai hē tōn zōiōn en autois physis.*
63. *Ennead* II.6.3. On the purely qualitative existence of the individual, see the extensive discussion of Wurm 1973.
64. *Esti d' autōn hē hoion hroē ek mias pēgēs, ouch hoion henos tinos pneumatos ē thermotētos mias, alla hoion ei tis ēn poiotēs mia pasas en autēi echousa kai sōi zousa tas poiotētas, glykutētas meta euōdias, kai homou oinōdēs poiotēs kai chylōn hapantōn dynameis kai chrōmatōn opseis kai hosa haphai ginōskousin.*

65. *Dio kai eitis auton apeikazei sphairai zōsēi poikilēi, eite pamprosōpon ti chrēma lampron zōsi prosōpois eite psychas tas katharas pasas eis to auto syndramousas phantazoito ouk endeeis.*
66. See Reinhardt 1924, 116–117.
67. VI.7.13, 1: *alla poikila panta hosōi hapla, touto de hosōi mē syntheta kai hosōi energeiai.*
68. *Ouden estin autou, ho ti mē allo, hina allo on kai touto syntelēi.*
69. Davidson 1980, 61.
70. **References For Works Cited:**

Alfonso, M. 1990: "Plotinus on the Possibility of Non-Propositional Thought," *Ancient Philosophy* **8**, 273–284.

Barnes, J. 1983: "Immaterial Causes," *Oxford Studies in Ancient Philosophy* 1.

Beutler, R. and Theiler, W. 1960–1971: *Plotins Schriften* (Hamburg); Griechischer Text, deutsche Übersetzung, Anmerkungen, Bände II, III, IV, V a-b, VI.

Blumenthal, H. 1987: "Neoplatonic Elements in the De Anima Commentaries," *Aristotle Transformed*, ed. R. Sorabji (Ithaca: Cornell, University Press).

Code, A. 1985: "Aristotle: Essence and Accident," *Philosophical Grounds of Rationality*, eds. R. Grandy and R. Warner (Oxford).

Cooper, J. 1987: "Hypothetical Necessity and Natural Teleology," *Philosophical Issues in Aristotle's Biology*, ed. A. Gotthelf and J. Lennox (Cambridge).

Corrigan, K. 1981: "The Internal Dimensions of the Sensible Object in the Thought of Plotinus and Aristotle," *Dionysius* 5, 98–126.

Davidson, D. 1980: *Essays on Actions and Events* (Oxford).

Dillon, J. 1977: *The Middle Platonists* (Ithaca: Cornell University Press).

Gotthelf, A. 1987: "Aristotle's Conception of Final Causality," *Philosophical Issues in Aristotle's Biology*, eds. A. Gotthelf and J. Lennox (Cambridge).

Graeser, A. 1972: *Plotinus and the Stoics* (Leiden).

Gurtler, G. 1989: *Plotinus, the Experience of Unity* (New York).

Hadot, P. 1988: *Plotin, Traité 38 [VI 7]* (Paris).

________. 1987: "Structure et themes du Traite 38 [VI,7] de Plotin," *Aufstieg und Niedergang der Romsichen Welt Band* 36.II.

Hancock, C. L. 1985: *Energeia* (Dissertation: Loyola University).

Lee, J. S. 1978: *The Omnipresence of Being: A Study in Plotinian Metaphysics* (Dissertation: University of Connecticut).

Leroux, G. 1990: *Plotin Traite sur la liberte et la volunte de l'Un* (Paris).

Lloyd, A. C. 1955–1956: "Neoplatonic Logic and Aristotelian Logic," *Phronesis* 1, 58–72 & 146–160.

________. 1969–1970. "Non-discursive thought: An Enigma of Greek Philosophy," *Proceedings of the Aristotelian Society* 70, 261–274.

________. 1986: "Non-Propositional Thought in Plotinus," *Phronesis* 31, 258–265.

________. 1990: *The Anatomy of Neoplatonism* (Oxford).

Mackie, J. 1974: *Cement of the Universe* (Oxford).

Peuch, H. 1957: "Plotin et les Gnostiques," *Entretiens Hardt* V (Geneva).

Putnam, H. 1983: *Realism and Reason* (Cambridge).

Reinhardt, K. 1924: *Kosmos und Sympathie* (Munich).

Rist, J. 1967: *Plotinus: The Road to Reality* (Cambridge).

Roloff, D. 1970: *Plotin: Die Großschrift* III, 8–V, 8–V, 5–II, 9 (Berlin).

Schroeder, F. 1980: "Representation and Reflection in Plotinus," *Dionysius* 4, 37–59.

________. 1992: *Form and Transformation* (Montreal).

Schubert, V. 1968: "*Pronoia* und *Logos*: Die Rechtfertigung der Weltordnunb bei Plotin," *Epimeleia* 11 (Salzburg).

Sorabji, R. 1983: "Myths About Non-Propositional Thought," *Time, Creation, and the Continuum*, ed. Sorabji (Ithaca: Cornell University Press).

Strange, S. K. 1981: *Plotinus' Treatise On the Genera of Being: An Historical and Philosophical Study* (Dissertation: University of Texas).

________. 1987: "Plotinus, Porphyry, and the *Categories*," *Aufstieg und Niedergang der Romischen Welt* 36.2 (Band).

Wagner, M. R. 1982: "Plotinus' World," *Dionysius* 6, 13–42.

________. 1982: "Vertical Causation in Plotinus," *The Structure of Being*, ed. R. Baine Harris (New York& International Society for Neoplatonic Studies), 51–72.

Wallis, R. T. 1987: "Scepticism and Neoplatonism," *Aufstieg und Niedergang der Romsichen Welt* 36.I (Band).

Wurm, K. 1973: *Substanz und Qualität* (Berlin & New York).

PROVIDENCE: THE PLATONIC DEMIURGE AND HELLENISTIC CAUSALITY

Gary M. Gurtler

Plotinus' discussion of providence and theodicy combines elements from diverse parts of the Greek philosophical tradition. The notion of providence, for example, owes much to the Stoic doctrines of sympathy and seminal reasons, while its actual operation relies on Aristotle's notion of causality. It remains true nonetheless that the context for both of these contributions is the teaching of Plato, especially concerning the role of the Demiurge in the *Timaeus*. The centrality of Plato in this instance, as in many others, is not without its difficulties. Plato, in his usual deliberate way, describes the relation between the world of Forms and the sensible world, and the consequent perfection of that world of nature, in terms of a myth, with the Demiurge having a key but mysterious role. Plotinus' more systematic approach means that he must give an exegesis of this Platonic myth in such a way that it fits coherently into his own metaphysical structures without at the same time doing violence to the Platonic text. His exegesis is indeed a conscious one, aware of the literal meaning of the text and of the principles he is using to interpret it.

Under and within this Platonic superstructure, moreover, Plotinus inserts the contributions of the Stoics and Aristotle with hardly a nod of recognition. They have been assimilated as contributing detailed analyses of particular facets of a reality that remains thoroughly Platonic in its orientation. From Plotinus' point of view they do not need exegesis, though he will at times indicate how they must be changed to fit a Platonic world. They are rather tools ready at hand for his more crucial task of understanding what is often obscure in the text of Plato.[1]

My emphasis will be on four treatises where Plotinus provides either a discussion of demiurgic activity or a direct exegesis of the text of the *Timaeus*, two relatively early (V.1[10] & III.9[13]) and two from late in the middle period of his writing (V.8[31] & VI.7[38]). As indicated above, two different kinds of problems emerge. One is strictly exegetical: how to make sense of the vocabulary Plato uses to discuss the activities of the Demiurge. The second includes a systematic component: the nature itself of demiurgic activity in relation to the corresponding natures of Intellect, the Hypostasis Soul and the world soul. By looking at these two areas we can begin to see how Plotinus develops a carefully nuanced doctrine of providence and also a philosophical method for its articulation within the Platonic tradition. The particularly neuralgic character of the doctrine of providence presents us, therefore, with a glance at the way Plotinus actually went about philosophizing, the issues he considers crucial and the meaning of the texts he regards as foundational.

It is in the context of the doctrine of providence that Plotinus adumbrates how it is that the intelligible world serves as the archetype of the sensible and, in paradoxical fashion, how our knowledge of the sensible serves as the basis for our knowledge of the intelligible. In this regard, he shows great subtlety in moving from concepts or analogies that have their original meaning in relation to sensible experience to the nature and functioning of these ideas when transferred to the realm of the intelligible. Providence thus can be understood not only as a cosmic ordering principle or theodicy but as a peculiar version of the argument for the existence of God in terms of design.

1. The Demiurge and Its Planning

In the two early treatises (V.1[10] & III.9[13]), Plotinus sets out to qualify the two key areas that will allow for the possibility of providence, the nature of the Demiurge itself and the language describing its planning activity. His procedure is similar in both cases, moving from an univocal to an analogical understanding of the areas involved. The Demiurge, for example, is identified in the strictest sense with the Intellectual Principle itself, but to operate in the generation of the sensible world its activities must be spread out to include the Hypostasis Soul and the world soul.[2] In a similar way, Soul's reasoning or planning [*dianoia* or *logismos*] must be carefully distinguished from the discursive mode of human thought from which it gets its name and with which it is analogous. The two moves delineate the intermediate nature and function of the soul, which serves as the ontological link between the intelligible and sensible worlds and thus as the locus where providence operates in the Plotinian system. In the later treatise considered in this part, V.8[31], Plotinus specifies the planning of the Demiurge by means of a contrast to human artistry, thus completing the groundwork for the major discussion in VI.7[38].

1.1 *The Soul as Demiurge*

The first passages, from the treatise 'On the Three Primary Hypostases' (V.1[10]), are taken from the middle of the treatise, omitting the preliminary and final sections about the ascent of the individual soul, which begins with its initial identification with the world soul. In this middle section, Plotinus shifts the analysis to the radically different point of view of the relation of the hypostasis Soul to Intellect and the One, on the one hand, and to the sensible cosmos, on the other. The shift is subtle and not all commentators recognize it, but two mutually supportive factors provide strong evidence for it.[3] First, Plotinus begins to discuss the emanation of Soul from Intellect and, second, there is an implicit recapitulation of the relation of this Soul, as the Hypostasis and source, to the world soul and individual souls as its participants. Two passages in particular specify characteristics of the Soul that make it different from Intellect and thus crucial in determining its demiurgic role. They occur at the beginning and end of this middle section, at VI.1.3 & 7.

> But one must understand that the activity on the level of Intellect does not flow out of it, but [remains in itself while] the external activity comes into existence as something distinct. Since then its existence derives from Intellect soul is intellectual, but its intellect is in reasonings [*logismois*], and its perfection comes from Intellect, like a father who brings to maturity a son whom he begat imperfect in comparison with himself. Soul's establishment in reality, then, comes from Intellect and its reason [*logos*] becomes actual in its seeing of Intellect. (V.1.3, 12-15: adapted from Armstrong translation)

There is a good bit of ambiguity in this passage. The closeness of Soul and Intellect is both affirmed and denied. The Soul is like the Intellect as having the same intellective nature, like a son to a father, but its intellection is described as reasonings and reason and its sonship is of a peculiar kind not maturing to eventual equality of being. The ambiguity is deliberate, with Plotinus indicating the nature of the Soul as on the border of the intelligible and sensible worlds with its own function as the generative mediator between the two. This function of the soul is clearly demiurgic, preserving the transcendence of the Intelligible world and allowing for the generation of the sensible, while at the same time defining the nature of soul in terms of its own being and knowing. For our purposes, however, the terms used for the soul's knowing present a further problem.

The soul analyzed here is definitely the Hypostasis Soul, but Plotinus uses the terms *logismos* and *logos* to describe its knowing in contrast to the *nous* (intellect) and *noera* (intellectual activity) that characterize Intellect itself. The meaning of these terms comes directly from the discursive character of human reasoning, but such discursiveness is impossible in the case of the Hypostasis Soul, which is completely within the Intelligible world. On the one hand, Plotinus is attempting to convey the demiurgic function of the Soul as the repository of the rational, creative, formative principles (*logoi*) that operate in the generation of the sensible world. On the other hand, as V.1.7 points out, the proper activity of the soul is nonetheless intellectual, with the inferior activities connoted by *logismos* and *logos* actually belonging to an inferior type of soul.

> And the offspring of Intellect is a rational form [*logos*] and an existing being [*hypostasis*], that which reasons [*to dianooumenon*]; it is this which moves round Intellect and is light and trace of Intellect and dependent on it, united to it on one side and so filled with it and enjoying it and sharing in it and thinking [*nooun*], but, on the other side, in touch with the things which came after it, or rather itself generating those things which must necessarily be worse than soul; about these we must speak later. (V.1.7, 42-48: adapted from Armstrong translation)

The problem thus centers on the application of *logos* and *dianoeisthai* to the soul. *Dianoeisthai* adds a crucial word that also carries the connotations of planning and deliberation, modeled on the discursive character of human making. The caveat to a simple and literal interpretation of either of these terms, with their full discursive character to the fore, is once more pressed home by the divided character of the soul. The Soul is lower as a certain *logos* and hypostasis different from Intellect, one which reasons (*to dianooumenon*), but is so close to Intellect on its higher side as to be filled with it and think (*nooun*), only on its lower side producing things worse than itself. Since Intellect itself is described in this treatise as a *logos* of the One (V.1.6, 45), it is clear that Plotinus is using this term in a technical sense which indicates ontological subordination rather than discursive thought or reason. In addition, the consistent way Plotinus posits the soul's own true activity as intellective, using *nous* and *nooun,* makes sense only if *logismos* and *dianoeisthai* can also mean something other than discursive thought in these passages. More evidence is needed, however, to confirm this initial reading and to fill out more completely what Plotinus means by it and how he actually understands the analogy between their use with reference to the human soul and to these higher levels of soul.

The second treatise in this early period, the first note of Various Considerations (III. 9[13].1), provides more abundant material for resolving these issues. First of all, it is a specific exegesis of *Timaeus* 39e7-9, particularly concerned with the relation of the Demiurge to Plotinus' own threefold division of reality into the One, Intellect and Soul. Secondly, although only *dianoeisthai* and *dianoia* are used, the same problem emerges of applying this term in its strict discursive sense to either Intellect or Soul as Demiurge.[4] This treatise thus provides a glimpse at Plotinus' exegetical problem, how to make sense of a Platonic passage that seems, at least linguistically, not to fit his own philosophical position.

> 'Intellect,' Plato says, 'sees the Ideas contained in the living creature which is.' Then the Demiurge, he says, 'planned [*dienoethe*] that this universe too should have the things, which Intellect sees in the living creature which is.' (III.9.1, 1-3: following Igal III-IV, 265)

Plato himself uses *dianoeisthai,* with Plotinus supplying the Demiurge as it subject. Parallel passages (V.1[10].10; IV.4[28].12; II.9[33].6; V.8[31].6-8; VI.7[38].1) contain the same juxtaposition of demiurgic function and planning, each attempting to unravel the seeming contradictions between the description of this function as planning and the ontological nature of Intellect and Soul, which excludes any kind of movement in Plotinus' theory of intellectual knowledge.

In the present passage, therefore, Plotinus first determines whether or not the living creature and Intellect are in fact the same thing, distinct only in thought, stating that there is nothing to prevent this identification from being Plato's intention (III.9.1, 10-15). Nor do the words of Plato rule out the possibility of two Intellects, one the intelligible object which is at rest and the other the Intellect that sees it (III.9.1, 15-22). This exegesis admits openly that the text of Plato supports a number of interpretations, only one of which corresponds to his own and one of which was current in the generation before him. He argues for his own position, the second hypostasis as Demiurge, but combines it with the thesis of two Intellects, the middle Platonic position which he normally rejects, as Igal notes (III-IV, 266 n9), putting his conclusion in these terms:

> This, then, is that which planned [*dianoethen*] to make in this universe the four kinds of living creatures which it sees in the intelligible. (III.9.1, 21-22: Armstrong translation)

This, however, raises an *aporia*, that the planning function of the Demiurge is in fact not appropriate for the Intellect, whether in its middle Platonic formulation or his own, so some other alternative must be sought. In a very revealing way, moreover, Plotinus indicates that the text of Plato is in itself of no help, and that the solution comes from principles supplied by the interpreter. Exegesis cannot force the text to say something that it does not, although a good exegete, using principles consistent with a Platonic system, should be able to give a consistent, if not conclusive, interpretation.

> It seems, nevertheless, that Plato is trying obscurely to make the planner [*to dianooumenon*] something other than those two. But to others it will seem that the three are one, the living creature which exists in itself, the intellect, and the planner [*to dianooumenon*]. Rather, as in many cases, proceeding from different premises, there are different ways of understanding that there are three. (III.9.1, 23-26: following Igal III-IV, 267: Cf. Armstrong III, 409)

The difficulty concerns the activities ascribed to the Intellect on the basis of the passage in the *Timaeus*. The Intellect would not only plan what is to be made in the physical universe, but actually carry out the making and dividing, which are clearly functions inappropriate for its eternal and undivided nature. Thus Plotinus is forced to conclude that there must be a third, other than Intellect and the living creature, which actually does something closer to planning than Intellect can and, more importantly, is able to do the dividing necessary in the generation of the sensible world.

> We have already spoken of two, but who is this third, who itself planned [*dienoethe*] to construct and make and divide into parts the things that Intellect sees lying in the living creature? (III.9.1, 27-29: following Igal III-IV, 267)

The nub of the problem is the dividing that is done. The Demiurge makes the four kinds of living things (III.9.1, 22)—heavenly beings, birds, fish, and land animals—and a parallel division into types of soul—gods and men, animals and plants. In a way this division comes from Intellect, but the dividing must be the work of Soul, and especially the world soul, a position that becomes a commonplace in the later treatises of the *Enneads*. Thus, as in V.1[10], Soul is identified with the Demiurge that planned:

> Because of this Plato says that the division belongs to the third and is in the third, because it planned [*dienoethe*], which—the planning [*dianoia*]—is not the work of Intellect, but of Soul, which has a divided activity in a divided nature. (III.9.1, 34-37: adapted from Armstrong translation)

Though it is appropriate that Soul be that which plans, the strict sense of *dianoia* as discursive thought must still be guarded against. This is true for both the hypostasis Soul and the world soul. We might say that Soul has a planning-in-itself that precedes the actual division into bodies, which is accomplished by the world soul.[5] The world soul in its planning also does not deliberate in carrying out the division, a point that will be made abundantly clear in VI.7[38].1. Thus the terms Plotinus uses here in III.9[13] and earlier in V.1[10], *logismos* or *dianoia* and their cognates, cannot have the discursive character in the Hypostasis Soul and the world soul that they do in the human soul. Why then are they used? Plotinus wants to distinguish two aspects of soul's being and knowing, in conformity with his theory of two acts: the full intellectual act by which it is identified with the Intellect and that act by which its own identity as soul is revealed in generating the sensible cosmos. This second act gets its name from what it produces, but must still have a nature more compatible with the Intelligible. Another aspect of Plotinus' method is implicit in this instance, that our terminology for describing reality, whether sensible or intelligible, derives from sensible experience, and will need appropriate redefinition when we begin to apply it to the higher realms of Soul and Intellect. The next treatise, V.8[31], from the middle period, provides a more explicit contrast to clarify the difference between sensible and intelligible and to indicate the kind of corrective needed to make the move from knowledge of the sensible world to an understanding of the higher realms of Soul and Intellect.

1.2 *Planning in the Demiurge and the Human Artist*

In V.8[31], the second installment of the long treatise against the Gnostics, Plotinus discusses the nature of beauty and distinguishes two kinds of making, that of nature and that of art. This provides a context in which the deliberative and discursive character of the human artist can be contrasted with the non-discursive and non-deliberative character of nature in its generation of the sensible world. Plotinus is able in this way to confirm the interpretation of the earlier passages in V.1[10] and III.9[13].1 as not implying the same kind of discursive character that is always present in their use with human knowing. At the same time he is able to describe more fully how he understands the activity of the Hypostasis Soul and the world soul as actually taking place. This second area opens up an ancillary topic, the element of design in the world and how it is traceable to a transcendent source. In this instance, moreover, the source under consideration is not Plotinus' ultimate principle or God, but an intermediate being a bit further down the ontological ladder. It is thus all the more useful for shedding light on this controverted area, since Plotinus' peculiar vantage point gives him a certain neutrality with regard to issues that emerge later in the debate about the argument from design.

In the case of both art and nature, 'reason' and 'form' (*logos* and *eidos*) are employed to describe the process of making, although they are present differently in the two different makers. *Logos*, as in the early treatises, denotes the active principle behind the making, while *eidos* picks up the content or model according to which the object is being made. Thus far art and nature are quite similar, and the one can shed light on the other. The difference between art and nature concerns, rather, how *logos* and *eidos* are present to or in each of the makers. Plotinus' contrast is between a presence that is internal in the case of nature and external in the case of the human artist.

> But certainly nature which produces such beautiful works is far before them in beauty, but we, because we are not accustomed to see any of the things within and do not know them, pursue the external and do not know that it is that within which moves us: as if someone looking at his image and not knowing where it came from should pursue it. (V.8.2, 31-35: Armstrong translation)

Plotinus, taking his cue from Plato's *Symposium* and *Phaedrus*, enunciates in this passage the clear orientation of human experience toward the external, the sensible world, and the role of beauty in awakening the ascent of the soul toward the internal, the Intelligible world. This has a moral dimension, alluded to in Plotinus' own allusion to the story of Narcissus, where his pursuit of his reflection leads to his self-destruction. In a similar way, the general human determination by the external, sensible world is understood by Plotinus as the circumstance allowing for moral evil and, like Plato, he finds beauty as a first corrective to this moral descent. Implicit as well is the need for an intellectual corrective, so that nature and art are understood from the point of view of the Intelligible world, reversing this natural orientation outward and the constant misunderstanding of the intelligible in terms either of the sensible or of the discursive character of human thought.

Again here, while Plato's corrective appears as the move from dialectic to myth, Plotinus feels obliged to give a more systematic articulation. He is unusually clear throughout this treatise, for example, in giving the limitations of experience and how they can be corrected, but is equally clear in dealing with the difficulties presented by Plato's often laconic or confusing *modus dicendi*. The following passages indicate some basic principles and areas of Plotinus' program of correction.

> But we have not arrived at understanding this, because we consider that the branches of knowledge are made up of theorems and a collection of propositions; but this is not true even of the sciences here below. But if someone wants to dispute about these, let them go for the present; but about the knowledge there—which Plato observed and said 'that which is not a knowledge different from that in which it is,' but how this is so, he left us to investigate and discover, if we claim to be worthy of our title [of Platonists]. (V.8.4, 48-55: Armstrong translation)

For Plotinus, the non-propositional character of authentic knowledge is the key corrective for understanding the nature of knowledge at any level above human knowing, whether nature, Soul or Intellect itself. Thus when reason or planning are used of these higher agencies, they cannot be understood in a discursive sense, but rather as indicating their relative subordination to one another at this higher level. These terms will thus be applied to nature and soul not as claiming that they operate discursively in generating the multiplicity of the sensible world, but to differentiate them from the more unified character of Intellect as abiding more completely in itself. As in earlier works, these differences are articulated in reference to the Platonic Demiurge, whose functions Plotinus must carefully parcel out.

> For this reason Plato, wishing to indicate this by reference to something which is clearer relative to ourselves, represents the Craftsman approving his completed work, wishing to show by this how delightful is the beauty of the model, which is the Idea....
>
> Plato deliberately makes it clear that he refers the 'was delighted' to the model by the words which follow: for he says, 'he was delighted, and wanted to make it still more like its model,' showing what the beauty of the model is like by saying that what originates from it is itself, too, beautiful

> because it is an image of the intelligible beauty. (V.8.8, 7-11, 15-20: Armstrong translation)

Besides indicating Intellect as the ultimate source of the beauty of the sensible world, Plotinus also makes reference to his method. The sensible world is the beginning of our experience, so our concepts and ideas begin from here as the realm that is clearer to us. That is, we begin with things known through the senses and our knowledge is expressed in propositions, which indicates, in the Greek tradition, the reasoning process of combining and dividing concepts. As we advance in the ascent to the intelligible, we must therefore engage in an ongoing critique of our experience and language so that what seems initially clearer might not interfere with our appreciation of that which is in itself clearer, the intelligible realm as such, and so that our articulation of its nature might qualify the discursive character of our own expression.

At this point, we have reached the end of this preliminary investigation. Passages from three treatises—V.1[10]; III.9[13].1; and V.8[31]—have been used to identify the issues and relevant terms for a discussion of the role of the Demiurge in the generation of the sensible world. The Demiurge itself is identified with Intellect, the Hypostasis Soul and the world soul to accommodate basic principles of Plotinus' ontology. The language applied to the activity of the Demiurge, 'planning' or 'reasoning,' needs to be distinguished in the other direction from its origins as characteristic of human knowing. Finally, the mode of operation of the Demiurge or nature, as it were combining the previous two points, is fundamentally distinct from human making. What is not yet clearly on the table is the relationship of all these points to the problem of providence. The final treatise to be considered, VI.7[38], brings these issues together precisely in terms of a discussion of providence.

2. The Nature of Providence

The beginning of the treatise, 'How the Multitude of the Forms Came into Being, and on the Good' (VI.7[38]), presents a tightly woven argument that focuses all the elements scattered in the three earlier treatises on the problem of providence. It begins with a clear statement of the *aporia* to be resolved: the presence of natural evil in the sensible cosmos and the remarkable way sense creatures are adapted to this hostile environment. This is the evidence for providence; but the problem is showing whether such providence is possible and, if it is, how it works. He begins by making the contrast to human making more precise. The artist must necessarily use a reasoning process that includes foresight. This in a sense is nothing more than the combination of induction and deduction involved in the production of the object. That is, Plotinus recognizes that discursive reasoning tends to work from abstract or mental plans which seek to address the variability that results from combining these plans with an appropriate matter and from the vulnerability of these products to other natural forces, which can be just as hostile to the work of art as they are to the various beings that form part of the world of nature. The Demiurge, on all its levels—Intellect, the Hypostasis Soul or the world soul—differs on both these fronts. It does not need to plan, or form a hypothesis, nor does it need to foresee, or make deductions, since its product is not a combination of plans and matter as separate and discrete elements, precisely because it does not work with an already existing contingent thing or things where alternatives and multiplicities are involved. The sensible world is instead produced as a whole, illustrating Stoic *sympathy*, albeit in a radically modified form, and the demiurgic activity occurs within nature, paralleling Stoic seminal reasons.[6] To establish the Demiurge as an effective agent in the production of the sensible world, however, he relies upon a transformation of the Aristotelian notion of causality, allowing it to operate between levels of reality rather than within the physical world alone. All this, nonetheless, seems to leave little room for a notion of providence as planning and foresight in the generative agent. Plotinus, therefore, must either deny the idea of providence or understand it in some other way.

Finally, this exegesis of the Platonic Demiurge illustrates once more his philosophical method. In part this method implies a hermeneutic for understanding philosophical texts, especially those of Plato. Without the historic or developmental categories of modern exegesis, Plotinus is forced to find ways around the literal meaning of a text that still come from the text itself. We have already seen an example of this in the exegesis of III.9.1, where he delicately balances the literal meaning of the text and the principles he needs to give it a reasonable interpretation in terms of his own system. He uses an analogical sense of language, but is nonetheless cautious in solving his difficulties by this means, even though analogy is a fundamental principle with deep roots both in his ontology and theory of knowledge. Analogy provides one of the major correctives needed in going from familiar discourse about the sensible world to authentic discourse about the intelligible, but it must be supplemented by and subordinate to a synthetic grasp that begins, as we have seen, from an overall understanding of the Platonic system, moving from there to some problematic area. In addition, there is room within this hermeneutic for the detailed analyses of the Stoic or Aristotelian traditions as ways of filling out the more schematic and sometimes enigmatic approach of Plato.

2.1 *Providence and Planning*

Plotinus begins VI.7[38] with a recognition that sense powers adapt their possessors to the world which they inhabit, which is both other and hostile (VI.7.1, 19-20). The *aporia* to be resolved is whether such adaptation is the result of rational planning (*logismos*), and if it is, of what kind. Providence (*pronoia*) is the indicated mode of such planning and thus the topic of investigation. The difficulty is to determine how providence can operate in the Intelligible world and, more specifically, if it does, what is its nature.

> This is the providence, that they might be saved being in evil, and this is the plan [*ho logismos*] of God (Cf. *Tm* 34a8) and rational planning [*logismos*] in general. (VI.7.1, 19-21)

The statement of the problem includes as well the major objection to providence or design: the presence and influence of evil. In this context, of course, Plotinus is referring to natural evil, the result of the generation of a level of reality that is divided into parts, with the necessary result that some of those parts will be in conflict with one another. Though providence with regard to ensouled creatures involves their being protected from evil through the use of their senses, the evil itself is a necessary part of the system. Providence is therefore analogous to the rational plan and foresight needed to deal with the contingencies of sensible existence, as in the case of human making. His first argument, however, begins with an attack on this parallel to human making by inquiring into the principles through which providence operates in governing the cosmos.

> But what are the principles of these rational plans [*logismon*]? For indeed, if they are from other plans [*logismon*], it is necessary to go back in all cases to something or some things before rational planning [*logismou*]. What then are the principles? Either sensation or intellect. But sensation is not yet, therefore intellect. But if the premises are intellect, the conclusion is knowledge; therefore there is nothing about the sensible. Where a principle

> is from the intelligible and reaches completion in the intelligible, how is it possible for this same disposition to reach completion in discursive thought [*dianoesin*] about the sensible? (VI.7.1, 21-27)

It is a commonplace among the ancients that reasoning is necessarily a process that uses principles that function as the starting points for the arguments that lead to truth or for the rational plans that lead to the making of an object. Such principles stop the regress of thought because they are eternal, unchanging and outside the system. Plato and Aristotle are both in agreement about this, although they express it in radically different ways. The difference is that Plato associated planning with the Demiurge as some kind of intelligent agent that ontologically precedes the generation of the sensible world, while Aristotle's elimination of the world of forms makes the causes somehow immanent in nature, with the different problem of relating this causality to a first- principle transcending nature. Plotinus is ironically quite content with Aristotle's mode of immanent causation, and exerts far more effort to explain Plato's description of the Demiurge as actually planning, given that such a mode of thinking seems incompatible both with intelligible knowing and with immanent natural causality.

Plotinus uses a complex dialectical argument to examine the relation between intellect and reason, investigating the original problem of the Intellect's provision for the needs of sensible creatures. He begins with an explanation of Plato's affirmation that providence is from rational planning, based on the analogy to human making, where the wise, working with things that already exist in the world of becoming, must plan how they should be arranged and foresee how they will be used.

> So providence from reasoning [*logismou*] is neither about a living being nor about this particular universe at all, since there is really no reasoning [*logismos*] there, but reasoning [*logismos*] is affirmed [by Plato] in reference to an indication from the universe in this way, as another wise maker works from reasoning [*logismou*] on things that are later, and foreseeing is also affirmed, because it is in this way that someone wise would pre-know it. (VI.7.1, 28-32)[7]

Two aspects of human making are highlighted in this analogy used to explain the vocabulary Plato ascribes to the Demiurge: the inductive type of reasoning needed to use the material available profitably, and the deductive type needed to predict possible problems with the product and how to correct them. It is an indication, on the one hand, of how well nature is constructed and adapted to innumerable contingencies and, on the other hand, of how much the analogy limps when one actually looks at the operation of the Demiurge. This second aspect occupies the next major section of the argument.

> For among those things that do not come about before reasoning [*pro logismou*], the reasoning faculty [*ho logismos*] is useful for want of a power which is before reasoning [*pro logismou*], and foreseeing [*proorasis*], because the one who foresees does not have the power according to which he does not need foreseeing. Thus foreseeing [*proorasis*] occurs that it might not be *this* but *that*, and, so to speak, is afraid that it not make something of a particular sort. But where it is only this, there is no foresight. Likewise the reasoning faculty [*ho logismos*] makes a *this* before a *that*. But when there is only one alternative, what will it reason [*logizetai*]? (VI.7.1, 33-39)

Foresight and reasoning are shown to derive their function from the need of a creature who works with a material that is already at hand and therefore has to anticipate how the object will interact with other things, also not of one's making, that may well interfere with its purpose. The contrasting situation of the Demiurge is central for Plotinus' understanding of the effortless working of providence in the ordered generation of the sensible world. He proceeds:

> How indeed does the alone and one and simple have that which is unfolded, '*this* that it might not be *that*,' and 'for it would be *this*, except it is *that*,' and '*this* appeared plainly useful and salutary having become *that*'? Did it then foresee and did it then pre-plan [*proelogisato*], and in particular—what has been said now from the beginning—did it give the sensations and their faculties through this means, even granting that the giving and its mode are especially hard to understand? (VI.7.1, 39-45)

I have adopted Hadot's reading[8] of the second sentence here as a question, which has the advantage of making Plotinus' position consistent and setting up the precise conditions of the *aporia*: that without any kind of planning or foreseeing the Demiurge can still produce providentially. His solution, given in the rest of the chapter, is to show how Intellect can maintain its unity and also become the source of sensible multiplicity. Intellect, as a unified and perfect act, already combines present and future, so that the future is already in it, and everything that will come to be is already always there. When it is unfolded in time, then, it is as if it has been thought out beforehand, but this means only that there is nothing deficient since the act of Intellect is perfect and complete, the internal cause (*en heauto kai tēn aitian*) of the unfolding (VI. 7.1, 45-57). Thus Plotinus posits preexistence, a preexistence that is perfect and complete and that acts from within, instead of the planning and foreseeing that characterize human making, as the nature and method of providence. With this structural change in understanding the nature of the unity of the cosmos, Plotinus is able to establish Stoic *sympathy* without Stoic materialism. We shall see later how he uses the notion of immanent causality in connection with the Stoic seminal reasons.

An analogy from human activity, moreover, might clarify this model of making from within, and it has the advantage of being used by Plotinus himself, though in a slightly different context, to understand the immateriality and consequent interpenetrability of the Intelligible world. It is the development of a science and its theorems (cf. above, V.8.4). For our purposes, it is perhaps easier to switch the analogy to the origin and development of a language. In any case, it makes no sense to say that a language or science is planned, much less that its development is foreseen. It is, as it were, contained whole and entire in the human capacity for communication. When a particular group begins to speak, this capacity for communication is unfolded as a system of meaning that cannot be radically deficient, otherwise communication could not take place at all, but is always moving unerringly toward further completion, with the rules of development operating unconsciously and immanently within it. This makes sense not only in terms of what Plotinus means by the notion of providence and the workings of the Demiurge, but also in relation to the argument for the existence of God from design. Thus the analogy of God to a clockmaker can be justifiably critiqued, but a more subtle argument about the development of order in the universe along the lines of Plotinus' position is both much more cogent and more than likely the model behind the classical Medieval formulations of the argument. This kind of argument is, moreover, implicit in the above passage, where an indication from this universe is used to understand the nature of the intelligible.[9]

This brief section has set out the first part of Plotinus' program, with the silent incorporation of Stoic *sympathy* transformed into Plato's sense of the integral unity of the cosmos and the internal operation of its causality. What is left is Aristotle's analysis of causality and Stoic seminal reasons transformed into the crucial ingredients to explain the relationship between the sensible and intelligible worlds. Plotinus turns first to the Aristotelian position in the next section of the text.

2.2 *Providence and Causality*

In VI.7[38].2, he begins to reflect on the nature of causality as it appears in the sense world, where cause and effect are usually different things, in contrast to the intelligible, where they are always identical. His effort is to show how the substance (*ousia*) and essential nature (*to ti en einai*) of a thing (VI.7.2, 14-15) necessarily include both that it is and the reason why it is, such that the cause of the thing is within it as an integral member of the Intelligible world. This pairing of terms has a reference back to V.8[31], where *eidos* and *logos* are similarly joined, and forward to VI.7.4 & 5, where soul and *logos* will be analyzed in a similar way. The terms are Aristotelian, but Plotinus changes the way they are related. For Aristotle, substance is a *pros hen* equivocal, with *to ti en einai* as one of its meanings. In Plotinus, on the contrary, the two terms are related as co-principles, somewhat like form and matter in Aristotle, with one term expressing the activity of the thing and the other the thing as receiving that activity in a particular way.

Plotinus is moving the terms out of the Aristotelian context of sensible substance to the ontological context of the Intelligible world, where their relationship and function are radically altered. He thereby attempts to describe the dual operation of Intellect in the generation of its own content and ultimately of the sensible world. *Ousia* (substance) and *to ti en einai* (essential nature) thus allude to the two poles of the Intelligible world, being and knowing, both of which must contribute to, and be aspects of, any intelligible being. The relationship between these two aspects of the Intelligible world is something like that of Aristotle's act and potency, but the absence of matter in the Intelligible world changes the nature of the relationship from the horizontal generation of something similar in kind to the vertical generation of something different in substance, as lower and less unified.

This generation also proceeds from the very nature of Intellect as an act, and thus does not involve planning of any sort. Its own content is thus shown not to be planned, but to form an integrally and mutually constitutive unity-in-diversity. Each member of the Intelligible world is generated as an activity, but an activity that resides in some substance, always keeping the essential duality of the Intelligible world. In generating the sensible world, the same dual causality is at work, not making atomistic parts that need to be assembled in some secondary step, but proceeding immanently to create a whole where the parts emerge from within it and at the same time act as co-agents in constituting its ongoing development.

He singles out one instance, the relation between the intelligible Man and the secondary man of becoming, to illustrate further this different kind of causality. At the beginning of VI. 7.3, he repeats the initial question, specifically asking if deliberation is a factor in the making of the sensible man.

> What then prevents deliberating [*probouleusasthai*] about him before hand? Rather, he is according to that intelligible Man, so that neither is it necessary to take away nor to add anything, but [the Demiurge is said] to deliberate and to have reasoned [*to bouleusasthai kai lelogisthai*] by hypothesis: for [Plato] hypothesized for things that become. In this view there is deliberation and reason [*hē bouleusis kai ho logismos*], but by demonstrating an 'eternal becoming,' he denies that the [Demiurge] reasons [*logizetai*]. For it is impossible to reason [*logizesthai*] about the eternal. (VI.7.3, 1-6)

No new point is added to the initial discussion, but the restriction to a particular case clarifies the implications. As a result, Plotinus can argue that Plato does not use 'deliberation' and 'reasoning' in their strict discursive sense, but rather that the providence and rationality apparent from the sensible world show how closely it is an image of the Intelligible. Plato's hypothesis is, therefore, more like a metaphor, which he corrected by positing an eternal becoming. In a sense, qualifying the words of Plato is not merely an exercise in school loyalty, but an indication of the nature of philosophical discourse. Our understanding of the nature of things begins with experience of the sense world, but this implies a necessary critique that understands the sensible world and our way of knowing it as images that point to a reality, the nature of which is gradually articulated precisely as it is distinguished from the sensible. Plotinus thus exploits the ambiguity of the text, on the literal level, to indicate more than just clever exegetical *legerdemain*, since it articulates a critical principle in his own philosophical method, especially prominent throughout this treatise.

In the next chapter, Plotinus spells out how the intelligible Man is present in the man of becoming. He does so by means of an examination of *logos*, which has been linked in all the treatises considered here with the causality or activity of a higher reality on a lower level. This has been in conflict, however, with a sense of *logos* that is associated with human reason or the sensible cosmos alone. We have in the present context, for example, the Stoic notion of seminal reasons, which Hadot oddly takes as the Platonic productive logos in contrast to the Aristotelian definitional logos (*Traite 38*, 217). It is not clear what he means by this Platonic productive logos; Stoic spermatic logoi seem the more obvious reference. It should also be noted that Aristotle's definitional logos is not meant in an exclusive sense, but as one of its technical usages. It remains to be seen, moreover, how Plotinus purports to bring these different meanings of *logos*, Stoic and Aristotelian, into harmony with one another.

Let us begin with his own sense of *logos* as an active principle. We have seen in V.1[10] that the Hypostasis Soul looked at as a whole can be described as a *logos* of Intellect, which emphasizes that it is the act of Intellect expressed in an external and secondary way. In V.8[31], art and nature use a *logos* as the active principle of their making, with form supplying the content. In the present context, the problem is the relationship between this *logos* as an active principle and the soul as that which receives it. On the one hand, soul and body form the composite living being; but, on the other hand, Plotinus argues, *logos* and soul must also be different, forming a type of composite on the level of the intelligible. Soul thus relates to the sensible composite as the logos of Aristotle's definition (VI.7[38].4, 17-28), and to the active *logos* coming from the intelligible Man itself as the *ousia* defined by this *logos* as *to ti en einai* cited earlier at VI.7.2, 14-15. Soul, by being what it is, generates something further in the sensible world, and the *logos* of the intelligible Man, as the active principle united with this soul, continues its active role by giving to the sensible man all the powers it needs to function. Like the power to communicate, this generation by soul and its *logos* does not need to be planned, because it is either there as a whole or it is not there at all.

He concludes this argument at the beginning of VI.7.5, where he links the intelligible Man and the sensible man by means of the *logos* that specifies the activities of a specific kind of soul and the composite being it establishes in the sensible world.

> It is necessary, therefore, that man is a forming principle [*logos*] other than the soul. What prevents man from being something composite, a soul in such a forming principle [*logos*], where the forming principle [*logos*] is like a type of activity, but an activity that cannot be without that which acts? This is the case for the forming principles [*logoi*] in seeds, for they are neither without souls nor souls simply speaking. These forming principles [*logoi*] that make are likewise not soulless, and it is not at all amazing that these forming principles [*logous*] are such substances. (VI.7.5, 1-8: Armstrong translation)

In terms of previous treatises, soul is the *eidos* or *ousia* of the sensible man, while the *logos*, as the active principle coming from the intelligible

Man, is the *to ti en einai* that defines exactly what this kind of soul is as a substance or the spermatic *logos* that directs its unfolding in the sensible world.

At this point, Plotinus' anthropology can be seen in all its complexity.[10] He has the intelligible Man, the identity of *logos* and soul, which is the generative cause of the sensible man, the image of man made by soul and body (VI.7.5, 14-15). The various meanings of *logos* now fall into place. *Logos* as the active principle is used to explain the duality of the Intelligible world Plotinus inherits from Plato, but it also incorporates the immanent cause denoted by the Stoics in their spermatic logos. Next the sensible composite of soul and body provides for the definitional logos of Aristotle's categorical theory. It is clear, moreover, that the rational forming principle (*logos*) is the key relating the intelligible and sensible, operating with the interior causality established earlier. Thus, whether in the case of the sensible universe as a whole or in that of one being within it, the result is the same. As an image of the intelligible it does not need to be made by any kind of planning or foresight, but proceeds as a whole from a whole, though it is unfolded in time.

A final passage continues this reflection on human nature. Plotinus repeats that reasoning as such is not in the Intelligible, but then asks why this faculty is only present in human nature in the sensible world.

> For neither is the reasoning faculty [*to logikon*] There: for perhaps the reasoning faculty [*to logikon*] is here, but There that which is before reasoning [*logizesthai*]. Why does this man reason [*logizetai*] here, but no other living thing? Rather, since there is a difference There in thinking [*tou noein*] between Man and other living things, so there is also a difference in reasoning [*to logizesthai*]; for many activities of reason [*dianoias*] are in some way possible also for other living things. (VI.7.9, 9-14)

The major addition of this brief passage is to underline the analogous use of language that is behind Plotinus' whole discussion. 'Reason' is analogous in two different directions. Usually it shows the continuity between reason and intellect, but it can also indicate the continuity of reason in lower forms of knowing and perception.

Plotinus has shown in this section the subtlety of his position. What was implicit in the earlier treatises is faced with considerable frankness. It is interesting that the problem of evil is not the main sticking point in justifying providence; evil rather confirms the presence of providence in the sensible cosmos. The main problem concerns the possibility of providence given the nature of the Intelligible world. Our sense of how providence works might begin with an anthropomorphic model, but Plotinus is relentless in showing that the reasoning and foreseeing of the human artist are at best ways around the defective character of human knowing and making. The Demiurge, as soul or Intellect, is not handicapped in this way and thus operates without such planning and foreseeing. It acts in a way that is both different and difficult to articulate. As the artist works premeditatively and externally, the Demiurge works without any deliberation at all and internally. When Intellect generates something, it has a dual aspect: It is a substance that has as well its own active principle within it. This establishes a chain of causality that moves from higher to lower levels of reality, reaching finally to the sensible world itself. This chain of causality is similar to Aristotle's, as composed of active and passive elements, but is radically different, as proceeding vertically rather than horizontally.

3. Conclusion

The discussion of providence afforded by these four treatises is far from complete. They provide instead an introduction to a topic that occupies Plotinus' attention at different times throughout the whole period of his writing. As a good introduction, they indicate the basic themes and problems that arise in relation to providence but none of them provide an exhaustive treatment of the problem, with objections and counter positions given and discussed. For that one needs to turn to the later treatise on providence, III.2 & 3[47 & 48]. Nonetheless they illustrate in a remarkable way how Plotinus goes about dealing with an issue, collecting his thoughts about one detail or another and building a case that is clearer and stronger as he goes along.

Another advantage of these four treatises is that the problem of providence is discussed in terms of the Platonic Demiurge, which means that Plotinus is forced to reflect a little more fully on the actual mechanism that allows providence to work. The problems he faces in this pursuit occur in multiple areas: the identity of the Demiurge itself, Plato's description of the demiurgic activity in mythical terms that are highly anthropomorphic, the difference between human reasoning and the thought of Intellect, and the difficulty in finding a proper way to articulate the causal activity of the Demiurge, whether as the world soul, the Hypostasis Soul, or Intellect itself. These problems come to focus in two major difficulties: the exact nature and functioning of the Demiurge as providential and the proper exegesis of the Platonic *Timaeus*. While the description of the Demiurge is of central concern, the exegetical problem, tackled in one treatise after another, reveals some interesting insights into the way Plotinus actually philosophizes. Taking Plato as his model doesn't imply abdicating his own rational powers, nor does it imply an uncritical rejection of other philosophers, like Aristotle and the Stoics. In the texts examined, in fact, one of the main problems is elucidating what Plato means, given his use of myth and consequent lack of rational precision. While Plotinus' interpretation of the Platonic text is not exactly critical according to today's standards, it is not particularly fanciful. He respects the literal meaning of the text and articulates his own principles of interpretation. Where he can, he bases his interpretation on some facet of the text itself; where he cannot, he admits that he is following certain principles to explain what Plato has put incompletely or enigmatically. In the process, he is outlining a theory of analogy that is not without connection to his overall purpose in enunciating the principles of providence, that is, indicating the nature of the sensible as an image of the intelligible.

In summarizing his discussion of providence, however, he shows first that the providential role of the Demiurge must itself be spread out among various levels of his own hierarchy of Being. The role of Soul as an active agent must be distinguished from that of Intellect, to preserve the perfection of the Intellect itself. World soul must in turn be distinguished from the Hypostasis Soul for similar reasons. With the agency thus parceled out, the attention shifts to the process, the planning, reasoning or foreseeing, that is used to introduce providence into the sensible world. The planning and foreseeing of the Demiurge are sharply differentiated from the processes of human thought, which give them their names and to which they are analogous. Plotinus moves in two directions at once, distinguishing the role of the soul from Intellect and then making a similar distinction between soul's activity and human thinking. Thus he applies planning and foreseeing to the activity of the Soul in distinguishing it from Intellect, but provides a critique of this usage to avoid an anthropomorphic understanding of providence. Such a critique is particularly crucial in terms of the natural tendency to understand the intelligible world and its operations in terms of concepts derived from the sensible world and human activities operative within it. Plotinus thus has two tasks, to indicate the foundation of the analogy in the nature of the sensible world and human thinking as images of the intelligible and to distinguish the actual nature and activity of the intelligible from these sensory images and models.

Plotinus provides a dialectical movement of affirmation and negation to accomplish his purpose and to safeguard both the relative validity of sense experience and the possibility of authentic knowledge of the intelligible itself. Finally, he must provide a positive understanding of the relation of the Intelligible and sensible worlds through a causality that can adequately link them. He tacitly admits that Plato's works do not provide such a causal theory. He must therefore borrow from Aristotle, especially his understanding of act and potency, but needs to do a bit of reworking to allow causality to operate between different ontological levels. What results is a very subtle account of providence based squarely on the Platonic position that the sensible cosmos is a beautifully complex image of the Intelligible world.

Boston College

NOTES

1. More information on the Stoic notion of providence and its relation to that of Plotinus can be found elsewhere in this volume in the chapter by Laura Westra, "Freedom and Providence." Her discussion focuses on the impact of providence on human freedom and moral responsibility, both among the Stoics and in Plotinus himself. My discussion emphasizes the Platonic sources for providence especially in earlier treatises and thus is complementary to Westra's discussion of III.2 & 3[47 & 48]. It also provides support for her contention that Plotinus "should not be resolved into his sources," by showing how those sources fit into a Platonic context. In addition, the inclusion of Aristotle's theory of causality forms part of the general metaphysical aim showing how providence functions within the confines of a Platonic theory of reality. Further analysis of Plotinus' relation to Aristotle in terms of his metaphysical interests can be found in my article, "Plotinus and the Platonic *Parmenides*," *International Philosophical Quarterly* 32 (1992), 441-445. Thus, while Westra concentrates more clearly on the anthropological and ethical repercussions of the doctrine of providence in Plotinus' major discussion of the topic, this paper focuses on ontological and noetic issues scattered in several earlier treatises.
2. Armstrong, *Plotinus: Enneads*, Loeb Classical Library: 7 volumes (Cambridge, MA: Harvard University Press, 1966–1988), states that Plotinus always identifies the craftsman with Intellect, and never with Soul (volume 5, 40 n1), but the passages examined here state rather unambiguously that the Demiurge is concerned with the universe more directly than is possible for the Intellect. It is much simpler to follow Igal's thesis, *Plotino: "Enéadas" I–II, III–IV* (Madrid: Editorial Gredos, 1982, 1985), I–II, 73, 79–83, 405 & III–IV, 267–268, that the demiurgic function is analogous, with Intellect the true maker and Demiurge (V.9[49].3, 25–26), the Soul, as receiving the *logoi*

from it, the planning principle, and lastly the world soul making the actual divisions in the sense world (III.9[13].1 and II.3[52].17 & 18). My book, *Plotinus: The Experience of Unity* (New York: Peter Lang, 1988) confirms Igal's thesis by showing how it fits into the major structural paradigm that undergirds both Plotinus' ontology and psychology. Atkinson, *Plotinus: Ennead V, 1, On the Three Principal Hypostases* (Oxford University Press, 1983), 22–23, also admits the different references of the Demiurge in Plotinus' usage.

3. Armstrong, neither in his synopsis nor in the translation, indicates the change from world soul to the Hypostasis Soul. This is not surprising, since his notes on IV.9 do not indicate that Plotinus distinguishes the Hypostasis from the world soul, although his translation is accurate enough to express it (e.g. at IV.9.1, 13). H. J. Blumenthal, "Soul, World-Soul and Individual Soul," *Le Néoplatonisme* (Paris: Éditions de Centre de la Recherche Scientifique, 1971), 55–63, and Igal III–IV, 545, both maintain that Plotinus does distinguish the Hypostasis from the world soul, but are somewhat hesitant about how early this takes place in Plotinus' writings. In the context of V.1, the unity of chapter 3–7 about the Hypostases and the parallel between chapters 2 and 10 on the relation of the world soul and the individual soul, for both of which the Hypostases are described as external, indicate that the distinction is operative, despite Plotinus' laconic transitions. Atkinson, *Ennead V, 1,* 62 & 89, presents Plotinus' argument as if the same soul is being discussed all the way through, with the resultant complaint of inconsistency.
4. Igal III–IV, 268 n18, makes this question of the meaning of *dianoeisthai* and *dianoia* explicit, which Armstrong implicitly supports by translating them as 'plan'. Armstrong's problem, as noted, is the identification of the Demiurge with soul, which he argues Plotinus never does (vol. 5, 40 n1). Igal, both in III–IV, 267 n13, and in I–II, 73, argues that Plotinus posits three Demiurges: Intellect, Hypostasis Soul, and world soul. Igal's position reflects the fact that Plotinus divides the various functions of the Demiurge in the *Timaeus* so that each function is matched with an appropriate level of Being, which Armstrong reluctantly admits in his note on the present treatise (volume 3, 410 n1).
5. The same difficulty can be found in terms of time and eternity, where the Soul is described as eternally in the Intellect, and yet as temporal. P. Manchester, "Time and the Soul," *Dionysus* 2 (1978), 128–136, explains this paradox by showing that there is a Time-in-itself in the hypostasis Soul and a successive time in the sensible order. In a similar way, the content of the Hypostasis Soul is both less unified than that of Intellect, since its movement is directed outward, but more unified than its successive unfolding in Nature. Though unified in itself as within the Intelligible world, this focus outward to the division of sensible bodies makes the term 'planning' a more fitting description of its activity.

6. It is worthwhile to compare this internal agency with the comments of Laura Westra about the Stoic background in the second part of her chapter in this volume. she points out the immanent way in which the world soul operates and the impersonal character of the logos which establishes the unity of the natural order. Providence for the Stoics, she observes, has three goals: to structure, to complete, and to beautify the world. These three aspects of providence are part of Plotinus' own program, but they are not so much goals as means to achieving the goal of conforming the sensible world to its intellectual archetype. Westra pushes this a bit further back to the Good or One as the aim of all things. This is indeed true, although the particular interest of my argument is restricted to the relation of providence to the Intelligible and sensible worlds alone.
7. There is some textual difficulty at VI.7.1, 30–32, with Harder deleting *allos sophos* and Theiler deleting *en tois hysteron* (Cf. critical apparatus in H-S²). Theiler's deletion has been followed, since it makes no essential difference to the meaning. Harder's deletion, however, is another matter. I take both clauses as referring to human making in contrast to the providence of the world soul or Intellect, and thus "the other wise one" is the human craftsman, who works from a plan and on materials that already exist. This is consistent with Plotinus' usual point of contrasting the discursive nature of human reason and the non-discursive nature of higher souls and, especially, of Intellect (Cf. IV.4.12). The alternative is that the world soul, as the making Demiurge, is contrasted with Intellect. This does not, however, seem to account for all the elements as easily as the human craftsman. 'On Providence I&II' (III 2 & 3[47 & 48]), moreover, provides a confirmation of this reading.

    The ordering of the universe, then, corresponds with Intellect in such a way that it exists without rational planning [*logismou*], but exists so that if anyone could plan rationally [*logismō*], as well as possible, he would wonder at it because planning [*logismos*] could not have found out another way to make it; something of this is observed even in individual natures, which come into being continually more conformed to Intellect than they could be by an ordering which depended on rational planning [*logismou*]. (III.2[47].14, 1–6: Armstrong translation)

8. Pierre Hadot, *Traite 38 (VI 7)* (Paris: Les Éditions du Cerf, 1988), 195–197. While one or another point might be disputed, this translation and commentary is invaluable for understanding this complex treatise. It is particularly helpful in the part immediately after the texts that are of concern here, where he discusses Plotinus' anthropology in a rather full way.
9. The claim that Plotinus has anything like the argument for the existence of God from design is on the face of it quite improbable. The transcendence of the One and its necessary lack of interest in the emanations from it are both

emphatically and consistently maintained throughout the Plotinian corpus. The argument presented here in fact gives indirect confirmation of this central Plotinian thesis. It is thus not in relation to the One that a version of the argument from design can be found, but rather in the role of the Demiurge in generating the sensible cosmos from its intellectual archetype.

This different context gives the argument a character much different from later versions working from Christian presuppositions. Plotinus argues that the sensible cosmos, including the evil that is present within it, must have its immediate origin in the Intelligible world, focusing his attention on the nature and mode of design itself. In agreement with later authors, Plotinus thus sees the issues of providence and theodicy as at the heart of the argument from design, but they operate in a strange sort of way. The agent, here the Platonic Demiurge, must be kept as far as possible from any whiff of pre-planning or deliberation. This is a corollary of his general principle, already mentioned above, that a higher reality is transcendent in such a way as to be uninvolved with what follows from it as well as his specific principle that the mode of knowing in the Intelligible world is non-discursive. This joint metaphysical and epistemological restriction gives his argument a sophistication that is not without relevance for understanding the cogency of such arguments in contemporary debate. Plotinus' scheme makes quite clear why design or order or reason are discernible in the workings of the physical universe, and thus how that design is discoverable by the human mind and expressed in discursive sciences. This in no way means, however, that the agent, whether looked at as Intellect, Soul or world soul, has a similarly discursive plan or model. In other words, Plotinus maintains a clear distinction between the operations of nature and those of human making. Thus design has nothing in common with William Paley's version of the argument in his *Natural Theology*, which makes a jump from inferring a watchmaker upon finding a watch to inferring a divine agent upon finding a stone. Our explanation of the stone can be logical and reasonable, but that does not entail that nature itself has a blueprint that somehow corresponds to our explanation. Plotinus is explicit, moreover, that nature cannot in fact operate in the way a human agent does in making an object. The sensible world, therefore, is ordered and unified not because nature is a conscious cause working with a plan, but because the alternative, as neither ordered nor unified, could not even exist.

The medieval argument from design, as found for example in Aquinas's fifth way, where things that lack knowledge still act for an end, depending on an intelligent being which directs them to their ends, hasmore in common with Plotinus' argument than Paley's. It is intelligence as such, and not the capacity to form a plan, that directs beings toward their ends, which are seen as part of an ordered and unified whole. The difference in this case is that Plotinus' ordered hierarchy of causes pushes the problem of design away from God as first principle and toward divinities (Intellect and Soul) as mediating principles. From this point of view, certain issues become clarified in greater detail, as can be seen in V.8[31] and VI.7[38], where the distinction between divine and human production can be seen with a subtlety that Christian theism tends to find superfluous. Plotinus has a middle position between full intelligence, expressed in Intellect and Soul at their highest, and the discursive character of human thought. This middle position allows for a more complex analysis of the actual working out of design, the conclusions of which can be used to supplement the more tersely described operation of design in a system where creation takes the place of generation.

10. Igal, "Aristoteles y la evolución de la antropología de Plotino," *Pensamiento* 35 (1979), 315–346, and "Introducción General" I–II, 52–62, shows how Plotinus combines Aristotle's division of the soul into vegetative, sensitive and rational with Plato's different division into rational, spirited and appetitive parts. H. J. Blumenthal, *Plotinus' Psychology* (The Hague: Martinus Hijhoff, 1971), 21–22, 48, 103–104, 135, argues very strongly that Plotinus rejects Plato's tripartition of the soul, only using it in ethical contexts where it seems less in conflict with his general theory of soul. Accounting for evil obviously confronts Plotinus with a different set of problems than the cognitive operations for which he favors Aristotle's faculties. Plotinus must preserve the soul's impassibility while at the same time giving it some role in the explanation of evil. Plato's two lower parts, the appetitive and spirited, provide the context in which evil can take place, but the role of the rational part is also recognized as causative. There is no reason, however, to see this as in conflict with the use of Aristotle's psychological faculties to explain various sensory processes, such as perception and imagination.

FREEDOM AND PROVIDENCE IN PLOTINUS[1]

Laura S. Westra

I contend that *freedom* represents the central notion in the philosophy of Plotinus. Although there are only four instances of 'free' (or 'freedom') in the *Enneads* as a whole, with the exception of the intensive discussion of the concept in *Enneads* VI.8, if the One is Absolute Freedom and the One represents the culmination of Plotinus' philosophy as well as our highest ideal, my contention is defensible on textual grounds. Yet, although our ascent to the One is through virtue and this assumes at least some possession of freedom, so that we can be viewed as moral agents, a question remains: What is the relationship between the 'self' (or our 'upper soul') and universal laws? If such laws are rational, ordained, eternal, and immutable, what does this imply for individual freedom? Can we maintain the position of staying determinedly aloof, uninvolved and free—as Plotinus counsels—even though we are part of the cosmic organism and thus subject to its laws?

1. Introduction to the Problem

Pronoia, the Greek term for providence, means 'pre-knowing.' Now, this notion seems to imply a fixed series of circumstances, with the one following upon the other in a relentless sequence, whereas *freedom*, in both its fullest sense (as descending or as originating from the One) and its derived sense (as ascending, as a commitment and an ideal from our standpoint) seems out of place in such a context. As we will see, Plotinus' views on providence are played out against the background of the Stoic conception, for he accepts some of the tenets of the Stoics and rejects others.[2] In the final analysis, the problematic we are dealing with here (i.e. the role, and even the possibility, of freedom in a universe under the rule of providence) will give us an answer to the question whether providence as Plotinus discusses it is—and can be—mainly Stoic.

The notion of Plotinian 'virtue' may be viewed as progressively freeing us from involvement—and even connections—with others as much as possible.[3] There are difficulties in trying to reconcile the way this term is understood in ordinary language with its meaning for Plotinus. In the case of virtue there are three possible senses to deal with: virtue in its religious sense, virtue in its moral but non-religious sense, and moral virtue in its Plotinian sense. Examination reveals that there are serious differences between the third sense and the first two senses, and that these differences are rooted in the central notion in Plotinus' thought, namely, freedom, which has a special meaning for him and plays the central role in his metaphysics. Freedom is a notion that tends to illuminate the more obscure aspects of his thought.

The problem of the conflict between providence and freedom is even more acute because the ordinary-language understanding of the former is exclusively religious. We may speak, for example, of 'providing for someone' or of an event as 'providential,' but the noun does not really lend itself to nonreligious uses. Furthermore, we must remember Rist's warning about "not dissolving Plotinus into his sources."[4] In few contexts is this danger so acute as in the case of providence; in fact, if the role of freedom in his philosophy is not properly understood, the difference between Plotinus and the Stoics when it comes to providence will appear minimal. And this may lead to further misunderstandings. For instance, A. Graeser, after comparing a number of Plotinian texts with texts found in the Stoics, concludes by calling Plotinian free will "a precursor to Kantian good will." Not only does this appear anachronistic, it is a conclusion that totally disregards the meaning of the ascent and the supernoetic nature of its goal for Plotinus.[5] He adds: "Plotinus, to be subjected to this intelligible environment is evidently guarantee of its liberty,"[6] which is hardly the whole story. The 'intelligible environment,' for Plotinus and also in some sense for us, is a given against whose limits and confines our individually-won quest for personal liberty is to be fought out. Moreover, the 'intelligible environment' is not just limit and background but also the embodied reminder of our own intelligible beauty and of our capacity (which, unfortunately, is not guaranteed to succeed) to reach beyond it, to freedom.

Bréhier provides us with another example of what can go wrong when we limit ourselves to Plotinus' sources in trying to understand him. Bréhier suggests: "The name 'One' contains perhaps nothing but the negation of the manifold." He then quotes Dean Inge to the effect that "perhaps Plotinus utilizes the word 'One' only because the Greek had no symbol for zero."[7] Even a cursory glance at *Enneads* VI.8 and many of the passages examined in this study flatly rules out such an interpretation. Neither sheer Unity (an interpretation apparently based on the Pythagoreans) nor 'zero' can even begin to do justice to the multifaceted Act, Being, Good, and Freedom in the One, especially in His providential role. Therefore neither of these interpretations captures Plotinus' originality.

The problems we face in this essay, then, are twofold. On the one hand, we must guard against reading too much of his background and sources in his notion of 'providence.' To make sure that inherited concepts are kept separate from what is original in Plotinus, I will begin with a brief examination of the Stoics. On the other hand, we must be equally careful not to import later and alien meanings into his conception of providence. To guard against this danger, I will also discuss briefly the difference between the Christian understanding of providence and the view held by Plotinus. In the process I will draw directly on the Gospels rather than taking up the treatment of providence in this or that Christian philosopher or theologian. In relation to both of these problems, the original Plotinian meaning of freedom will suffice to steer us away from misunderstandings. In the former case, we will see that the main difference between the Stoic conception of providence and the plotinian one hinges on the meaning of freedom. And in the latter instance we will have to rely on 'freedom' as well to keep Plotinus' view of providence separate from the conception to be found in ordinary language.

2. The Stoic Background

The background to Plotinus' doctrine is to be found in the Stoics. The main meaning of Providence in the Stoic context is "foreseeing and foreseeing correctly."[8] Plutarch regards Zeus and Providence as two possible separate roles played by the same entity, although this interpretation might not be accurate.[9] Reale instead emphasizes Providence as "a consequence of the affirmation of finality" and as a concept that is largely original with the Stoics, although he notes that "it does not have anything to do with the providence of a personal God."[10] He views Providence as an expression of "universal finality," since every being is part of the logos (reason) and is therefore good in that sense. It is the "immanent artificer, the World Soul," Reale says, citing Cicero.

Reale's claim about the lack of a personal God as a major component of the notion of Providence is the main point to be defended in any effort to show that there is a difference between a religious understanding of Providence and the Plotinian/Stoic counterpart of this notion. Therefore I will cite a few Stoic sources and discuss them. Cicero says the following about Zeno's doctrine: "Such being the nature of the world-mind, it can therefore correctly be designated as practical wisdom, or Providence (for in Greek it is termed *pronoia*), and this Providence is chiefly directed and concentrated upon three objects, namely, to secure for the world first, the structure best fitted for survival, next, absolute completeness, but chiefly consummate beauty and embellishment of every king."[11] All three 'objects' are creatively intellectual. Providence is planning and organizing the whole, ensuring that the world is fit to survive, complete and beautiful, that is, intellectually organized. In the providential relation, the relata are 'Providence' and 'the world,' and no personalized concern for any individual part of aspect of the world is required. The relation is that of a far-seeing planner to his well-put-together plan. The result is 'good' in the sense of being emotionally charged with goodwill toward any human being or entity.

In another passage Cicero praises God's power and his ability to accomplish anything "without toil," which is unlike the way our mind directs our actions and decisions. He says: "the moulder and manipulator of the universal substance is Divine Providence, withersoever it moves, is able to perform whatever it will."[12] Reale here draws the obviously correct conclusion I mentioned earlier, namely, that providence is not concerned with individual human beings. But a further point can be made beyond the one Reale mentions: Providence appears to have a will. The passage cited indicates not only the ability to perform any chosen action but also the freedom to do so. In this way Providence manifests freedom in its activity, which is a point not explicitly argued for but well worth keeping in mind when we return to Plotinus.

Finally, Stobaeus discusses 'fate' in Zeno and Antipater. Fate can also be called 'nature' or 'necessity' as well as 'Providence.' Other appropriate terms that could be used are 'truth,' 'cause' and 'logos.'[13] This represents an interesting move away from the dichotomy of Ideas/Demiurge (on the side of reason) and 'necessity' as sheer unformed matter in Plato's *Timaeus*. Reason is no longer just external and in opposition to the matter of the Universe; instead it is an immanent principle of regular, forming and organizing/planning power. Therefore freedom is necessarily in Providence, as is rationality. This is no longer Plato's doctrine, but it is not quite Plotinus' either, as we shall see.

This is not the place to rehash the abundant literature on the problem of freedom in the Stoics, who wish to retain morality (as based on personal responsibility and thus on free choice) while at the same time upholding Fate (as Necessity? or as Providence?). Rist has analyzed this aporia. Some actions, after all, are in our power: for instance, we affirm our freedom by means of the ultimate choice open to man (i.e. suicide) in certain appropriate circumstances. This position was held by the Stoics, and by Plotinus as well: "Obviously we shall die; that is fate. But there is no necessity (in Chrysippus' sense) for us to die at any time other than the time we choose."[14] This sentence is not obviously true, for one might decide to commit 'therapeutic' suicide tomorrow but be struck down by lightning or robbers today. Nevertheless the sense of being able to choose freely is clearly part of the decision to commit suicide when understood along the lines of the Stoics and Plotinus. Rist says: "Fate for Chrysippus is what will be, not what must be, and that still allows for something to be in our power (*eph' hemin*)."[15] If this is so, then fate and necessity are not one, nor is Providence interchangeable with these notions. And freedom is Fate's (or Providence's) unlimited power to choose, but then it is drastically altered in its meaning as far as we are concerned. Plotinus' freedom of the self goes beyond "the ability to be a co-worker with fate" and then to go along willingly as the wise man must do (he is the only one who is truly free, in Stoic terms), as opposed to those who are "dragged along behind the cart."[16]

Yet, if Providence, at this point, means no more than that certain law-like regularities obtain (necessarily) through the connections of causes which "make any object *qua* object what it is and not another thing,"[17] then we can at least conclude that Providence is not in conflict with Freedom, for it belongs to a different category of things. Freedom, for humans, is a state acquired through virtue, but is not come by easily. Freedom is not to be understood as a description of a state of affairs which obtains and of the natural laws within whose gambit human beings' quest for well-being and their ascent must take place.

We can therefore see what Reale means when he speaks of Providence and 'finality': It is the goal of the perfect, completed design of the world as it is and as it will be. Individuals indeed participate in this 'Providential order' as fitting parts of it, not as persons with specific interests, needs or concerns aside from those that are appropriate to their role within the totality of the world.

3. Plotinus and Providence

What is Providence for Plotinus? As we noted, the Greek expression means 'foreknowledge'; it is a noetic, not an effective, term. It does not seem to have anything to do with 'providing' or 'taking care' of things or people. All that is involved is perceiving beforehand. This much one can pick up from studying the Liddell-Scott Greek lexicon.

Plotinus begins *Enneads* III.2 by rearticulating an often repeated concern: We must not attribute the existence of all that is to chance or accident. Furthermore, Providence should not be confused with our sort of providence—viz. foresight—"which is a calculation before action how something should happen or not happen in the case of things which ought not to be done, or how we may have something or not have it" (III.2.1, 11–14). Thus, in its individual meaning, at least, Plotinus understanding of Providence clearly involves a judgment and an anticipatory calculation about future actions and contingencies. It does not involve others, except perhaps as components of the actions and situations we might deliberate about.

As far as the divine aspect of this notion and its meaning is concerned, it is to be understood as "the foreseeing and calculation of the divine [probably soul: *proosasin tina kai logismon theou*] about how all this might come into existence, and how things might be as good as possible" (III.2.1, 18–19). This does not entail a time when the universe did not exist or a prior deliberation and decision that was followed by a coming to be of all that is. Rather, as we have seen, we are to think in terms of a "spontaneous outflow of creative power," as Armstrong puts it in his note to the translation of this passage.[18] It is the manifestation of the One's Freedom: It is not so much a direct 'outflow' as an outflow that proceeds through Intellect, who is prior in nature and is the cause of the universe as a kind of archetype and model, the universe being an image of it and existing by means of it (III.2.1, 23–27). "Each part is not cut off from the whole," says Plotinus, echoing Parmenides.[19] The universe as a whole "lives and thinks all together as one," so that even if individual parts are opposite to one another, they still belong together. No single part of the universe "has become merely other, estranged from the rest" (III.2.1, 33–34).

The manifestation of individual ascending freedom does not require as primary that we consider others specifically and individually, whereas it does need respect and admiration from our Source and what comes from There, that is, the universe as a whole.[20] We can now see that its counterpart, the manifestation of the freedom of the One (Providence) also entails consideration for the Intellectual unity of the Universe and its appropriateness as a whole.

The freely creating power of the One, "the power to produce something else, without seeking to produce it" (III.2.2, 12–13), brings about the Intellect, which in turn, through Soul, without effort or means, creates the interconnected intelligible beauty which is the universe. Providence thus appears to consist of the freely produced completeness of the whole. By way of example, Plotinus points to the relation between Providence and man: "But the divine exists also as things are; and has come to something other than itself, not to destroy the other but, when a man, for instance, comes to it, it stands over him and sees to it that he is man; that it, that he lives by the law of providence, which means doing everything its law says" (III.2.0, 4–8).

Two points emerge here. The first relates to the lack of planning on the part of the One and to the Intellect's free outflow, to which Plotinus returns in V.8.7, which is entitled 'On Intelligible Beauty.' The intelligible world order is a principle, he says, and "in this sense it is well said that we should not enquire into the reason why of a principle" (V.8.7, 43–46). And since 'principle and goal' together form a whole and are to all intents and purposes one and the same, no imperfection or deficiency can arise within it: It is—as a whole—beautiful. It was not laboriously designed through planning or syllogism, and it was not the result of rational inquiry, that is, using the rationality of Intellect. Clearly, no rational argument or inquiry and debate is possible at the level of the One—only effortless, free production. When intellectual endeavour is possible, as in the second Hypostasis (Intellect), then we still do not have process—nothing prior (deliberation) followed something posterior (the formed world), for the two coexist eternally in the form of Beauty as principle and Beauty as completed, perfected goal.

The second point also hinges on the true meaning of freedom and its import in Plotinus. The question that arose in connection with the Stoic meaning of Providence and Fate was: How could individual freedom and a thoroughly complete world order coexist? The passage cited above can help us understand how Plotinus was able to speak on the one hand of the 'law of providence' and 'doing everything which the law says,' while on the other hand still describing freedom as the highest ideal to which man can aspire. Today most people agree that we are basically free to choose our course of action, even when we take into consideration a number of limiting and qualifying factors; to make this affirmation is not to deny the interconnected material, psychical and logical laws that govern us. Thus, whereas the existence of a personally determined, 'providing' Providence might be viewed as intruding on our personal freedom, the existence of universal laws and regularities does not. It appears that Plotinus had the latter in mind rather than the former.

Such a harmonization is the "concord" of "intellect and necessity" (*nou kai anangkas*: III.2.2, 33–34) to which Plotinus refers. This 'harmony' reconciles destruction with coming into being, parts which are friendly with others that are hostile, and those that are better with those that are worse. Because of this concord, it would be unreasonable to "blame the whole because of the parts, as if one were to take a hair of a whole living being, or a toe and neglect the whole man, a wonderful sight to see" (III.2.3, 14–16).

All things aim toward the Good, but they attain it in varying degrees, in proportion to their own receptive power. This is the point Plotinus makes in *Enneads* II.9. The excellence of the Source does not permit us to criticize that which proceeds from Him. However, we can and must try to understand, for all things do not participate in being and life in equal ways: "One must not demand equal gifts in things which are not equal" (III.2.3, 39). Nor should hostility and destruction surprise us: They are necessary in beings that are not meant to last forever. They have come into being as they are "because they all exist There, in the upper heaven" (III.2.4, 19). On the other hand, human beings act "under their own control," inclining to turn to "what is better" and "what is worse." Thus the necessary law-like design of the whole includes the existence of freely acting beings. It is only when these beings act according to the good that they live in well-being. Justice prevails either here or in future times; yet the prize of well-being lies essentially within our grasp, if we make the effort to be virtuous. Even poverty and sickness do not affect this well-being; moreover, they are "not without usefulness for the coordination and completion of the whole" (III.2.5, 8–9).

And so evil is explained without recourse to religious arguments, but in a way that will eventually be useful to Christians. Even the definition of evil is similar to the one to be found later in Augustine and Aquinas: "In general we must define evil as a falling short of good" (III.2.5, 26). Such a definition should not surprise us, for it is quite consistent with Plotinus' doctrine in general. We know where the true good is to be found. The 'evils' we perceive and have to accept do not affect our true well-being.

Plotinus' argument begins with the admitted prevalence of evils. And not only are evils prevalent, but their distribution appears unjust: bad men are masters of good ones and appear to have more than their fair share of worldly goods. Against this background it appears as though "Providence does not reach as far as the Earth" (III.2.7, 34). But note that Plotinus is not wondering who will provide for the unfortunates of the world; his concern here is rather about the extent of the rational pattern of the universe. We cannot deny that even animals and plants share in it. Do we perhaps need to doubt its power?

Again we might be misled into considering some of these parts (evils) in isolation from the whole, as we are tempted to approve of the good while censuring the bad. It is as though we were to claim that heads are fine while the rest of the human body is not quite right, which would be improper from the standpoint of logic and would also fail to show proper respect for the Source of all creation. Logic will not permit us to demand that one part of the integrated organism be dismissed as unworthy; piety and reverence ought to restrain us in our complaining. The first of these two grounds appears more philosophically sound than the second. In general, even the prevalence of evil and injustice should simply be considered part of the whole. The very fact that we perceive evils as such attests to our lack of preparation (III.2.8, 15–16).

Many evils exist simply because of our choices: "But the wicked rule by the cowardice of the ruled; for this is just, and the opposite is not" (III.2.8, 51–52). Despite the many evils we see around us, therefore, we can conclude that Plotinus' arguments for the existence of Providence are based on three separate kinds of premises: (a) ethical, (b) ontological, and (c) noetic.

The ethical arguments are strictly arguments *quoadrios*: The fact that the One is the Good does not make Providence an extension of goodwill or of love. The objective of Intellect is to create according to rational laws and form, to produce the most beauty possible, and to achieve completeness. This was the position of the Stoics, and we have no reason to suppose that Plotinus differed with them substantially on this point. The ethical explanations connected with evils in this world are also of three kinds. (a) We choose the wrong thing.[21] (b) We are not sufficiently 'trained' or prepared to understand the 'evils' that befall us and others in an accepting and understanding frame of mind.[22] Both of these represent inappropriate attitudes which are neither moral nor good, attitudes which are not conducive to our well-being.

From the noetic or epistemological standpoint (c), we persist in misunderstanding the composition of the universe in all its aspects. We expect it to be all light when what it actually presents us with is an infinite variety of plays of light and shadow (III.2.11, 9–17). Therefore we need the sort of understanding that arises out of a different perspective (d), an understanding that is no longer particularized but global, one that is not centered upon our own problems or those of our friends and kin but rather on the admirably law-like regularities that are entailed by a rational forming of the universe. Finally, we must not demand "unmixed excellence" (e) (III.2.7, 2), but should only expect from the rational forming principle "as much as the mixture can receive" (III.2.7, 6–7).

Finally, the metaphysical-ontological reasons have to do with our understanding of the true nature of man. These considerations might also be subsumed under the heading of 'epistemological reasons,' but what is required is not a change in approach but a truer grasp of man's nature. Thus man's nature is not all of one piece (f): The "shadow of man" cries and moans for the external difficulties of life be encounters. But only the "seriously good part of man is capable of taking serious doings seriously; the rest of man is a toy" (III.2.15, 51–54). Cilento speaks of these passages as the most tragic ones in the *Enneads* and the most powerful commentaries Plotinus offers on the human condition.[23] And what are the 'serious doings' Plotinus is talking about? It seems clear that only our true well-being needs to be taken seriously: All else is play on a stage and childish games. Even death is simply the removal of the "play-costume in which he was dressed" (III.2.15, 57–58). Furthermore, all opposites are part of "the single rational living being" (g) (III.2.16, 48–49). They are often in conflict, since an absolute homogeneity of parts and actions does not make for a good play or an organism that is rationally put together. Unformed uniformity of matter does not manifest a rational plan, but "since it is a rational pattern it has distinctions in itself, and the extreme distinction is opposition" (III.2.16, 53–54). It is necessary to differentiate all throughout nature, for form and limit are better than their lack.[24] Difference in the highest degree is opposition and hostility.

This is to be expected in a universe that is far less of a Unity than its original Source and is a well-differentiated multiplicity instead. Had the universe been different, the rational principle might have been blamed for bringing about simply unformed, homogeneous parts, "parts all alike and equal" (III.2.1.2, 5–7).

4. The Role of Freedom in Providence

In the tenth chapter, Plotinus once again takes up the problem of free will in relation to evil. If we have to accept the existence of evil in the world for the reasons cited above, is it the case that "men are unwillingly wicked" (III.2.10, 1–4) and that their wrongdoing is not their responsibility? Is the rational principle to blame instead? This is not the case, he says. Earlier in the treatise he had indicated, furthermore, that it is "neither pious nor reverent" to believe such a thing (III.2.7, 42–43). Human beings are not blameless and are not coerced by inflexibly predetermined principles: "men, too, are principles" (III.2.10, 19). Therefore their actions are their own, and they are responsible for them. Plotinus is rather brief here because 'On Providence' is a treatise meant to explain descending—rather than ascending—freedom. The focus of the argument is the necessary coexistence of good and evil in a universe brought about by the rational principle (Intellect)—thus by something that is good by definition.[25]

How does Plotinus manage to save freedom and moral responsibility while exonerating the rational principle from blame? In his clearest statement on this topic occurring in this chapter, he declares: "But as for the necessity, this does not mean that it comes in from outside but only that it is universally so" (III.2.10, 12–13). Thus it is not that the rational principle has erred; all it has done is to establish universal laws of which the amphibious nature of man is undoubtedly a part, so that man's capacity to act and to do "noble actions by their own nature" and to be a free and independent principle (III.2.10, 19–21) is simply a manifestation of one of the laws that govern everything.

Even a rational principle is only able to produce such effects as the recipient matter is capable of accomplishing. Just as stones have a fixed nature that permits them to be shaped and formed, to roll whenever pushed, but not to walk or feel, and just as an animal's nature permits it to move and feel and 'choose' according to instinctive desires, but not to philosophize, so too a human being is free to exercise and to enjoy his limited sort of freedom.

This freedom consists in part of a natural inclination to pursue the arduous, demanding task of achieving a much better sort of freedom through ascent.[26] The same sort of thing could be said of the laws governing the flow of a river: They are meant to keep the flow orderly and thus rational, thereby producing certain effects on its banks and in its bed, and also on the creatures on which it has an impact. It is possible, however, for the river to react to specific environmental stimuli and overflow, thus producing 'evils' which its natural inclination would not cause, or to dry up because of extreme climatic conditions, which would have equally adverse effects. The laws upon which the operation of the river are based are rational, but the evil possibilities are universal in the sense that under the same circumstances or stimuli, any river would perform in the same manner.

Plotinus insists that it is not right to criticize, for to do so would be to demonstrate the same lack of comprehension that one might exhibit in criticizing a painter for not painting a picture that includes all of the best things he is able to paint and nothing else, or in criticizing someone for not producing a play that portrays static perfection rather than action, movement and a mixture of elements (III.2.11, 13–17). Therefore, although freedom is limited by universal laws, it is still present.

Another questions remains to be explored: What about the freedom and rationality of the productive principle? Is it still represented through the multi-colored mosaic it produces? Can he still be understood as 'just'? Justice is manifested in two separate ways. First, one needs to adopt the timeless perspective fitting for an eternal Hypostasis such as Intellect or Soul. For instance, we need not judge the justice or injustice of a man's life simply by considering his present circumstances. Any evil he might suffer is surely either (a) part of his natural makeup, e.g. due to disease or death, or (b) the result of a wrong choice, e.g. not working hard enough to elect good rulers, or (c) retribution for misdeeds in past lives.

Once again the fault or responsibility is strictly ours. To think otherwise is simply to demonstrate a lack of understanding of how Infinite Freedom manifests itself. Our parts are prescribed for us in the universal play it designs, but our ability to carry them through in accordance with our talents—admittedly unequal—is due to ourselves alone (III.2.17, 26–33). If fact, our freedom to excel or to disgrace ourselves is much greater because of the universal magnitude of our 'play,' and also because of the basic differences we start out with (III.2.18, 1–3).

Freedom to express itself belongs to Intellect in much greater measure and, through it, to Soul, although we are liable to misunderstand this point because of our limited abilities. Both, however, are less than absolutely free, for both are 'constrained' by rational principles, unlike the One, who is supranoetic. Yet they enjoy a freedom that is not possible for us as complex human beings under the sway of a multitude of laws. We can indeed attain some measure of freedom through training and hard work, but only for our very self, our inner core, which is subject only to the laws governing non-material entities.

In chapter 4, the second part of the treatise entitled 'On Providence,' Plotinus returns to the question of man's freedom in order to decide whether he is to blame for wrongdoing or not, even though his main aim in this treatise is to show that Intellect and Soul are to be absolved from all blame. He argues that if man were simple, in the sense of being subject to immutable laws in *all* his aspects, as plants and animals are, he would be no more to blame than they are. But he is to blame because "he is not only what he was made but has another, free principle" (III.2.4, 7), which many men do not elect to use, instead choosing "a number of others, the worse ones" (III.2.4, 15–16).

Therefore man has a different status than those other entities, a status that depends on his kinship with the One and freedom, rather than simply on his reception of the rational principle. In the latter regard he is like all of creation, for all things, in one degree or another, receive the rational principle to the extent that their nature is able to. It is the recognition and choice of rationality on man's part, however, that makes freedom possible.

An interesting question remains to be considered. The One is Freedom in an absolute sense and is under no constraint in relation to His free production. This multifaceted and complex world is what He creates, through Intellect (*nous*) and Soul. Why does He not create everything and everyone good? Plotinus answers: Should we blame the Maker just because plants do not feel, animals do not reason, and human beings are not gods? Just as we can and must accept diversity in the world around us, so we must also accept that people have different capacities to perfect themselves and to act for the good (III.2.3, 8–12). It is not as though the Creator of the world had set out to make all the entities in the world perfectly equal (III.2.3, 19–20). Plotinus does not come right out and say it, but the implication is clear: The universe is diverse and was meant to be such. Why should this be the case? First of all, that there is ranking is simply a fact of life. But the strongest consideration is that while the One is Freedom and Intellect is second (and Soul third), individual souls are followed by individual beings which are "not only souls but diminutions of souls," and thus represent "a kind of fading away as the living things move farther away from their origins" (III.2.3, 25–27).

This is clearly the principle reason for the status of the Universe and its controversial condition. Even the One, through Rational Principle and Intellect, could not deny His own uniqueness and supremacy through His creation. He is and remains the only One to be absolutely free; all else is increasingly and progressively lower, thus possessing lower and lower levels of freedom. It is only man who has as much as the capacity for freedom through rationality. Thus, what we observe in the universe is unavoidable and rational, given the One's unique position. Any other form of creation would obscure the One's own 'nature' and role.

5. The 'Daimon' and Freedom

Plotinus devotes a short treatise to the 'daimon.' Are we to regard the existence of yet another superhuman influence on our lives as a further threat to freedom? Does the existence of daimons endanger our already precarious quest for freedom? On the contrary, Plotinus' *daimonia* help us understand why the upper soul is intrinsically inclined to seek freedom.

Other philosophers before Plotinus had grasped the unique nature of soul. Not just Thales but also Heraclitus had understood its depth: "You could not discover the limits of soul, even if you travelled by every path in order to do so; such is the depth of its meaning."[27] Heraclitus also anticipates the role of the demon: "Soul has its own inner law of growth."[28] Cilento says the following about the soul's destiny and nature: "Of this odyssey of the soul, who is the eternal nomad in the metaphysical realm, Plotinus is the last poet."[29] Why is the soul the 'eternal nomad'? Primarily because it is not totally tied to any predetermined state but is free to choose.

In this brief treatise, then, Plotinus explains why Providence's rational plans, which include the nature of the soul just as it is, do not preclude the possibility of human freedom but—on the contrary—require it. The notion of a daimon is alien to our present world-view, and those for whom this notion has meaning (mainly Christians and other religions) view demons as an evil, undesirable lot. For Plotinus, however, 'daimon' possesses a positive meaning, which emerges clearly from his treatment of the topic.[30]

In the title and body of *Enneads* III.4, Armstrong translates *daimon* as 'our allotted guardian spirit.' Cilento reserves the expression 'spirit' for Intellect, perhaps to distinguish it from the more laborious rationality of logos, or even to emphasize the spiritual component of the intellectual principle. He simply retains 'demone' (Italian for 'demon') for his own translation. Cilento also devotes one of his 'saggi' to the history and meaning of *daimonia*, tracing the notion from Homeric and even pre-Homeric times, beginning with Thales, for whom water and even "all" were "full of demons."[31] I will simply refer the reader to his rich and poetic presentation of the history of 'demons' in Greece. Cilento maintains that with Plotinus we have arrived at the last stage of Greek demonology.

Plotinus begins his treatise by clearly outlining the difference between: (a) fixed, unmoving being and reality, (b) the coming to be and flux of the "expression of some realities" (III.4.1, 1–2), and (c) the restless position of the soul, poised between the two. Cilento characteristics the soul as "a bridge thrown between *Nous* [Intellect] and the world."[32] This 'bridge' is therefore like neither side. Its main characteristic is its ability to change—first of all from state to state, choosing a life that is mired only in the sensual, or the purely vegetative, or perhaps choosing a higher, intellectual way of life. Furthermore, it also moves from life to life, through a "multitude of gradations, values and changing forms," as Cilento puts it.[33]

After an exposition of Platonic doctrine, Plotinus goes on. It is not the daimon that chooses us; rather, we choose the daimon and thus bear the responsibility of our choice. Again and again, we will turn into the sort of creature we deserve to be because of our behaviour. In chapter 3 Plotinus picks up the thread of his own doctrine. We need to choose the daimon above us so that our efforts in this life will be compensated for by the status we achieve in the next life. Plotinus does not say that a daimon exists as separate hypostasis or entity of any sort; still, his description confers on it a "degree of spiritual life" and makes it the highest 'I' that spurs us on—a mythical reified version of man's perennial striving and restlessness for change.

Cilento says: "The demon, like history, is Freedom."[34] And so when we presume to judge Providence for the effects of the Rational Principle which governs the universe and gives it its laws, we first need to understand the power of freedom within the Principle. It is this freedom that permits us to go beyond the myth of the metals, allowing each one of us to choose the better daimon and higher life. The talents we need in order to reach a progressively higher level of spiritual life are just that—spiritual talents; they are primarily spiritual rather that intellectual, because our ultimate goal is freedom. And freedom, in its highest form, is supranoetic.

6. Christian Providence and Evil

Contemporary philosophy of religion faces many of the same problems that plagued Plotinus, such as the conflict between the goodness of God (and thus Providence, in its Christian meaning) and the existence of what some people have called 'surplus evils,' that is, certain evils which, according to them, cannot even partly be explained by pointing to human error and sinfulness. Even though some 'non-disciplinary evils' might eventually be understood as fostering other human goods, and perhaps as leading to greater strength and happiness in the human beings affected by them,[35] there remain many that appear far beyond any and all rational explanations.

When confronting the cases in which it does not appear that God cares in a personal way—or any other way—for every sparrow, philosophers are often at a loss. Some try to rethink and rework the concept of God in such a way that He retains a sort of Kantian goodwill while His omnipotence is temporarily or occasionally curtailed.[36] In this study I will not discuss these cases or otherwise attempt to deal with this problem. However, I do wonder whether these arguments do not surrender as much as they gain. Is the 'God' who emerges from such well-meaning conceptual manipulation still the God whom the Christian or an individual belonging to any of the great monotheistic religions would wish to worship?

I also wonder whether Plotinus' concept of Freedom as Absolute, combined with an acceptance of the existence of grades of life and reality, might not say as much in the face of the problem of evil as some of these contemporary thinkers manage to say. Plotinus' position saves more of the Unity and Integrity of his Principle than some Christian thinkers are able to do. (We should not suppose, however, that we was limited by some religious orthodoxy; he was committed only to the inner consistency and coherence of his own metaphysical doctrines and to the necessity of accounting for the existent realities he was acquainted with.)

Is there any sense in which the One or Intellect cares about what happens to us? Rist, addressing the subject of prayer, observes: "The One of Plotinus is transcendent and ultimately remote and unconcerned with transient things."[37] There is nothing in the textual work I have undertaken to suggest any other interpretation. Therefore we should not expect much in the way of concern—or even sympathy—from that Source. On the other hand, some sympathy may be available from other quarters.[38]

It is an important part of the Christian faith to believe that God is a loving Father whose function in regard to man is not limited to His role as Creator. The Christian is told: 'Ask, and ye shall be answered.' Parables attest to the power of prayer and supplication bolstered by faith, which is the prelude for the granting of favours and requests—and perhaps even for miracles that subvert that natural order of laws. Our hope—and sometimes even our success in being granted what we ask for—is grounded in God's infinite love for us. Belief in these matters is central to being a Christian: faith, hope and charity are Christian virtues *par excellence*. Yet they are not to be found in Plotinus, with the possible exception of 'neoplatonic faith,' as Rist call it.[39]

What could Plotinus possibly mean by 'prayer,' then? What could it mean to pray to a Providence (or a God) who does not love men and cannot ultimately justify their hopes? In chapters 30 through 45 of *Enneads* IV.4, Plotinus distinguishes between two separate meanings of 'prayer.' The first one comes up in connection with his treatment of magic and cults, a domain of activity which he places below the realm of the World Soul. When prayer actually works, he argues, it is not because the gods hear and listen and react; rather, it succeeds because our action mobilizes the 'sympathetic' reaction of various parts of the organism we call the universe. We make these prayers, argues Plotinus, "to the sun and other men to the stars,"[40] and sometimes our wishes (whether good or bad) are granted. But how can a rational entity grant the wishes of an evil man? That this happens should not surprise us, says Plotinus, since both the good man and the evil man can draw water from the river. From this we see that natural bounties are available to all on an indiscriminate basis (IV.4.41, 15–17). Medicine, agriculture, rhetoric, and music all influence things and men to some degree. The first to help "natural things to be in a natural state" (IV.4.31, 17–19), whereas the latter two "influence the soul" and "lead men to better or worse by changing them" (IV.4.31, 21–23). The question is why this should be the case, and the answer we seek ought to be able to explain the effects of prayer and magic. In a lengthy discussion Plotinus considers and rejects various arguments and finally comes to the following conclusion: "This All is a 'single living being which encompasses all the living beings within it'; it has one soul which extends to all its parts, insofar as each individual thing is a part of it...."[41]

The whole universe is 'bound together' as one organism. What is felt by one part is felt by all, just as the pain in one finger is experienced by us as a general feeling (IV.4.32, 21–23). This whole 'organism' exhibits a "harmony of action and experience" (IV.4.33, 2–5). It possesses a great deal, and not just in the way of rational principles, for it also has an "unbounded store of varied powers" (IV.4.36, 1–2). These powers are somehow alerted or awakened by our prayers or magic. Therefore it is not the case that the gods or heavenly bodies are responsible for the effects of our prayers; rather, "the nature of what is done" is responsible (IV.4.38, 5–6). Hence, "magic spells work," according to Plotinus, "by sympathy and by the fact that there is a natural concord of things that are alike and the opposition of things which are different" (IV.4.40, 1–4).[42]

This sort of prayer or magic is irrational, that is, not subject to rationality or deliberation. It is an 'enchantment' that affects "anything bodily," but "he himself" (i.e. a person's true self) would be unharmed (IV.4.43, 11–1 2). This enchantment is perhaps on a par with the enticement of the "care of children and concern for marriage" and with other activities such as "political activity and the pursuit of power." All of these are caused primarily by "our passionate spirit," and they "entice man since they give pleasure to their carnal desires" (IV.4.44, 7–12). We have come along way since Plato's *Republic* with its philosopher-king!

All of these lower 'enchantments' are contrasted with contemplation, pure and entirely self-directed, and of such a nature that "it alone remains incapable of enchantment" (IV.4.44, 1–3). It seems as though the good man has no need of this sort of prayer; it may even be the case that resort to it or to other 'magic' is a sure sign that one has not yet become either virtuous or free. The second sort of prayer is instead nothing more than a final 'waiting'; it is something we engage in when we attempt to reach for the One at the end of our journey of ascent: Alone to the Alone. It is not a prayer of request or petition; it is rather a prayer of silence, "...first invoking God himself, not in spoken words, but by stretching ourselves out with our soul into prayer to him..." (V.1.6, 10–12).

Therefore the usual Christian understanding of Providence as the work of a being to whom we can pray in the hope that love will come our way is not to be found in Plotinus, nor is the faith that our prayers will be heard and possibly even answered and that praying is a virtuous enterprise in itself. What he has in mind instead is a free but rational ordering of the universe, a virtuous goal which is conducive to our well-being but does not primarily involve an acquisition of traits or habits: Instead it is to be understood as a new becoming. It is the pursuit of immanent freedom, and it is based on a progressive detachment from everything that is not, or does not foster, the reunion of freedom in ourselves with Freedom itself.

Sympathy exists within various parts of the universe, and it manifests its interconnected wholeness and the powers we can summon from within it—provided we do not expect anything that might run counter to the providential laws that govern and direct us. Any care or concern that we would deem 'natural' is natural for Plotinus as well, but it is therefore to be dismissed, or controlled and—if possible—unlearned. It is a "passionate impulse" belonging to our "play costume," and not to our real self or to our serious work. The latter leads us to the One, but the One is not a personal God, much less a Loving Agent.[43] It is simply not a nurturing or providing entity. It appears that the only one thing the One provides us with is a respect of a certain sort. He arranges effortlessly for cosmic laws subject to Intellect, but He allows us to retain our freedom, and thus also the kinship to Him that we need in order to ascend.

The term 'respect' is used by Plotinus himself and seems to capture the most that a good man is allowed to feel for his neighbour. For example, he says: "Since you can respect the soul in another, respect yourself" (V.1.2, 51).[44] It is also in the respect for our freedom that we find the main difference between the Stoic meaning of providence (*pronoia*) and the meaning Plotinus assigns it. The latter bases his interpretation of it on the addition to his universe of the One as beyond Intellect and thus beyond the rational principle of providence. Thus the metaphysics of Plotinus adds a new dimension to the universe envisioned by the Stoics, since our ultimate goal, in his view, is to go beyond Intellect, or at least to try to do so. And we should remember that the final step of the ascent is supranoetic. When we consider the Stoic meaning of providence, then, we can clearly affirm that Plotinus does not hold the same view at all.

When we turn to the problem of the meaning of 'providence' in ordinary language, a meaning with an undeniably Christian flavour, we are equally far from the thought of Plotinus. The main reason for this is the emphasis on God's infinite love, a notion that would be even more anachronistic within the Plotinian context than the human love discussed earlier. Rist, who makes much of certain similarities between human *eros* in Plotinus and the Christian notion of *agape*, points out some differences: "The parable of Jesus, the writings of Paul and John, tell us the nature of Agape. Agape leaves the ninety-nine sheep in the wilderness to seek the one which is lost (Luke 15:4)."[45] What would Plotinus make of this parable? On the basis of the texts we have examined, we would have to say that his main concern would be for the justice of the case rather than for love shown to the lost individual. He tells us his own parable of the underdog, of those who are weaker, 'unprepared.' It would not be just, he says, for us to step in and save such people; in fact, it would be just if they were to be punished, even if those who triumph are the wicked (III.2.8, 16–26).[46]

Therefore, we must cast aside the limited perspective that would have us view all such cases as injustices (immediate injustices) instead we should take the longer-range view urged upon us by Plotinus: Providence will see to it that justice is served at some time—but not necessarily during our own time, or when we deem it appropriate. We cannot and need not get involved, since it is our freedom alone that leads to the well-being that is our desired and natural aim.

All involvement with the human needs of others—and even with our own needs—is to be cast aside. As for prayers and other forms of magic, even if they are successful, they simply reaffirm our kinship with the rest of the universe; they do not bring us any closer to our well-being or to the One. It is only progressive freedom, which increases as many of our involvements decrease, that leads us to our goal. This freedom is not really in conflict with the rational laws of providence; it simply helps to clarify its reach and limitations. Perhaps this respectful freedom to choose to be what we can be is the highest sort of providing that man should wish for. In other words, it may be that we should think not in terms of a Christian love for the lowest, for the poorest, for sinners, but in terms of a transcendent 'toughlove' instead, to use a current expression. Such 'love' is all that human beings can expect, according to Plotinus. It may even be enough.

7. Conclusion: Freedom and Providence

Although individual human freedom is discussed in the two treatises on providence, the main thrust of the argument is intended to answer the two following questions. (a) How can free creation, which arises from the Good, retain the rationality of the principles according to which it operates when evil exists in the products of its creation? (b) Why is it that no blame for *what is* needs to be ascribed to the One or to other Hypostases? The defense of human freedom is also included, but the purpose of including it is to explain and defend the reach and limitations of rational universal laws and the possible conflict between freedom and necessity.

Another way to approach the problem of how to summarize Plotinus' teaching on providence is to look at it from the standpoint of freedom—in two senses. First let us consider the meaning of Providence against the background of the conflict between freedom and necessity; here the problem is one of global freedom. Against the same background, we could (secondly) raise the question of individual freedom. In both cases, the existence of evil is the catalyst. How can the existence of evil be rendered consistent with the One's creation as both free and good, and thus be uncoerced in respect to the evil that exists?

The first point (the global one) is answered by Plotinus as follows: all things are as good as it is possible for them to be. In other words, the limits to the goodness of the things in the world do not result from any impotence in the One, who creates everything freely and spontaneously—and not according to any plan. On the contrary, in view of the fact that (1) the One is free, and that Intellectual Principle and the soul are second and third and so on, everything else has to manifest a progressively fading unity, freedom and goodness. The existence of levels and grades emanating from the centre like rays from the sun, each one weaker than the one before as the high power and concentration of light recedes, simply follows from the primacy of the One and is necessitated by His status within the universe. It is not an evil choice, then, that makes Alaska less warm and sunny than the countries through which the Equator passes.

Secondly, there is no conflict between universal necessity and absolute freedom in the One. The conflict that appears to be present is resolved once we realize that the One's free and spontaneous creation in the Good engenders just Intellect, the Intellectual Principle. Therefore the rest of the universe, including Soul and our own souls, is under the sway of rational laws. Freedom is retained through the creative process, for contemplation and freedom are one. Hence the 'self' is always There, maintaining and preserving this higher element even in its fall. After all, the higher element is what inclines the self to reascend to its 'true self' and to its Father and Country once again. Therefore, through freedom the two main difficulties that arise with regard to Providence's universal aspects can be solved.

And what about Providence considered from the individual standpoint? How are souls to be good and bad, and how can men be moral agents (and therefore necessarily free) while they are under the sway of immutable laws? Are we free, or are we coerced by those laws? We have just noted that the self remains akin to the One (Freedom) and longs to reascend. We also saw earlier that the self is a principle, and as such is free. It is clear that the self, since it is immaterial, aloof and free, is under the control of no law, for freedom and the limits of an essence (the rational form) cannot mix. However, the rest of our soul, and the composite that is humanity, are indeed governed by universal fixed laws. This is the reason why our instincts, for example, are no more blameworthy than those of animals. But there is more to us than this aspect, and it is precisely the other aspect, which is akin to the highest (and not just akin to Intellect) that makes our individual action free and thus enables us to retain our moral responsibility. Our responsibility extends even beyond our life. For the rationality of Providence ensures that good is rewarded and evil is punished—if not in this live, then in the future. The section on the 'daimon' also makes this point forcefully: We must freely choose a higher life. Justice prevails throughout the universe, as is reasonable.

And so we see again that when the role and nature of freedom are kept clearly in mind (at least to the extent that such an open-ended notion permits clarity), the apparent contradictions in Plotinus' conception of Providence are resolved. What remains is a coherent and consistent doctrine.

The University of Windsor

NOTES

1. Reprinted with modification, by permission, from: Laura Westra, *Plotinus and Freedom: A Meditation on Enneads 5: 6.8*, Studies in the History of Philosophy series, volume 9 (Lewiston, NY: The Edwin Mellen Press ©1990), 147–174.
2. J. M. Rist, *Plotinus: The Road to Reality* (Cambridge: Cambridge University Press, 1967), 173.
3. This notion raises a problem which has been discussed elsewhere: see Westra, *Plotinus and Freedom*, chapter 6.
4. Rist, *Road to Reality*, 169.
5. Graeser, *Plotinus and the Stoics* (Leiden: E. J. Brill, 1972); see also Graeser, "Plotinus on Man's Free Will," where he writes: "This idea appears to be a striking anticipation of Immanuel Kant..." (124).
6. Graeser, *Plotinus and the Stoics*.
7. Bréhier, *The Philosophy of Plotinus* (Chicago: University of Chicago Press, 1958), 157 & n6.
8. J. M. Rist, *Stoic Philosophy* (Cambridge: Cambridge University Press, 1969), 126.
9. Rist, *Stoic Philosophy*, 163–164.
10. Giovanni Reale, *The Systems of the Hellenistic Age*, translated by J. R. Catan (New York: SUNY Press, 1985), 248–249.
11. Reale, *Hellenistic Age*, 250.
12. Reale, *Hellenistic Age*, 250 (citing Cicero, *De natura deorum*, 2.22.57ff.).
13. Reale, *Hellenistic Age*, 251 (citing Stobaeus, Anth. 1.78.18ff.).
14. Rist, *Stoic Philosophy*, 129.
15. Rist, *Stoic Philosophy*, 122–128; see n1, where he cites Reesor.
16. Rist, *Stoic Philosophy*, 130; see also 127, where he cites Zeno and Chrysippus.
17. Rist, *Stoic Philosophy*, 121.
18. In n1 on pages 44–45 in reference to *Ennead* III.2.1. Armstrong states: "Plotinus frequently attacks the idea that God first planned the universe and then created it, and insists that it is everlasting and not the result of divine

deliberation and choice but of spontaneous outflow of creative power without beginning or end." See also V.8.7.

19. Parmenides, "The Way of Truth" (DK 4): "Gaze steadfastly at things which, though far away, are yet present to the mind. For you cannot cut off being from being: it does not scatter into a universe then reunify": P. Wheelwright, *The Presocratics* (New York: Odyssey Press, 1966), 96.
20. See Westra, *Plotinus and Freedom*, chapter 6.
21. *Ennead* III.2.7, 2-21 & III.2.9, 14–17.
22. *Ennead* III.2.8, 14–16 & III.2.15, 36–39.
23. "Il senurnento tragico," in Cilento, *Saggi su Plutino*, 255–259.
24. Rist, *Road to Reality*, 23–24.
25. The question of free will and of human responsibility is the counterpart to the main question that is under consideration, is discussed in Westra, *Plotinus and Freedom*, chapter 6.
26. Outlined in Westra, *Plotinus and Freedom*, chapter 4.
27. DK 45 (Wheelwright, *Presocratics*, 7).
28. DK 115.
29. Cilento, *Saggi*, 35.
30. Regarding the Platonic references in chapter 2 of this treatise, see Armstrong's translation in the Loeb edition, 144–146 nn1–3 & 146 n1.
31. Cilento, *Saggi*, 29–41 (especially page 35, for the history of this notion prior to Plotinus).
32. Cilento, *Saggi*, 35.
33. Cilento, *Saggi*, 35.
34. Cilento, *Saggi*, 37 (also 31).
35. Peter Bertocci, "A Theistic Explanation of Evil," *The Challenge of Religion* (New York: Seabury Press 1982), 334–335.
36. Bertocci, "Theistic Explanation,", 336.
37. Rist, *Road to Reality*, 208.
38. Rist, *Road to Reality*, 208.
39. Rist, "Neoplatonic Faith," *Road to Realty*, 231–246.
40. *Enneads* IV.4.30, 4–5. See 225 n3 in Armstrong's translation (Loeb Classical Library edition) for historical details and sources.
41. *Enneads* IV.4.32, 5–8; see also Plato, *Timaeus*.
42. See the discussion of this topic in Rist, "Prayer" *Road to Reality*, 199–212.
43. P. Bertocci, "The Person God Is," *The Challenge of Religion*, 56–57.
44. The expression *agaidai* seems to allow this translation, although the primary meaning of this term is connected with wonder or admiration: *aga* has 'reverence' as one of its possible meanings.
45. "Some interpretations of AGAPE and EROS," *The Philosophy and Theology of Anders Nygren*, ed. Charles W. Kegley (Carbondale: Southern Illinois University Press, 1970), 160.

46. Plotinus here tells the tale of tough, well-trained boys who are "inferior in soul" to those they beat in a match, and whom they then rob of "their food and their dainty clothes". He asks: "is this anything but a joke?" It is the "good boys" fault that they allowed themselves to become weak and soft, through laziness. It is right not to interfere.

THE NOTION OF BEAUTY IN THE STRUCTURE OF THE UNIVERSE: PYTHAGOREAN INFLUENCES ON PLOTINUS

Aphrodite Alexandrakis

The aim of this paper is two-fold. First, I will attempt to set forth the aesthetic terms and principles involved in the Pythagorean theory of the construction of the universe. I shall discuss the two central Pythagorean concepts of harmony and symmetry and their relationship to beauty as well as to the Pythagorean mathematical model of the universe. This analysis will establish the importance of harmony and symmetry in the Pythagorean system. Secondly, I shall trace the Pythagorean influence on Plotinus' conception of the cosmos as a harmonious whole and his concern with World Harmony. On the basis of this discussion, I shall argue that the concept of beauty played a fundamental role in both the Pythagorean and the Plotinian models of the structure of the universe.

While it is true that the Pythagoreans did not pursue "aesthetics as an independent science,"[1] their interest in beauty is reflected in their study and analysis of aesthetic elements. The fact that they did not give a name to the study of aesthetic elements—such as harmony, rhythm, and symmetry—does not mean that they did not think of beauty as such. In fact, for the Pythagoreans harmony *is* beauty, and beauty arises from proportion (*symmetria*).[2]

I

The Pythagorean theory of the universe rests on the basic premise that the world is constructed mathematically. According to Aristotle, the Pythagoreans thought that the principles of mathematics were "the principles of all things."[3] They conceived of the universe as "a musical scale and a number." They arrived at their theory through a recognition of the numerical properties in all things.[4] Furthermore, they observed empirically that the properties and ratios of harmonious musical scales depend upon numbers.[5] The cosmic significance that the Pythagoreans attributed to number arose from their attempt to "discern cosmos within chaos."[6] The term *kosmos* (cosmos) suggests order and the main characteristic of order is measure. Measure leads to balance, which implies proportion (*symmetria*). The concepts of order and proportion are thus deeply aligned with the concept of harmony in the Pythagorean model of the universe.

In the Pythagorean system, the Cosmic structure was conceived as a sphere consisting of a central fire surrounded by Counterearth, Earth, Moon, Sun, the five planets, and "the outer sphere of the universe which carried the fixed stars."[7] According to this Philolaic structure, ten bodies are moving in ten orbits around the central fire.[8] According to Philolaus' *fragments*—which are the only direct sources of Pythagorean philosophy[9]—Pythagoras conceived of a universal harmony produced by the movements of the planets. In their movements the planets followed a geometric pattern, an astronomical order "conceived both geometrically and musically."[10] This structure is the basis for the doctrine of the *Music of the Spheres* in which, according to Aristotle,

> ...the movement of the stars produces a harmony, i.e. the sounds they make are concordant...[11]

And, as Plato says,

> ...as the eyes are framed for astronomy, so the ears are framed for the movements of harmony.[12]

The Pythagorean belief that "the whole heaven is harmony and number" is expressed by Philolaus:

> Since the principles or origins [*archai*], namely, those from which the world order was formed, the limited and unlimited in numbers, as the odd and even, were not similar nor of the same kind, it would have been improbable for them to be set in order, if there had not supervened a fitting together [*harmonia*]. It was necessary that they be fastened together by an *harmonia* such that by it they could be held together in order.[13]

As indicated in the above passage, the term *harmonia* has more than one definition. On the one hand, it means a 'fitting together;'[14] on the other hand, it describes a mathematical relation. For Pythagoras, according to Aristotle, "the attributes of numbers are present in a musical scale and in the heavens and in many other things."[15] In Pythagorean thought the notion that the universe consisted of numbers, and that numbers are tied up with harmony, is the foundation of the harmonic conception of the universe. The Pythagoreans observed a musical harmony in the stars and in their movement. This harmonic conception of the universe was connected to the musical scale which they referred to as an 'harmony.' Philolaus explains the intervals of the musical scale in terms of ratios: 1:2 [the octave]; 3:2 [the fifth]; and 4:3 [the fourth]. This proportional theory was based on the observation of vibrating strings. According to Philolaus, "these ratios are the fundamental principles of cosmic order."[16] Thus, harmony takes on a 'scientific' character. As a result, the Pythagorean cosmology was based on harmonic relationships contained in the Tetractys or the Decad—which represents the totality of mathematical order, for as Aristotle says: "It symbolizes the 'elements of number' which are the elements of all things."[17] The Tetractys has been described as the discovery

> of the chief musical intervals, the octave, fourth, and fifth, expressed as the numerical ratios 2:1, 4:3, 3:2, of the fact that the first four integers add up to ten, and that the diagonal of the square is incommensurable with its side.[18]

The Tetractys has been identified by Iamblicus with the cosmic harmony, and was called by Plutarch 'cosmos', 'Heaven' (*ouranos*), and 'All' (*pan*).[19] Thus, harmony brings together and puts in a certain order the 'mixed elements' of the universe. The Pythagorean principles of the limited and the unlimited are "combined by a harmonic process"[20] of a metaphysical nature. The result is an orderly, harmonious universe, founded on a structure of numbers. The Tetractys or Decad, was conceived as divine and perfect—"containing all things in itself"—and it was "the focus of a positively religious veneration."[21]

II

In addition to the concept of *harmony*, the concept of *symmetry* was of great importance to the Pythagoreans. Symmetry seems to be the result of the order which exists in the Pythagorean cosmos. Plato, whose

Pythagorean influence is apparent, confirms the importance of measure and symmetry in beauty.[22] He says:

> ...any compound, whatever it be, that does not by some means or other exhibit measure and proportion, is the ruin both of its ingredients and, first and foremost, of itself.[23]

As J. J. Pollit points out, order cannot be conceived without measure—"which involves both definition [marking the boundaries of things] and analysis of the interrelationships of discrete forms."[24] In fact, for Plato, "it is precisely by this effort they make to maintain the due measure that they achieve effectiveness and beauty in all that they produce."[25]

Plato's definition of order (*taxis*) is clearly rooted in the Pythagorean theory. For him, order refers to "how correctly is the object produced"[26] or, in other words, how correctly its parts are arranged.[27] Indeed, he goes even further to suggest that measure and beauty are identical.[28]

III

In contrast to Plato and the Pythagoreans, Plotinus *rejects* symmetry as a component of beauty.[29] Beauty, for Plotinus, is not found in the symmetrical parts of the object: The One is Beauty (*kallos*), and the One has no parts.[30] Plotinus' One stands for 'zero' (null), or what Scotus Eriugena calls 'Nothing'[31]—that is, the negation of multiplicity in the nature of the One. It is interesting, however, to note that in discussing the One's singular nature, Plotinus refers to the Pythagoreans: "...the Pythagoreans symbolically indicated it to each other by the name of 'Apollo'..."[32] The word '*Apollo*' derives from *a*- ['not'] and *pollon* ['of many']. Plotinus' comment indicates his knowledge of and interest in Pythagorean theory.

Plotinus prefers to use the concept of harmony rather than symmetry in his description of the universe. In his view, the universe consists of a rational principle out of which springs "the battle of conflicting elements."[33] He refers to the World Harmony as the result of 'adverse elements'—akin (syggene) and opposed (*enandia*). He compares the rational principle of the universe to the plot of a play: There is warfare (*polemos*) and strife (*machē*) in the world, just as there are conflicts in the play whose plot is one. When these conflicts are brought together into one *harmonia*, then the play is a harmonious whole. In music, as well, melody "results from the conflicting sounds." What Plotinus has in mind here is the Pythagorean combination of higher and lower sounds into an *harmonia*. He discusses how the high and low (*oxy kai vare*) sounds "come together into a unity into the melody itself..." (*syniasin eis en, ondes harmonias logoi*...).[34] The oneness of reason, or of the universe, is the result of the combining of different and opposite elements—such as "white-black, hot-cold, winged-wingless."[35] Like the Pythagoreans, Plotinus extends the notion of *harmonia* to its mystical significance. He refers to the person whose prayers do not reach the heavenly bodies directly but through and because of the presence of an *harmonia* which brings them together.[36] He further compares the World Harmony to the vibration which passes from one lyre to another in so far as *harmonia* exists.

IV

For the Pythagoreans, harmony is the core of mathematics, music, and their components: symmetry, order, and measure. Consequently, harmony is an aesthetic, scientific, metaphysical, and practical notion.[37] Although there is no use of the term 'beauty' in Pythagoras' theory, it is likely that the Pythagoreans "employed rather the term 'harmony' in place of beauty."[38] Hence, the scientific and religious "character of the Pythagorean movement is reflected in its aesthetics."[39]

Finally, according to Philolaus, it is the presence of *harmonia* which puts in order the causes (*archai*), that is, the principles of the limiting and the unlimited. As a result, harmony, or beauty, takes on a metaphysical aspect which Plato called the 'Idea of Beauty.' The order—the perfect structure and appearance of the planets and the heavenly bodies—results in beauty. Plotinus' notion of harmony, which acts as a 'peace-maker,' a complete serene whole, and a principle of measure, is of Pythagorean origin. He considers *harmonia* from the metaphysical and the aesthetic point of view. It is through *harmonia* that the 'akin' and 'opposing' elements return and unite in order to form the World Harmony. Similarly, the return to the One is the return to humanity's harmonious origin. Both Pythagorean and Plotinian thought are directed towards an ordered rational system: the Tetractys and the One. The Tetractys is a complete, harmonic whole, but it consists of parts. Plotinus' One is a complete, harmonious whole, without parts. The One is Beauty. The One is the principle of measure itself.[40] The One is Harmony.

Barry University

NOTES

1. W. Tatarkiewicz, *History of Aesthetics* I (Paris: Mouton, 1970), 80.
2. H. Diels, *Fragmenta* 40a3 (Galen, *De Placitis Hippocratis et Platonis* 5, ed., Muller, 425).
3. *Metaphysics* 985b26; 968a1–2; 1080b19; 1090a21–23.
4. *Metaphysics* 1.5, 955b23–35 & 986a1–3.
5. *Metaphysics* 1090a23–24.
6. J. J. Pollitt, *The Ancient View of Greek Art* (Yale University Press, 1974), 16.
7. D. R. Dicks, *Early Greek Astronomy* (Cornell University Press, 1970), 66.
8. Dicks, 68.
9. C. H. Kahn, *Pythagorean Philosophy Before Plato: The Presocratics*, ed. A. P. Mourelatos (Anchor books, 1974), 172.
10. P. Wheelright, ed., *The Presocratics* (New York: Odyssey Press, 1966), 208.
11. Aristotle, *De Caelo* II.9, 290b12.
12. *Republic* 530b.
13. Quoted in W. Burkert, *Lore and Science in Ancient Pythagorianism*, translated by E. L. Minar (Cambridge, MA: Harvard University Press, 1922), 'Philolaus' b6.
14. G. S. Kirk, *Heraclitus* (Cambridge University Press, 1954), 43–44. The noun appears in Homer in reference to concrete fittings-together.
15. *Metaphysics* 1090a23–24.
16. Kahn, 177.
17. F. M. Cornford, *Mysticism and Science in the Pythagorean Tradition*, ed. Mourelatos, 147.
18. Dicks, 65.
19. Cornford, 147.
20. E. A. Lippman, *Musical Thought in Ancient Greece* (Columbia University Press, 1964), 14.
21. A. H. Armstrong, *Plotinus* (Cambridge University Press, 1964), 14.
22. In *Philebus* 55e, 64d, and 65d, Plato refers to measure (μέτρον). In the *Politicus* 283d, he refers to measure, and measurement (μετρίτικη), as "length and shortness, excess and deficiency in general."
23. *Philebus* 64e.
24. Pollitt, 15.
25. *Politicus* 284b.
26. *Laws* 669b.
27. In *Laws* (669), Plato's requirements for a work of art are: symmetry, order, and harmony (the correct shapes and colors).

28. *Philebus* 64e; *Politicus* 284a-b.
29. For Plotinus' refutation of symmetry, see J. Anton "Plotinus' Refutation of Beauty as Symmetry," *Journal of Aesthetics and Art Criticism* 23 (1964–1965).
30. *Ennead* I.5.6.
31. Inge, *The Philosophy of Plotinus* (London: Longmans, Green and Co., 1929), 107–108.
32. *Ennead* V.5.6.
33. *Ennead* III.2.16.
34. *Ennead* III.2.16.
35. *Ennead* III.2.16.
36. *Ennead* VI.4.41.
37. The tuning of an instrument.
38. Tatarkiewicz, 80.
39. H. Diels, *Fragmenta* 40A3 (Galen, *de Placitis Hippocratis et Platonis* 5, ed. Muller, 425).
40. Armstrong, 26.

THE ONE: SUBSTANCE OR FUNCTION?

Reiner Schürmann

When metaphysicians speak of a supreme being, they call it 'the Good,' 'the Beautiful,' 'Truth,' or 'the One.' Each of these epithets results from a definite human experience, leading to a specific cognitive interest under which that being is considered. It appears as the Good insofar as man's desire for irrevocable possession finds rest in it.[1] It appears as the Beautiful since it orders all things into a cosmos, an order that can be mastered by reason.[2] It is the Truth, for it is known by the mind's return upon itself.[3] Each of these three points of view thus corresponds to a given human interest: appropriation, domination, and reflection. But in virtue of what interest, what intellectual temperament, do metaphysicians call the supreme being 'the One'? I wish to suggest that the *one* (*to on*), at least according to a few decisive texts by Plotinus, is not primarily to be understood as a predicate of the supreme being, nor of any being. If *metaphysics* is the doctrine of the nature of things and of their ultimate grounding, then a discourse about the One, *henology*, has overcome metaphysics. If the One is not the supreme noumenon, its 'nature' will have to be discovered in the way it functions among phenomena. It will be 'the First' only as the ordering factor of beings and their constellations. It will not function as ground—neither of things, nor of our knowledge of them.

1. Negative Henology versus Negative Theology

The One is not a being, not something. This is clearly implied in the first lines of Plotinus' treatise 'On the One': "It is due to the One that all beings are beings."[4] Why can the One not be called 'something,' a being? "The One is in all respects the First, but mind, as well as the ideas *and being* are not first."[5] The derivative status of *being* is a consequence of its chief quality, intelligibility. All that there is, all that exists, can be understood. But the One is beyond the reach of intellection. Hence it is not a being. Conversely, *being* is secondary since it is of the same order as mind (*nous*) and the ideas.

Plotinus' denial of knowability and being in the One amounts to turning Plato against himself. With Plato, he holds that *to be* is to be intelligible. But against Plato, he discovers that when we speak of things intelligible we always speak of things manifold, be it only of the duality of knower and known. And what is manifold, what implies otherness, cannot be the First. Mind and Being are derivative because they are intrinsically manifold. This is why, in the Plotinian universe, no being can claim ultimacy. Thus, if it is due to the One that all beings are beings, the One is not itself to be found among them. It is 'non-being.'[6] Here, then, the phrase 'supreme being' would be a contradiction in terms.

It may be all too rash to read the statements quoted, and others like them, as a negative discourse about a divine First—as negative theology. Such is the received opinion about the Neoplatonists: Since the One ranks beyond mind and being, it is 'higher' than these. Its simplicity makes it unknowable to us, but also supreme. The distinction between the One and intelligible Being has led to a few equations for which one would find ample support in the Neoplatonist corpus, both Christian and non-Christian: To be one is to be *inconceivably* actual, spiritual, changeless, powerful, causative, eternal. Thus the One remains something after all. Only, according to what could be called a metaphysics of radical transcendence, it is beyond our reach—being beyond Being, mind beyond mind, cause beyond cause. Despite its apophatism, the discourse of this so-called emanationist metaphysics remains squarely onto-theological, a discourse about being 'as such' which seeks its legitimation in 'a' being that is supreme and divine, although beyond our grasp.

By his distinction between the One and *being*, Plotinus disrupts onto-theology understood in this fashion. He retrieves a characteristic of *being* that has been lost under the predominance of onto-theology since Plato. The English participle 'being', just as the Greek '*on*' (*one*), contains an ambiguity. A participle is that grammatical form which 'participates' in both noun and verb. *On*, or the archaic *eon*, is an essentially equivocal concept. About this equivocity, Heidegger writes: "*On* says 'being' in the sense of *to be* a being; at the same time it names *a being* which is. In the duality of the participial significance of *on* the distinction between 'to be' and 'a being' lies concealed."[7] In Plotinus, it is clear that *on* is a noun. But as such it is precisely derivative. As 'a being' it is not the First. Heidegger thinks that the 'verb' connotation of the participle *on* has been obscured since Plato by the identification between nominal *on* and the supreme being.

The distinction between One and *being* in Plotinus makes it impossible to reduce the First to nominal being—substance (*ousia*), as he also says.[8] The *on* assuredly is God (*theos*)[9] for him. But Plotinus' onto-theology is his penultimate word, so to speak. It is not his last word. It has to be distinguished from his henology as the second hypostasis, *Noūs* (Intellect, Mind), is from the first hypostasis, *Hen* (the One). Plotinus has seen that any onto-theological discourse about the One necessarily commits the metaphysical fallacy of treating what is First as a being; or what is ultimate, as a substance.

Against the Platonic and Aristotelian metaphysics of form, Plotinus holds that it is *not* due to their substantial form that all beings are beings: "It is due to the One that all beings are beings." The metaphysical difference in both Plato and Aristotle between *substance* (whether divine or sensible) and *being* is displaced in Plotinus. He conceives a henological difference between the *One* and *being*. Since the One is non-being—*mē on*—we had better speak of negative henology.[10] It has to be 'negative' since *logos* constitutes the thresholds between the hypostases and is for that very reason subsequent to the One. In negative henology, the ontological difference is between One and *being*, or between *non*-being and *being*.

2. Metaphysical and Henological Difference

Negative henology achieves what negative theology can never achieve, namely, an understanding of the difference between *non*-being and *being* as the difference between the verbal and the nominal participle—between 'to be' and 'a being.' The One differs from Mind as a process or an event differs from the noun. Plotinus himself never equates *to hen* with *to einai*. In a later Neoplatonist, however, we read these lines:

> The One that is beyond substance (*ousia*) and beyond being (*ontos*) is neither being, nor substance, nor act, but rather it acts and is itself pure acting, so that it is itself 'the to be' (*to einai*), that which is prior to being (*ontos*).

The editor of this striking text first attributed it to Porphyry, and later to the 'Anonymous of Turino.'[11] The One here is not only called 'pure acting' and is thereby desubstantialized, but it is also identified with the verb 'to be.' Here the ontological difference between the first and the second hypostases is clearly expressed as the difference between 'to be' and 'a being'; between the indeterminate or pure 'is' and the determinate sum of all beings; between the verbal and the nominal participle.

This desubstantialized notion of the One designates no transcendent reality—no thing—and in that sense, nothing. The 'verbal' understanding of the One is also irreducible to the later Scholastic notions of *ipsum esse subsistens* and *actus essendi*. Although these notions rehabilitate the infinitive in the ontological discourse, the verb there serves to express the principle of intelligibility, which is the Neoplatonic *second* hypostasis.

We thus have to distinguish between two versions of the ontological difference. Because of the sweeping influence that Aristotle's *Physics*—"the hidden foundational book of Western philosophy"[12]—has had over the tradition, the terms of the ontological difference have remained confined to problems connected with fabrication. Metaphysicians have not 'forgotten' the ontological difference, but, at least within the Aristotelian tradition, it has remained a physicalist difference. Its discovery was altogether linked to the question of technique: How to produce a universal *being* or form (*eidos*) in individual matter. Thus the terms of the historically predominant concept of difference have been: *ousia* and *on*, *entitas* and *ens*, or, in Heidegger's language, *die Seiendheit* ('beingness') and *das Seiende* ('beings'). This is the *metaphysical* difference. It has imposed itself upon reflection through the observation of physical change. For Plotinus, it constitutes the realm of mind. "The first substance," that is, Mind (*Noūs*), he writes, "has all things and is all things."[13] With the physicalist-metaphysical difference, we are in the realm of onto-theology: the substantiality of things—*ousia*—is treated as an entity, as the hypostatic mind, as a God.

Both Plotinus and Heidegger take a step backwards from this metaphysical difference between substantiality and things to the 'One' or to 'being' understood verbally. What appears with this step can be called the *phenomenological* difference, which is of another kind than the metaphysical difference between a thing and its substantiality. The phenomenological difference secures no transcendent most-real ground; it amounts only to a transcendental condition for the appearance of phenomena. Plotinus' henological difference between the One and substantial *being* shares, as we shall see, the chief feature of Heidegger's phenomenological difference between *to-be* and substantial *being*, namely, the character of event. These separate steps, 1) from *ousia*, or 'beingness,' to *einai*, or 'to be,' and 2) from *on* or *onta* ('beings') to *ousia* ('beingness') are heterogeneous. Their heterogeneity is completely lost when the One is called *hyper-on*, 'a being beyond being,' as in later Neoplatonists.

One of the most revealing treatments of the relation between the One and *being* is found in Plotinus' commentary on Plato's *Parmenides*. Plotinus there equates each of Plato's hypotheses with one of the three hypostases. The first hypothesis[14] is, 'the One is one.' In Plotinus, it is said to correspond to absolute unity, the primordial One.[15] 'The One is one' amounts to saying that we cannot speak of it because we cannot treat it as an entity. On the other hand, the proposition, 'the One is,' which corresponds to the hypostatic Mind, expresses a unity of many entities.

> Whatever has existence and *is*, is by that fact determined numerically...[In the second hypostasis] this multiplicity is seized as a unity; to be utter multiplicity is denied of it, it is unit-multiple. Therefore it ranks below the One, since it possesses multiplicity.[16]

The Mind is the unity of all intelligibles, the first substance, and as such the beingness of all beings. The argument for breaking up the identification between the One and the supreme being rests not on the distinction between the universal and the particular, but on that between unity and multiplicity. *Ousia* or 'beingness' is a derived unity because it comprises multiplicity. Consequently, substantial *being* cannot in any way be predicated of the One.

The full ontological difference, embracing both the metaphysical ground and the phenomenological condition of possibility, thus unites three terms. In Plotinus they are 'beings, substance, One.' In his fourth century disciple, they are 'beings, substance, to-be.' In Heidegger they receive several descriptions: 'beings, beingness, to-be' or 'things present, their presence, presencing' (*das Anwesende, die Anwesenheit, das Anwesen*), or 'things manifest, their manifestness, manifestation' (*das Offenbare, die Offenbarkeit, das Offenbaren*).[17] In each of these descriptions, the third term is a verb: to be, to presence, to manifest.

To point out these parallels concerning the ontological difference in Plotinus and Heidegger is not to claim that the former was a phenomenologist of *being* or that the latter was a negative henologist. Heidegger wanted to convey the impression that he was barely acquainted with the *Enneads*.[18] But his understanding of the ontological difference, uniting three heterogeneous terms, is helpful in showing how negative henology overcomes metaphysics insofar as metaphysics is conceived as the quest for a most-real ground on which knowledge can find certitude—and life, peace. It is the verbal sense of *on* which shows all substantive notions of the First to be derivative. The verbal participle *on*, Heidegger writes, obviously echoing Plotinus, "indicates what is purely and simply singular, what in its unity is unique and, as unique, is the unifying One before all number."[19]

3. The 'One' as Event

The One, both as no-thing (*mē on*) and as the to-be (*to einai*) is best described as event. It repels any notion of substantiality; hence we cannot say that it does something, that it acts. Unifying is not its act in the sense that thinking and speaking are the acts of a human substance or agent. And yet, the One is what unifies each thing as well as each order of things: "Deprived of unity, a thing ceases to be what it is called: no army, unless a unity. A chorus, a flock must be one thing. Even house and ship demand unity, one house, one ship; unity gone, neither remains."[20] Unification is not the act of the One, but the One *is* altogether unification; *hen* is *henōsis*.[21] Plotinus never calls the One a hypostasis. The example of the army in movement, borrowed from Aristotle, illustrates his concept of the One as pure function. An *archē*, principle, is nothing in itself, it is mere ordering—"like a rout in battle," Aristotle writes, "stopped by first one man making a stand and then another, until the original formation has been restored."[22] It is through this line of argument that we have to understand the One. Plotinus calls it 'the principle of being' (*archē ontos*).[23] As a function, as the differentiating principle among things, "the First is present without any coming and, while it is nowhere, there is nothing where it is not."[24] This is to say, the One is the factor of coordination in all things without which all would disintegrate. It is their pure constellation, uniting bricks into a house, soldiers into an army, cities into an empire. But far from being the epitome of power, as the modality of phenomenal interaction it is most inconspicuous.

Here again, the alliance between metaphysical apophatism and onto-theology obscures the phenomenological discovery contained in negative henology. This discovery can now be stated in a paraphrase of the initial quote from the *Enneads*: It is due to unification—to their entrance into an order of interconnectedness—that all beings are beings. In negative theology, on the contrary, we hear that the One is the supreme being, of which we do not know *what* it is, although we know *that* it is. But if the One as *henōsis* is a resurgence of the verb-connotation of the participle, then we can think, although not know, what it is—we can think its nature:

It is the very movement of *nasci*, or *phyein*, of coming-to-presence, in all that there is. It is the *phainesthai*, the appearance as such, in all phenomena. It is their origin in the sense of pure *oriri*, showing-forth. These verbs, *nasci*, *phyein*, *phainesthai*, *oriri*—and although the two Greek ones are not central to the Plotinian terminology—indicate never-the-less how the One is an event. It is the event by which any phenomenon whatsoever enters into a constellation, an economy of presence. These terms also indicate how we have to understand the apophatic negations in Plotinus: the One has no 'form', he says, no 'substance', no 'this' (*tode ti*), and "even this name, the One, contains no more than the negation of plurality." To speak of it, he adds, it might be more appropriate to use "the symbol Apollo," composed of the privative '*a*-' and '*pollōn*' ('of many'). All these negations are meant to discourage us from conceiving the One as position, as *thesis*.[25] They should also discourage us from conceiving it as simply a more intense mode of *being* than anything we experience phenomenally.

The difficulty in understanding the radically non-metaphysical notion of the One stems primarily from the difficulty of separating it from causal representations. The One assigns all things their locus, their site, in a given economy of presence. It does so, however, not as a demiurge (and even less as a creator), but as a principle, *archē*—this term understood as the mere function by which things present enter into commerce, as the coming about of their mutual rapport. It is true that in Neoplatonism causality is exclusively 'descending.' There is no ascending efficacy of sensible things upon intelligible things. But how can the One be called a cause? "It is cause of the cause" which is the Mind. It gives the second hypostasis (*Noūs*) its orientation so that the Mind's causality is actively unifying. But the One is not active, no more than a geometrical law is active when three lines enter into a certain relation so as to form a triangle. The Mind, the active fullness of reality, is thus immediately unified, but is only mediately unifying. According to received imagery, the One imparts an 'upward' direction to all causes, the *epistrophē* or return. It also imparts to them a 'downward' direction, the *proodos*, or process. It orders substance back to its source and ahead towards appearance. Only as this directionality of substance can the One be called "what is most causative and the true cause."[26]

For this entire set of premises—the One as factor of unification; as denoted by the verb 'being' and not as supreme entity denoted by the noun 'being'; as directionality of phenomena and not as their efficient cause—I find no better term than Heidegger's notion of *Ereignis*, 'event of appropriation.[27] Again, I am not claiming that it is from Plotinus's *hen* or *henōsis* that Heidegger has worked out this concept, nor am I saying in this context that Plotinus sheds light on the later Heidegger (although that would be a consequence of my claim). Rather, my point is that the later Heidegger is useful for understanding Plotinus. Indeed, one can identify a line of authors whose thinking has remained on the margins of metaphysics precisely because they attempted to retrieve a 'verbal,' non-substantialist, understanding of being. This line would go from Plotinus' 'unification' to Meister Eckhart's 'ground,' to Schelling's 'longing' in all beings to break out of darkness into manifestation, to Heidegger's *Ereignis*.

The 'firstness' of the One remains incomprehensible in terms of efficient, formal, final or material causality.[28] The One can be called the universal 'cause' only insofar as it imposes the directionality of process and return upon all things intelligible and sensible. Since the entire vocabulary of cause is inadequate for an account of the One, negative henology revealed itself to be irreducible to negative theology. Moreover, the difference between the One and *being* is irreducible to the metaphysical difference. The One *is* the directionality of all things. As such, it is primordial time.

4. Primordial Time

Does the notion of *Ereignis* allow one to raise the question—heretical within the tradition of Neoplatonism—of the temporality of the One? Before seeing how far one can go in temporalizing the One, it may be useful to recall briefly the three decisive moments in the Western philosophies of time. We will then be able to place henology within that framework.

The first of these moments results from the chief experience that strikes the Greek mind in the classical age, namely, the experience of change effected by man. Substantial motion as it occurs in sculpting, building, and so forth, received its theory in Aristotle's *Physics*. Correspondingly, the classical notion of time has to do with movement: "Time is the number of movement according to a before and an after."[29] Without motion no time could be represented. Only through the sequence of individual moments in becoming do we reach concepts such as 'before' and 'after.' Even if the soul experiences such a movement in its own life, this concept of time is worked out from the phenomenal domain of material transformation. In Heidegger's words, "the Aristotelian interpretation of motion was the most difficult task for thinking in the entire history of Western metaphysics."[30] Since this classical concept of time is derived from physical change, time cannot occur outside the world of sensible substances.

The second moment is one of interiorization. It is most evident in Augustine. To be sure, Augustine knows the concept of time that arises from the observation of change. Following Aristotle, he expresses this as numbering the 'mutations' of forms in matter.[31] But with Augustine the locus of our experience of time shifts from manual production to the life of the mind. The soul itself appears to him as stretched out between past and future: "It seemed to me that time is nothing else than extendedness; but of what sort of thing, I do not know; and it would be surprising if it were not an extendedness of the mind itself." In much the same fashion as Aristotle's physicalist concept of time, this mentalist notion, too, applies only to the earthly world of change. Eternity is entirely beyond time. In eternity there is no alteration. Change is the essence of time,[32] which is therefore not simple: "Time is threefold, namely the present of things past, the present of things present, and the present of things to come."[33]

The third moment in this history of Western thinking about time is Heidegger's discovery of ecstatic temporality. This notion can, in a way, still be viewed as an offspring of the Augustinian *distentio animi*.[34] However, it breaks with that entire tradition in the following ways: The ecstases by which human existence 'steps out of itself' into past, present and future replace the representation of a linear time-flux; the preeminence of the future replaces the traditional primacy of the present; and the three co-originary, 'equiprimordial,' dimensions of time replace the construction of past and future as prolongations of the present. In the metaphysical tradition up to and including Husserl, these elements—the *linear* sequence of 'now-moments,' the origination of the stream from the *present*, and the genesis of past and future by acts akin to *protention* and *retention*—form a system.

To these historical points of juncture two more must be added, both of which occur in the development of Heidegger's writings. He described the first of these breaks as the transition from time as 'the sense of being' to time as the history of 'the truth of being.'[35] This break constitutes what he called 'the turning' in his thinking. It results from the discovery that being-in-the-world is not the neutral structure it appears to be in *Being and Time*, but that it has itself a history, which Heidegger calls the 'history of being.' There are the Greek, Roman, Medieval, modern and contemporary modes of being-in-the-world. Thus ecstatic temporality turns into epochal temporality. The continuity with the existential analytic is nonetheless striking. An epoch, a sudden instauration of a constellation of presencing and absencing, in *alētheia* (truth), unites the three dimensions of time in a *non-linear* upsurge of a phenomenal arrangement that will hold for awhile. Furthermore, since it is the advent of such a new arrangement of things, the epoch is *future*-directed. Lastly, as the phenomenal origin of past, present and future, the epoch unites these dimensions *equiprimordially*. Thus from ecstatic to epochal temporality the basic features in Heidegger's new understanding of time remain preserved, although they become historicized.

The other break is described by Heidegger as the transition from 'the truth of being' to 'the topology of being.'[36] With this last stage in the reflection about time the primordial condition of all previous notions has been reached. Time here is the 'sense' of *being* inasmuch as *being* 'assigns' to all phenomena their site or their place in any given constellation of presencing and absencing. Such assigning must not be misconstrued as referring to any mythical agency. It is nothing but the entrance of beings into an order. This entrance, for which Heidegger also has recourse to such traditional terms as *phyein*, coming-forth, and *phainesthai*, appearing, is what the term *Ereignis* is meant to capture. It may indeed be most suitably translated as 'event of appropriation'; but there is no agent, human or otherwise, who appropriates things, who makes them his own. Nor does the 'proper' (*eigen*) suggest a metaphysic of full presence. Rather it points to the way things belong to one another in any given order, the movement by which they enter into mutual propinquity. Quite as in ecstatic and epochal temporality, it is the *Sinn* as directionality ('sense', not 'meaning') that is at stake here. The directionality of time is, however, no longer understood in relation to either man or history, but merely in relation to presence and absence. It is understood as the emergence from absence into presence.

It should be clear in what way the last phase of Heidegger's thinking remains indebted to the transcendental tradition. Time as 'event' makes possible ecstatic as well as epochal temporality.[37] However, in Heidegger, transcendentalism is divorced from the typically modern preoccupation with subjectivity. The event is primordial time, operative 'always already' in lived time and rendering possible all transmitted concepts of time, be they physicalist or mentalist.

5. Time as 'Bad Eternity'

How does Plotinus fit into this history of the concept of time? At first sight his place is obvious. It is indeed from Plotinus (*via* Porphyry) that Augustine learned to understand time in relation to the soul rather than to physical motion. On the soul's *distentio* (extension) into past, present and future, Augustine merely repeats Plotinus. After having rejected all previous definitions of time, particularly the Aristotelian one, Plotinus gives this one as his own:

> It is the extendedness (*diastasis*) of life that takes time, and the ceaseless forward movement of life takes ever new time, quite as life past took past time. Would it then not be sound to define time as the life-process of the soul in movement as it passes from one state of life into another?[38]

Plotinus rejects all time concepts derived from spatial representations, that is, time as identified with either a thing moved (Pythagoras), movement (Plato), or some quality of movement (Aristotle). To understand time in terms of itself, he turns inward—a displacement that presages not only Augustine, but Kant as well. Time, then, is the life of the soul. This definition also rejects Plato's theory of time as the product of the demiurge: "It is the soul that made time."[39] As the soul's life, time is 'prior' to the sensible world. Without time there would be no such world. For the classical tradition, on the contrary, there would be no time without the world. The soul, according to Plotinus, temporalizes[40] itself and thus the world. This is a new way of thinking that he states with some apology to his predecessors: "Possibly these [previous] thinkers did not yet theorize in this reversed fashion, and possibly we simply do not understand them."[41] The apparently obvious place of Plotinus in the history of the concept of time is the moment of its interiorization.

But what exactly is his 'reversed fashion' of thinking? Time "is something upon the soul, inherent in it, quite as eternity is to the [intellectual] realm above."[42] His new way of thinking can be stated in the proportionality:

time : soul :: eternity : mind.

It is the relation between time and eternity that separates Plotinus not only from the authors of early Antiquity but also from those in late Antiquity. His new way of thinking consists in understanding time out of eternity. In a strictly parallel way, because the soul can only be known once the mind is known, he can define time as the life of the soul. This definition is thus not originary. It depends on the more fundamental premise enunciated in the proportionality above. His new way of thinking requires an examination of the *model* of time in the second hypostasis, the Mind. This model is eternity. However, it too is derivative. The new way of thinking, then, cannot stop short of the question, What is the model of eternity, in the One itself? It cannot stop short of the question of primordial time.

The Plotinian 'method' consists in always following a descending *hodos*, or path, of explanation. There can be no action of the sensible upon the intelligible within such an outlook. It is for this general methodological reason that inwardness cannot be Plotinus' last word about time. He does not conceive of time in relation to sense experience at all, be it located in the inner or the outer sense. It is true that his inquiry—as opposed to his explanation—proceeds from the exterior to the interior to the superior, but this itinerary does not properly constitute an ascent. He retains only the heuristic function of *anagogē*, at least as far as the issue of time is concerned.[43] Thus he describes how a perceived outward movement of becoming, for instance in animal life, *reveals* the inward movement of psychic life, time; the life of the soul in turn *reveals* the life of the mind, eternity. In this regress of upward discovery it is clear that the One can be neither in time nor in eternity. It is the direct source of eternity and the indirect source of time. In keeping with the understanding, established earlier, of *to hen* as *to einai*—of the One as 'the to be'—the issue of primordial time can now be formulated in another proportionality:

the One : Mind : Soul :: 'to-be' : being : becoming :: X : eternity : time.

How are we to describe this unknown 'X'?

We may learn something about this unknown principle of eternity and time if we look at the way in which eternity mediates between the One and the life of the soul. Every mediating term must participate in the two terms that it connects, otherwise there would be no mediation. More specifically, the mediating hypostasis must have two *logoi*; it must be two-sided, turned both toward the hypostasis from which it proceeds and toward that which proceeds from it. Thus Proclus will later say: From the point of view of the One, the ideas are 'henads,' but from the point of view of the many, they are 'monads.' Furthermore, given the general framework of participation by deficient similitude, the lower degrees of *being*, the images, manifest the higher ones, the models. Plotinus must therefore distinguish two aspects of eternity as both image of the One and model of time. "*Everlastingness* is the state pertaining to the substrate that stems from it and inheres in it; *eternity*, on the other hand, is the substrate [itself], together with the state which carries it into manifestation." As the image of the One, eternity is a *hypokeimenon* (substrate), even a god. But as the model of time, it is a *katastasis* (state), of that substrate; it is a world. "Eternity is a god; he manifests himself, shows himself in his essence, namely the to-be without jolt or change, and therefore as also the firmly living."[44] If everlastingness is "that state which carries [eternity] into manifestation," then eternity *appears* as everlastingness, as unvarying duration. Christian followers of Plotinus will conclude from this distinction between the essence of eternity and its appearance that everlastingness is only an inadequate analogy of the 'standing now' in which 'all is simultaneous.' In its appearance, eternity both manifests and obscures itself.

Something is lost, then, when we call eternity the model of time. Such an inductive proposition is incommensurate with the second hypostasis because the measure of eternity is the One. The commensurate way of thinking about eternity would have to be deductive. It would be more commensurate with the nature of time to call it the image of eternity. Any phenomenon is correctly understood only when it is placed in the light of the degree above it—which is the reason why there can be no knowledge of the One. Such is Plotinus' reversed way of thinking.[45] Due to the merely heuristic function of anagogical reasoning, the treatise on eternity amounts to a negative treatise on the One. "Eternity is around the One."[46] The ascending order of discovery—as opposed to the descending order of foundation—is spelled out clearly when Plotinus says:

> It is now appropriate to state what *time* really is. To this end we must go back to the state we affirmed of *eternity*, unwavering life, undivided totality, limitless, knowing no divagation, at rest in the *One* and intent upon it.[47]

From time to eternity to the One, what is the primordial condition of all derivative concepts of time that we reach?

6. Being as Time[48]

We saw that each of the traditional metaphysical attributes of the absolute—the Good, the Beautiful, Truth—originates in a specific human experience. In Plotinus it is a general axiom that we can only philosophize about what we also 'touch,' that is, experience: "What understanding would succeed failing some point of contact? And what contact could there be with the utterly alien?"[49] We are indeed in contact with each of the hypostases: Through the experience of want, we are in contact with that of soul and time;[50] through the experience of intellectual intuition, with that of Mind and eternity;[51] through the experience of "going forth from the self (*ekstasis*), simplifying oneself (*haplōsis*), renouncing (*epidōsis*), reaching towards contact and resting (*stasis*),"[52] with the One and primordial time.

This description of the way we are in touch with the One may sound like moral discourse. There is indeed a Plotinian imperative: *Become restful.* But such an injunction is possible only because we are already in touch with the One ontologically. The One does what man does when he is 'wise,' when he follows his nature and "lets all things be what they are."[53] Unification and simplification in Plotinus thus constitute essential traits both of man and of the One. Likewise, in Heidegger, *Gelassenheit*, 'releasement,' constitutes the essential trait not only of man when he becomes thoughtful, but more basically of *being* as an event. Even though Heidegger seems to wish to connect his 'letting' with the verb *parechein*, 'to offer, to make possible, to exhibit'[54] rather than with *eaein*, this identity of man's way of living and *being*'s way of presencing seems to me one indisputably common element between Plotinus and Heidegger. The One is no thing, no hypostasis, but sheer process—*eaein, einai, henōsis*.[55] Likewise Heidegger's 'being' is no-thing,[56] but a process, 'letting-be.'[57] Man's life-process is formally identical with the being-process, be this called 'unification' or 'letting-be.'[58]

Two key terms in Plotinus point to the One as event of appropriation, which is to say, as primordial time. These are *dynamis* and *archē*. The One is "the potential (*dynamis*) towards all things."[59] As such, it lets all things emerge from itself without suffering any diminution. Such letting-appear (a wholly unAristotelian notion of *dynamis*) occurs neither in time nor in eternity; it is the condition of both. At least as far as Heidegger's topological understanding of *Ereignis* is concerned, his reach towards what ultimately conditions all phenomena is not unlike Plotinus' reach. The One as ultimate potential is that event by which phenomena are left to their *topoi*, to the place that is theirs in the universal order of presencing and absencing. As the 'potential towards all things,' it *differs* from all. It is neither one of them nor their sum total. 'Potency' thus must not be misunderstood as the power of a supreme being. It is the condition that enables all beings to appear; it is appearance as such. This phenomenological difference between appearance and the appearing in Plotinus is particularly evident when he warns us not to conceive of potency as a virtuality for things not yet existent: "It is not possible that anything else come into existence. There is nothing that did not come into existence when the all came about. [The One], however, never was the all."[60] As *dynamis*, the One is the movement by which the all becomes the 'uni-verse,' 'turned towards the One.' It is that sweeping *vertere*, turning, it is directedness as such.

As to *archē*, this term always refers to the One when used without qualification. It is frequently followed by a genitive: The One is "origin of process, origin of life, origin of the mind as well as of all things." As such it is something quite familiar to each of us: "We indicate it by virtue of what in ourselves is like it."[61] What is it in us that is like the *archē*? It is the fact that the body, the soul with its many layers, and the mind are integrated into one human being. It is humanity as a *principle of order* in us, as an ordering, that is like the One. The Greek *archē*, however, implies a motility that neither its Latin equivalents—*imperium, regimen, princeps, principium, primum*—nor the English 'principle' preserve. In the text quoted earlier from Aristotle, this motility was likened to a battle that is forming. When an army takes flight, the disarray does not stop because one or two soldiers regain courage. But suddenly all may take up their formation. Then the activities of each turn into the action of all. So it is that the One is a forming of order, absolutely. It is nothing but the entrance of many factors into a constellation, nothing but the emergence of such a constellation. If on the contrary *archē* designated some *being* that dominates—although we may not know the nature of its dominion—then the Neoplatonic discourse about the One would indeed amount to negative theology. But the origin as *archē* is nothing other than *archein*, beginning, *oriri*. The subject-matter of negative henology is not divine world-government but something rather more tenuous: the event of arising from absence into presence. This event is impossible to hypostatize or to deify. Nor can it occur either in time or in eternity. It is not possible to construe such an arising as the emptiest genus of all types of unification, sensible and intelligible. It is, rather, the condition (*dynamis*) of these types, their coming-about (*archein*) as such. The One as *archē* is the condition that makes possible all and any forms of time.

It should be clear in what sense this concept of the One as unifying factor in all phenomena, as unification, 'overcomes' metaphysics. To overcome it is not to reject it. Quite the contrary. As we saw, the metaphysical difference is integrated into henology as the step by which the mind transcends the visible. But the step by which, according to Plotinus, we can also transcend the intelligible is not metaphysical since it leads neither to the nature of substances nor to their ultimate ground. This second step of transcendence amounts to a 'working through'[62] of the hypostatic Mind, a working through of metaphysics. The possibility of going beyond substance arises from the very *dynamis* of the One itself, not from some human faculty. Only when the One is understood as an event can it be claimed that negative henology is an overcoming of metaphysics.

Is it not a very minimalist reading of Plotinus to interpret the One as unification? Is it not utter functionalism to so radically de-substantialize the One that it is best designated by a verb rather than a noun? What, then, are we to make of those best known and most puzzling texts in which Plotinus speaks of an experience that is quite personal and datable? The *Ereignis* in no way refers to some lived experience, some *Erlebnis*. Porphyry, on the other hand, tells us that his master "achieved the supreme goal four times during the period I passed with him, by no mere latent fitness but by the ineffable act."[63] The *Ereignis* is nothing that happens to human beings, rather a *singulare tantum*. How, then, can the One as mere factor of economical ordering inspire lines like these?

> Several times it has happened: awakening from the body to return to myself; leaving behind all things and becoming self-encentered; beholding a marvelous beauty; then, more than ever, assured of community with the loftiest order; enacting the noblest life, acquiring identity with the divine; stationing within it by having attained that activity; poised above all other intellectual beings: yet, there comes the moment of descent....[64]

In light of the imperative mentioned earlier, we can answer: Here Plotinus speaks of those rare moments when it was given to him to 'let' all things be quite as the One lets them all be. His experience would constitute the opposite of the original classical Greek experience as reflected in Aristotle's *Physics*—the experience of making, fabricating, mastering nature. Plotinus stands outside the prevailing tradition in the West because to all forms (including theological) of domination he opposes *henōsis*, the experiential side of which is 'letting-be.' Practical *Gelassenheit* is however only a consequence of the *Gelassenheit* which is primordial time.

In Heidegger the ultimate condition of all forms of time is called, as we saw, the 'event of appropriation.' However, he adds that *being*, understood in this way, is not an unobstructed object for thought. "We must never forget that expropriation (*Enteignis*) belongs essentially to appropriation (*Ereignis*)."[65] In Plotinian terms: We must never forget that the One as such is ineffable, that there can be no full manifestation of the One. It is part of its essence to hide itself from our thinking. Only as a consequence of this self-revealing, self-concealing nature of the One will any henology have to be essentially negative.

How, then, is the One primordial time? It is as the literally 'dynamic' identity of *being* and nothingness. After having described the transcendental step backwards from epochal temporality to primordial time, Heidegger adds: "The absence of [epochal] destiny from the event of appropriation thus does not mean that it lacks any 'motility'." The event is primordial time as "turning towards us in withdrawal."[66] In a comparable fashion, the One as *to einai*, 'the to-be,' renders itself absent as it renders itself present. While it remains wholly at rest, this interplay of presencing and absencing makes it the condition of all modalities of time.

What cognitive interest is operative when the absolute is called 'the One'? It may well be the attempt to understand *being* as time.

The New School of Social Research

NOTES

1. Cf. Plato, *The Republic* 358a, 571a, 580b.
2. Cf. Plato, *Philebus* 64e.
3. Cf. Augustine, *Confessions*, Book VII, chapters 10 & 16.
4. Plotinus, *Ennead* VI.9.1, 1.
5. *Ennead* VI.9.2, 30 (emphasis added).
6. *Ennead* VI.9.3, 39.
7. Martin Heidegger, *Holzwege* (Frankfurt, 1950), 317; translated by D. F. Krell and F. A. Capuzzi, *Early Greek Thinking* (New York, 1975), 32. About the duality contained in the participial form, Cf. M. Heidegger, *Was heisst Denken* (Tübingen, 1954), 133f.; translated by F. D. Wieck and J. G. Gray, *What is Called Thinking?* (New York, 1968), 220f.
8. Substance, *ousia*, is what is most intensely or authentically, *ontōs on*: *Ennead* VI.3.6, 1 & 30.
9. E.g. *Ennead* IV.7.8.(3), 12.
10. I borrow this term from Pierre Aubenque, "Plotin et le dēpassement de l'ontologie grecque classique," *Le Nēoplatonisme*, Editions du CNRS (Paris, 1971), 102.
11. Pierre Hadot, *Porphyre et Victorinus*, volume II (Paris, 1968), 104. For the change in attribution, see Pierre Hadot, "L'âtre et l'ētant dans le nēoplatonisme," *Etudes nēoplatoniciennes* (Neuchâtel, 1973), 30.

12. M. Heidegger, *Wegmarken* (Frankfurt, 1967), 312; translated by T. Sheehan, "On the Being and Conception of *Physis* in Aristotle's *Physics* B, 1," *Man and World* IX (1976), 224. Cf. M. Heidegger, *Der Satz vom Grund* (Pfullingen, 1957), 111.
13. *Ennead* I.8.2, 16 & 22.
14. Plato, *Parmenides* 142b.
15. *Ennead* V.1.8, 23–26.
16. *Ennead* VI.6.3, 1–7. For a commentary see Pierre Hadot, "L'Etre et l'étant dans le néoplatonisme," 29 & 32f.
17. Cf. *Zur Sache des Denkens* (Tübingen, 1969), 32; translated by J. Stambaugh, *On Time and Being* (New York, 1972), 30.
18. In conversation—to disantiate himself, it seemed—he said about Plotinus: "But is that not one of the Neoplatonists?"
19. Heidegger, *Holzwege* 318; Capuzzi, *Early Greek Thinking* 33; translation modified.
20. *Ennead* VI.9.1, 3–9.
21. Cf. *Ennead* VI.1.26, 27.
22. Aristotle, *Posterior Analytics* II.19, 100a11–13. See the commentary by Hans-Georg Gadamer, *Kleine Schriften*, volume I (Tübingen, 1967), 110.
23. *Ennead* VI.9.9, 1.
24. *Ennead* V.5.8, 23f.
25. *Ennead* V.5.6, 6s. & V.5.6, 26–31.
26. *Ennead* VI.8.18, 37.
27. Concerning the meanings of this word I have nothing to add to Henri Birault's enumeration: "Firstly, *das Ereignis* commonly signifies 'the event' or 'the happening.' Secondly, *das Ereignis* derives from the word *eigen*, which means 'own,' 'proper,' or 'properly.' From this sense stem, for instance, *die Eigenschaft*, 'property' in the sense of 'attribute,' and *das Eigentum*, 'property' in the sense of 'possession,' but also the now quite obsolete philosophical notion *die Eigentlichkeit*, 'authenticity.' Fourthly, *das Ereignis* refers to the old German verb *er-äugen*, which is construed from *das Auge*, 'the eye' or 'the glance'": *Heidegger et l'expérience de la pensée*' (Paris, 1978), 41.
28. The first three types of causality are frequently ascribed by Plotinus to the One. As to matter, it is said to paradoxically resemble the One: It is formless (*Ennead* I.8.8, 21 and II.5.4, 12), not-being (*Ennead* II.5.4, 11), boundless (*Ennead* I.8.3, 13), and mere potentiality (*Ennead* II.5.5, 5).
29. *Physics* IV.11, 220a24.
30. Heidegger, *Wegmarken*, 353; translated by Sheehan, "On the Being...," 255.
31. "Ipsa mutabilitas...in qua sentiri et dinumerari possunt tempora, quia rerum mutationibus fiunt tempora," *Confessions*, Book XII, chapter 8, 8.
32. Cf. *The City of God* XI, 6, and *On the Trinity* IV.18, 24. Plotinus, in his treatise on time, called eternity *adiastatōs*, non-extended, *Ennead* III.7.3, 15.
33. *Confessions* XI.26, 33 and XI.20, 26.

34. Heidegger cites *Physics* IV.14—"if there were no soul time would be impossible"—and *Confessions* XI.26, 33 as examples of the 'ordinary' time concept. He adds: "The interpretation of Dasein as temporality does not lie outside the horizon of the ordinary concept of time," *Sein und Zeit* (Tübingen, 1957), 427; translated by J. Macquarrie and E. Robinson, *Being and Time* (New York, 1962), 479f.
35. M. Heidegger, *Vier Seminare* (Frankfurt, 1977), 73.
36. Heidegger, *Seminare*, 73.
37. "The event always grants the time-span out of which history takes the while that guarantees an epoch," M. Heidegger, *Nietzsche*, volume II (Pfullingen, 1961), 490.
38. *Ennead* III.7.11, 42–46. I follow Hans Jonas, "Plotin über Ewigkeit und Zeit," in *Politische Ordnung und menschliche Existenz, Festgabe für Eric Voegelin* (Munich, 1962), 310f., in translating *zoē* as 'life-process' and *bios* as 'state of life.'
39. *Ennead* III.7.13, 47.
40. *Chronoun* (*Ennead* III.7.11, 30). According to H. R. Schwyzer, "Plotinos" in *Realencyklopädie der klassischen Altertumswissenschaft* XXI, 1 (525 n14), this verb is probably a neologism forged by Plotinus himself.
41. *Ennead* III.7.13, 13.
42. *Ennead* III.7.11, 64.
43. In the early treatises, however, there are several paraphrases of the ascent according to Plato's *Symposium*, e.g. *Ennead* I.6.7 & 8.
44. *Ennead* III.7.5, 16–22. My reading of the distinction between everlastingness (*aidiotes*), and eternity (*aion*), as the two *logoi* of the mediating hypostasis differs from that of H. Jonas, "Plotin über Ewigkert und Zeit," 297 n3, who admits of no difference in meaning between these two terms. The two-sidedness of eternity as a middle term, which I am trying to exhibit, provides the architectonic ground for the remark by Werner Beierwaltes—*Plotin: über Ewigkeit und Zeit* (Frankfurt, 1967), 156–158—for whom these terms are names of the same subject-matter, seen from two points of view. The later Latin authors make frequent use of the distinction between everlastingness and eternity, for instance as *sempiternitas mundi* and *aeternitas dei*. As to the substantivized verb *to einai* in this quote, it confirms my earlier distinction between negative henology and negative theology. Plotinus equates "the 'to-be'" with eternity, a god, the firmly living, that is, with the hypostatic mind. The same equation makes him speak of *to d'estin* (III.7.6, 18) and *esti monon* (III.7.3, 34), both of which refer to eternity.
45. "We begin with eternity, since when the stable exemplar is known, its representation in image which time is understood to be will be clearly apprehended. But it is of course true, admitting this relationship of time as image to eternity as the original, that if we chose to begin by identifying time we could thence proceed upwards by recollection (*anamnēsis*) and thus

become aware of [eternity]" (III.7.1, 21–24). Plotinus does not carry out this inductive, upwards reasoning.

46. *Peri to hen* (III.7.6, 2f.). Eternity is *kentro-eidēs*, it looks to the center of which it is the periphery.
47. *Ennead* III.7.10, 16–11 & 4.
48. "Thinking the most difficult thought of philosophy, means thinking being as time," M. Heidegger, *Nietzsche*, volume I, 28; translated by D. F. Krell, "Nietzsche," *The Will to Power as Art*, volume I (New York, 1979), 20.
49. *Ennead* III.7.7, 3f.
50. What is in time 'lacks' (*elleipein*: III.7.4, 15) being, 'attracts' it (*helkon to einai*: III.7.4, 30), it must constantly 'acquire' (*epiktasthai*: III.7.4, 20) being, 'strive' (*ephesei tini ousias*: III.7.4, 31) after it as after what is to come (*ephesis to mellontos*: III.7.4, 34). From phrases like these it appears that "for Plotinus the future is what is properly temporal about time, the mode of its temporalizing," H. Jonas, "Plotin über...," 298. Possessing their end is therefore not the lot of things sensible; the Aristotelian concept of *entelecheia* here does not apply to the sublunary world.
51. Eternity differs from time because there is no futurity, no net-yet in thinking: the act of *noesis* is identical with its object, the *noeton*. On the other hand, eternity also differs from the One, since noetic identity unites two terms: "The mind is number, but number and the like has its origin in the One. Further, the mind is together what thinks and what is thought, so that it is a duality" (*Ennead* III 8.9, 4f.).
52. *Ennead* VI.9.11, 23f.
53. *Eph' heauton eāsai einai*: *Ennead* V.5.12, 49.
54. Heidegger, *Wegmarken*, 136; translated by J. Barlow and F. M. Cornford, *Philosophy in the Twentieth Century*, ed. W. Barrett and H. D. Aikens, volume III (New York, 1962), 265.
55. It is thus impossible to distinguish between the One and unification as between a substance and its act. H. Jonas seems to intend this impossibility when he writes: "*relatedness to* the ground is itself the ground" ("Plotin über...," 304).
56. "What is entirely different from all beings is non-being; this 'nothing,' however, is the essence of being": Heidegger, *Wegmarken*, 101f.
57. Being is *Anwesen*-lassen (with the emphasis on '*lassen*'), '*letting*-presence': *Heidegger, Vier Seminare*, 103.
58. It is Meister Eckhart, mediating between Plotinus and Heidegger on this point, who is most explicit about the process-like identity between the essence of being and that of man; see the term *Ereignis* in the index of my *Meister Eckhart, Mystic and Philosopher* (Bloomington, 1978).
59. *Ennead* III.8.10, 1. This usage of *dynamis* is irreducible to that of Aristotle. When predicated of the One, Plotinus' concept of potentiality or potency is neither kinetic (potency as "the origin of movement or change": *Metaphysics* IV.12, 1019a15) nor hyletic ("matter is what exists potentially": *Metaphysics*

VIII.2, 1042b9). I take his usage in this context rather to be an excessive appropriation of Plato's, who writes: "As to potency, I solely consider to what it is related and what it effects." Plotinus' use here is excessive since for Plato there are many *dynamai*, "the strongest being knowledge" (*Republic* V, 477c-d). For Plotinus there can ultimately be only one *dynamis*, the One itself.

60. *Ennead* V5.12, 48f.
61. *Ennead* III.8.9, 39f. & 24.
62. Heidegger says *verwinden*, which is reminiscent of the Freudian *durcharbeiten*—working through suffering or a neurosis. "This *Verwinden* is similar to what happens when, in the human realm, one gets over grief or pain": *Die Technik und die Kehre* (Pfullingen, 1962), 38; translated by W. Lovitt, *The Question Concerning Technology* (New York, 1977), 39.
63. Porphyry, "Life of Plotinus," in *Plotinus: The Enneads*, 2nd edition, translated by Stephen MacKenna (New York, 1962), 17.
64. *Ennead* IV.8.1, 1–10.
65. Heidegger, *Zur Sache des Denkens*, 46; translated by Stambaugh, *On Time and Being*, 43. Expropriation is related to appropriation as *lēthē* to *alētheia*: Cf. *Zur Sache…*, 44; *Time and Being*, 41.
66. Heidegger, *Zur Sache…*, 44; *Time and Being*, 41.

PLOTINUS ON THE ORIGIN OF MATTER

William J. Carroll

Our aim in this study is to determine what Plotinus considers to be the origin of matter, both corporeal and intelligible.[1] Does he conceive of matter as the end product of the procession which started with the separation of the Intellect from the One, or does he understand it as a principle independent of this procession and, in fact, one which impedes and ultimately halts it? Emile Bréhier states the problem as follows: "Either matter is the last term in the procession of the realities, that is to say, the sterile stage in which the productive force which has proceeded from the One at last dies out," or it "is a term distinct from the realities which proceed progressively from the One, and it may set itself against these realities."[2] As long as the 'sterile stage' or ultimate reality is the last in the line of procession from the One, this endproduct cannot be at the same time separate from or independent of that procession.

But the question to be pursued is whether Plotinus' monism is consistent in accounting for the origin of matter, or whether it devolves into a dualism because it makes no provision for this origin. Is the opposition of the sterile stage to the power of the One nothing more than its character of being the last, or is this opposition due to the presence of an independent reality?

The problem cannot be solved by turning to Plotinian scholars, for they are divided over the origin and role of matter in the Plotinian universe. A number of them specifically point out the difficulties involved in Plotinus' thought between considering matter as part of the overflow process from the One and positing it as an independent reality thereby setting it in opposition to that process. Among such authors, John Rist insists that matter is good when it is viewed as a product of a higher reality and evil only when considered in itself apart from the emanative process.[3] Emile Bréhier is also aware of this problem and says that if matter were eternal, then it would indeed be an independent reality. However, he speaks of the eternal participation of matter in the good and of the soul's engendering the sensible world when it encounters matter. Strangely enough, Bréhier suggests that matter is independent of the One but at the same time maintains some type of participation in the Good.[4]

Yet some authors believe that matter is independent of the One. Phillippus Pistorius contends that matter is pure negation, that all creativity is an activity of idea upon matter and that matter is eternal. He calls it "the imaginary point where God is not, and where there is, therefore, an absolute lack of reality...absolute evil."[5]

A number of authors are inclined to believe that for Plotinus the production of matter is in some way an activity of the One. E. R. Dodds, for example, strongly asserts that Plotinus will have none of the dualism which results in admitting an independent origin to matter or in making any kind of active source of evil. And, since matter is from the One, "incarnation as such is not necessarily an evil state."[6] Paul Henry contends that Plotinus has made the decisive jump from the One to matter by means of the emanative process.[7] A. H. Armstrong finds a paradoxical situation in Plotinus' account of matter since it is the principle of evil as well as "the last and lowest stage of procession from the Good."[8]

Among those authors who view matter as the endproduct of the emanative process, Dean Inge insists that matter must not be equated with absolute nothingness. He says that it is not "absolutely non-existent," and that below it, "there can be nothing, for the next stage below matter would be absolute non-entity."[9]

Jean Trouillard and Dennis O'Brien are perhaps the best spokesman for the monism of Plotinus. Trouillard says that "Plotinian matter is needed by the Good, and proceeds from it." It is "total indetermination," and still it is "integrated into the total process."[10] O'Brien says that there can be evil only "*subsequent* to the soul's production of matter."[11]

There remains yet another group of authors. They have no interest in the controversy over the origin of matter, but consider the problem to be meaningless. In general they say that because matter is such a weak and limiting concept this precludes its being an endproduct of the emanative process or an independent reality opposed to that process. John Murray says that matter is "nothing more positive than a determined limit" for the activity of the mind.[12] Joseph Katz calls matter 'complete powerlessness,' which does not exist, and is just "the furthermost limit of power."[13] Of this latter group of authors, Cletus Carbonara is the most forceful. He maintains that Plotinus rejects dualism, but this rejection does not mean that matter is a part of the monistic overflow. Matter is not an independent reality in the Plotinian universe, not a creation of the One; it is pure negation.[14]

Clearly, Plotinian scholars do not agree on the origin and function of matter in the Plotinian universe. In fact, three possible positions have been noted: (i) matter is independent of the One and opposed actively or passively to it; (ii) matter is the end product of the procession from the One; and (iii) the question of the origin of matter is meaningless since matter is nothing at all.

The purpose of this study is to determine which, if any, of these positions best characterizes Plotinus' thought on the origin and role of matter—both corporeal and intelligible. Our method will be one of textual analysis; that is, several key texts,[15] representative of Plotinus' early, middle and late literary periods, will be analyzed.[16]

1. Key Text A: *Ennead* II.4[17]

The title of this treatise is given by Porphyry in the *Life* as 'On the Two Kinds of Matter' (*Peri tōn duo hylōn*)[18]. It is number twelve in the chronological order and was written at a time when Plotinus did not seem to be particularly interested in the origin of corporeal matter. The treatise is important for our purposes, however, because Plotinus does indicate that intelligible matter is produced by the One.

The treatise begins with an acknowledgment that men generally agree that matter is a certain 'substrate' and 'receptacle' of form. This agreement dissolves, however, when they begin to question concerning the nature of matter and "how it is a receptacle and what of."[19] Chapters 2 through 5 are devoted to an analysis of intelligible matter while the remainder of the treatise is concerned with corporeal matter. It is important that we consider the function and origin of divine intelligible matter because matter Here is in some way an image of the matter There.[20]

Plotinus first presents the argument against there being matter in the intelligible world saying: "If what is of the matter kind must be indeterminate and formless, and there is nothing indeterminate or formless among the beings there, which are the best, there would not be matter there."[21] He counters this argument by pointing out that we must not despise the undefined or the idea of shapelessness since Soul itself is shapeless before being shaped by Intellect and Reason. The matter There is different from the matter Here in that the latter is always receiving different forms while the former always possesses the same form.

> In the intelligible world matter is all things at once, so it has nothing to change into, for it has all things already. Accordingly, matter is never without form in the intelligible world since even the matter here is not, but each of them has form in a different way.[22]

Moreover, since the ideas are many, each must have something that is properly its own—its form (*morphē*) and that which is common to all, matter (*hylē*). Thus, if there is form in the intelligible world, there must also be matter which underlies and receives the form.[23] In fact, while the intelligible world is certainly indivisible, still it is, in a sense, divisible and matter exists in it. The intelligible world is unity amidst diversity, and the diversity is that of many forms. Take away the diversity of forms and what remains is formless and indeterminate (*amorphon kai aoriston*), viz. intelligible matter.

> So, it must be formless before it is varied; for it you take away in your mind its variety and forms and forming principles and thoughts, what is prior to these is formless and undefined and it is none of these things that are on it and in it.[24]

And so that on or in which these intelligible realities have their unity amidst diversity is intelligible matter. Plotinus describes the origin of this matter as follows:

> For Otherness There is eternal and produces intelligible matter for this is the principle of matter, this and the primary Movement. For this reason Movement, too, was called Otherness, because Movement and Otherness sprung forth together. The Movement and Otherness which came from the First are undefined, and need the First to define them; they are defined when they turn to It. But before the turning, matter, too, was undefined and the Other and no way good, but unilluminated from the First. For if light comes from the First, then that which receives the light before it receives it has everlastingly no light; but it has light as other than itself, since the light comes to it from another.[25]

Rist explains how this 'otherness' characterizes matter both Here and There. "All beings, that is, everything associated with any kind of matter, possesses 'otherness'; intelligible matter is 'other' than the One, that is than what is 'beyond Being,' matter 'here' is other than Being."[26] And that which is other There is intelligible matter which has its source in the One.

> As 2, 4, 5, 30, makes abundantly clear, it is the very characteristic of the first product of the One, namely the substrate of the intelligible world of 'intelligible matter,' to be 'other' than its source.[27]

This 'otherness' of matter does not wish to remain such and continually strives to be filled from the same source that made it 'other.'[28] Now since everything after the One is other than It, all things have some characteristics of matter.[29] They are all produced in an initial overflow as indefinite, and through a conversion to their source they are informed and so complete hypostases.

Chapters 6 through 16 of II.4 are devoted to an analysis of corporeal matter as that which underlies changing beings. Change is not a coming to be from absolute non-being nor is destruction a total perishing into non-being. If this is true then that which changes and perishes must be a composite and as such it must be composed of matter and form. So beings that are destroyed "must be composed of matter and form: form is in relation to their quality and shape, and matter to their substrate, which is indeterminate because it is not form."[30]

Now matter which underlies form is without quality. "We must not attribute to it lightness or heaviness, density or rarity, and indeed not even shape and so not size either."[31] All the qualities that are seen in matter are brought to it by form. "So when the form comes to matter it brings everything with it; the form has everything, the size and all that goes with it and is caused by *logos*."[32] Therefore, since matter is without qualities, it is difficult to speak of it as anything other than a mere potentiality without potency. It is qualityless (*apoios*) (I.8.10), non-being (*mē on*)(II.5.4 & 5), only a potentiality of being (II.5.5). But even devoid of qualities and other than being, matter still has its own particular characteristic which is simply its being 'other' than others. Rist calls this otherness of matter its nature.

> This 'otherness' is its nature (*physis*), a nature which is not essentially quantified but continually admits a flux of changing qualities. Plotinus finds no difficulty in the idea of entities being unqualified (2, 4, 13). If this is so—and nobody disputes the existence and discussability of Quality— then the mere absence of qualities does not rule out the potential 'existence' of matter, or prevent its 'possession' of a nature.[33]

Rist's contention that matter in some sense has a nature appears to be correct. Plotinus himself asserts that just because matter is non-being does not mean that it is not.

> Non-being here does not mean complete non-being but only something other than being; not non-being in the same way as the movement and rest which affect being, but like an image of being or something still more non-existent.[34]

Apparently, Plotinus here employs Plato's work in the *Sophist* on negation. Plato had found it necessary to distinguish between the kinds of negation. His conclusion was that 'not being something' is not the same as non-existence.[35] And so when something is said to be non-being, it is not necessarily non-existence but only something other than being. In this way, Plotinus can claim that matter has no being;[36] it is non-being (*mē einai*), and that non-being has some kind of existence that is identical with privation. "Therefore, though it is non-being, it has a certain sort of 'being' in this way and is the same thing as privation."[37]

Now one can not consign matter to the realm of non-being or privation and then forget about it. For although formless and indeterminate, it is the substratum of things.

> There is need for some one kind of vessel or place to receive bodies; but place is posterior to matter and bodies, so that bodies would need matter before they need place...it is not an empty name but it is something underlying, even if it is invisible and sizeless.[38]

Matter is analogous to a mirror but does not have the real existence that a mirror does over and above the appearances in it.[39] The images of bodies that enter into it enter as 'falsity into falsity.' Matter is not visible like a mirror and must not be thought of as an object as the mirror is an object. The mirror is an analogy only insofar as it, too, is a 'receptacle' in which images come and go.

Finally, since matter has such a strange type of existence, it can be apprehended only by an equally strange kind of reasoning. Plotinus refers to the 'bastard reasoning' of the *Timaeus* saying that such reasoning does not originate in the mind, but in some illogical way.[40] In order to 'see' matter, one must use "another intellect which is not intellect," an intellect that is devoid of all form and being. Intellect must leave its own light, as it were, and go outside, "to experience something contrary to itself." It must negate itself and become intellectless in order to see matter which exists outside of being.[41]

And so in the twelfth treatise, Plotinus has presented a valuable analysis of the two kinds of matter. Our own analysis of the text has demonstrated that although intelligible matter has its origin in the overflow of the One, no such claim, on the basis of this treatise, can be made for corporeal matter. The text does indicate, however, that the matter Here is an image of the matter There. It is without quality, a container of bodies, and identical with privation. In its very privation it can be said in some sense 'to be' but as to the source of this 'being' the text is silent.

2. Key Text B: *Ennead* III.4.1

This text, number fifteen in Porphyry's list, helps clear up some of the uncertainty concerning the origin of corporeal matter. In II.4 we saw that specific mention was made of the origin of intelligible matter, but no mention was made as to the origin of corporeal matter. Plotinus clears up this deficiency by saying that absolute indetermination (*aoristian pantelē*) is produced by Soul. The text is quoted at length because of its importance.

> Some realities [the One and Intellect] remain unmoved when their off-spring come into being, but Soul has already been said to be in motion when it brings forth sense perception, which is a hypostasis, and the power of growth, which also extends to plants. Now Soul has the power of growth when it exists in us, but this power does not dominate because it is only a part of Soul; in plants, however, it dominates because it has, as it were, been isolated. But does this power of growth produce anything? It produces a thing altogether different from itself, for after it there is no more life and what is produced is lifeless. What is it then? Everything which was produced prior to this was produced formless but received form by turning towards its producer and being, as it were, reared to maturity, so here, too, that which is produced is not anymore a form of Soul—for it is without life—but absolute indetermination.[42]

But what is this 'absolute indetermination'? Harder, in commenting on this text, asserts that absolute indetermination is matter.[43] Plotinus himself lends credibility to this interpretation since he refers to matter as indetermination many times.[44] Armstrong in commenting on the meaning of 'others' in II.4.13 adds further clarification.

> To say something is 'other' than something else is a way of helping to define it, to show it as a distinctive unity; this remarkable plural is an attempt to exclude all definition, to speak of matter as absolutely indefinite and incoherent with no sort of distinctive unity.[45]

In addition, the very metaphysical structure of bodies requires that matter be indeterminate. This is indicated by several texts but especially by III.4.1 itself.

> When it [absolute indetermination]is perfected it becomes a body, receiving a form proper to its potentiality, a receptacle for the principle that produced and nourished it.[46]

Now in another treatise Plotinus speaks of fire, air, water, and earth as the four kinds of bodies.[47] It is the indetermination of matter that is raised to the level of bodies by the introduction of form. Without form coming to matter there would be no bodies. Why?

> Because there would not be compounded bodies or even a simple body in reality, without the soul which is in the universe, since it is a rational principle coming into matter which makes a body, and that rational principle does not proceed from any other than Soul.[48]

That which raises matter to the perfection of body is the very principle that produced it. It is first generated by Soul and then becomes the recipient (*hypodochēn*) of its generator. "It is not the body that is the recipient (*hypodochēn*), but the indeterminate matter."[49] Once the power of growth generates and raises it to the level of body other forms can then be superimposed on the matter. For example, a living being is a result of the imposition of the forms of corporealness, element, and life on matter.[50]

Body becomes the meeting place, as it were, between the higher realities and matter here below. "And only this form in bodies is the last trace of that above in the last depth of that below."[51] That which is 'the last depth of that below' is matter.

> Now it is necessary that what comes after the First should exist, and as a result that the last should exist, and this is matter, which has nothing at all of the Good.[52]

Plotinus' universe has reached the point of no emanation, no overflow and no Being. Each stage of the emanatory process is characterized by the ability of the less perfect product to turn to its source and be filled, but matter, which is not perfect at all, is unable to turn towards its generator and so remains unformed and in darkness. Previous generations always possessed something of their generator in themselves, even though it may have been 'indetermination without form,' but matter possesses nothing of the principle of growth which generated it and so is absolute indetermination.

The importance of this text is evident. Matter under the guise of absolute indetermination is explicitly linked with the chain of realities that ultimately has its source in the One.

3. Key Text C: *Ennead* III.6.14

The next text for consideration is from treatise number twenty-six, according to Porphyry's list. This treatise, along with the others written during Plotinus' middle literary period, may be more useful for an understanding of the Plotinian doctrine on the origin of matter than the more popular treatises such as I.8 and II.4. This is so because II.4, one of the earlier treatises, is representative of Plotinus' early thinking on matter, and I.8 is representative of his later thought "when his power was already failing."[53] This treatise, then, written when his mental power was "at its height"[54] should present to us, more than any other, his mature thought on the origin of matter. Moreover, if there is any development of his thinking on matter, this treatise should be a keystone in that development, coming between his earlier and later thinking.

The treatise entitled, 'On the Impassibility of Beings Without Body' seeks to demonstrate that both soul and matter are not subject to affections or modifications. With regards to matter Plotinus builds on a discussion just completed in II.5.5.

> But if matter really was participant and received being as is commonly thought, what comes to it would be swallowed and sink into it. But, it is apparent that it is not swallowed but matter remains the same and receives nothing, but checks the approach as a repellent base and a receptacle for the things which come to the same point and there mingle: it is like the polished objects which one sets against the sun when he wants to get fire (and he fills some of them with water). Hence, the ray, being hindered by the resistance within, can not pass through but will be concentrated on the outside. So matter becomes in this way the cause of coming into being, and the things that are brought together in it are brought together in this way.[55]

In II.5.5 Plotinus indicates that matter is 'cast out' and 'utterly separated' from all reality. The above citation adds credibility to this independence thesis; in fact, it would seem to suggest that matter is an independent reality which repels and halts the overflow process.

How does matter 'repel' this procession? It repels it "like the polished objects that one sets against the sun." This analogy is reinforced when Plotinus compares matter to a mirror and the beings that are in it to the images in a mirror.

> The being which is imagined in it is not 'being' but only a fleeting frivolity; accordingly, the things which seem to come to be in it are frivolities, nothing but phantoms on a phantom, just like something in a mirror which really exists in one place but is reflected in another; the mirror seems to be filled but actually holds nothing while seeming to have all. 'Images of real beings pass into and out of it.' Phantoms into a formless phantom, visible because of its formlessness. They seem to act on it but produce nothing, for they are ghost-like and feeble and have nothing to resist them. They go through it without making a cut, as if through water, or as if someone in a way projected forms in the void.[56]

This analogy aptly illustrates Plotinus' whole doctrine of matter and of bodies (and so the sensible world). If the images that we see in a mirror were really there, likewise the images present in matter would be there, but, of course, what is reflected in a mirror is not actually there.[57] For a mirror appears to possess everything when actually it possesses nothing at all. Just as a mirror is not affected by the images in it, matter is not affected by the images on it.[58] Moreover, matter is non-being and as such its reflections are non-being. The sensible world is a 'phantom on a phantom.'[59] Thus both matter and the sensible world have 'the being' of non-being: "The being of these is the being of things that do not exist."[60]

Our text further states that matter is the cause of the generated beings, indicating that in some sense matter 'is' before these other things come to be. This is similar to the account given in III.4.1 where matter is first generated and then raised to the level of body. The coming to be of body is a result of the combination of form and unmodifiable matter. Once again the analogy of the mirror is useful. Just as a mirror must first exist before the images in it can come to be, matter must first exist before the things contained in it can come to be.

> Well, then, if matter did not exist, would nothing come into existence? No, just as there would be no image, if a mirror or something of the sort did not exist. For that whose nature is to come into being in something else would not come into being if that something else was not, for that is the nature of an image, to be in another.[61]

Since the sensible world is a 'phantom on a phantom' or an image on an image, matter must first exist before it can come to be. Matter must be before it can unite with form to produce body and so the sensible world.

In this text an interesting development has taken place in Plotinus' thought. Key Text B said that matter was first produced by the power of growth in Soul and it was only then that it was 'informed' by its producer. Through this information of matter by the power of growth in plants, bodies are produced. Our present text is much different in language as well as content. Matter is no longer produced and perfected by form, but is the cause of things as a repellent base. There appears to be no union of matter and form but only reflection. Matter is no longer referred to as being produced but that which halts production. Concerning matter's origin, if it has one, the text is conspicuously silent.

4. Key Text D: *Ennead* V.8.7

In this, the thirty-first treatise according to Porphyry, Plotinus says that the visible universe comes into being as a whole; it is not planned and then made part by part by proceeds without thought or effort from Intellect—even corporeal matter.

> Everything Here comes from There, and exists in greater beauty There; for here it is intermingled, but There it is pure. All this universe is occupied by form from beginning to end, matter first of all by the forms of the elements, and then other forms upon these, and then again others; hence, it is difficult to find the matter hidden under so many forms. Since matter too is a sort of ultimate form, this universe is all form, and all things that are in it are form.[62]

In attempting to understand this text, the first half in which Plotinus says that everything is "occupied by forms from beginning to end" is relatively clear since everything that is Here is also There and "Intellect as a whole is all the forms."[63] Even the statement that matter is first of all occupied by the forms of the elements presents no difficulty since it is compatible with the earlier statement that matter is raised to the level of body through its union with form.[64] A difficulty arises, however, when Plotinus calls matter 'a sort of ultimate form.' The Greek simply says *eidos ti eschaton*, which literally means that "it [matter] is the last [or lowest] form."

This passage is both unique and difficult. Unique in that it is one of the only places in the *Enneads* that Plotinus implies that matter is a form;[65]

and difficult when we try to reconcile this account of matter with the very strong assertions that matter is formless.[66] At first glance it appears that Plotinus is involved in a contradiction saying that matter is both formless and a form. This difficulty can be clarified, however, by calling to mind Proclus' notion of the extension of power, a notion also operative in Plotinus.

Proclus says in his *Elements of Theology* that a cause is more perfect and powerful than its consequents (Prop. 7), and so it will have a greater number of effects, for greater power produces more effects (Prop. 57).[67] Even those things produced by secondary causes are produced, in a greater measure, by prior and more determinate principles (Prop. 56). Thus the primal cause can be said to operate prior to its consequents, in conjunction with its consequents, and posterior to these same consequents.

> From this it is apparent that what Soul causes is also caused by Intelligence, but not all that Intelligence causes is caused by Soul; Intelligence operates prior to Soul; and what Soul bestows on secondary existences Intelligence bestows in a greater measure; and the level where Soul is no longer operative Intelligence irradiates with its own gifts things on which Soul has not bestowed itself—for even the inanimate participates Intelligence, a creative activity of Intelligence, insofar as it participates form.[68]

Clearly, the Primal Cause of all, the One, has an extension which is beyond the secondary causative powers of Soul and Intelligence. Likewise, Intelligence has a greater causative power than Soul. This notion of the extension of power can be diagrammed as follows.

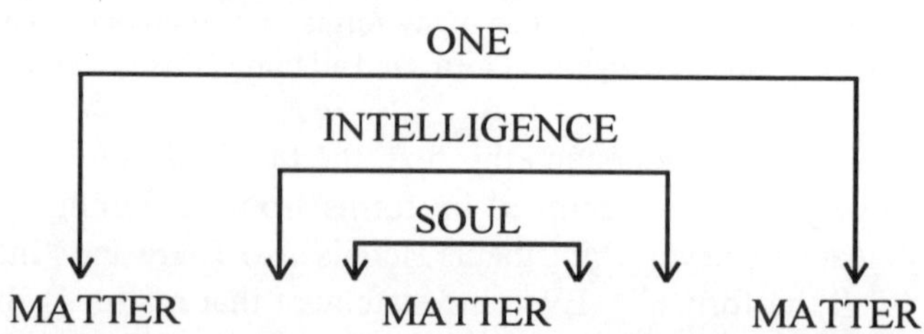

In the diagram we see that the One includes in its extension the secondary causes of intelligence and Soul, while Intelligence is inclusive of the causative power of Soul. As a causative power, the One goes beyond the productions of Intelligence and Soul and produces matter.

Thus, for Proclus, the causative power of the One extends to the whole universe. Everything in the universe, including unformed and chaotic matter derives its reality (or non-being) from the One. The activity of Intelligence does not reach down as far as the One's precisely because it is not the primary principle or causative power. Intelligence does not generate matter. This is not to say, however, that Intelligence in no way effects matter. It shapes it like a potter shapes his clay, but as a potter does not cause clay to be clay, Intelligence does not cause matter to be matter.

Admittedly, there is not a one to one correspondence between Proclus' and Plotinus' respective positions. But through an analysis of Proclus' notion of the extension of power, much light is shed on Plotinus' position in V.8.7. It is our contention, in the remainder of our analysis of this text, that Plotinus includes matter as a 'sort of ultimate form' to demonstrate the scope of Intellect's causative power. He states at the outset of the text that "all that is here below comes from There" but this does not necessarily include matter. The whole universe, "from beginning to end," is occupied by form. Therefore, matter which is the Last[69] must also be occupied by form. It is first occupied "by the forms of the elements, and then other forms upon these, and then again others; hence, it is difficult to find the matter hidden under so many forms." The text concludes by saying that "matter too is a sort of ultimate form." This statement, which appears contradictory at first, now takes on a broader meaning as a result of our analysis of causal extension. Plotinus has said that everything is occupied by form, even matter since it is evident that matter is within the extension of Intellect's power. Since the content of Intellect is all the forms, Plotinus is able to conclude that because matter is affected by the power of the Intellect, it "too is a sort of ultimate form." But the fact that matter is an ultimate form does not necessarily imply a causal connection with Intellect. As we saw in our analysis of Proclus, matter is not dependent on Intelligence for its 'existence.' Rather, Intelligence effects and shapes matter, but it does not cause matter to be. Similarly in V.8.7, Plotinus demonstrates that the power of Intellect extends to matter, but a statement of causal connection is not present. For both Plotinus and Proclus, then, Intellect (Intelligence) shapes matter like a potter shapes his clay, but as the potter does not cause clay to be clay, the Intellect (Intelligence) does not cause matter to be matter. Its contact with form Here is, at best, a pale glimmer of union of matter and form There.

5. Key Text E: *Ennead* III.2.2

This treatise, number forty-seven in Porphyry's list, which Plotinus wrote towards the end of his life, is devoted to the traditional theme of providence. The text explains how belief in the existence and goodness of divine providence can be justified in the face of all the apparent evils in the world. The opponents he has in mind in writing this treatise are the Epicureans, who denied providence; the Peripatetics, who denied that it extended to the world below the moon; and most of all the Gnostics, who propounded the theory that the material world is the work of an evil creator.

The notable characteristic of this treatise is that in it alone Plotinus speaks of a rational forming principle, a *logos*, of the whole universe which appears to be a distinct hypostasis over and above the One, Intellect and Soul. However, Bréhier says, and here we concur with him, that the *logos* of this treatise is not that of a distinct hypostasis but is a way of speaking of the living, forming and directing matter which is derived from the Intellect. It keeps the material universe in the best possible order and brings it into a unity-in-diversity of contrasting and clashing forces which, far inferior to the unity of the intelligible world, is the best possible image of that world here below.[70]

But a unity-amidst-diversity is a universe that is not only one: there is a separation in it and therefore conflict. It is not the result of any kind of reasoning but flows necessarily from above.

> This universe has come into existence, not as a result of the process of reasoning that it ought to exist but because it was necessary that there should be a second nature; for that true All was not of a kind to be the last of realities. For it was the first and had much power, indeed, all power, and this is the power to produce something else without seeking for it to be produced. For if it had sought, it would not have had it of itself, nor would it have been of its own substance, but it would have been like a craftsman who does not have the ability to produce from himself, but as something acquired, and gets it from learning. So Intellect, by giving something of itself to matter, made all things without itself being moved; this something of itself is the *logos* flowing from Intellect.[71]

This *logos* or rational forming principle, which Intellect gives to matter is not a distinct hypostasis but the presence of Intellect in everything that comes after it.[72] The world of Intellect is the archetype of the material universe. Everything that is Here is also There, but There everything is alive and united in the rich fullness of eternal life.[73]

Just as the One must produce, the Intellect, the perfect image of the One, must also produce and this production is a movement towards matter.

> Just like the One, Intellect produces pouring forth much power. Just as That, which was before it, poured forth its likeness, so what Intellect produces is a likeness of itself. This activity springing from being is Soul, which comes into being while Intellect remains unchanged: for Intellect too comes into being while That while is before It remains unchanged.[74]

Soul is matter in the sense that it is posterior and inferior to the Intellect in which it has its source. This concept of Soul as matter is wholly relational, as Dean Inge aptly demonstrates.

> Matter is Matter only in relation to that which is next above it, and which gives it form, and indefinite existence. Thus the same thing may be form (*eidos*) in relation to what is below it. A thing is matter insofar as it is acted upon by a higher principle. It is a purely relative term; every stage in the hierarchy of being, except the highest, is *hylē* (matter), every stage except the lowest is *hylē*. Every *eidos* makes its own *hylē*. But *hylē* is generally the name for the lowest rung in the ladder.[75]

Thus in the hierarchical structure of the Plotinian universe each stage except the First and the Last is both *eidos* (form) and *hylē* (matter). The soul is both matter and form in that it is matter in regards to what comes after it. As form it is the extension of 'the *logos* flowing from Intellect.'

> The Soul is, in effect, the *logos* of all things; as the *logos*, it is the last of the intelligi ble realities or of things included in the intelligible realm, and the first of things included in the sensible universe. It is therefore related to two worlds, happy and brought to life on the one hand; and on the other hand deceived by its resemblance to the First. And it descends here as if under the influence of a magical charm.[76]

Now Soul has two levels: the higher one which acts as a transcendent principle of form, order and intelligent direction; and a lower level, nature, which operates as an immanent principle of life. Nature, as an extension of the higher soul and ultimately Intellect, also produces according to the *logos* in it, but its formation is weak and poor since it is far removed from Intellect.

> Intellect gives to the Soul of the All, and Soul (the one which comes next after Intellect) gives from itself to the soul next after it, illuminating it and impressing form on it, and this last soul immediately makes as if under orders. It makes something without hinderance, but in others, the inferior ones, it is impeded. In as much as its power to make is derived, and it is filled with *logoi* which are not the First ones, it will not simple make according to the forms but there would be an offspring of its own, and this is clearly inferior. Its product is a living being, but a very imperfect one, and one which finds its own life hateful since it is the worst of living things, ill conditioned and savage, made of inferior matter, a sort of sediment of the prior realities, bitter and embittering.[77]

John N. Deck explains the relationship of soul, *logoi* and matter:

> The soul, containing the logoi of all things in the visible universe gives logoi to the bodies of the visible universe (ch. IV.3.10.38-42). This giving of logoi is the producing of these bodies; that is, a body together with its size and extension, is brought about by a coming of logoi upon matter (ch. IV.7.2.22-25). This coming of logos is, from different aspects, a coming of unity, of form, of beauty, of life (Cf. I.6.2.13-24; IV.3.10.38-42). The trace of unity is the trace of form and beauty is the trace of intellectual beauty, and so again of the Nous.[78]

This being the case, it is through the logos or rational formative principle that the power of the Intellect extends to the ends of the universe. The Soul, with its higher part in the realm of Intellect and its lower part reflecting these true realities on matter, is the vehicle by which the power of Intellect is disseminated. This dissemination of the power of the Intellect continues downward until it reaches the Last, matter, which is 'the lowest rung on the ladder.'

Key Text E has sought to demonstrate that Intellect has given something of itself in order to produce all things. This something of itself is the *logos*. Our analysis has shown that Intellect's 'movement towards matter' begins in its production of Soul. Through Dean Inge's conception of the relatively of matter, we are able to ascertain that all things, except the First and the Last, are both form and matter. We can further conclude that the One, as the First, can be said to be Form in relation to all things and matter to none since It is the First prior to which there is nothing. Likewise, the Last is matter to all things and form to none since it is the Last and there is nothing that comes after it. Concerning the origin of this matter, it appears that Plotinus has avoided the problem. The text says that "Intellect, by giving something of itself to matter, made all things," but we are left in the dark with regards to the status of this matter before Intellect gave something of itself to it.

6. Key Text F: *Ennead* I.8

The last text is from the eighth tractate of the first treatise, the famous treatise on evil. It is the fifty-first treatise, according to Porphyry, one of the last nine which were "written when his power was already failing." In fact, it was one of the last four treatises in which this waning of power is most evident.[79]

Plotinus begins his study by asking what evil is and what is its nature. By so doing, he seeks to discover its source and whether it exists. But first an epistemological question concerning the nature of how we arrive at knowledge must be answered. Do we come to a knowledge of evil by something already in use? "But there would then be no way to discern by which powers in us we know evil, if knowledge of all is by likeness."[80] Or by knowledge of opposites?

> But if opposites are known by the same kind of knowledge and evil is opposite to good, the knowledge of good is also the knowledge of evil, then those who wish to know of evils must have a clear perception of the good, since the better precedes the worse and the better is Form, and the worse is not, but rather privation of Form.[81]

Plotinus chooses the latter approach and begins a discussion of the nature of the Good.

> It is that on which everything depends and to which all beings aspire, they have it as their principle and need It: but It is without need, self-sufficient, lacking nothing, the measure and limit of all things, giving from itself Intellect and Being, Soul, Life and intellectual activity. Up to It all things are beautiful. But it is beautiful beyond all beauty and is king of the intelligible realm.[82]

Nowhere in the life of the Good do we find any trace of evil or in the things that are necessarily related to It.

> The Intellect is the first act of the Good and the first substance; the Good stays still in Itself, but Intellect moves about It in its activity, as also it lives around It. And Soul dances round Intellect outside, and looks to it, and in contemplating its interior sees God through it. 'This is the life of the gods,'

> without sorrow and blessed; evil is nowhere here, and if things had stopped here there would not have been any evil, only a first, a second and a third goods.[83]

If we are to discover the nature of evil, we will not find it in the realm of being. But through a knowledge of the nature of the Good we have gained an insight into the nature of evil. The Good is characterized by measure, form and self-sufficiency, that to which all beings aspire. Evil, being opposite the Good, is characterized by its lack of measure and form and is such that no being should aspire to it.[84] It cannot be a part of being since the whole of reality contains some order and measure.

> One is able to conceive of evil as a kind of unmeasuredness in relation to measure, and unboundedness in relation to limit, and formlessness in relation to the cause of form, and perpetual neediness in relation to what is self-sufficient; always indeterminate, nowhere stable, completely passive, insatiate, complete poverty; and all this is not accidental to it but the essence of evil itself.[85]

These characteristics deprive evil of any claim to being. It is beyond being not in the sense of the One which is supra-being but as infra-being. The very essence of this non-being is privation. If we say that something is not good because it lacks something, then this is evil accidentally. Evil so conceived is contained accidentally in something else and must itself be something before it can be contained in something else—it must be something else even if we cannot properly call it substance.

> For if evil occurs accidentally in something else, it must be itself first, even if it is not a substance. Just as there is the Good Itself and good as an attribute, so there must be evil itself and the evil derived from it which inheres in something else...So, that which underlies figures and forms and shapes and measures and limits, decked out with an adornment which belongs to something else, having no good of its own, only a shadow in comparison to real being, is the substance of evil, if there really can be a substance of evil; this is what our reason discovers to be primal evil, evil itself.[86]

So just as there must be an absolute good that is the source of all that is good, there must be an absolute evil that underlies all that is evil. Evil in a particular soul is the lack of a good (form) that ought to be there. Such a soul cannot be considered as primarily evil since it still shares in the good.[87]

Now the medium which produces this falling short in the soul and is itself the farthest removed from the good is matter.[88] Just as the good must exist, evil must exist and this is matter.

> One can grasp the necessity of evil in this way. Since not only the Good exists, there must be the last end to the process of going out past It, or if one prefers to put it like this, descending or going away; and this last, after which nothing else can come into being is evil. Now it is necessary that what comes after the First exists, and therefore that the Last exists; and this is matter, which possesses nothing at all of the Good.[89]

We have now reached a crucial stage in the analysis of this treatise. Does Plotinus mean, in the above citation, that matter is the last thing produced by the emanative process? Or is it the point at which this process is halted and turned back? The First interpretation would hold that matter is ultimately produced by the One, whereas the second would conceive matter as apart from and opposed to the productive power of the One.

At this point we must distinguish between the two matters in regard to this text and the notion of evil in general. In chapter two of this treatise, Plotinus has said that evil is nowhere to be found in the intelligible realm.[90] Now intelligible matter belongs to this realm[91] and so it cannot be identified with evil. Clearly, the matter with which Plotinus is concerned in this text, and the treatise itself, is corporeal matter. This matter has nothing to call its own and is characterized by its privation. We cannot even call privation a quality of matter but a negation of quality. For Plotinus, such negations of quality are not themselves to be considered a quality. For example, noiselessness is not a quality of sound or anything else; rather, it is the absence of quality. To assert a quality of anything is to speak positively concerning it. Matter is without quality and as such it can be considered to be in a state of potentiality without potency. It is qualityless (*apoios*),[92] non-being (*mē on*),[93] only a potentiality of being.[94]

Yet, to say that matter is non-being is not to say that it does not exist. "Non-being here does not mean absolute non-being but only that which is other than being; not non-being in the same way as movement and rest which affect being, but like an image of being or something still more non-existent."[95] Apparently, Plotinus here makes use of Plato's work in the *Sophist.* Plato had found it necessary to distinguish between the kinds of negation. His conclusion was that 'not being something' is not the same as non-being. Thus when it is said that matter is non-being, this does not mean that it is not, but only that is other than being. In this way Plotinus can claim that matter has no being[96] and its non-being is identical with privation.[97]

Thus matter is and is not. As there is a First, there must be a Last, and this is matter. As the Last, the Plotinian universe has reached the point of no production, no overflow and no Being. Concerning the problem of whether matter is the last stage produced by the overflow process or the extrinsic stone wall which halts this process, two additional texts are available which would appear to support the independence thesis.

The first text is taken from the first of two proofs for the necessity of evil—the second of which is given on the preceding pages.

> The All must be composed of contrary principles; it would not exist at all if matter did not exist. 'For the generation of the cosmos was a mixed result of the combination of intellect and necessity.' What comes to it from God is good; the evil comes from the 'ancient nature.'[98]

In this text there is an apparent dualism. On the one hand, everything that comes into the All from God is good. On the other hand, everything that comes into the All from the 'ancient nature' is evil. What are we to understand by this 'ancient nature' (*tēs archaias physeōs*)? Once again we must remember that in this text, as in the previous one, Plotinus' emphasis is on the necessity (*anangkēs*) of evil (matter), and not on evil's origin.

Matter must be because the universe is a combination of Intellect and necessity.[99] Apparently the 'ancient nature,' for Plotinus, refers to the unformed matter which is indeterminate and pure potentiality. The sensible universe is, as it were, the point at which matter and Intellect meet. That which is good in this universe is from 'God' (*via* Intellect) and that which is evil is from matter. Thus there are two sources of influence in the sensible universe, and the possibilities of a dualistic interpretation of this text are evident.

A second text which lends support to the dualistic thesis is one which traces the evil in the soul to matter:

> This is the fall of the soul, to come in this way to matter and to become weak, because all its powers do not come into action; matter hinders them from coming by occupying the place soul holds which results in a kind of cramped condition, and making evil what it has got hold of by a sort of theft—until soul is able to regain its higher state. Accordingly, matter is the cause of the soul's weakness and vice and is itself evil before soul and is primarily evil. Even if soul had produced matter, being affected in some way, and had

> become evil by communication with it, the presence of matter in it would have been the cause of its evil.[100]

Just as there is a primal good for the soul there is a primal evil, which, as the texts indicate, is matter. Matter has been called evil, non-being, the ancient nature, and now it is called the primary evil (*prōton kakon*). Nowhere in this treatise has Plotinus indicated that matter has its origin in the Good. In fact, he has consistently placed it opposite the First in the sense of a limit to the power of the One and as the Last. As the primary evil its evil is absolute and as such it has no share in the Good. If it had its origin in the Good through the emanatory process, however remote it is from the Good, this would be sufficient to warrant its having some share in the Good. The closest the text comes to indicating that matter might have its origin in the emanatory process is the statement: "Even if the soul had produced matter..." (*kai gar hei autē hē psychē tēn hylēn egennēse*).[101] But the use of εἰ with the aorist indicative *egennēse* indicates a very remote possibility, if not impossibility, that the soul is the producer of matter.

The result of this treatise is that Plotinus leaves us with a great amount of uncertainty as regards the status of corporeal matter. While it is true that he is not interested, in this treatise, with the problem of the origin of matter *per se*, nevertheless, in talking about the necessity of matter he uses a language full of dualistic implications.

7. Summary and Conclusions

Our analysis of several key Plotinian texts has discovered three distinct positions regarding the origin of matter. First, matter is not nothing but its position in the Plotinian universe is an unknown—even to Plotinus himself. Secondly, matter is independent of the One and therefore a principle opposed to It. Thirdly, matter is dependent on the One and as such is the end product of the overflow process. Our conclusion differs from the conclusions of other Plotinian scholars in that our study has shown that Plotinus held all three of these positions at specific times in his philosophical career. This conclusion can be verified by summarizing the key texts:

II.4[12]

The analysis of this text has shown that intelligible matter has its origin in the One, but no such claim is made for corporeal matter. The text does indicate that the matter Here is an image of the matter There. It is devoid of quality, a container of bodies, identical with privation. In its very privation it can be said to exist but as to the source of this existence the text is silent.

III.4[15].1

The importance of this text cannot be questioned. Corporeal matter, under the guise of absolute indetermination is explicitly linked to the chain of realities that ultimately have their source in the One.

III.6[26].14

At this point in Plotinus' philosophical speculations, matter is no longer spoken of in terms of being produced, but it is that which halts all production. Concerning matter's own origin, if it has one, the text is silent.

V.8[31].7

Plotinus demonstrates that the power of Intellect extends to matter, but a statement of causal connection is not present. Intellect shapes matter like the potter shapes his clay, and as the potter does not cause clay to be clay, the Intellect does not cause matter to be matter.

III.2[47].2

The One which is the First can be said to be form in relation to all things and matter to none since It is the First prior to which there is nothing. Matter, being the Last, can only be matter to all things and form to none since it is the Last and as such there is nothing that is after it. Concerning the origin of this matter, Plotinus avoided discussing the problem. The text states that "Intellect by giving something of Itself to matter, made all things," but we are left in the dark with regards to the status of matter before Intellect gave something of Itself to it.

I.8[51]

The result of this treatise is that Plotinus leaves us with a great amount of uncertainty as regards the status of corporeal matter. While it is true that he is not interested, in this treatise, with the problem of the origin of matter *per se*; nevertheless, in talking about the necessity of matter he uses a language full of dualistic implications. There is no indication whatsoever that matter is linked to the higher realities. It is the 'ancient nature' that is the cause of all evil in the world.

That the problem of the origin of matter plagued Plotinus throughout his philosophical career should now be evident. Of the three positions discovered in our analysis of the texts, the one which appears to predominate is the first: matter is not nothing; but Plotinus simply did not know where to place its origin in his philosophical system. This is most evident in his earliest treatises in which many characteristics of matter are discussed. Concerning its origin, the texts are painfully silent. There is a breakthrough, however, in II.4 in which Plotinus inextricably links the origin of intelligible matter to the overflow of the One, but no such claim is made for corporeal matter.

The situation changes with III.4.1 in which Plotinus' monism is most evident. Corporeal matter now has an origin and this origin is 'the power of growth in plants.' Matter is called 'absolute indetermination,' yet it is an indetermination that is tied to the chain of realities flowing from the One. But Plotinus' position of the origin of corporeal matter does not remain stable. After asserting that matter (absolute indetermination) has its source in the higher realities (III.4.1), he once again lapses into his state of uncertainty. Matter is no longer produced but is that which halts all production (III.6.14). This movement away from an emphasis on the origin of matter reaches its peak in I.8 in which Plotinus adopts the third position: matter is independent of the One and the point at which the power of the One is halted.

Plotinus' changing position on the origin of corporeal matter may be diagrammed as follows:

A	**B**	**C**	**D**
II.4[12]	III.4[15].1	III.6[26].14 V.8[31].7 III.2[47].2	I.8[51]

Tables B and D are indicative of Plotinus' monistic (matter appears to have its origin in the One) and dualistic (matter appears not to have its origin in the One) positions respectively. Tables A and C are transition periods in Plotinus' philosophical development when he was at a loss as to where to place the origin of matter, if it had one, in his philosophical system. The uncertainty of A culminated in the monism of B while the uncertainty of C culminated in the dualism of D.

The question pursued in this study was whether Plotinus' monism is consistent in accounting for the origin of matter, or whether this monism devolves into a dualism because it makes no provision for this origin. At this point we can say that Plotinus' monism does devolve into a dualism but a dualism of implication rather than intent. At no time does Plotinus say that matter is not a product of the One, but his silence in this regard, especially in the later treatises, deals a deadly blow to his monistic inclinations. The problem of the origin of matter and its position in the universe can be termed the Plotinian albatross—a problem that was with Plotinus throughout his philosophical career and that weighed most heavily upon him in his later years. This is especially true in I.8 in which by the implication of his own language Plotinus appears to embrace a dualism which he heretofore would have avoided.

Ohio Dominican College

NOTES

1. Matter is always to be understood as the primary participant. For Plotinus and later for Proclus, this participant is identical with intelligible matter in the trans-sensible world and with corporeal matter in the sensible world.
2. Emile Bréhier, *The Philosophy of Plotinus*, translated by J. Thomas (Chicago: University of Chicago Press, 1958), 180.
3. See John M. Rist, "Plotinus on Matter and Evil," *Phronesis* 6 (1961), 154–66.
4. See Emile Bréhier, *The Philosophy of Plotinus*, 174–181.
5. See Phillippus Villiers Pistorius, *Plotinus and Neoplatonism* (Cambridge: Bowes and Bowes, 1952), especially 129–30.
6. E. R. Dodds, "Numenius and Ammonius," *Les Source de Plotin*: Dix epossées et discussion par MM. A. H. Armstrong, P. Vincenzo Cilento, E. R. Dodds, H. Dorrie, P. Hadot, R. Harder, P.-P. Henry, H.-Ch. Peuch, H. R. Schwyzer, W. Theiler (Paris: Klincksieck, 1960), 21–22.
7. Paul Henry, "Discussion of Dorrie's 'Die Frage nach dem Transzendentem im Mittelplatonismus,'" *Les Sources de Plotin*, 236–37.
8. A. H. Armstrong, *Plotinus* I (Cambridge, MA: Harvard University Press, 1966), xxiv.
9. W. R. Inge, *The Philosophy of Plotinus*, 2 volumes (London: Longman's, Green and Co., 1918), especially 129–144.

10. Jean Trouillard, *La procession Plotinienne* (Paris: Presses Universitaries de France, 1955), 15.
11. Dennis O'Brien, "Plotinus on Evil," *The Downside Review* 87 (1969), 68–110. The quote is from page 102.
12. John Murray, "The Ascent of Plotinus to God," *Gregorianum* 32 (1951), 223–246. The quote is from page 234.
13. Joseph Katz, *Plotinus' Search for the Good: A Study of the Moral Motivation of His Metaphysics* (New York: Kings Crown Press, 1950), 44.
14. Cletus Carbonara, *La Filosofia di Plotino* (Napoli: Libreria Scientifica Editrice, 1954).
15. These texts are referred to as 'key texts' because in them Plotinus himself speaks of the origin and role of matter.
16. We shall employ Porphyry's chronological listing of the *Enneads* as presented in his "On the Life of Plotinus," which is contained in Armstrong's *Plotinus* (Volume I). All references to Porphyry's work will be to this edition.
17. The *Enneads* are cited throughout this study as follows. References to the Greek text of *Enneads* I–III are taken from A. H. Armstrong's *Plotinus* in the Loeb Classical Library Editions (Cambridge: Harvard University Press, 1966–67); to *Enneads* IV–V, from P. Henry and H–R Schwyzer's *Plotini Opera: Minor Edition* (Oxford: University Press, 1977); to *Ennead* VI, from E. Bréhier's *Ennead* VI (Paris: Société d'Edition *Les Belles Letters*, 1956). In my translations I am greatly indebted to Armstrong's English and Bréhier's French translations, which accompany the Greek text. I have also consulted Stephen MacKenna's English translation—*Plotinus: The Enneads* (London: Farber and Faber, 1956); the Italian translation of V. Cilento—*Plotini Eneadi* (Bari: Gius, Latera & Figli, 1947 s); and Richard Harder's German translation—*Plotins Schriften* (Hamburg: Felix Meiner, 1956).
18. Porphyry, "On the Life of Plotinus," 4, 45.
19. *Ennead* II.4.1, 5–6.
20. *Ennead* II.4.15, 21–23.
21. *Ennead* II.4.2, 2–5.
22. *Ennead* II.4.3, 13–19.
23. *Ennead* II.4.4, 7–8.
24. *Ennead* II.4.4, 18–21.
25. *Ennead* II.4.5, 28–39.
26. Rist, "Plotinus on Matter and Evil," 155–156.
27. John Rist, *Plotinus: The Road to Reality* (Cambridge: University Press, 1967), 219.
28. See A. H. Armstrong, "Spiritual or Intelligible Matter in Plotinus and St. Augustine," *Augustinus Magister* I (Congrès international augustinien, Paris: 21–24 Sept., 1954) Bréhier, *Enneads* II, 49; Carbonara, *Filosofia Di Plotino* (Napoli: Libreria Scientifica Editrice, 1954), 21; Leo Sweeney, S. J.,

"Infinity in Plotinus," *Gregorianum* 38 (1957), 526.

29. See *Ennead* II.5.3. & V.9.4.
30. *Ennead* II.4.6, 17–20. This notion of coming to be is characteristic of Aristotle's concept of matter (Cf. *Metaphysics* Λ.1 & 2, 1069b). The criticism of pre-Socratic views found in chapter 7 is also based on Aristotle (Cf. *Metaphysics* A.7, 988a27ff.; Λ.2, 1069b20–23).
31. *Ennead* II.4.8, 9–11.
32. *Ennead* II.4.8, 23–26.
33. Rist, "Plotinus on Matter and Evil," 156.
34. *Ennead* I.8.3, 7–10.
35. For example, Plato says in 257b: "When we speak of 'that which is not,' it seems that we do not mean something contrary to what exists but only something that is different...So, when it is asserted that a negation signifies a contrary, we shall not agree, but admit no more than this—that the prefix 'not' indicates something different from the words that follow, or rather from the things designated by the words pronounced after the negative": translated by F. M. Cornford in *The Collected Dialogues of Plato*, ed. E. Hamilton and H. Cairns (New York: Pantheon Books, 1966), 1003–1004.
36. *Ennead* I.8.5, 8ff.
37. *Ennead* II.4.16, 3–5.
38. *Ennead* II.4.12, 11–14 & 23–25. On matter as a receptacle see III.6.14, 28–37.
39. For Plotinus' use of the analogy of the mirror in describing matter see III.6.13, 35–55.
40. *Ennead* II.4.10, 6–13: "That which wants to be a thought about it [matter] will not be a thought but a kind of thoughtlessness; or rather the mental representation of it will be spurious and not genuine, compounded of an unreal part and with the diverse kind of reasoning. And it was perhaps because he had observed this that Plato said that matter was apprehended by a 'spurious reasoning'." This reference is to the *Timaeus* 52b2.
41. *Ennead* I.8.9, 15–27.
42. *Ennead* III.4.1, 1–2. III.9.3, 7–14 also speaks of the Soul's production of the indeterminate.
43. Richard Harder, *Plotins Shriften* Ib, 540.
44. Texts in which matter is identified with indetermination are: II.4.4, 20; II.4.10, 34; I.4.11, 32 & 41; II.4.13, 6. As indefinite, "it is not quality but the substrate and the matter that we are looking for" (II.4.13, 6).
45. *Ennead* II.4.13, 28–33 (page 140 n1). The text that he is commenting on is as follows: "Other things are not only other but each of them is something as form, but this would appropriately be called nothing but other; or perhaps others, so as not to define it as a unity by the term 'other' but to show its indefiniteness by calling it 'others'."
46. *Ennead* III.4.1, 14–17.
47. *Ennead* IV.7.2.

48. *Ennead* IV.7.2, 22–25. II.7.3, 8–14, gives a similar account of the coming to be of bodies.
49. Harder, Ib, 542–543. "Aber nicht der Korper ist sondien das Umbestimmte, die Materie...."
50. One is inclined to say a 'collection' of forms of matter but in VI.3.8, 26, Plotinus uses the word *migma* which means 'mixture.' Commenting on this text, Bréhier says: "But in Plotinus, as there is no such union of matter and forms, forms can be added to one another without the concrete ever becoming one. The sensible substance is, as it is in Locke, 'an aggregate of qualities and of matter'" (*The Philosophy of Plotinus*, 175).
51. *Ennead* III.4.1, 17–18.
52. *Ennead* I.8.7, 21–22.
53. Porphyry, "On the Life of Plotinus," 6, 26–36.
54. Porphyry, "Life," 6, 26–36.
55. *Ennead* III.6.14, 26–37.
56. *Ennead* III.6.7, 22–33. The analogy of matter as a mirror is used again in IV.3.11, 6–14.
57. *Ennead* III.6.13, 49–51.
58. *Ennead* III.6.11, 15–18 & 36–41.
59. *Ennead* III.6.7, 24.
60. *Ennead* III.6.6, 32–33. On the point of the sensible world as non-being, we must be careful not to misinterpret Plotinus. The sensible is beautiful (V.8.8, 7–23), but it is not the intelligible world—the world of true reality. It is an imitation: "Surely, what other fairer image of the intelligible world could there be?" (II.9.4, 22–23) This world is the best possible image of the world There. The plants There are the paradigms of the plants Here (VI.7.11, 6–17).
61. *Ennead* III.6.14, 1–5.
62. *Ennead* V.8.7, 18–29.
63. *Ennead* V.9.8, 4. For other examples of Intellect containing all the forms see VI.7.15; VI.7.22; V.9.6; V.8.3 & 4; VI.7.9; VI.7.12; V.1.4; VI.2.21.
64. *Ennead* III.4.1.
65. He says in I.8.3, 5, that matter is "a sort of form of non-existence...."
66. Examples of the formlessness of matter are: *Ennead* III.6.7, 28–30: "Imitation of real beings pass into and out of it [*Timaeus* 50c4–5]—ghosts into a formless ghost, visible because of its formlessness"; I.3.5, 23–24: "...ugliness is matter not mastered by form..."; II.4.8, 23–25: "So when the forms come to the matter it brings everything with it..."; I.8.8, 19–24: "For matter masters what is imaged in it and corrupts and destroys it by applying its own nature which is contrary to form, not bringing cold to hot but putting its own formlessness to the form of heat and its shapelessness to the shape and its excess and defect to that which is measured, till it has made the form belong to matter and no longer to itself...."

67. Proclus, *The Elements of Theology*, translated by E. R. Dodds (Oxford: At the Clarendon Press, 1964).
68. Proclus, *Theology*, Prop. 57 (Dodds Translation).
69. *Ennead* I.8.7, 20–22. "Now it is necessary that what comes after the first exists, and therefore that the last exists, and this is matter...."
70. See Bréhier's "Notice" to his translation of III.2.2. & 3. Also see II.9.1, 31–33, in which Plotinus himself says that λόγος does not constitute a separate hypostasis.
71. *Ennead* III.2.2, 8–17.
72. *Ennead* III.2.2, 18: *to gar aporreon ek noū logos*.
73. See *Ennead* VI.7.9 & VI.7.12.
74. *Ennead* V.2.1, 13–18.
75. Inge, *The Philosophy of Plotinus* I, 131. Plotinus himself refers to Soul as matter in II.5.3, 13–14: "...the soul, which is form, can be matter to something else." This 'something else' is Intellect.
76. *Ennead* IV.6.3, 5–10.
77. *Ennead* II.3.17, 15–24. Also see IV.3.10, 38–42 & IV.7.2, 22–25.
78. John N. Deck, *Nature, Contemplation, and the One* (Toronto: University Press, 1967), 60–61.
79. Porphyry, "Life," 6, 26–36.
80. *Ennead* I.8.1, 7–10.
81. *Ennead* I.8.1, 13–18.
82. *Ennead* I.8.2, 2–10.
83. *Ennead* I.8.2, 21–29. The reference is to *Phaedrus* 248a1.
84. Perhaps a coined word such as 'despire' is more appropriate.
85. *Ennead* I.8.3, 12–17.
86. *Ennead* I.8.3, 22–25 & 35–40.
87. *Ennead* I.8.11, 15–20. I.8.12 continues the discussion begun in the previous chapter. "But what is the answer if someone says that the vice and evil in the soul is not absolute privation of good, but only a (particular, limited) privation of good? In this case, if it has some good and is deprived of some, it will be in a mixed state and the evil will not be undiluted, and we have not yet found primary, undiluted evil: and the soul will have good in its very substance, but evil as some kind of accident."
88. Concerning the notion of matter as the cause of the soul's failure to achieve its proper goal see: I.6.5; I.8.4 & 5; II.3.12, 9–11.
89. *Ennead* I.8.7, 17–23.
90. *Ennead* I.8.2, 26–28.
91. *Ennead* II.4.5. See Key Text A above.
92. *Ennead* I.8.10, 2.
93. *Ennead* II.5.4, 11–19.
94. *Ennead* II.5.5, 6–8.
95. *Ennead* I.8.3, 7–10.
96. *Ennead* I.8.5, 8–13.

97. *Ennead* II.4.16, 1–10.
98. *Ennead* I.8.7, 3–9. By 'ancient nature' Plato meant the underlying matter not yet set in order by some god. The citation is from *Timaeus* 47e5–48a.
99. Plotinus here echoes Plato who says in *Timaeus* 47e5: "For the creation of this world is the combined work of necessity and mind" (B. Jowett translation: *The Collected Dialogues of Plato*, ed. E. Hamilton and H. Cairns,) 1175.
100. *Ennead* I.8.14, 39–54.
101. *Ennead* I.8.14, 52–54. In I.6.5, 45–50, Plotinus says that the soul's ugliness has come from the addition of alien matter and, if it is to be beautiful again, it must cleanse itself and be as it was before. For the means of purification, see I.8.9, 8–9 & I.9.

PLOTINUS' SET OF CATEGORIES FOR THE *KOSMOS AISTHĒTOS*[1]

Christos Evangeliou

Plotinus certainly is not known as a philosopher who was fond of writing polemical essays and refuting the doctrines of other philosophers of the past or his contemporaries. Many of his admirers would have difficulty imagining him in the role of a dialectician or advocate. As a rule, he does not engage in polemics in the *Enneads* which is a book of finding and stating the truth positively. Yet, the treatises II.9 and VI.1 stand as notable exceptions to the rule. It is known that II.9 is directed against the Gnostics—more precisely, a certain sect of Gnostics who seem to have had an interest in the philosophy of Plato and some connection with the school of Plotinus in Rome.[2] In this treatise Plotinus not only refutes the Gnostic tenets as follies but he also discharges the task of effectively defending Hellenism against the attacks which it received from Barbarism in the third century A.D.[3] In VI.1, on the other hand, Plotinus advances a rigorous criticism of the Stoic and the Peripatetic theories of categories both of which he rejects as being inadequate to account for the Intelligible realm.[4]

According to Porphyry's thematical arrangement, VI.1 is followed by two treatises, VI.2 and VI.3, which share with it the characteristic title 'On the Genera of Being.'[5] In VI.2, Plotinus presents the Platonic doctrine of the five 'highest kinds' (*megista genē* or *maxima genera*) as found in the *Sophist*,[6] and he defends it as the only sound account of the 'genera of being' compared to the rival Aristotelian and Stoic categorial schemes. He also makes it clear that "new genera must be found" for the sensible cosmos (*kosmos aisthētos*).[7] This is the reason why VI.3 is devoted to the search for the needed 'genera.'[8] The list, which was finally adopted by Plotinus, is a fivefold division of 'genera' or categories of Becoming. This obviously corresponds to the five 'highest kinds' of Plato, and the correspondence can hardly be coincidental. What is more important for our purposes here is that the names of the Plotinian categories for the Sensible realm are the same as those of Aristotle's list with one exception.[9]

In this study my purpose is to attempt a critical analysis of Plotinus' proposed new set of categories for the Sensible world in connection with its Aristotelian background. From this analysis it will become clear why it was that Plotinus found Aristotle's categorial scheme defective and how he thought he could improve upon the Stagirite in this important area of philosophical inquiry. However, before I proceed to deal with the analysis and evaluation of Plotinus' arguments regarding the 'genera' of Becoming and their relationship to the 'genera of Being,' it will be well to draw attention to certain facts which indicate clearly, I think, the importance of the treatise under consideration. Such a clarification is necessary in view of the fact that modern scholars speak of this part of the *Enneads* as, to use Inge's expression, "one of the most obscure and least interesting."[10]

First of all, it is the case that in VI.3 Plotinus is concerned with the Sensible cosmos and its problems theoretically. This interest is rather unusual for the otherworldly philosopher and, therefore, significant. Presumably, Plotinus would not have bothered to write this treatise had he not been convinced that there was much confusion regarding the ontic problem of the 'genera of Being' and its relation to the problem of the categories of Becoming. Second, it is also the case that in VI.3, unlike VI.2, Plotinus challenges Aristotle in the field of his expertise, that is, the realm of the Sensible cosmos. The claim of Plotinus that Aristotle's set of categories, as it stands, is superfluous and cannot adequately account for the phenomena of this world, which it was supposed to explain, is a very serious charge. If Plotinus were right that the categorial scheme of Aristotle needs a drastic (fifty percent) reduction and certain other fundamental changes, which we will discuss in due course, in order to function well within the realm of nature, it would follow that Aristotle did not know what he was doing when he developed his theory of categories in the way he did. It is significant, I think, that subsequent generations of Neoplatonists, beginning with Porphyry, found it difficult to follow Plotinus' anti-Aristoteliantactics in so far as the doctrine of categories was concerned. Fourth, in this light, it would not be an exaggerationto suggest that the problematic of Aristotle's categories caused a schism in the Neoplatonic school in Rome in the middle of the Third Century A.D., and that Porphyry, in opposition to Plotinus, emerged as a champion of the movement towards a deeper reconciliation of Platonism and Aristotelianism by accepting and defending Aristotle's doctrine of categories in its entirety.[11]

I

The third tractate of the sixth *Ennead* opens in the following characteristic way:

> We have now explained our conception of Reality (True Being) and considered how far it agrees with the teaching of Plato. We have still to investigate the opposed principle (the principle of Becoming)....
>
> The subject of our discussion is the Sensible realm: Sensible Existence is entirely embraced by what we know as the Universe: our duty, then, would seem to be clear enough—to take this Universe and analyze its nature, classifying its constituent parts and arranging them by species. (VI.3.1, 1–11)

From this passage at least two things are evident: (1) The sharp contrast between the realm of 'True Being' and the realm of mere 'Becoming,' this Universe which Plotinus terms 'the opposed principle' (*hetera physis*); and (2) the purpose (duty) which Plotinus poses to himself in the present tract is to determine under what genera the constituents of this Universe fall, and whether or not these 'genera' are similar to (or the same as) the genera of the other realm, i.e. the Intelligible cosmos (*kosmos noētos*).

Given, however, that this realm of Becoming is a 'mixture' (*migma*) of Body and Soul, Plotinus alerts us that the investigation should not take into consideration that element of the mixture which is 'alien,' viz. Soul. For, as he explains:

> True, it involves the parallel existence of Body and Soul, for the Universe is a living form: essentially however Soul is of the Intellectual and does not enter into the structure of what is called Sensible Being.
>
> Remembering this fact, we must—however great the difficulty—exclude Soul from the present investigation, just as in a census of citizens, taken in the interests of commerce and taxation, we should ignore the alien population. (VI.3.1, 23–28)

As to the question whether the genera posited for the Intelligible sphere will do well also with regard to the Sensible sphere, Plotinus' answer seems to be negative. Inasmuch as the two realms are different, Plotinus thinks that distinct and "new genera must be sought for this Universe" (VI.3.1, 20). The new 'genera,' consequently, can be called so only in an analogous way and homonymously.[12] In no way can they be regarded as 'primary genera.'

> Substance (Real Being) requires no more than these five constituents; but when we have to turn to the lower sphere, we find other principles giving rise no longer to Substance (as such) but to quantitative Substance and qualitative: these other principles may be regarded as genera but not primary genera. (VI.2.15, 15–18)

And again:

> Our first observations must be directed to what passes in the Sensible realm for Substance. It is, we shall agree, only by analogy that the nature manifested in bodies is designated as Substance, and by no means because such terms as Substance or Being tally with the notion bodies in flux; the proper term would be Becoming. (VI.1.3, 1–4)

Accordingly, ontologically important terms, such as Substance (*ousia*) and Being (*to on*) may be used in reference to the sensible world, but only homonymously, since the so-called 'beings' (*onta*) of this sensible realm are just reflections and images (*eidōla*) of the real Beings of the true and 'Authentic Being.' Thus, the relation between these two realms of existents is analogous to the relation of a living being and its portrait. While 'Up There' everything is both 'simple' and 'substantial,'[13] 'Down Here' everything is 'composite' and 'shadowy.'[14] At the end of the second tract (chapter 23) Plotinus used the following characteristic expressions in reference to this sensible realm: *indalma*, *eidōlon*, *eikōn*, *mimēma*, *phantasma*, *graphē*—all of which have the connotation of copy or ectype. Consider, for example, the following:

> Up to the production of the image, the Intellectual realm is wholly and exclusively composed of Intellectual Beings: in the same way the Sensible world representing that in so far as it is able to retain the likeness of a living being, is itself a living being: the relation is like that of a portrait or reflection to the original which is regarded as prior to the water or the painting reproducing it. (VI.2.23, 36–40)

Again:

> Observe also how in other things Motion or life is clearly separated from Being—a separation impossible, doubtless, in True Being, but possible in its shadow and namesake. In the portrait of a man much is left out, and above all the essential thing, life: the 'Being' of sensible things is just such a shadow of True Being, an abstraction from that Being complete which was life in the Archetype; it is because of this incompleteness that we are able in

the Sensible world to separate Being from life and life from Being. (VI. 2.7, 8–15)

In VI.3.3, Plotinus makes several tentative proposals about the 'genera' or categories of the Sensible realm and finally adopts a fivefold division which includes Sensible Substance or pseudo-substance, as MacKenna renders it[15] (*ousia legomene* or *aisthētē*), Quantity (*poson*), Quality (*poion*), Motion (*kinēsis*), and Relation (*pros ti*). A simple comparison of this list to that of Aristotle's categories reveals that, at least in name, four of them correspond to the cardinal Aristotelian categories of Substance, Quantity, Quality, and Relation. Plotinus' newly coined category or 'genus' of Motion is called in to substitute for two Aristotelian categories: action (*poiein*) and passion (*paschein*). Whether the Plotinian 'genera' and the Aristotelian categories share in everything else except for their common names will become apparent from the discussion of each of them separately.

The remaining twenty-five chapters of the present tractate are devoted to the discussion of the proposed five 'genera' of the Sensible realm. In accordance with the role which they play in the Plotinian theory, the proportional length devoted to each of these 'genera' is as follows:

(a) Substance—seven chapters.
(b) Motion—seven chapters.
(c) Quantity—five chapters.
(d) Quality—five chapters.
(e) Relation—one chapter.

They are considered and discussed in the following order: Substance, Quantity, Quality, Motion, and Relation.

As expected, priority is given to the 'genus' or category of Substance (*ousia*) in respect to both length and order. After Substance comes the Plotinian category of Motion which is new and needs to be well considered and established. With regard to the categories of Quantity and Quality, nothing is unexpected. It is surprising, however, that the discussion of Relation has been compressed into one small chapter, in a way which contrasts sharply with the treatment given to the same category in the first tract. How is this discrepancy to be explained?

Without intending to offer a full explanation of this issue, it may be observed that Relation in a wider sense encompasses the other three Plotinian categories—viz. Quantity, Quality and Motion—as it is clear from the following:

> Thus we have five genera, counting the first three entities as one. If the first three are not massed into a unity, the series will be Matter, Form, Composite, Relation, Quantity, Quality, Motion. The last three may, again, be included in Relation, which is capable of bearing this wider extension. (VI.3.3, 17–32)

Therefore, it may be argued that Plotinus found it unnecessary to discuss this category at length, since he had done so with regard to the other three. However that may be, it will be worthwhile to examine very briefly how Plotinus considers each of his categories or 'genera' of the Sensible world. In my discussion I will follow the same order as Plotinus, so I will begin with Substance.

Plotinus opens the discussion on Sensible Substance (*ousia aisthētē*) by raising the question: "What, then, we have to ask, is the constant element in the first three entities? What is it that identifies them with their inherent Substance?" (VI.3.4, 1–2). Seeking for the 'constant element' which will allow the three entities—Matter, Form and Composite—to be regarded as one 'genus,' Plotinus raises the further questions:

> But what, we may ask, have Matter and Form in common? In what sense can Matter be conceived as a genus, and what will be its species? What is the differentia of Matter? In which genus, Matter or Form, are we to rank the composite of both? It may be this very composite which constitutes the Substance manifested in bodies, neither of the components by itself answering to the conception of Body: how, then, can we rank them in one and the same genus as the composite? How can the elements of a thing be brought within the same genus as the thing itself? Yet if we begin with bodies, our first-principles will be compounds.
>
> Why not resort to analogy? (VI.3.2, 9–16)

Resort to analogy—which would mean to conceive Matter and Form as analogous to the genera of the 'True Being,' i.e. Substance and Motion respectively—is excluded for reasons given in the rest of chapter two of this tract. Instead, Plotinus goes on to consider five alternative 'constant elements,' some of which resemble Aristotle's 'peculiar character' (*idia*) of Substance, as will be seen presently.

According to the first alternative, the 'constant element' is identified as *hedra* or *hypobathra*—i.e. 'having the capability to serve as base.' This may be true with regard to Matter or with regard to Composite, Plotinus remarks. But apparently it can not apply to Form which, on this ground, would not be allowed to be considered as a Substance. So the first candidate must be rejected.

According to the second alternative, the 'constant element' is identified as "that which is not said of anything else" (VI.3.4, 7–8). This is evidently true in cases of Composite, e.g. Socrates. But what about Form and Matter? Are not they said to be the Form and Matter *of* something? To meet objections of this sort, Plotinus proceeds to distinguish, correctly I think, between that which is 'said of something else' because it is a part of that something considered as a whole, and that which is 'said of something else,' though they differ from each other. It is to the former where both Matter and Form belong. Whereas attributes, such as white, which are predicated of something distinct from itself, belong to the latter. In this connection, Plotinus states:

> We conclude that nothing belonging to something else and predicated of it can be Substance. Substance is that which belongs essentially to itself, or, in so far as it is a part of the differentiated object, serves only to complete the Composite. Each or either part of the Composite belongs to itself, and is only affirmed of the Composite in a special sense: only *qua* part of the whole is it predicated of something else; *qua* individual it is never in its essential nature predicated of an external. (VI.3.4, 20–26)

According to the third alternative the 'constant element' is identified as *hypokeimenon*—i.e. 'having the capacity to be a subject.' Plotinus thinks that this property is common to all three entities—viz. Matter, Form and Composite— but not without some qualifications (*allōs*). For example, Plotinus contends that Matter is said to be *hypokeimenon* to Form in a sense which is not the same as when the Composite is said to be *hypokeimenon* to accidents, activities, consequents etc. (VI.3.4, 34–35).

According to the fourth alternative the 'constant element' is identified as 'not being present in a subject' (*mē ēn hypokeimenō*). Plotinus observes that this characteristic can not be applied to all entities called Substances, unless: "...presence in a subject be stipulated as not including the case of the part present in the whole or of one thing combining with another to form a distinct unity" (VI.3.5, 8–10). Thus, Form will not be present in Matter as 'in a subject,' nor will man be present in Socrates. For, as Plotinus explains, 'Man is part of Socrates' (VI.3.5, 13), not in the sense in which Socrates' hand is part of Socrates, but in the sense that Socrates is composite of Matter and Form.[16]

It may be recalled here that Aristotle did not, in the end, admit this characteristic as the 'peculiar character' of Substance, on the ground that it did not characterize Substance solely.[17] For it is applicable to *differentia* as well. Plotinus seems to reject the view that differentiae, like

Substances, are not 'in a subject.' To support this thesis he argues along the following lines:

> It may be objected that non-presence in a subject is not peculiar to Substance, inasmuch as the differentia of a substance is no more present in a subject than the substance itself; but this objection results from taking a part of the whole substance, such as 'two-footed' in our example, and asserting that this part is not present in a subject: If we take, not 'two-footed' which is merely an aspect of Substance, but 'two-footedness' by which we signify not Substance but Quality, we shall find that this 'two-footedness' is indeed present in a subject. (VI.2.5, 23–29)

According to the fifth and last alternative, the 'constant element' is identified as 'neither being present in a subject nor being predicated of a subject' (VI.3.5, 14–15). The expression 'neither...nor,' it may be recalled, states the peculiar characteristic of primary substance in the Aristotelian text.[18] As it is stated, however, this formula can apply only to the Composite. In order to make it fit all other entities, which Plotinus calls categories, he had to modify the formula a little by adding 'neither...nor predicated of *another as other*' (VI.3.5, 15). This little modification is very important because it allows Plotinus to draw the fundamental distinction between predicates predicated of a subject from which they differ essentially (e.g. 'a piece of wood is white') and predicates predicated of a subject from which they do not differ essentially (e.g. 'Socrates is a man'). For, according to Plotinus:

> When I predicate Man of Socrates, it is as though I affirmed, not that a piece of wood is white, but that whiteness is white; for in asserting that Socrates is a man, I predicate Man (the universal) of a particular man, I affirm Man of the manhood in Socrates; I am really saying only that Socrates is Socrates, or that this particular rational animal is an animal. (VI.2.5, 17–23)

In other words, cases of *essential predication* seem to be reducible to cases of *self-predication*, i.e. tautologies. For example, to predicate 'man' of an individual is the same, according to Plotinus, as to say that 'Socrates is Socrates.' The problem of predication, however, is very complex and cannot be considered here.[19] Suffice it to emphasize here that the formula 'neither...nor...' as modified by Plotinus can encompass both Aristotle's secondary substances and Plato's eternal Forms. Even so, Matter is left outside. Realizing this, Plotinus gives up the effort to find a formula which will provide the needed 'constant element' and concludes in the following way:

> The truth is, however, that the 'Substance' of our enquiry may be apprehended in directly opposite ways: it may be determined by one of the properties we have been discussing, by more than one, by all at once, according as they answer to the notions of Matter, Form and the Couplement (VI.2.5, 35–39)

Although he has said much about this issue, Plotinus is aware that he has not clarified the category of Sensible Substance, nor has he provided a 'definition' of it as yet. Thus, he is ready to attempt another approach in order to discover what is that peculiar characteristic which distinguishes Substance from the other 'genera' of Becoming. Eventually he will find a solution to this problem in what I shall call the doctrine of *double dependence*. I shall explain what this expression is supposed to mean, after I have quoted Plotinus once again on the equivocation of the term 'existence' (*einai*), as applied to different categories of the sensible realm. Plotinus argues:

> What, then, is the meaning of 'existence' as applied to fire, earth and the other elements? What is the difference between this existence and existence in the other categories? It is the difference between being simply—that which merely is—and being white. But surely the being qualified by 'white' is the same as that having no qualification? It is not the same: the latter is Being in the primary sense, the former is Being only by participation and in a secondary degree. Whiteness added to Being produces a being white; Being added to whiteness produces a white being: thus, whiteness becomes an accident of Being, and Being an accident of whiteness. (VI.2.6, 8–18)

Also:

> The Being of the Sensible resembles the white in not originating in itself. It must therefore be regarded as dependent for its being upon the Authentic Being, as white is dependent upon the Authentic Whiteness, and the Authentic Whiteness dependent for its whiteness upon participation in that Supreme Being whose existence is underived. (VI.2.6, 28–32)

Now it is somewhat easier to explain what distinguishes sensible substance from the other 'genera' of the sensible realm. The distinction is based on the formula of double dependence. For, as it is evident from the two passages quoted above, especially the second one, while the sensible

Substance is dependent upon the 'Authentic Being' for its existence, the sensible white depends upon the 'Authentic Whiteness' which in turn is dependent upon the 'Authentic Being' ultimately. That is to say, in the category of sensible substance we have *simple dependence*, whereas in the other sensible categories or 'genera' the dependence is *double*.[20] It is in this respect that Sensible Substance is differentiated from the other 'genera' of Becoming.

Let us turn our attention now to another point of importance which Plotinus discusses in this connection—viz. the problem of priority between the two constituents of the Composite: Matter and Form. This is not an easy problem to solve because its solution, that is, priority of the one constituent over the other seems to depend on the viewpoint from which one considers the whole matter.

> That Matter is not a Primary we have established elsewhere. If it be urged that other things can have no subsistence without being implanted in Matter, we admit the claim for Sensible things. But though Matter be prior to these, it is not thereby precluded from being posterior to many things—posterior, in fact, to all the beings of the Intellectual sphere. Its existence is but a pale reflection, and less complete than that of the things implanted in it....
>
> But once concede that Form is higher in the scale of Being than Matter, and Matter can no longer be regarded as a common ground of both, nor substance as a genus embracing Matter, Form and the Couplement. True, these will have many common properties, to which we have already referred, but their being (or existence) will nonetheless be different. (VI.2.7, 3–16)

Evidently, by 'things implanted in Matter' Plotinus means the Forms which are "higher in the scale of being than Matter," we are told (VI.2.7, 12–13). Now, granted that "when a higher being comes into contact with a lower, the lower, though first in the natural order, is yet posterior in the scale of Reality," (VI.2.7, 16–18) the conclusion seems to follow, as Plotinus puts it:

> If Being does not belong in equal degrees to Matter, to Form and to the Couplement, Substance can no longer be common to all three in the sense of being their genus: to their posteriors it will bear a still different relation, serving them as a common base by being bound up with all alike. Substance, thus, resembles life, dim here, clearer there, or portraits of which one is an outline, another more minutely worked. By measuring Being by its dim manifestation and neglecting a fuller revelation elsewhere, we may come to regard this dim existence as a common ground....

> We conclude that the term 'Being' must have different connotations as applied to Matter, to Form and to both conjointly, in spite of the single source pouring into the different streams. (VI.2.7, 12–30)

It is clear, therefore, that Plotinus realizes finally that the term 'to be' (*einai, to on*) is a *pollachōs legomenon*, as Aristotle had pointed out; it is a term with 'focal meaning' to use contemporary terminology.[21] Be it as it may, the conclusion reached by Plotinus—viz. that the 'being' does not mean the same thing when applied to Matter, Form, Composite, entities of the Sensible or the Intelligible Realms—led him to declare that:

> The division into elements must, in short, be abandoned, especially in regard to Sensible Substance, known necessarily by sense rather than by reason. We must no longer look for help in constituent parts, since such parts will not be substances, or at any rate not sensible substances.
>
> Our plan must be to apprehend what is constant in stone, earth, water and the entities which they compose—the vegetal and animal forms, considered purely as sensibles—and to confine this constant within a single genus. (VI.3.8, 1–6)

Thus, it would seem that we are back again at the point from which we started, viz. the composite entities of the Sensible World. But now the emphasis will be put, not on the constituents, but on the composite things as such (*syntheta*), which are considered as (a) "actually many substances in one" (VI.3.8, 9), though (b) "not everything which composes the amalgam is Substance, but only the amalgam as a whole" (VI.3.8, 29–30). It may be objected here that (a) and (b) as stated above seem to be incompatible with each other. Whereas the first asserts that 'composites' are actually a collection of many substances,[22] the second seems to deny it by considering as Substance only the amalgam 'as a whole.' For Plotinus, the two statements are not necessarily contradictory or incompatible; they are the outcome of two different considerations. For (a) considers 'composites' sensible being—as composed of such elements as fire, earth, air and water, which in themselves are composites of Matter and Form (VI.3.8, 7–12). But (b) considers a 'composite' sensible being as Composite of Matter, Form, Qualities, Activities and all other Accidents (*symbebēkota*) which go with 'composite,' and which separately can not be called Substance in the same sense (VI.3.8, 13–27).

Apart from the above objection, what really bothers Plotinus is that, if (b) is taken literally, it would seem that sensible substances are derived from non-substances, which is somehow disturbing. For how can

Substance come out of something which is not substantial? Such a claim would seem to amount to its being created *ex nihilo*, and this certainly is neither rational nor acceptable to a Platonist, like Plotinus. Much of the confusion, however, may be cleared up if we recall that the discussion here is about Sensible Substance, which is but a mere 'reflection' and 'shadow' of the Authentic Substances of the Intelligible realm. Plotinus explains:

> And let no one take exception on the ground that we produce Sensible Substance from non-substances. The whole amalgam itself is not True Substance; it is merely an imitation of that True Substance which has Being apart from its concomitants, these indeed being derived from it as the possessor of True Being. In the lower realm the case is different: the underlying ground is sterile, and from its inability to produce fails to attain to the status of Being; it remains a shadow, and on this shadow is traced a sketch...the world of Appearance. (VI.3.8, 30–37)

That is the way in which Plotinus considers the Sensible World whose 'genera' he tries to determine. This Universe is simply a picture or sketch (*zōgraphia*) drawn on a shadow, that is, the barren Matter (*agonon*). Such a conception is evidently very different than Aristotle's conception of this World. Plotinus thinks that he has said enough about the 'so-called' substance (*legomenē ousia*), or 'pseudo-substance,' as MacKenna renders it. Next he proceeds to examine the kinds (*eidē*) of Sensible Substance, which will provide him with the opportunity to criticize Aristotle's distinction between primary and secondary substances. I shall consider this issue briefly here.

To begin with, Plotinus postulates body (*sōma*) as the highest 'genus' with reference to the Sensible world. Then, by applying the Platonic method of division he is able to obtain a scheme of subordinate species and genera in a way which closely resembles the 'Porphyrian Tree.'[23] This division of sensible substances is given in the following passage:

> But what are we to posit as its species? How divide this genus?
>
> The genus as a whole must be identified with body. Bodies may be divided into the characteristically material and the organic: the material bodies comprise fire, earth, water, air; the organic the bodies of plants and animals, these in turn admitting of formal differentiation. (VI.3.9, 3–6)

This is not the only possible division, according to Plotinus. On the contrary, he mentions two more: (a) The division which is based on such qualities as hot, dry, cold, moist; and (b) the division which is based on forms or shapes (*morphai*). Both (a) and (b) are related to sense-perception. He observes: "Since our discussion is concerned with Sensible Substance, it is not strange that it should turn upon distinctions related to sense-perception: This Substance is not Being pure and simply, but the Sensible Being which we call the Universe" (VI.3.10, 12–15). Once again, Plotinus felt it necessary to stress the differences which separate the two realms, that of Becoming and that of Being.

With regard to the Aristotelian distinction between primary and secondary substances, Plotinus seems to agree that there are not different kinds of Substances, because they do not differ essentially from each other. Yet, he rejects Aristotle's view expressed in the *Categories* according to which the particular (i.e. primary Substance) is prior to the universal (i.e. secondary Substance).[24] Plotinus thinks otherwise on this issue as it is evident from what follows:

> We may be told that Man (the universal) is Form alone, Socrates Form in Matter. But on this very ground Socrates will be less fully Man than the universal;...
>
> Besides, the more general is by nature prior; hence, the Form-Idea is prior to the individual: but what is prior by nature is prior unconditionally. How then can the Form take a lower rank? The individual, it is true, is prior in the sense of being more readily accessible to our cognisance; this fact, however, entails no objective difference.
>
> Moreover, such a difference, if established, would be incompatible with a single Reason-Principle of Substance; First and Second Substances could not have the same Principle, nor be brought under a single genus. (VI.3.9, 32–42)

It may be noted here that the distinction between 'prior by nature' (*physei proteron*) and 'prior with regard to us' (*pros hēmas proteron*) is parallel to Porphyry's distinction between 'prior by nature' and 'sensibly prior' (*aisthēsei proteron*).[25] The Plotinian insight here, like the Porphyrian, is that for *x* to be prior to *y* in one sense does not imply necessarily that it will be prior to that in every sense. This formula, indeed, played an important role in Porphyry's efforts to reconcile the Aristotelian doctrine of the concrete individual (*tode ti*) with the Platonic theory of Forms (universals), as well as the Platonic-Aristotelian theories of the Sensible World with the Platonic-Plotinian theories of the Intelligible realm.

In conclusion it can be said that Sensible Substance is accepted by Plotinus as a 'genus' of the sensible world. But no one should be misled as to the fact that the 'being,' to which this 'genus' refers is only an image of the 'Authentic Being.' Thus, the use of the term 'Substance' (*ousia*) in its double reference covers a case of homonymy.[26]

II

As in the *Categories*, Quantity occupies the second place in Plotinus' list of the 'genera' of the Sensible world. In his discussion of this 'genus,' Plotinus wants to make clear from the very beginning that (a) only quantities related to matter—but not Absolute Quantity—will be considered here, and (b) only number (*arithmos*) and magnitude (*megethos*) are to be regarded as true quantities. He states:

> Passing to Quantity and the quantum, we have to consider the view which identifies them with number and magnitude on the ground that everything quantitative is numbered among Sensible things or rated by the extension of its substrate: we are here, of course, discussing not Quantity in isolation, but that which causes a piece of wood to be three yards long and gives the five in 'five horses.' (VI.3.11, 1–5)

Accordingly, three of the seven Aristotelian 'kinds' (*eidē*) of quantities are left out. These quantities are identified as Place or Space (*topos*) and Time (*chronos*)—which Aristotle classified with the continuous quantities—and *logos* (speech, discourse)—which Aristotle considered as discrete quantity. According to Plotinus, these quantities (*posa*) are reducible to the other 'genera' which were mentioned above. Of these the first two can be assigned to Relation, while the third must be referred to Motion. The justification of this reduction is stated by Plotinus in the following way:

> Now we have often maintained that number and magnitude are to be regarded as the only true qualities, and that Space and Time have no right to be conceived as quantitative: Time as the measure of Motion should be assigned to Relation, while Space, being that which circumscribes Body, is also a relative and falls under the same category; though continuous, it is, like Motion, not included in Quantity. (VI.3.11, 6–11)

Also:

> Syllable and discourse are only indirectly quantities or substrates of Quantity; it is voice that is quantitative: but voice is a kind of Motion; it must accordingly in any case (quantity or no quantity) be referred to Motion, as must activity also. (VI.3.12, 25–28)

In agreement with Aristotle, Plotinus rejects as non-quantities those comparatives which Porphyry, commenting on this category, called 'comparative quantities' (*aorista posa*)—e.g. 'more,' 'less,' 'more beautiful' etc.—on the ground that they belong to relatives. For the same reason 'large' and 'small'—as in the expressions 'a large tree,' 'a small mountain' etc.—are reducible to comparatives, and ultimately to relatives. For Plotinus, as for Aristotle, these expressions are equivalent to 'a tree larger (i.e. taller) than another tree' and 'a mountain smaller than (i.e. not as high as) another mountain' respectively. Apart from that, Plotinus, unlike Aristotle, wants to assert that "it is some kind of Quantity which gives greatness to the great." He queries:

> On the other hand, why do we not find in the category of Quantity 'great' and 'small'? It is some kind of Quantity which gives greatness to the great; greatness is not a relative, though greater and smaller are relatives, since these, like doubleness, imply an external correlative. (VI.3.11, 12–14)

Similarly with 'the beautiful' (*to kalon*):

> In sum, just as there is a Reason-Principle of Beauty, so there must be a Reason-Principle of greatness, participation in which makes a thing great, as the Principle of beauty makes it beautiful. (VI.3.12, 17–19)[27]

Considerations such as the above led Plotinus to accept that there is *contrariety* in the category of Quantity—which Aristotle had denied.[28] The possibility of receiving contraries was, for Aristotle, an indication that the 'quantities' involved were in fact not quantities, but relatives. Plotinus takes the opposite view:

> ...we must allow contrariety to Quantity: whenever we speak of great and small our notions acknowledge this contrariety by evolving opposite images, as also when we refer to many and few; indeed, 'few' and 'many' call for similar treatment to 'small' and 'great.' (VI.3.12, 1–5)[29]

And again:

> To judge from these instances, there is contrariety in Quantity. Place we may neglect as not strictly coming under the category of Quantity; if it were admitted, 'above' could only be a contrary if there were something in the universe which was 'below': as referring to the partial, the terms 'above' and 'below' are used in a purely relative sense, and must go with 'right' and 'left' into the category of Relation. (VI.3.12, 19–25)[30]

Finally, Plotinus accepts the Aristotelian distinction between *continuous* and *discrete* quantities and also the basis for this distinction as given by Aristotle:

> It has been remarked that the continuous is effectually distinguished from the discrete by their possessing the one a common, the other a separate limit. (VI.3.13, 1–2)

Number, according to Plotinus, belongs to the latter and can be subdivided into odd and even numbers. On the other hand, magnitude belongs to the former and is subdivided into lines, surfaces, and solids. But to speak of division here is rather misleading. This procedure should be called enumeration (*katarithmēsis*) for the reason that the distinction prior/posterior is involved in the different magnitudes, whereas simultaneity characterizes the species of the divided genus. In this connection Plotinus states:

> But how are we to differentiate the continuous, comprising as it does line, surface and solid? The line may be rated as of one dimension, the surface as of two dimensions, the solid as of three, if we are only making a calculation and do not suppose that we are dividing the continuous into its species; for it is an invariable rule that numbers, thus grouped as prior and posterior, cannot be brought into a common genus; there is no common basis in first, second and third dimensions. Yet there is a sense in which they would appear to be equal—namely, as pure measures of Quantity: of higher and lower dimensions, they are not however more or less quantitative.
>
> Numbers have similarly a common property in their being numbers all; and the truth may well be, not that One creates two, and two creates three, but that all have a common source. (VI.3.13, 9–20)

Now, if line is a quantity, and if a triangle is the product of three lines, then to the question "Why is not the product of three lines included in Quantity?" Plotinus' answer is that "a triangle consists not merely of three lines but of three lines in a particular disposition, a quadrilateral of four lines in a particular disposition: even the straight line involves disposition as well as quantity" (VI.3.14, 8–11). He seems to share Aristotle's view that one and the same entity can be classed under two different categories provided that each time it will be considered from a different point of view:

> If however by classing the triangle and the rectangle as qualia we propose to bring figures under Quality, we are not thereby precluded from assigning the same object to more categories than one: in so far as it is a magnitude—a magnitude of such and such a size—it will belong to Quantity; in so far as it presents a particular shape, to Quality. (VI.3.14, 18–22)

Consequently, it is not absurd that Geometry, which deals with figures[31]—viz. triangles, quadrilaterals, etc.—"is the study of magnitudes" (VI.3.14, 16). Thus, Plotinus is able to claim that "if we are told that equality and inequality are characteristic of Quantity, that is not to deny that similarity also may be predicated of certain quantities" (VI.3.15, 4–7). This is evidently an allusion to Aristotle's *Categories*, where equality and inequality are presented as the 'peculiar character' of Quantity.[32] This brings the discussion on the 'genus' of Quantity to an end. But there is a last point which needs to be considered before I proceed to examine the next 'genus' of the sensible world.

The point which Plotinus makes at the end of chapter 15 is that, in contrast to Aristotle's strong position that the individual or primary substance signifies a concrete individual, the sensible substance (*legomenē ousia*) is rather a 'qualified something' (*poion ti*). Hence, that which signifies substance and essence (*to ti einai*) is not the individual but the universal as expressed by *logos*. Compared with what Aristotle states about the expression 'this-such' (*tode ti*) in the *Categories*[33] and about the expression 'what something *is*' (*ti ēn einai*) in the *Metaphysics*,[34] the following quotation may show that Plotinus confused the two expressions and their different meanings:

> We have spoken of Quality as combining with other entities, Matter and Quantity, to form the complete Sensible Substance; this Substance, so called, may be supposed to constitute the manifold world of Sense, which is not so much an essence as a quale. Thus, for the essence of fire we must look to the Reason-Principle; what produces the visible aspect is, properly speaking, a quale.
>
> Man's essence will lie in his Reason-Principle; that which is perfected in the corporeal nature is a mere image of the Reason-Principle, a quale rather than an essence.

> Consider: the visible Socrates is a man, yet we give the name of Socrates to that likeness of him in a portrait, which consists of mere colours, mere pigments: similarly, it is a Reason-Principle which constitutes Socrates, but we apply the name Socrates to the Socrates we see: in truth, however, the colours and shapes which make up the visible Socrates are but reproductions of those in the Reason-Principle, while this Reason-Principle itself bears a corresponding relation to the truest Reason-Principle of Man.—But we need not elaborate this point. (VI.3.15, 23–37)

Unfortunately, Plotinus did not think it necessary to elaborate the point which he is making here, though an elaboration would be most welcome. He seems to distinguish between *logos* of man (i.e. definition, or 'Reason-Principle,' as MacKenna renders it) and *logos* of individual man, e.g. Socrates. But it is not clear (a) on what grounds this distinction is based, and (b) what is meant by *logos* in the case of Socrates. If we interpret *logos* in the second case as having the same meaning as in the first case, then it would seem to follow that for Plotinus even individuals are definable, which Aristotle had denied.[35] Such an interpretation may lead to the further hypothesis that Plotinus accepted 'Forms' of individuals, as has been suggested by modern scholars.[36] But it is possible that *logos* in the second case (i.e. *logos* of Socrates) does not mean 'definition' as in the first case, but rather description.[37] Thus, while the '*logos* of man' will give the essence (*ti esti*) of man in general, the '*logos* of Socrates' will qualify and specify—more precisely, atomize—the 'individual' (*ti*) by adding a collection of (accidental) properties, so that it will produce a 'qualified something' (*poion ti*). In this light, the meaning of the above quotation will be the following: As the portrait of Socrates stands to the living sensible Socrates, so the *logos* (*hypographē*) of Socrates (the individual man) stands to *logos* (definition) of man (the universal). The implication of this analogy is that the universal is more real than the particular, in spite of all Aristotelian assertion to the contrary.

III

With regard to Quality, considered as a separate 'genus' of the Sensible world, there are three main issues which Plotinus discusses: (a) Its distinction from the other 'genera,' (b) its different kinds, and (c) its special characteristics—i.e. its *idia*, as Porphyry called them. Of these three issues it is on (a) that Plotinus' views come very close to Aristotle's.

On (b) and (c), their views diverge, as will become clear from the discussion which follows.

It has been repeatedly stated by Plotinus that the sensible substance or 'pseudo-substance' (*legomenē*) is not simple but complex. It is the amalgam, the concrescence or coming together of many entities (*to ek pollōn*: VI.3.15, 26). Its constituents are not only Matter and Form but also Quantity, Quality, and Motion or absence of Motion, according to Plotinus. Quality, taken separately from the amalgam, can be said to signify 'the distinct mark' or 'the type of a thing.' Thus:

> When each of the entities bound up with the pseudo-substance is taken apart from the rest, the name of Quality is given to that one among them, by which without pointing to essence or quantity or motion we signify the distinctive mark, the type or aspect of a thing—for example, the beauty or ugliness of a body. This beauty—need we say?—is identical in name only with Intellectual Beauty: it follows that the term 'Quality' as applied to the Sensible and the Intellectual is necessarily equivocal. (VI.3.16, 1–7)

It is important to note here the 'equivocation' of the term 'Quality' as applied to the two realms—the Sensible and the Intelligible—because Plotinus' discussion in the next several pages seems to rest on this homonymy. On this basis he distinguishes the virtues, arts and sciences which are classed with 'Sensible Quality' from those which "necessarily belong to the...Intellectual." He states:

> Geometry and arithmetic are, we shall maintain, of a twofold character: in their earthly types they rank with Sensible Quality, but in so far as they are functions of pure Soul, they necessarily belong to that other world in close proximity to the Intellectual. This, too, is in Plato's view the case with music and astronomy.
>
> The arts concerned with material objects and making use of perceptible instruments and sense-perception must be classed with Sensible Quality, even though they are dispositions of the Soul, attendant upon its apostasy.
>
> There is also every reason for consigning to this category the practical virtues whose function is directed to a social end: These do not isolate Soul by inclining it towards the higher; their manifestation makes for beauty in this world, a beauty regarded not as necessary but as desirable. (VI.3.16, 19–31)

The outcome of this procedure would seem to be, as Plotinus realizes, "a distinction between psychic and bodily qualities, the latter belonging specifically to body" (VI.3.17, 1–2). By subdividing the psychic and bodily qualities, many and different kinds of Quality may be obtained, which are not the same as those presented in the *Categories*.[38] But here a serious question is raised and discussed by Plotinus: How is it possible to divide Quality into different kinds? For such a division, *differentiae* are needed. Where are they to be found? If qualities (*poiotētes*) serve as differentiae of substances (*diaphorai ousias*), then what would serve as *differentiae* of qualities (*diaphora poiotētos*)? It cannot be qualities, because that "would be no less absurd than setting up substances as differences of substances." The problem is not solved even if we take as basis for the distinctions of different kinds of qualities 'the variety of sense-organs':

> Here a difficulty may be raised: we divide the varieties of Substance and their functions and activities, fair or foul or indeed of any kind whatsoever, on the basis of Quality, Quantity rarely, if ever, entering into the differences which produce species; Quantity, again, we divide in accordance with qualities of its own: how then are we to divide Quality itself into species? what differences are we to employ, and from what genus shall we taken them? To take them from Quality itself would be no less absurd than setting up substances as differences of substances.
>
> How, then, are we to distinguish black from white? how differentiate colours in general from tastes and tangible qualities? By the variety of sense-organs? Then there will be no difference in the objects themselves.
>
> But waiving this objection, how deal with qualities perceived by the same sense-organ? (VI.3.17, 3–19)

Eventually Plotinus accepts the view that not all qualities constitute differentiae (VI.3.18, 16–20). He then proceeds to put down as a rule that (a) "Quality is never a differentia of quality, any more than Substance is a differentia of substance, Quantity of quantity" (VI.3.18, 30–33); and (b) "while in general it is necessary to look for differences by which to separate things from each other, to hunt for differences of the differences themselves is both futile and irrational" (VI.3.18, 1–3). The reason why it is futile to seek for 'differences of differences' is not difficult to understand, though not stated by Plotinus. For, it would seem that such an attempt leads to an infinite regress. But it is not clear on what grounds such a procedure can be characterized as irrational. Perhaps the reason for this is to be found in that only essential qualities (*ousiōdeis poiotētes*) can serve as differentiae by means of which definitions are obtained. Now, definitions seem indispensable to discursive reason in performing its function, which is to give explanations supported by arguments. But sense-perception and intellect, as cognitive faculties, can dispense with definitions and arguments, since they do not aim at explanation, as Plotinus puts it:

> Sense-perception and intelligence may be trusted to indicate diversity but not to explain it: explanation is outside the province of sense-perception, whose function is merely to produce a variety of information; while, as for intelligence, it works exclusively with intuitions and never resorts to explanations to justify them; there is in the movements of intelligence a diversity which separates one object from another, making further differentiation unnecessary. (VI.3.18, 7–12)

In connection with the problem of the different kinds of qualities and the basis of their differentiation, it should be noted that Plotinus agrees here with Aristotle in grouping together (though with some qualifications) qualities and *qualia.* The qualifications suggested here by Plotinus are as follows:

> With Quality we have undertaken to group the dependent qualia, in so far as Quality is bound up with them; we shall not however introduce into this category the qualified objects (*qua* objects), that we may not be dealing with two categories at once; we shall pass over the objects to that which gives them their (specific) name. (VI.3.19, 1–4)

In so far as the 'peculiar characteristics' (*idia*) of quality are concerned, it may be recalled that Aristotle asserted in the *Categories* that qualities admit (a) contraries and (b) a more and a less. Plotinus has some objections with regard to both (a) and (b). First of all he can not accept the Aristotelian view of contrariety as 'the greatest possible difference.'[39] He rejects it by arguing in the following way:

> It may be urged that the products of a contrariety exhibit the greatest diversity. But 'the greatest diversity' is clearly meaningless, unless we can point to lower degrees of diversity in the means. Thus, we cannot speak of 'the greatest diversity' in reference to health and disease. This definition of contrariety is therefore inadmissible. (VI.3.20, 20–23)

Secondly, Plotinus accepts the basic Aristotelian distinction between contraries without intermediaries (*amesa*) and contraries with intermediaries (*emmesa*).[40] Thus, health and sickness, for example, belong to the former, while virtue and vice or black and white belong to the latter.

But there is a difference between these last two examples which Plotinus tries to clarify:

> We have to ascertain whether there is not to every quality a contrary. In the case of virtue and vice even the mean appears to be contrary to the extremes.
>
> But when we turn to colours, we do not find the intermediates so related. If we regard the intermediates as blendings of the extremes, we must not posit any contrariety other than that between black and white, but must show that all other colours are combinations of these two. Contrariety however demands that there be some one distinct quality in the intermediates, though this quality may be seen to arise from a combination. (VI.3.20, 1–7)

Hence the conclusion seems to follow that:

> If these observations be sound, colours which have a common ground will not be contraries. But there will be nothing to prevent, not indeed every colour from being contrary to any other; and similarly with tastes.—This will serve as a statement of the problem. (VI.3.20, 35–38)

As for (b) Plotinus thinks that only *qualia*—objects participating in Quality—admit of degrees, but Quality as such is excluded:

> As for Degree (subsisting in Quality), it was given as our opinion that it exists in the objects participating in Quality, though whether it enters into qualities as such—into health and justice—was left open to question. If indeed these qualities possess an extension quite apart from their participants, we must actually ascribe to them degrees: but in truth they belong to a sphere where each entity is the whole and does not admit of degree. (VI.3.20, 39–42)

IV

Can Motion be established as a 'genus' of the Sensible world? This question has to be considered first for two reasons: (1) Because Aristotle did not consider Motion as one of his categories; and (2) because Plotinus thinks that the positing of Motion as a new 'genus' is possible. Plotinus' claim depends on three conditions which he specifies as follows:

(a) "That it cannot rightly be referred to any other genus";

(b) "That nothing higher than itself can be predicated of it in respect to its essence";

(c) "That by assuming differences it will produce species" (VI.3.21, 1–5).

With regard to (a) Plotinus argues that Motion (*kinēsis*) cannot be referred to any other of the 'genera' which he has postulated for this world. According to him, Motion is neither Substance, nor quality, nor quantity, nor relation. It is, as Plotinus puts it, *heteron*: other, something else, different. It cannot be Substance because it presupposes Substance. Although attributive, Motion has an independent reality in the same sense in which Quantity and Quality are said to have independent realities. It is this characteristic which distinguishes Motion from Relation. Plotinus explains:

> If we are agreed that Quality and Quantity, though attributive, are real entities, and on the basis of this reality distinguishable as Quality and Quantity respectively: then, on the same principle, since Motion, though an attribute, has a reality prior to its attribution, it is incumbent upon us to discover the intrinsic nature of this reality. We must never be content to regard as a relative something which exists prior to its attribution, but only that which is engendered by Relation, and has no existence apart from the relation to which it owes its name. (VI.3.21, 12–17)

Before proceeding to answer the question "What is that entity, called Motion, which, though attributive, has an independent reality, which makes its attribution possible?" Plotinus finds it necessary to make sure that "there is nothing prior to Motion and predicated of it as its genus" (VI.3.21, 21–24). This was condition (b) as stated above. Change (*metabolē*) is the most serious candidate to be considered as 'genus' of Motion. But upon inspection it appears to be a species rather than the 'genus' of Motion, because "change signifies merely the substitution of one thing for another, whereas Motion involves also the removal of a thing from the place to which it belongs, as is shown by locomotion" (VI.3.21, 42–44). It may also be the case that 'change' is but another name for Motion, because if it were another 'genus,' then the genera would have to be not five but six (VI.3.21, 25–26).[41]

Since change is not the only species of Motion, as Plotinus understands it, he goes on to specify its other species (*eidē*). Among them are to be found not only generation (*genesis*), alteration (*alloiōsis*) and augmentation (*auksē*) (chapter 21) but also actions (*poiēseis*) and passions (*peiseis*) (chapter 28). Accordingly, the condition (c) is satisfied and, therefore, Motion is established as a 'genus' of Becoming. An additional reason that Motion, in Plotinus' view, must be considered as one of the highest 'genera' is the fact that it can not be defined: "That Motion is a genus we may be all the more confident in virtue of the difficulty—the impossibility even—of confining it within a definition" (VI.3.22, 19–21).

Having established in this way that Motion is a 'genus,' Plotinus felt it necessary to search for the 'constant element' of this 'genus' which appears in all its species. The outcome of this search is stated in the following passage:

> In short, the common basis of all Motion is the existence of a progression and an urge from potentiality and the potential to actuality and the actual: everything which has any kind of motion whatsoever derives this motion from a pre-existent potentiality within itself of activity or passivity. (VI.3.22, 47–50)

Accordingly, "the view would not be unreasonable which, taking some Forms to be active, others inactive, regarded Motion as a dynamic Form in opposition to the other Forms which are static, and further as the cause of whatever new Form ensues upon it" (VI.3.22, 12–16).[42]

In addition to its being a dynamic Form, Plotinus characterizes Motion as (a) "passage from potentiality to its realization" (VI.3.22, 3–4);[43] (b) "being itself perpetual difference" (*aei heterotēs*) (VI.3.22, 43–44); (c) being distinguished from 'moved objects,' since "by walking we do not mean the feet but the activity springing from a potentiality in the feet" (VI.3.23, 4–5), and (d) "being always qualified" and "taking its quality from the moved" (VI.3.23, 31–33). Thus:

> Now, when the potentiality of Motion consists in an ability to walk, it may be imagined as thrusting a man forward and causing him to be continually adopting a different position; when it lies in the capacity to heat, it heats; when the potentiality takes hold of Matter and builds up the organism, we have growth; and when another potentiality demolishes the structure, the result is decay, that which has the potentiality of demolition experiencing the decay. Where the birth-giving principle is active, we find birth; where it is impotent and the power to destroy prevails, destruction takes place—not the destruction of what already exists, but that which intervenes upon the road to existence. (VI.3.23, 20–28)

In chapter 24 Plotinus considers the contrary motions with regard to locomotion, such as: ascending and descending, circular and linear. He concludes that "it appears in general that locomotion is a definite unity, taking its differences from externals" (VI.3.24, 14–15). As for integration (*synkrisis*) and disintegration (*diakrisis*), which are considered in the next chapter (chapter 25), Plotinus thinks that (a) they should not be identified with condensation (*pyknōsis*) and rarefaction (*araiōsis*) because "to suppose that they were would involve the admission of a vacuum" (VI.3.25, 34), and (b) they are in a sense reducible to local motions. For:

> If integration implies that one element proceeds towards another, implies in short an approach, and disintegration, on the other hand, a retreat into the background, such motions may be termed local; we have clearly a case of two things moving in the direction of unity, or else making away from each other. (VI.3.25, 5–9)

The last point which Plotinus discusses with regard to Motion is its opposite. Whether this opposite is Stability (*stasis*) or Rest (*ēremia*) is problematic. The distinction between these two notions is subtle and must be carefully considered. Their difference consists in that the former belongs to that which is immovable (*akineton*), while the latter pertains to that which is movable (*kineton*) but for some reason rests or has come to a stop. In this respect, it is understandable that "we should, no doubt, be well advised to assign Stability to the Intellectual, and to look in the lower sphere for Rest alone" (VI.3.27, 3–4). Accordingly, Rest appears to be the negation of Motion in the Sensible realm, though in the Intelligible realm Stability does not negate Motion.

> Why, then, did we not in discussing the Intellectual realm assert that Stability was the negation of Motion? Because it is not indeed possible to consider Stability as an annulling of Motion, for when Motion ceases Stability does not exist, but requires for its own existence the simultaneous existence of Motion; and what is of a nature to move is not stationary because the Stability of that realm is motionless, but because Stability has taken hold of it; in so far as it has Motion, it will never cease to move: thus, it is stationary under the influence of Stability, and moves under the influence of Motion. In the lower realm, too, a thing moves in virtue of Motion, but its Rest is caused by a deficiency; it has been deprived of its due motion. (VI.3.27, 27–35)

The implication is that Stability is not to be found in this Sensible world in which everything is either in Motion or at Rest, that is, in slower or relative Motion. In other words, every entity of the Sensible world must be always in Motion in reference to the Absolute Stability of the Intelligible realm. And there is no other frame of reference. Plotinus argues:

> Now, if Rest means coming to rest, it must be regarded as a motion which has not yet ceased but still continues; but if we suppose it to be incompatible with Motion, we have first to ask whether there is in the Sensible world anything without motion. (VI.3.24, 11–14)

This then is Plotinus' theory of relative Motion in the Sensible world.[44]

V

The last and short chapter of the present tractate (chapter 28) is devoted to the fifth 'genus' of Becoming—i.e. Relation (*pros ti*)—which was discussed at length in the first tractate. In passing, Plotinus notes that: (a) "We have already indicated that Activity and Passivity are to be regarded as motions;" and (b) "as for the remaining so-called genera, we have shown that they are reducible to those which we have posited" (VI.3.28, 1–4). Then he states the following with regard to Relation, which he had characterized as 'manifestly an offshoot' (VI.2.16, 1):

> With regard to the relative, we have maintained that Relation belongs to one object as compared with another, that the two objects coexist simultaneously, and that Relation is found whenever a substance is in such a condition as to produce it; not that the substance is a relative, except in so far as it constitutes part of a whole—a hand, for example, or head or cause or principle or element. (VI.3.28, 4–8)

Consequently, Plotinus seems to agree with Aristotle in that (1) relations are closely connected with substances; (2) they presuppose a plurality (at least two) of substances which must exist simultaneously; and (3) no substance is a relative. This last point, it may be recalled, was very controversial. It was discussed by Aristotle at length in the *Categories* and was the main reason why he modified the definition of relatives. Unlike Aristotle, Plotinus is prepared to accept that in some cases Substances can be regarded as relatives. These cases are specified as parts, causes, principles and elements. Now, Aristotle might have objected to this, that in all these cases substances are not considered substances. As Porphyry puts it, it is not Socrates *qua* primary Substance, but Socrates *qua* father of his sons, who can be regarded as a relative (efficient cause).[45]

At the end of his discussion, Plotinus mentions an ancient division of relatives which reads as follows:

> We may adopt the ancient division of relatives into creative principles, measures, excesses and deficiencies, and those which in general separate things on the basis of similarities and differences. (VI.3.28, 8–11)

In this light, it is easy to see how the category or 'genus' of Relation was able, in the Plotinian scheme, to absorb all the Aristotelian categories except for Substance.[46] Although this development led Plotinus away from Aristotle's categorial many-fold, it certainly brought him back to the old Platonic dichotomy between Substance and Relation, or Absolute and Relative Being, as is customary to render the Greek expressions *kathauto on* and *en allō on*.[47] Having thus determined the number and nature of the 'genera' of Becoming, Plotinus closes the tripartite treatise 'On the Genera of Being' with the satisfaction that he has provided a set of five categories which is sufficient, he thinks, to account for this Sensible cosmos, the image and reflection of the Intelligible cosmos.

VI

It was the purpose of this study to examine Plotinus' proposal of a new set of categories or so-called 'genera' of Becoming and its relationship to Aristotle's categories most of which Plotinus found redundant and, therefore, reducible. In view of Plotinus' criticism and rejection of the Aristotelian categorial set as presented in VI 1, it was necessary to emphasize the point that in VI 3 Plotinus was concerned with finding a new set of categories. Since Aristotle's categories in their ontic claims had been found inadequate to account for the Intelligible realm and had been rejected in favor of Plato's 'highest kinds', Plotinus thought it necessary to restrict his investigations to the Sensible realm in order to examine the applicability of the Aristotelian scheme to the sensible cosmos (*kosmos aisthētos*). Because of this restriction, Plotinus also thought that one should not speak of 'genera of Being' but rather of so-called 'genera' or categories of Becoming in view of the all-important Platonic and Neoplatonic ontological distinction between the Sensible cosmos and the Intelligible cosmos. The dangers of homonymy are always present in Plotinus' mind and this explains a great deal of both the terminology he uses and the criticism he advances against his predecessors. As revealed in the preceding discussion and analysis, Plotinus' views can be summarized as follows:

1) Given their ontological inadequacy, the applicability of Aristotle's set of categories must be restricted to the realm of Becoming. But even within this realm, the Aristotelian number of ten categories is too large compared to the five genera which Plotinus found sufficient to account for the realm of Being.

2) Plotinus recommends a drastic reduction of Aristotle's categories which amounts to fifty percent, and justifies it on the grounds that the omitted categories are redundant and reducible, or that they are more specific than general, or that they lack the required unity and simplicity. Thus six Aristotelian categories are absent from the Plotinian set, because they fail to meet these criteria.

3) Even those of Aristotle's categories which can pass the Plotinian tests of generality, unity, simplicity, and irreducibility must be modified before they can be accepted as 'genera' of Becoming in the Plotinian sense of the term. The specific ways of such modifications and Plotinus' arguments to support them we have seen in our discussion above in detail.

4) Of the five categories for the Sensible world to be found in Plotinus' list four correspond, at least in name, to Aristotle's categories of Substance, Quantity, Quality, and Relation. The fifth Plotinian category, Motion, which substitutes for Aristotle's categories of Action and Passion, has certainly a Platonic origin, since it is found also in the list of Plato's 'highest kinds'.

5) In some sense, then, the Plotinian categorial scheme comprises elements borrowed from Plato and Aristotle. It was left to Porphyry to effectively continue and deepen this process of reconciling the two philosophies, so that he can be rightly considered as the originator of an Aristotelian Neoplatonic tradition regarding Aristotle's doctrine of the categories.

6) The important point to keep in mind is that Plotinus remained to the end anti-Aristotelian regarding the doctrine of the categories, in spite of all the borrowings and similarities in terminology. Since he could not accept Aristotle's categories in their ontological claims, and since he had to restrict their application to the realm of Becoming, it was inevitable that the function of Plotinus' new categories would be formalistic and nominalistic, as has been observed.[48]

Towson State University

NOTES

1. For a more extensive discussion of the issues addressed in this essay, see my *Aristotle's Categories and Porphyry*, Philosophia Antiqua 48 (Leider: E. J. Brill, 1988).
2. I have discussed this problem in "Plotinus' Anti-Gnostic Polemic," *Neoplatonism and Gnosticism*, eds. R. Wallis and J. Bregman (Albany: ISNS & Suny Press, 1992), 111–128.
3. In all probability, Plotinus' Gnostic opponents were Christians. However, for the Neoplatonists of that time, both movements, Gnosticism and Christianity, were considered as barbaric in spirit, that is, non-Hellenic. (See my "Plotinus' Anti-Gnostic Polemic.")
4. The expression used by Plotinus is *kosmos noētos*.
5. The division of the treatise into three parts is probably due to Porphyry's editorial intervention to reach the desired number, 54 (i.e. 6 x 9).
6. Especially, 254a–256e.
7. Enneads VI.2.1, 19–20: MacKenna's translation, which I shall follow throughout unless stated otherwise.
8. In Plotinus' view, the expression 'genera of Being' can be properly used only in reference to *kosmos noētos*. As for the so-called 'genera' of Becoming, they should be termed 'categories' because they lack real generic power and unity. On this point, see VI.1.5, 22–26; VI.1.9, 27–30; and VI.1.10, 40–42.
9. The exception is Motion (*kinēsis*), which is not a category for Aristotle.
10. *The Philosophy of Plotinus* (New York: Longmans, 1948), 194.
11. It has been reported that Porphyry was the author of two commentaries on the *Categories*: see Simplicius, *Commentaria in Aristotelem Graeca* VIII, ed. C. Kalbfleisch (Berlin, 1907), 1–2.
12. For Aristotle's conception of homonymy, or rather *homōnyma onta*, see the opening paragraph of the *Categories*.
13. With regard to simplicity and unity the three *Hypostaseis* are characterized as follows:
    - a. The One as *pantelōs hen* (Absolute Unity) (VI.2.9, 30) and *adiaphoron on* (Undifferentiated Being) (VI.2.9, 9).
    - b. The *Nous* as *to ek pantōn* (Unity in Plurality) (VI.2.19, 9) and *holon hen* (Total Unity) (VI.2.6, 16).
    - c. The Soul as *polla kai hen* (one and many) (VI.2.4, 31–32).
14. That is the reason why they lack the unity which a genus of Being must possess.
15. Plotinus occasionally refers to this entity as *syntheton* or *synamphoteron*—meaning that which is made up of two entities, Matter and Form.
16. That is to say, the Form of a human being.
17. *Categories* 3a21–27.
18. *Categories* 1b3–8.

19. I have dealt with the problem of essential and accidental predication and its role in determining the nature of Aristotle's four predicables in "Aristotle's Theory of Predicables and Porphyry's *Isagoge*," *Journal of the History of Philosophy* 23 (1985), 15–35.
20. This Plotinian doctrine is in sharp contrast to Aristotle's doctrine that *ousia* is not dependent. In *Metaphysics* he states: "Of the other categories none can exist independently but only substance" (1028a35–35). Also *Categories* 2a34–35.
21. E. G. W. Leszl uses the expression 'focality of meaning' in *Logic and Metaphysics in Aristotle* (Padua: Editrice Antenore, 1970), 99. Aristotle's expression for this is *pro hen legomena*.
22. In VI.3.8, 19–20, we are told that the sensible substance is *symphorēsis tis poiotētōn kai hylēs* (a concrescence of matter and qualities: translation mine).
23. *Isagoge*, 4 (21–25).
24. *Categories* 2a11–18.
25. Commentary to the *Categories*, 91 (4–27).
26. In this way homonymy, which was used by Aristotle for cases such as a living human being and its portrait, is extended by Plotinus so as to cover the whole Sensible universe.
27. The question of self-predication of the Forms in the *Enneads* has been ably discussed by J. Rist in *Eros and Psyche* (Toronto: University of Toronto Press, 1964), 59–61.
28. *Categories* 5b11 ff: 'a quantity has no contrary.'
29. The same examples of 'few and many' have been used by Aristotle, *Categories* 5b.
30. According to Aristotle, "it is most of all with regard to place that there seems to be contrariety of a quantity" (*Categories* 6a11–12). See also Porphyry's *Commentary*, 107–108.
31. It may be noted here that geometrical figures (*schemata*) were considered as a kind of quality by Aristotle: *Categories* 10a11–15.
32. *Categories* 11a15–19.
33. *Categories* 3b10–23.
34. *Metaphysics* 1029b13, 20, 27; 1031b9; 1032b14; 1035b16.
35. For Aristotle, individuals admit the definition of their species (*Categories* 2a19–34).
36. On this see J. Rist, *Plotinus: The Road of Reality* (Cambridge: Cambridge University Press, 1967), 86–87.
37. *Hypographe* is used by Porphyry and other commentators to give a description of concepts, like the highest genera, which cannot be defined by genus and differentia.
38. *Categories*, chapter 8.

39. In *Metaphysics* (1061a12) Aristotle identified contrarieties with 'the first differences of being' (*protas diaphoras tou ontos*). Also, *Categories* 6a17–18.
40. *Categories* 11b38–12a25.
41. In *Physics* 18b19 and *Metaphysics* 1065b14, Aristotle uses *kinēsis* and *metabolo* as synonyms.
42. This remark echoes the *Sophist* 247e, where Plato states: "I am proposing as a mark to distinguish real things that they are nothing but power."
43. *Physics* 201a11: *he tou dynamei ontos entelecheia.*
44. A comparative study of Plotinus' theory of Motion and Einstein's theory of Relativity should be interesting.
45. Porphyry's *Commentary*, 140–141.
46. See, for instance, *Ennead* VI.3.3, 30–32.
47. On this distinction, see J. Dillon, *The Middle Platonists* (Ithaca, NY: Cornell University Press, 1977), 8.
48. C. Rutten, *Les catégories du monde sensible dans les 'Enneads' de Plotin* (Paris: Les Belles Lettres, 1961), especially 48–56 & 112–115.

SYMPATHY: STOIC MATERIALISM AND THE PLATONIC SOUL[1]

Gary M. Gurtler

Sympathy holds a unique place in Plotinus' philosophy of nature. It seems, on the one hand, to be simply a characterization of the organic unity of the physical cosmos. From this point of view, sympathy becomes the explanatory key for prayer, magic and divination as diverse ways in which parts of the cosmos influence and interact with one another.[2] But, on the other hand, this organic unity is essential for Plotinus' thematization of sensation and perception. Thus sympathy also has a role in Plotinus' anthropology, playing the objective correlate to the subjective unity of consciousness, signified by the term *synaisthesis* ('consciousness'). Both of these terms derive from Stoic sources and both require appropriate dematerialization to fit the overall Platonic character of his thought, but in each case the appropriate dematerialization is close to being opposite. *Synaisthesis* is almost totally dematerialized and, consequently, its elaborate structure can be applied to any level in the hierarchy of reality, whereas sympathy needs only the bare minimum of dematerialization for its function in the sensible world.[3]

Using these two terms, sympathy (*sympatheia*) and consciousness (*synaisthesis*), moreover, Plotinus is able to construct a comprehensive account of nature and experience. This account is comprehensive in a new and original way. It attempts to combine the work of Plato and Aristotle, where the internal operations of the soul are analyzed, with the Stoic emphasis on the necessary organic unity of the cosmos as the external basis for perceptual awareness of any kind. It, thus, addresses simultaneously the two opposite poles of experience: the unity of the external world and the unity of the internal states of awareness or knowing.

It is part of Plotinus' genius to see these two aspects of experience and, in addition, to construct a theory that will handle both of them adequately.[4] In articulating the unity of a subject's interior cognitive states, for example, he faces the problem of other minds with a directness that disappeared in much of classical modern thought, only to be labored over anew by contemporary thinkers. It is not enough to unify the experiences of one mind alone, but the unity must include all other minds, without at the same time sacrificing the integrity of individual experience. From the side of the object, there is a similar bifocal character. Thus, it is not enough to posit a multitude of independent external objects that can be sensed and known, but this multiplicity of objects must already form a unity before sensation or knowledge can take place. Mere physical juxtaposition is not sufficient to explain sensation or perception, but only the cosmic unity established through the analysis of sympathy.

The elaboration of sympathy, finally, shows Plotinus' method of philosophizing, borrowing from the major traditions of Greek philosophy, but making the changes and adaptations necessary for the consistency of his own system. In this instance, the Stoic term, *sympathy* fills out the Platonic notion that the universe is a single living organism (*Timaeus* 30d3–31a1). The change is simple but radical: Stoic materialism must be replaced with the immateriality of the Platonic soul. Sympathy, like *synaisthesis*, is thus rooted in the soul, but the difference is that the relevant soul for sympathy is the world soul and not the individual soul at the center of human consciousness. With this accomplished, Plotinus can adapt the Stoic analysis of sympathy to explain the elusive Platonic characterization of the universe as a single living thing.[5]

1. Against Materialism

Four treatises in Plotinus' first period (A.D. 253–263), use sympathy in two major contexts: the inadequacy of materialism to explain the sympathy within or between beings and the corresponding reduction of sympathy to the soul. Finally, a unique usage of sympathy is broached in two treatises, I.2[19] and VI.4[22], overlapping the first and second of Plotinus' literary periods and showing a continuity of issues arising in different contexts. The problem giving rise to this usage is the problem of evil, a difficult point in relating a Platonic soul to the material world.

1.1 *Soul as Principle of Unity*

The first series of treatises to be analyzed come from the very first years of Plotinus' writing, A.D. 254–258, with their focus primarily on the relation of soul and body and secondarily on the interrelation of bodies in the cosmos. Thus, the treatise, 'On the Immortality of the Soul' (IV.7[2]), is a scholastic defense of the Platonic doctrine of the soul's nature and immortality, arguing against the materialistic views of the Epicureans and Stoics as well as the non-materialistic, but still objectionable, views of the Pythagoreans (the soul as a harmony) and the Peripatetics (the soul as entelechy). In the subsequent treatise, 'On Destiny' (III.1[3]), Plotinus shifts to a defense of Platonic causation, with the freedom and integrity of the soul opposed to the determinism of the astrologers and their materialistic allies, the Stoics and Epicureans.

The treatise, 'On the Essence of the Soul' (IV.2[4]), returns to the problem of the nature of the soul and its relation to bodies by introducing the scheme of the indivisible and divisible from *Timaeus* 35a1–4. As applied to the dualism of soul and body, this yields a fourfold structure, with its three higher elements presaging the structure of unity that emerges with more and more clarity in later works. The last treatise in this section, 'If All Souls Are One' (IV.9[8]), in fact, summarizes these earlier discussions on the nature of the soul and points forward, as Armstrong (IV, 427) notes, to the richly complex analyses in VI.4 & 5[22 & 23] and IV.3[27].1–8. Igal, for his part, maintains that this treatise presents the first hesitant attempt to distinguish individual souls and the world soul from the Hypostasis Soul as Plotinus gropes for a way to express adequately the unity and individuality of souls (III–IV, 545–548).

In these discussions of soul, Plotinus gradually unfolds the structure and meaning of sympathy. In IV.7[2], the passage containing sympathy argues against the atomism of the Epicureans.

> But if someone says that it is not so, but that atoms or things without parts make the soul when they come together by unity and community of feeling [*homopatheia*], he could be refuted by their [mere] juxtaposition, and that not a complete one, since nothing which is one and united with itself in community of feeling [*sympathous*] can come from bodies which are without feeling [*apathon*] and unable to be united, but soul is united with itself in community of feeling [*sympathes*]. But no body or magnitude could be produced from partless constituents. (IV.7.3, 1–6: Armstrong translation)

Plotinus, in his usual fashion, is using the same argument to cover two points: Epicurean atomism and Stoic materialism. With a twinge of irony,[6] he uses Stoic sympathy to indicate the absurdity of the atomists and then the inconsistency of the Stoics themselves, an argument which continues to IV.7.8[3]. The attack on the atomists is more fundamental, since their position renders explanation and experience impossible. These Epicureans may not have been troubled by the lack of explanation, but Plotinus presses home to the actual problem of their position, that the world itself becomes absurd and impossible. Atoms, Plotinus reasons, can only be next to one another. They cannot be formed into unities with some kind of common feeling, since their juxtaposition is never complete and their interaction only mechanical.

His alternative theory derives from Plato's *Timaeus*,[7] with its four elements and Platonic soul, Plotinus adding only the qualification that the soul is sympathetic to itself. This extremely laconic description should not serve to discount its crucial importance in Plotinus' argument, for in establishing the connection between sympathy and the soul, he is moving toward that first level in his structure of unity, a transcendent source in relation to those things which participate in it on a lower and more multiple level. The description of the soul as self-sympathetic also removes at the same stroke Stoic materialism. Sympathy is a function of the immaterial Platonic soul, and it is, consequently, from soul that it derives its power to unify the realm of bodies.

In the present context, however, Plotinus only states his position, with its development in the later treatises to be considered actually showing some evolution in his thought as he struggles to articulate the intricate relation of soul and body. Finally, the alternative explanation of atomism in this passage (IV.7.3, 5–6), that things without parts make the (corporeal) soul when they come together, is dismissed with utmost brevity: No body or magnitude is derived from what is partless. As Bréhier points out, this is the habitual mistake of confusing the mathematical point with the physical atom (IV, 191 n2). Thus atoms are eliminated because they cannot be unified, and partless things because they add up to nothing. Soul, on the other hand, has the power to unify what is lower and more dispersed than itself, with sympathy the description of this unifying power.

When Plotinus turns to the discussion of causation in the treatise, 'On Destiny' (III.1[3]), he maintains that the Platonic account is more complete than the Aristotelian (III.1.1 & 2) and more cogent than the various forms of determinism, whether Epicurean or specific types of Stoicism (III.1.3–7). The discussion thus hinges on the conflict between the immateriality of the Platonic soul and various forms of materialism, or, as expressed here, between freedom and determinism. Plotinus begins by accepting the evidence of the astrologers for the causal role of the sphere of the stars and the wandering planets, disagreeing only with their interpretation.

> The evidence for this is that by divination from the planets people foretell what is going to happen in the All and about each individual, what sort of fortune and, in particular, what sort of thoughts he is going to have. And they say that one can see that the other animals and plants grow and diminish under the sympathetic influence [*sympatheias*] of the planets, and are affected by them in other ways; and the regions of the earth differ from each other according to their position in relation to the All, and particularly to the sun; and not only do the other animals and plants correspond to the regions but also the forms and sizes and colours, the tempers and desires and ways of life and characters of human beings. (III.1.5,4–15: Armstrong translation)

The neuralgic point is the attribution to the stars and planets of a direct causal role in human thought and character, undermining the nature of the Platonic soul as an independent substance. This passage thus gives the *aporia* to be resolved in the exposition of his own position in III.1.8–10.

Plotinus' solution is to situate the human soul within the context of the universe as a whole. Thus any limitation on human freedom is due to the interweaving of a multitude of cosmic factors, including the individual's own choices, and not to a denial of freedom as such. From this point of view, the sympathy mentioned in this passage is a positive contribution to his own argument. By rooting sympathy in the soul, Plotinus derails the kind of complete causality operative in the materialistic view of the astrologers, and substitutes a concatenation of causes that is ultimately traceable to soul itself. At the same time, a secondary aspect of sympathy is introduced, the interrelation of the participants within a comprehensive whole.

The last treatise in this initial trilogy, 'On the Essence of the Soul' (IV.2[4]), is a short addition to IV.7[2], in which Plotinus establishes a further dichotomy in being and becoming, yielding a fourfold division. Thus, in the realm of being, there is the primary indivisible, the Intellect itself, and the secondary indivisible, the soul; and in the realm of becoming, the secondary divisible, the forms immanent in bodies, and the primary divisible, sensible magnitude and mass.[8] Appropriately, sympathy occurs in the section dealing with the secondary indivisible, the soul.

> But again, next to that altogether indivisible nature there is another reality following upon it and deriving from it, having indivisibility from that other nature, which pressing eagerly on in its progress from the one to the other nature, established itself in the middle between the two, the indivisible and primary and the 'divisible which is in the sphere of bodies', which is upon bodies: [it does] not [behave] in the same way in which every colour and quality is the same in many places and many bodily masses, but the quality or colour in one mass is totally separate from that in the other, just as much as one mass is separate from the other; and even if the magnitude is one, yet what is the same in each part has no community [with any other] leading to a common experience [*homopatheian*], because this 'same' is one thing here, another there: for what is the same is an affection [*pathema*], not the same substance. (IV.2.1, 41–53: Armstrong translation)

In the first part of the passage, the soul is established as between that which is indivisible essentially (the Intellect) and that which is divisible in the sphere of bodies (the qualities of bodies). Soul is thus between the primary indivisible and the secondary divisible, and will be characterized by attributes of both.

Unwittingly, Plotinus has stumbled on the structure of unity that will dominate his later discussions, a completely unified source, individually unified beings, and something in between which unifies these individual beings by its closeness to the source. In the present context, however, the groundwork for this structure is still being established. Central to this enterprise is the carefully wrought distinction between qualities and soul as they relate to bodies. Qualities are formally the same wherever they occur, but are numerically distinct and separate as attributes of material bodies. Soul, on the other hand, because it is a substance and not merely an affection of a body, keeps the indivisible nature it shares with the Intellect, and thus is divisible in bodies without loss of its integral unity.

The term in which this dual character of the soul comes to focus is sympathy, which describes the particular kind of unity soul gives to bodies that goes beyond mere physical juxtaposition. The present passage offers, therefore, an important clarification of the discussion in IV.7.3 by its more precise distinction between physical proximity and sympathetic unity. At the same time, it prepares for later discussions by its sharper focus on the relevant issues, the comparison of soul and qualities in relation to body and the very structure implicit in the fourfold division of being.

The next treatise, 'If All Souls Are One' (IV. 9[8]), provides an opposite perspective in Plotinus' treatment of the problem. It is not the relation of souls to bodies, but rather their relation to one another that becomes problematic. The first passage, therefore, presents an objection to the thesis that all souls are one precisely on the basis of the unity of experience that sympathy implies.

> But, before this, we must discuss whether it is correct to say that all the souls are one soul, like the soul of each individual. For it would be absurd if my soul and anyone else's were one soul: for if I perceived anything another would have to perceive it too, and if I was good he would have to be good, and if I desired anything he would have to desire it, and in general we should have to have the same experiences [*homopathein*] as each other and as the All, so that if I had an experience [*pathontos*] the All would share in the perception of it [*synaisthanesthai*]. (IV.9.1, 13–19: Armstrong translation)

Plotinus is caught here in a dialectical examination of the positions outlined in the three previous treatises. In two of them, IV.7[2] and IV.2[4], he has defined sympathy in terms of soul's unification of the body, and in the other, III.1[3], in terms of the relations of separately ensouled bodies in the universe to one another. In reversing his perspective, he introduces the problem of monism, the exact inverse of the atomism criticized so thoroughly earlier.

The *aporia* now becomes not the relation of soul and body nor the problem of freedom and determinism, but a unity that does away with any individuality at all, the unity, in other words, which was instrumental in solving his former difficulties. He begins in IV.9[8].2 by drawing out the implications of his former position for the present situation. In a reversal of the argument in IV.2.1, he now applies to souls the numerical distinction and separation that qualities had in relation to body. One might suspect inconsistency, but Plotinus is a very careful as well as subtle thinker. In the previous context, the contrast was in the relation of soul and qualities to one body, while here it is the relation of many souls to different bodies. Thus many souls, formally the same, are numerically distinct and separate, just like qualities, in relation to the many bodies they unify.

After establishing the individuality of souls in terms of their relation to individual bodies, Plotinus must reassert unity, lest his own position turn out to be as atomistic as the materialists'. He does so by examining the unity of the cosmos as a whole, the place where these individual souls take up their residency.

> For we do not say, either, that it is one in such a way as to be altogether without a share in multiplicity—this must be attributed to a higher

> nature—but we say that it is one and a multiplicity, and participates in 'that nature which is divisible in the sphere of bodies', and also in the 'indivisible nature', so that again it is one. But just as in me the experience of a part need not dominate the whole, but what happens to what is more essential has an influence on the part, in the same way the influences which come from the All to the individual are more obvious, and we are often affected [*homopathounton*] in the same way as the whole, but it is not clear whether what comes from us contributes anything to the whole. (IV.9.2, 24–33)
>
> Indeed, the argument deriving from facts opposed [to the assumption of complete separation of souls] asserts that we do share each other's experiences [*sympathein*] when we suffer with others from seeing their pain and feel happy and relaxed [in their company] and are naturally drawn to love them: for without a sharing of experience there could not be love for this reason. And if spells and magical acts in general draw men together and make them share experiences [*sympatheis*] at a distance, this must be altogether due to the one soul. And a word spoken quietly acts on what is far off, and makes something separated by an enormous distance listen; from this one can learn the unity of all because their soul is one. (IV.9.3, 1–9: Armstrong translation)

Again, IV.2[4].2 provides both the principle and illustrations necessary to resolve the present difficulty. The individuality of souls embodied does not imply complete division. Each soul not only unifies a particular body, but they are all related to the cosmos as a whole. The evidence for this is the sympathy operative between the All and its parts, and among the parts themselves. Plotinus admits that this evidence does not in fact explain how all souls are one, and gives a preliminary explanation in IV.9[8].4 & 5, using the analogy of a science and its parts. His full explanation comes in the middle period of his literary output in VI.4 & 5[22 & 23] and IV.3[27].1–8.

1.2 *Soul in Sympathy with Body*

The two treatises in this section consider, respectively, the ascent of the soul by means of the virtues (I.2[19]), and its descent made possible by its omnipresence and immateriality (VI.4[22]). They thus deal with the relation of soul to body from different perspectives, moral and ontological. Looked at morally, the soul has the task of fleeing the body and finding its identity in the Intellect, but, looked at ontologically, the very presence of soul to body needs to be explained. Despite this divergence of purpose, there is considerable connection between the two treatises, which is not surprising given their chronological proximity, separated only by Porphyry's arrival in Rome and attendance at Plotinus' lectures.

There is, for example, a distinction which is essential to both of them, the relation of image to archetype. In I.2, this appears as two types of likeness. One requires a reciprocal similarity between the objects that are alike, while the other precludes such reciprocity. The first type applies to the relation among objects from the same source, with the second, the relation of the objects to that source. Such objects are like the source, but the source is not reciprocally related to them nor even less is it like them (I.2.2, 4–10). An ontological distinction of the same sort dominates VI.4 & 5, as Plotinus tries to define the relation between the sensible and intelligible worlds. In VI.4.9, for example, he differentiates between partition and participation where the one and many are related as transcendent whole to its parts. The parts go out from it as powers, capturing the whole but as images on a lower and more multiple level. In the present context, VI.4.3 provides a similarly complex argument to show the independence of the source and the dependency of the parts.

A closer point of contact, however, is precisely in the use of sympathy, a use repeated only once outside these two treatises in II.3[52].13, 42. It seems to reverse the usual structure of sympathy by describing the soul as in sympathy with the body. In I.2[19], moreover, this particular meaning is seen in a wholly negative light.

> What then do we mean when we call these other virtues 'purifications,' and how are we made really like by being purified? Since the soul is evil when it is thoroughly mixed with the body and shares its experiences [*homopathes*] and has all the same opinions, it will be good and possess virtue when it no longer has the same opinions but acts alone—this is intelligence and wisdom—and does not share the body's experiences [*homopathes*]—this is self-control—and is not afraid of departing from the body—this is courage—and is ruled by reason and intellect, without opposition—and this is justice. (I.2.3, 10–19: Armstrong translation)

The good and evil states of the soul are distinguished precisely in terms of whether or not the soul is in sympathy with the body, with such sympathy defining its evil state. The summary in I.2.6 makes the same point.

> So the higher justice in the soul is its activity towards intellect, its self-control is its inward turning to intellect, its courage is its freedom from affections, according to the likeness of that to which it looks which is free from affections by nature: this freedom from affections in the soul comes

> from virtue, to prevent its sharing in the affections [*sympathe*] of its inferior companion. (I.2.6, 23–27: Armstrong translation)

To determine Plotinus' meaning in these two passages, it is necessary to keep in mind the moral tenor of the treatise. He is not discussing the ontological value of the sensible world, but the moral attitude of the embodied soul. The soul, moreover, is not seen as the source of sympathy in the sense world, but as itself in sympathy with the body it is unifying. This is diametrically opposed to the soul's ontological function and nature, wherein the soul's substantial nature is precisely what allows it to give the body sympathetic unity. In the present case, the soul seems to be overly sympathetic, taking upon itself the very limitations that its presence in the body was designed to overcome.

The treatise on the omnipresence of the soul (VI.4[22]) returns to the more familiar ground of the soul's ontological role in the making of the cosmos. There are two instances of sympathy, the first of which reverts to Plotinus' standard usage, and consequently adds no more than confirmation of the particular kind of unity the soul imparts through sympathy.[9] The second instance, on the other hand, occurs in the more general context of the relation of the Intelligible world to the sensible. This dense argument seems intended in fact to justify a positive understanding of the soul's sympathy with the body, the controversial usage of the immediately preceding treatise.

> (1) Are we to say the [Intelligible Being] is present itself, or, rather, that it exists independently, but powers go from it to all things and in this way it is said to be everywhere? They mean in this view that souls are like rays, so that it is set fast in itself, but they, as sent forth, become one living thing after another.
>
> (2) Rather, on the one hand, the one over these [many], by not preserving the whole nature which is in that intelligible itself, is present here only as the power of that by which it is present; but this is not to say that that intelligible is not completely present, since even then that intelligible is not cut off from its own power, which it gave to the sensible, but rather the recipient [i.e. the sensible] is able to take only so much of all that is present.
>
> (3) On the other hand, where all the powers are present, being itself is clearly present, though still separate. For if it became form of a particular, it would depart from being the whole and from being in itself everywhere, and would even accidentally belong to the other. But since it wishes to belong to nothing which would wish for it, as far as it is able, being draws near, not

becoming [form] of that particular (but that desires it), nor even less belonging to the other.

(4) It is then not surprising that it is in all of them in this way, because it is in no one of them so as to be dependent on them. In conclusion, to speak in this accidental fashion, that the soul is in sympathy with the body, is equally not absurd, if it were to mean that the soul is itself by itself, not becoming dependent on matter or body, but that it illuminates, as it were, the whole body throughout its whole self. (VI.4.3, 1–22)

In (1), the souls are set up as the means by which the intelligible is present in sensible things. The intelligible, however, retains its own independence, putting into ontological form the statement in I.2.2 that the source is not related to its products. In (2), the soul's power is present here in sensible objects precisely as one. This unity, however, is secondary and deficient. It is in the sensible object as spatially and temporally distinct, with only the power from the intelligible, since it cannot preserve the complete reality of the intelligible. Plotinus thus continues the distinction in IV.7.1 and IV.9 establishing the particular kind of unity the soul gives the living thing, analyzing it in terms of that power which comes from soul's relation to the Intellect.

The exact nature of the relation of soul's power to the Intellect is the major project of this treatise. There is brief indication here that the power must capture the intelligible as a whole, otherwise the intelligible would be cut off from its power. This power must, therefore, present the whole intelligible to the sensible object, with the limitation coming from the side of the sensible as recipient. All of the intelligible is present to it, but it can receive only so much. This relation of whole to part in terms of the notion of power receives more complete analysis later in the treatise at VI.4.9, where the power always brings its source as a whole, but on a lower level that is both different from and an image of the source.

In (3), the argument moves from the powers to being which is present along with them. There is thus a contrast between form and being, form becoming accidentally dependent on the particular, but being drawing near while keeping its independence, since it is the particular that desires it. The scheme in IV.2.1 can perhaps clarify Plotinus' point. Being can be identified with the secondary indivisibility of the intelligible (the soul), and form with the secondary divisibility of qualities in bodies. Soul in this scheme is able to maintain its independence and integral unity, while at the same time it is present to the divided particulars of the sense world.[10]

After this, the conclusion (4) is rather straightforward. With these distinctions in mind, it is not at all absurd to speak accidentally of the soul as in sympathy with the body, since negatively it preserves its independence and positively it illuminates the whole body as a totality.[11] It is clear, however, that speaking of the soul in this way is not strictly accurate. The two treatises, I.2 and VI.4, do not, therefore, advance the analysis of the structure of sympathy, but they do give an interesting insight into Plotinus' explanation of evil. It is not a problem of the soul's ontological function in producing and governing the cosmos, but of a moral attitude that reverses its proper relation to the body, becoming sympathetic to it rather than establishing sympathy within it.

2. The Universe and Its Parts

By the time we come to 'On the Problems of the Soul' IV.3 & 5[27 & 29], Plotinus has formulated the basic structure and the major issues concerning the operation of sympathy in his system, but has analyzed in depth only a few of them. The structure of unity establishes the soul as the immaterial source for sympathy in the cosmos. Sympathy, in turn, is the foundation for the kinds of mutual influence and interaction that manifest both the unity and diversity possible in the sensible world. The prologue of the treatise, IV.3.1–8, summarizes this material by making explicit the connection between sympathy and the structure of the Soul, the Hypostasis as transcendent source, with the world soul and individual souls as its participants.

> This then is how it is with the solution of this problem, and the fact of sympathy [*sympatheias*] does not hinder our arguments: for since all souls derive from the same from which the soul of the Whole derives too, they have a community of feeling [*sympatheis*]. (IV.3.8, 1–3: Armstrong translation)

As Plotinus begins this long investigation, applying his ideas to the experience and functions of the soul, he articulates the connection between his ontological analysis of the structure of the soul and the various states of awareness that characterize its operations. Sympathy is seen here in its cosmic dimension, relating individual souls to the world soul in one community of feeling. Two aspects of this community of feeling receive particular attention, the explanation of the awareness possible for the embodied soul, and the ultimate unity of the universe as a single living being.

2.1 *Perception: Between Soul and Object*

In discussing the relation of soul to body, three factors are involved, the soul's entrance into, presence in, and departure from the body. The first factor, as we have seen, is more strictly concerned with ontological problems, the relation of whole and part, and the omnipresence and immateriality of the soul. The next two factors add problems of a quite different sort that fall under two general headings: powers of awareness, analyzed in terms of memory, imagination and perception, and affections, whether pleasure and pain, the appetites, or anger. Plotinus defines these states from two points of view, the conditions necessary for their functioning, and the need they serve for the embodied soul.

The full range of these faculties and operations is unique to the human soul alone, with plants and animals not having all of them and the stars and planets, as divine beings, not needing any of them. In articulating the reason why the heavenly bodies do not need various perceptive powers, Plotinus begins with the occasional nature of human perception itself as linked to some specific need in the conjoint of soul and body. In the case of the stars, however, this experiential reason is only incidental, since the essential reason revolves around the perfection and unity of life shared by all the heavenly bodies and manifested in the music of the spheres.

> If, of course, the heavenly bodies themselves live a blessed life, and contemplate this life besides with their souls, by this direction of their souls towards one object and by the illumination which extends from them to the whole heaven-like strings on a lyre plucked harmoniously [*sympathos*] they sing a song which is naturally in tune—if this is how the whole heaven and its parts move, the heaven itself being self-directed and the different parts having the same direction in different ways (since their positions are different), then our account will be still more correct, since the life of all the heavenly bodies is still more one and uniform. (IV.4.8, 52–61: Armstrong translation)

The image of the strings of a lyre is common in this part of IV.4, capturing a movement that is at the same time a sympathetic interaction of all the parts together as well as the individual action of each by itself. This combination of perfect unity and individual freedom is pervasive, and is the motivating factor in Plotinus' adoption of sympathy in delineating the

Platonic notion of the cosmos as a single living being. As applied to the stars, it illustrates two points. Sympathy expresses the mutual perfection of the stars, allowing them to contemplate Intellect uninterruptedly, and also points to their materiality, allowing them to wield their mighty influence upon the events of earth.

Plotinus turns next from the music of the spheres to the perception of the mundane. At this point, the particular need for perception is not defined, but rather the elements necessary for the perceptual situation, preserving both the essential impassibility of the soul as well as the essentially passive character of perception itself. The solution is the introduction of the sense organ as between the soul and the sensible object and able to be in sympathy with either one.

> There cannot, then, be nothing but these two things, the external object and the soul: since then the soul would not be affected; but there must be a third thing which will be affected, and this is that which will receive the form. This must be jointly subject to like affections [*sympathes kai homoiopathes*] and of one matter with the sense-object, and it must be this which is affected and the other principle [the soul] which knows; and its affection must be of such a kind that it retains something of that which produced it, but is not the same as it, but as it is between the producer of the affection and the soul, it must have an affection which lies between the sensible and the intelligible, a proportional mean somehow linking the extremes to each other, with the capacity both of receiving and of transmitting information, suitable to be assimilated to each of the extremes. (IV.4.23, 19–28: Armstrong translation)

The synthetic character of Plotinus' thought can be seen in this passage. Is Aristotle the source of this description of the role of the organ of sense, the mean between object and knower, potentially the one and a potentiality of the other? Or, Plato, with the affections of the body reminding the soul of the forms within it? Or, the Stoics, with the affections coming together in the leading principle and judged as from the external object? One does not have to choose among them, but it is important to recognize that Plotinus is not merely putting things next to one another eclectically; their mixture is complete and completely his own.[12]

Having used the sympathy between the object and the organ in the explanation of perception, Plotinus turns to the more complex issue of the particular kinds of influence of heavenly bodies, illustrated, for example, by petitionary prayer or the effects of magic.

> Their knowledge of prayers is the result of a sort of linking and a particular disposition of things fitted into the whole, and the same applies to their accomplishment of what we pray for; and in the arts of the magicians everything is directed to this linking: this means that magic works by powers which follow on sympathetically [*sympathos*]. (IV.4.26, 1–4: Armstrong translation)

The effectiveness of both phenomena depends on the links and sympathy between parts of the universe. Prayer or magic, as a consequence, puts one in tune with the power of the stars as they form different configurations and patterns. It is, therefore, not a result of some kind of perception, but a communication of or participation in the power of beings in the universe, mediated through the cosmos as material but dependent on the nature of soul as spiritual.[13]

A similar argument holds for the earth itself in its providential care for the life it fosters, an essential element of its descent as soul.

> For even if the earth's body is difficult to move, it is certainly not immovable. But the earth's perceptions will not be of small things, but of great ones. But why? Because it is necessary, since there is a soul in it, that it should not be unaware of the greatest movements. And there is nothing to prevent the earth having perceptions for this reason, too, that it may make good arrangements for men, as far as the affairs of men concern it—it will make good arrangements by a kind of sympathy [*sympathos*]—and hearing those who pray to it, and answering their prayers, not in the way we do, and being subject to affection by the other senses in relation to itself. (IV.4.26, 8–17: Armstrong translation)

This last passage reiterates two points characteristic of this section. First, there is the necessary link between the presence of soul and awareness, though such awareness need not be at all like the familiar modes of human awareness. Second, and far more important for our purposes, there is the persistent theme of the unity of the cosmos, expressed through Stoic sympathy, but with its source very clearly in Plato's *Timaeus*, to which Plotinus now turns his attention.

2.2 *Sympathy: in a Single Living Thing*

The next series of passages all come from the same section, IV.4[28].30–45, which Igal describes as investigating the nature and scope of the influence of the stars (III–IV, 302). It is closely parallel to the treatise 'On Destiny' (III.1[3]), with the similar problem of freedom and determinism, but now arising against the background of the related aporia of atomism and monism (Cf. IV.9[8]). His solution involves a thorough analysis of the phrase from the *Timaeus*, that the universe is a single living being (30d3–31a1).

> First of all we must posit that this All is a 'single living being which encompasses all the living beings that are within it'; and it has one soul which extends to all its parts, in so far as each individual thing is a part of it...This one universe is all bound together in shared experience [*sympathes*] and is like one living creature, and that which is far is really near, just as, in one of the individual living things, a nail or horn or finger or one of the other limbs which is not contiguous: the intermediate part leaves a gap in the experience and is not affected, but that which is not near is affected...and since it is a living thing and all belongs to a unity nothing is so distant in space that it is not close enough to the nature of the one living thing to share experience [*to sympathein*]. (IV.4.32, 4–7, 13–17, 20–22: Armstrong translation)

As we have seen, Plotinus applied the primary aspect of his structure of unity to sympathy by showing its source in the Hypostasis Soul (IV.3.8), coming finally in this long section to apply its secondary aspect to sympathy as it occurs among participant souls. Sympathy in this secondary sense, therefore, has two foci: the comprehensive unity of the universe as a whole and, within that, the particular sympathy operative between or within its different parts.

The remainder of this section of the treatise explores the interrelation of these two foci, attempting a delicate balance between the demands of unity, which is the base of the whole structure, and the free and spontaneous movements of its parts, which is needed for their individual integrity.

> But since the heavenly bodies move according to reason and their relationships within the [universal] living being vary, and then here below these events occur in our own sphere in sympathy with [*sympathon*] those above, it is reasonable to enquire whether we should assert that these earthly occurrences follow on those above by correspondence, or whether the figures have the powers which bring about what is done, and whether it is simply the figures or the figures made by particular heavenly bodies. (IV.4.34, 9–14: Armstrong translation)

Plotinus, as we have seen in III.1 and IV.9, admits the influence of the stars, but wants to determine the exact nature of this influence: Is it merely correspondence, an external similarity, or is it causal, the figures actually having the power to bring about what happens? Assuming his earlier argument against determinism, he now argues for both aspects, making more explicit the role of the figures. Is the effect produced by a figure acting as a single entity, or as summing up all the causal factors occurring within it?

In opting for the effectiveness of all the causal factors, he undercuts the determinism of the astrologers by an argument already implicit in their own position, and substitutes an explanation linking both action and signification. A preliminary version of this argument was present in III.1[3].8–10, but Plotinus now illustrates it with the rich and varied images of this section, IV.4[28].30–45, mentioning next the image of the dance.[14]

> This argument, then, gives powers to the figures and powers to the bodies arranged: since with dancers each hand has a distinct power and so have the other limbs, but the figures also have great power, and then there is a third group of consequentially effective things, the parts of the limbs which are brought into the dance and their constituents, for instance the clenched fingers of the hand and the muscles and veins which are affected along with them [*sympathounta*]. (VI.4.34, 26–33: Armstrong translation)

In the ensemble of the dance, three elements in the configuration can be the focus of attention: the pattern of the whole dance, the movements of each dancer taken alone, and finally the gestures and movements of specific parts of the dancer's body. The dance as such depends on all three, but each element contributes both as part of the general pattern and as spontaneously moving in its own right, according to the particular sympathy operative within it. This is Plotinus' model for the living unity of the universe, a model that is taken from life itself.

The advantage of this model is that it does not reduce our experience to a formal antinomy of freedom and determinism, but substitutes a mixture of different kinds and levels of causes operating within an overall unitary scheme. It thus has, to use a modern analogy, the flexibility of Einsteinian relativity in contrast to Newtonian objectivity, of a multiplicity of possible perspectives instead of just one. In recapitulating these points, it is the sympathetic unity of the cosmos as one living being that is central for this mixture of unity and plurality.

> But if we remember that we posited that the universe is a single living thing, and that since it is so it was absolutely necessary for it to have an internal

> self-communication of its experiences [*sympathes*]; and if we remember further that the process of its life must be rational and all in tune [*symphonos*] with itself, and that there is nothing casual in its life but a single melody and order [*harmonia kai taxis*], and that the celestial arrangements are rational, and each individual part moves by numbers, as do the dancing parts of the living being, we must admit that both are the activity of the All, the figures in it and the parts of it which are arranged in figures,...and that this is the way the All lives. (IV.4.35, 8–17: Armstrong translation)

Plotinus begins, as he did in the image of the dance, with the universe as a whole, manifesting itself as a single living thing that is sympathetic to itself. Its life is unified, but not with a deterministic rigidity. In tune with itself, life weaves all else into a single harmony and order, whether the focus is on the whole or moves from part to part. Life fosters life, and thus neither the figures nor their parts are ultimate, but both together produce the flourishing state of the cosmos.

The last two passages in this section mention magic and prayer, both of which were also used to illustrate cosmic sympathy in IV.9[8].3 and IV.4[28].26.

> But how do magic spells work? By sympathy [*sympatheia*] and by the fact that there is a natural concord [*symphonian*] of things that are alike and opposition of things that are different, and by the rich variety of the many powers which go to make up the life of the one living creature. For many things are drawn and enchanted without anyone else's magical contrivance: and the true magic is the 'Love' and also the 'Strife' in the All. And this is the primary wizard and enchanter, from observing whom men came to use his philtres and spells on each other. (IV.4.40, 1–9: Armstrong translation)

The factors he lists follow the pattern of his description of the dance, the overview in terms of sympathy, and the interplay of specific parts as alike or different. The third point about the rich variety of powers in the cosmos is, as it were, the central point of his whole investigation. He can now rob magic of its magic by making it like any other power operative in the universe that attracts or repels, merely another illustration of Empedocles' reduction of all things to the interplay of love and strife. Petitionary prayer, too, comes under the same spell of universal sympathy.

> But the sun, or another heavenly body, does not hear his prayers. And that which he prays for comes about because one part is in sympathetic [*sympathous*] connection with another, just as in one tense string; for if the string is plucked at the lower end, it has a vibration at the upper. But often,

> too, when one string is plucked another has a kind of sense of this by its concord [*symphonian*] and the fact that it is tuned by the same scale [*harmonia*]. But if the vibration can even pass from one lyre to another in so far as a sympathy [*to sympathes*] exists, then there is also one single harmony in the All, even if it is composed of opposites; and it is in fact composed of parts which are alike and all akin, even when they are opposites. (IV.4.41, 1–9: Armstrong translation)

The musical image implicit in the previous passage becomes explicit here with the reemergence of the lyre, in fact, a whole series of lyres. This new twist to the image allows Plotinus to use sympathy not only to illustrate the internal unity of the parts of a thing, but also the relation between separate things that are mutually adjusted.

The discussion of sympathy in IV.4[28] provides, therefore, another example of the clarification Plotinus is able to give to one of his major ideas when he deals with it in a focused and systematic way. At no point does he disagree with the earlier series of treatises, but by drawing together the various themes dealt with in piecemeal fashion and for disparate purposes, he shows more clearly the unity and consistency of his thought. Sympathy, thus, clearly manifests the unity and diversity present between the world soul and individual souls as similarly participants in the Hypostasis Soul and similarly related to the physical universe. As such, IV.4 explores in rather thorough fashion the secondary type of unity in his structural scheme. He begins with individuals and their experience, the sympathy within and between each of them, but this sympathy itself must be traced back to the sympathetic unity of the cosmos as a whole. Without cosmic sympathy, these individual parts would fall into atomistic isolation, a point reinforced in IV.5[29], which examines the necessity of sympathy for sensation.[15]

3. The Soul's Causality

No new ground is broken in this final section on sympathy, but only a very late confirmation (II.3[52]) of the anomalous use of sympathy found otherwise only in I.2[19] and IV.4[22].3, and a fascinating study of the role of sympathy in sensation (IV.5[29].1–8). In discussing sensation, Plotinus is dealing with two ostensibly parallel cases, the necessity of the organ as the medium between soul and sensible object, developed at IV.4.23–25, and that of the corresponding medium between the organ itself and the sensible object. In both cases the interests of his Platonism determine the solution, demanding the medium in the first case to preserve the impassibility of the soul, and not demanding it in the second to accentuate the soul's essential role in grounding sensation in the sympathetic unity of the cosmos. The argument is very tightly drawn, showing Plotinus' ability to focus on a specific issue with all the resources of his system, thereby giving a concise critique of competing systems and the rich subtlety of his own.

3.1 *Perception: Between Organ and Object*

The issue was stated with deliberate precision in the previous paragraph, for it is a common interpretation that Plotinus rules out not only the necessity but even the possibility of the medium in the course of his argument. Evidence of this interpretation abounds: Bréhier's 'Notice' (IV, 57), presents the dichotomy that there either is or is not a medium; G. H. Clark, 'Plotinus' Theory of Sensation,' makes him develop a theory that "appears to be a case of transmission without a medium" (363–365). Armstrong (IV, 30) and Igal (III-IV, 305 & 453ff.) also state in their notes on the text that a medium is not necessary.[16] Plotinus' actual position, however, is somewhat more nuanced. It is not so much that the medium is not a necessary condition for sensation, but that it, along with the other necessary conditions discussed in IV.4[28].23–25, is not the sufficient condition. The sufficient condition involves both *synaisthesis* (as the internal intention to look) and sympathy (as the external unity of the physical cosmos). Thus the object between functions at a maximum as a hindrance to sensation or at a minimum as somehow manifesting the sympathetic connection between the sense and its object.

Plotinus begins the discussion with explicit reference back to the comments in IV.4.23–25, where the problem of the medium was first raised.

> This is why this knowledge comes through bodily organs; for through these, which are in a way naturally united to or continuous with sense-objects, the soul must somehow in some way come to a unity with the sense-objects themselves, and so a sort of common affection [*homopatheias*] with them must arise. (IV.5[59].1, 10–13: Armstrong translation)

Plotinus takes up the question postponed from IV.4.23, 42,[17] but moves outward from the sense organs to the objects with which they are somehow continuous, examining the other side of the organ's mediation. The distance, posited earlier as necessarily between the organ and the object, becomes here the problem to be examined, especially in the case of sight or hearing. The distance is assumed to be some kind of body, whether air, water or some other transparent material. Air, for example, is between object and organ, and must at least in the literal sense of the Greek be the medium. The problem is whether or not this medium is affected in the act of sensation, the very distinction Witt makes between air as medium and as instrument ('Plotinus and Posidonius,' 205). The nuance might be captured in English by stating that air, while between the eye and the object, does not act as a go-between.

Following from the premise that the air is the medium, Plotinus quite logically distinguishes between two types of bodies, dense or subtle. Dense bodies block sight and are therefore eliminated from consideration. Subtle bodies, as at least not blocking sight, are then examined to determine whether or not they can in fact be an aid to sight. Plotinus addresses this in two questions which dominate the discussion in IV.5[29].1–4. Does this object between have to be affected first in order for the affection to reach the eye? If, on the other hand, the eye is immediately affected by the object, then is the object between affected differently or not at all?

Plotinus immediately relates this second question to the issue of sympathy, giving the general direction of his answer, but certainly not its final form, a fact which interpreters of this passage have invariably overlooked.

> But really the discussion seems to be moving in the direction of the sympathies [*sympatheias*] we talk about. But if one thing is naturally disposed to be sympathetically [*sympathos*] affected by another because it has some kind of likeness to it, then the intermediary [*to metaxu*] between them, being unlike, would not be affected, or would not be affected in the same way. If this is so, then that which is naturally disposed to be affected would be so much more if there was nothing in between [*metaxu*] them, even if the intermediary [*to metaxu*] was of such a kind as to be affected also in some way itself. (IV.5.1, 34–40: Armstrong translation)

Plotinus' use of the plural, sympathies, seems hardly accidental, but a way of indicating the varieties of meaning established so clearly in earlier treatises, especially its immediate context in IV.4[28]. Two of these meanings are particularly relevant, the sympathy operative between or within specific parts of the cosmos and the cosmic sympathy which is their foundation.

The immediate concern is this first kind of sympathy, where the sense organ is 'to suffer sympathetically' with the object on the basis of some likeness to it. Plotinus is establishing, first, that sensation is for him to be understood as knowledge of like by like, maintaining at this juncture that the object between is not, in fact, like either of them. Consequently, it would not be affected at all, or at least not in the same way, and even if it is affected in some way, then the sense organ would be even more directly affected by the object if there were no such object in between. In either case, therefore, the object and the organ can be more directly related if there is, or perhaps could be, nothing between them. The premise of the argument remains, however, that there is in fact something between them, air, for example.

The subsequent review of previous theories concerning the relation of the eye to its object is typically brief (IV.5.2, 1–15), but does nonetheless cover the primary issues related to the discussion of each of his two questions. The first two theories, from Platonic sources, focus on the nature of light, which Plotinus will attempt to define in chapters 6 & 7. The first theory, from *Timaeus* 45b4–d3, joins the light coming from the eye with the intermediate light in the air-following Igal (III-IV, 310 & 455) rather than Armstrong (IV, 285). Plotinus is satisfied with Aristotle's objection that the alteration involved in this theory can just as easily take place in the eye alone without the intermediary (*De Anima* 418a29–b2). The other theory posits light as an efflux, needing an intermediary to keep it going in a straight line, which is again unnecessary since light is incorporeal (Cf. IV.5.6, 17–20).

The following pair of positions are both materialistic, but opposite in operation. The Stoics explain sight in terms of a resistance between the eye and the object, thus making it a material passage of the affection from the object to the eye. The Epicureans, on the other hand, positing images passing through a void, only require space to prevent an obstruction and thus would be quite happy with a theory that eliminates any need for an object between. In an exceedingly rare move, Plotinus admits favoring this Epicurean view, as if in some strange way it shares some common ground with his own position in terms of sympathy, which is the last theory in his list.

The next section, IV.5.2, 15–IV.5.4, 49, presents the thesis of sight by sympathy, and immediately puts it to the test by applying his two questions: whether the object between needs to be affected first (IV.5.2, 21–IV.5.3, 15) or the sensible object affects the eye directly with no role for the object between (IV.5.3, 15–IV.5.4, 49).

(1) But all those who say that seeing takes place by sympathy [*sympatheia*] will assert that one would see less well if there was any intermediary [*ti metaxu*], in that it would obstruct and hinder and weaken the sympathy [*sympatheian*]; but it would be more consistent to say that even that which is akin [*to syggenes*] in all circumstances weakens the sympathy, in so far as it is itself affected. Certainly, if a body continuous to the bottom is set alight by the application of fire, all the same the bottom of it will be less affected by the fire applied to it than the part before it. (IV.5.2, 15–22)

(2) But if the parts of one living being are in sympathy [*sympathe*] will they be less affected because there is something between [*metaxu*] them? Yes, perhaps they might be less affected, but the affection would be in the proportion which nature willed, and the intermediary [*to metaxu*] would prevent excess: unless what is conceded amounts to this, that the intermediary [*to metaxu*] is not affected at all. (IV.5.2, 22–26)

(3) But if sympathy [*sympathes*] depends on being one living thing, and we are affected because we are in one and belong to one, how is continuity not needed when there is perception of something far off? The answer is the continuity and the intermediary [*to metaxu*] are there because the living being must be continuous, but the affection is only incidentally of something continuous, or we shall have to say that everything is affected by everything. (IV.5.2, 26–31: Armstrong translation)

There is both a weak and a strong version of the objection that the medium, or object between, needs to be affected first (1). All would admit, he says, that any object between 'obstructs, hinders, and weakens' the sympathy, but he argues that the more logical position holds that even an intermediary that is totally akin to the organ and its object weakens the sympathy, precisely in being affected itself. He illustrates the point with the example of a continuous physical body set afire, and concludes that a material medium necessarily weakens the sympathy between the organ and its object, even though it establishes physical continuity between them. The primary target is, therefore, the Stoic explanation in terms of a materialistic transfer of the affection from the object to the eye.

Plotinus substitutes instead his own psychic explanation of sympathy, describing first an individual living being and then the cosmos itself as a unitary living being. In the case of an individual living thing (2), its parts are indeed affected less, because there are parts between them. This diversity in affection is precisely the work of nature, with the part between preventing that excess that would be destructive of some other part, or where the affection given is such that the part between is completely unaffected—again following Igal (III–IV, 457). Perhaps an example of the prevention of excess is the use of the hand to shield eye or ear from excessive light or noise, while the unaffected medium might be involved when reading a book or hearing a discourse conveys information but produces no affection in the body.

In turning to the universal living being (3), more importantly, Plotinus begins to define the nature and scope of sympathy, especially its difference from continuity and the object between establishing it. These two factors relate to the physical aspect of the universe, precluding a void and establishing some minimal physical connection between the distant parts of the universe. It is clear from this that his affinity with the Epicureans is merely incidental, with the only similarity a common immaterial operation, which is utter lack in the case of the void but the presence of soul in the case of sympathy. The physical continuity and the medium, furthermore, are incidentally, but necessarily, related to the affections that constitute sensation, which is precisely the affection of an embodied soul. Plotinus will clarify this complex interrelation when he explores in greater detail the relation of this continuity and medium to the sympathetic unity of the universe as a whole (IV.5.3, 15–21).

The conclusion from the argument so far is that the object between is not needed, and thus those who posit such an object for sight must show the need by some other method (IV.5.2, 34–35). He applies the conclusion himself to the two positions, Stoic and Platonic, that seemed to entail the medium in his cursory list at the beginning of the chapter. Stoic resistance, for example, seems to be explained here (IV.5.2, 35–48) in terms of the theory of reciprocal thrusts (*antiperistaseis*) as it applies to different bodies in the universe: bodies falling, fire rising, trees growing upward, and ourselves moving along. In all these instances, air is parted by bodies without being affected by them, with the corollary that air would need to part even less to allow for the passage of the forms which come to sight. In rare agreement with the Epicureans, Plotinus maintains that such forms do not pass through air as if through a stream, and this corroborates his conclusion that there is no need for the air to be affected first (IV.5.2, 49–50).

He next applies this conclusion to the Platonic thesis (IV.5.2, 50–IV.5.3, 15). Does the air between the object and the eye need to be illuminated? If the answer is yes, then seeing would be like being warmed. It would not be a perception of a distant object (Cf. II.8[35] & IV.6[41]), but of the immediately affected air before the eye, just as the body is warmed by the warm air next to it, and not directly by the more distant fire. That is, sight would take place by contact. But sight, as Aristotle pointed out (*De anima* 419a12–13), cannot take place by contact. Plotinus gives factual evidence to bolster his case: We see distant objects in daylight, but just as clearly we see, in the darkness of night, fires and beacons, and even distant stars. What is essential is that the object be in the line of sight, confirming once again the conclusion that the intermediary does not need to be affected.

This leads directly to the second question: that sight, in fact, takes place without an object between. Igal sees it clearly as a second objection, needing to be discussed and resolved. It thus cannot be, as it stands, the conclusion of the argument. Plotinus is rarely that simple. His position lies somewhere in between the alternatives posed by the two questions, revealed slowly in their dialectical interplay.

> But one might pause to consider this further point, whether it is not possible to see in the absence of an intermediary [*to metaxu*], not because there is no intermediary [*meden metaxu*] but because the sympathy [*sympatheia*] of the living being with itself and of its parts with each other, which depends on being one thing, will be done away with. For it looks as if any kind of perception depends on this, that the living being—this All—is in sympathy [*sympathes*] with itself. For if this were not so, how would one thing share in the power of another, and especially in power from a distance? (IV.5.3, 15–21: Armstrong translation)

Oddly enough this passage, far from eliminating the medium, sees it as a necessary manifestation of sympathy. What, however, can be the connection between sympathy and the medium? What can Plotinus mean?

The solution is readily available if the present context is compared to IV.4.23–25 concerning the necessary conditions for sensation. They may all be there, but without the soul's intention to look, there will be no sensation. The present case focuses similarly on the relation between the necessary and sufficient conditions for sight. The necessary conditions are the physical, and therefore minimal, manifestations of sympathy, precisely the continuity and the medium that his previous argument seems to eliminate, in the view of some interpreters. Consequently, he argues that the absence of these necessary conditions is actually the more radical problem of the absence of sympathy as the sufficient condition. Plotinus' logic is crystal clear, making allowances for the inversion caused by focusing on the external conditions for sight rather than its internal conditions within the sensitive being. Without sympathy, there simply cannot be physical continuity or a medium.

The inevitable conclusion is, paradoxically, that the medium is necessary, but not for the reasons its proponents had given. Plotinus' real difficulty is with a solely materialistic transmission of the affection. This is the point of the first section (IV.5.2, 15–IV.5.3, 15), and the second merely reinforces it (IV.5.3, 15–IV.5.4, 49). He begins again with an allusion to Stoic materialism. If the air in between were affected, it would have to be corporeally, the result of some kind of impression. Such an impression could, however, capture only a partial view of the object. He counters with this argument:

> But as it is, the whole object is seen, and all those who are in the air see it, from the front and sideways, from far and near, and from the back, as long as their line of sight is not blocked; so that each part of the air contains the whole seen object, the face for instance; but this is not a bodily affection, but is brought about by the higher necessities of the soul belonging to a single living being in sympathy [*sympathous*] with itself. (IV.5.3, 32–38: Armstrong translation)

There is an uncannily modern ring to this passage. It would be right at home in Twentieth Century phenomenology, for the object is seen as an integral whole. In perceiving it, one is aware at the same time that it can be perceived from any perspective. Such an awareness, Plotinus reasons, is not reducible to a bodily affection, but belongs to the soul precisely as self-sympathetic, that is, as itself a living whole.

The remainder of the treatise, IV.5.4–8, contains a mixture of positions—Platonic, Aristotelian and Stoic—held together by Plotinus' gradual explication of light in terms of his theory of two acts, in which light becomes structurally identical to soul. He begins with a parallel application of the present discussion about the object directly affecting the eye to the Platonic thesis of the mixture of the eye's own light with the light between it and the object, concluding that this intermediate light is needed for seeing at a distance, but remains itself unaffected (IV.5.4, 1–10). The relation of this intermediate light to air is mentioned, but its treatment is briefly postponed to consider an entirely new alternative, that sight is a movement out of the soul to the object, with the object inert and inactive. It comes in two forms, one which seems traceable to Galen (Igal, III-IV, 461 n23) and the other to the Stoics. Galen's version holds the connecting light to be ensouled as the soul moves through it to the object (IV.5.4, 10–38), whereas the Stoics have a materialistic interpretation, with the soul using the light like a stick to reach the object (IV.5.4, 38–46). The difficulty is the same for both: Seeing is reduced to a species of touch and the receptivity of sensation becomes inexplicable.

In IV.5.5–7, Plotinus finally considers the role of the intermediate air. In the case of hearing, he quickly establishes the same position as for sight: The intermediate air is affected only incidentally, with the colliding bodies a sufficient explanation for the vibrations of sound (IV.5.5). His argument in the case of light is against the Aristotelian position that light is an actuality of a transparent body (IV.5.6, 1–7), or alternatively is a modification of air (IV.5.6, 34–40). He reasons that light depends for its existence, not on air, but on fiery bodies. It is consequently not a quality of air, but an activity coming from such a body—a form of energy in modern parlance. It is therefore a second act, extrinsic to its source and incorporeal, in the same way that life is an activity of soul (IV.5.6, 7–34). As a secondary act, light never perishes, but color, its presence in the corporeal, can disappear, just as the trace of soul in matter can depart, not indicating that light or life perish, but that it is no longer present since nothing is there to pick up its image (IV.5.7, 1–49).

The parallel of light and life only emphasizes the centrality of the soul in Plotinus' account of sensation, expressing in visible form, as it were, the unity of the sense world as derivative of soul. The final passages using sympathy, in IV.5.8, capture this unity of the cosmos in a vivid image that illustrates the necessity of sympathy for any kind of sensory experience.

> But if there was a body outside the heavenly sphere and there was an eye looking from our universe with nothing to obstruct its vision, would it see what would not be sympathetically [*sympathes*] connected with our universe, if as things are sympathetic [*sympathes*] connection is due to the nature of a single living being? Now if sympathetic [*sympathes*] connection is due to the fact that perceiving subjects and perceived objects belong to a single living thing, there would be no perception, unless this outside body was part of our [universal] living being: for if it was, there would perhaps be perceptions of it. (IV.5.8, 1–7: Armstrong translation)

As Igal mentions (III–IV, 471 n50), Plotinus is positing a universe numerically distinct from our own, and as such outside the sympathetic unity requisite for sensation. He then gives it all the qualities and characteristics that would make it perceivable, making it seem absurd to claim that our senses fail to perceive their proper objects when they are present. Determining where the absurdity lies is a problem, moreover, that shows the intimate connection of this section on sight to the argument of the whole treatise, IV.3–5[27–29], that the soul is the principle of both the unity and plurality of the cosmos.

> It is that here, being in one and belonging to one, we act and are affected in this way. We must therefore investigate whether this is the reason why we do so. And if this has already been sufficiently shown, our demonstration is complete; if not, we must demonstrate it by other arguments as well. Now it is clear that a living being is sympathetically [*sympathes*] aware of itself; and if the universe is a living being, this is enough; so that the parts also will be sympathetically aware of each other in that they belong to one living being. But suppose someone were to say that this [sympathy] is because of their likeness? (IV.5.8, 14–19: Armstrong translation)

The absurdity comes, not surprisingly, in the conflict between the twin assumptions of Plotinus' theory of sensation. Sympathy precludes any awareness of that other world, but the principle of knowing like by like demands that we know it. The solution can come only by determining which one is prior, and Plotinus does this by tracing all likeness and kinship to the one soul, the source of all, as demonstrated ontologically in IV.3[27].1–5.[18]

3.2 *The Influence of the Stars*

The late treatise, 'On Whether the Stars are Causes' (II.3[52]), presents a final consideration of problems going back to his earliest writings, the treatise 'On Destiny' (III.1[3].5 & 6), and examined at great length during his middle period in IV.4[28].30–45 on the nature and scope of the influence of heavenly bodies. In both of these earlier treatises, sympathy plays a role in Plotinus' explanation of stellar influence, an explanation designed to counteract the determinism of the astrologists by situating the causality of the stars within the context of a wider interweaving of causal factors in the single unity of the universe as a whole. The first occurrence of sympathy in the present treatise, despite its textual dislocation,[19] continues the same line of argumentation, refuting the theories of the astrologers, while admitting their evidence (II.3.2–6).

> So, too, in the complete whole [of the universe] there is need of some organ like the gall and of some other directed to producing sweetness; others are the eyes of the universe; all are united in feeling [*sympathe*] by their correspondence. So the universe is one and a single melody. (II.3.12, 29–32: Armstrong translation but reading *analogo* [line 31] after E. Orth.)

Igal mentions that this is very much a capsule summary of the positions spelled out more fully in IV.4.28 & 32 (I-II, 395 n76 & n77), indicating that the general nature of sympathy remains consistent throughout Plotinus' writings.

Its second occurrence in this late treatise, however, is more significant, since it reiterates the usage and problem underlying the discussions in two other treatises, I.2[19].3 & 6 and VI.4[22].3. In only these three treatises does Plotinus speak of the soul's sympathy with the body, and only in I.2 and II.3 is sympathy seen negatively. The present context, in addition, emphasizes the dualism in the whole sensible order, affecting human nature and the entire cosmos, even the heavenly bodies. The soul gives rational order to the universe as a whole, but the parts of the universe share in that rationality by degree, as inanimate instruments or living beings with a variety of levels of contribution, from mere locomotion to rational thought. It is through this diversity of activity that Plotinus seeks to explain the origin and status of evil.

> So then living things are all conformed to the complete pattern of the All, both the ones in heaven and the rest which have been made parts in the whole, and no part, even if it is a great one, has power to bring about a complete change in the patterns or the things which happen according to the patterns. It can bring about a non-essential alteration in either direction, for better or worse, but it cannot make anything abandon its own proper nature. It makes a thing worse either by giving it bodily infirmity, or by becoming responsible for an incidental badness in the soul which is in sympathy [*sympathei*] with it and was given out by it into the lower region, or, when the body is badly put together, it may by means of it hinder the activity of the soul which is directed towards it: as when a lyre is not so tuned that it takes the melody [*harmonias*] accurately so as to make its sounds musical. (II.3.13, 34–47: Armstrong translation)

There are links here with the complex theodicy operative in IV.4.30–45, including the simile of the lyre, but that is only the context for the specific contribution of this passage in determining what Plotinus means by evil, especially moral evil.

To begin with, evil falls into the category of the non-essential change that any part of the universe can introduce, proportionate to its size and relation to soul. Such change can be either for better or worse, with change for the worse receiving more detailed analysis. Two examples of this kind of change concern physical evil, coming from bodily weakness or a situation where the body is described as badly put together, and thus a block to some activity of the soul. In either case, the problem has a more essential relation to the physical capacities of the composite, and does not affect the integrity of the soul.

The significant alternative is where the body is responsible for some accidental weakness, *phaulotetos*, in the soul, because of the soul's sympathy with it. This confirms the point made in I.2.3 & 6 that it is the soul's over-involvement with the body that brings about an evil that in some sense involves a moral dimension. Plotinus adds that the soul is somehow given over to the lower by the body, with reference perhaps to the theory of reincarnation recounted in Plato's *Republic* X. This specifies the weakness as the soul's sinking lower into the sense world, a position congruent with the analysis of evil in Rist, 'Plotinus and Augustine on Evil' (Atti del Convegno internazionale sul tema: *Plotino e il Neoplatonismo in Oriente e in Occidente*, Roma, 1970; Accademia Nazionale dei Lincei, 1974). There is an ambiguity here that Rist expresses well, that "the weakness of the human soul which is moral evil may at times be both an effect of matter and in some way prior" to matter as its cause (502). We find it here in the direct statement that the body is cause of the weakness of the soul, but that it acts as such a cause because of the soul's sympathy with it. A further ambiguity is introduced by describing this weakness of the soul as accidental, assuming strangely, as Rist also notes, that the soul can be affected somehow by the body. It seems that Plotinus tries to protect the impassivity of the soul by making the evil only accidental, but in so doing makes the soul more directly a cause of the evil. Even at the very end of his life, there is no movement beyond this radical ambiguity in his theory of evil and its relation to the soul.

4. Conclusion

In this analysis of sympathy, Plotinus shows remarkable consistency and ingenuity in the application of the basic structure of unity. The treatises of the first period, in fact, give some indication of the particular problems that served to refine Plotinus' thought to the point where the threefold structure of unity emerged with utmost clarity and could then be utilized in the lengthy treatises of the middle period. The first problem is the Platonic dualism articulated in IV.7[2] and IV.2[4]. In trying to delineate the connection between the sensible and Intelligible worlds, Plotinus proposes a fourfold division that contains the structure of unity implicitly in its three highest factors. In IV.9[8], the structure of unity has its first hesitant debut in the distinction of the Hypostasis Soul and its participants, world soul and individual souls. This treatise also brings into play the countervailing problem of monism, thus forcing Plotinus to steer the narrow course between atomism and monism.

The results of this tension come to expression in VI.4 & 5[22 & 23], a dense reexamination of the relation of sensible and intelligible in terms of the structure of unity. This is now firmly linked with the Platonic doctrine of participation and Aristotle's theory of act and potency, all transformed by his own keen sense of unity as immateriality. With these ontological distinctions in place, Plotinus can turn to an examination of soul in IV.3–5[27–29], its powers and affections. In terms of the discussion of sympathy, the problem of dualism appears in two forms, the relation of the individual soul to sensible objects through the medium of the senses, and the relation of the sense organs to their proper objects where there is a distance between them.

The first area, the soul in relation to the sense world, takes up the bulk of IV.4[28], with the possible interrelations between the parts of the sense world, whether perception, divination or magic, explainable in terms of the unity of the cosmos as a single living thing, combining Stoic sympathy with Plato's *Timaeus*. This emphasizes the two secondary levels in the structure of unity, that sympathy firmly rooted in the world soul as source and principle of the overall unity present in the physical universe, and of the final type of sympathy in the relation of one part of the universe to another. This last and most difficult aspect of sympathy receives thorough examination in IV.5[29] on the problem of sight. Here Plotinus sees the very material continuity of the universe, which functions under certain conditions as the medium between organ and object, as a manifestation of sympathy itself. Sympathy, as a power of the soul, gives the physical cosmos even that physical unity it is capable of having, showing how completely he has transformed this Stoic term.

One other problem occurs in the course of Plotinus' discussion of sympathy, the moral dimension of human life. It appears in III.1[3] as the problem of freedom and determinism, which Plotinus consistently solves by a careful exposition of the full range of causal factors involved in cosmic events and by a careful distinction of the different phases of the human soul. In I.2[19] and II.3[52], however, he addresses the more difficult issue of moral evil and its relation to the soul. His position is clearly subtle, but not enough to eradicate the ambiguity that moral evil presents to a consistently Platonic psychology. The ambiguity can be seen precisely in his use of the term *sympathy*, which ordinarily denotes the unifying activity of the soul in relation to the material world, allowing the parts of the world to have their own organic unity and, on that basis, to relate to one another. Sympathy in this respect is a decidedly positive phenomenon, manifesting the goodness and unity at the heart of Plotinian reality.

It is therefore all the more striking that sympathy should have some role in Plotinus' attempts to explain the problem of evil. The soul's sympathy with the body, thus, opens the door to moral evil and the soul's entrapment in the sense world. This usage is not only strange because of its association with evil, but this very association seems based on a reversal in the meaning of the term. In no other context does Plotinus claim that the soul, or any higher reality, is in sympathy with a lower. In fact, it is used precisely of the lower in relation to the higher, allowing it to be more unified and thus more in tune with its source. It must be admitted, however, that there is some basis for this usage in Plotinus' theory. He has defined *sympathy* from the very beginning as based in the soul and as expressing its relation to the material world.

The reversal in direction and the association with evil are, nevertheless, problematic, for they introduce an ambiguity in the soul itself. The dilemma is simple. Plotinus has been at pains, especially in controversy with the Gnostics, to show that the material world is not evil, and has thus tended to describe it as the occasion rather than cause of evil. These passages involving sympathy are fully in that tradition. This has the unwanted effect, however, of making the soul itself the implicit cause of evil, or perhaps, more accurately, some kind of co-cause. The ambiguity produced is both unavoidable, given the restrictions of his system, and subtle, given the extraordinarily delicate distinctions Plotinus is trying to make.

Boston College

NOTES

1. Reprinted with modification, by permission, from: Gary M. Gurtler, S.J., *Plotinus: The Experience of Unity*, Series 5, volume 43 (New York: Peter Lang Publishing © 1988), 91–137.
2. It is therefore not surprising that of its forty-five occurrences, twenty-seven of them can be found in IV 3–5[27–29], the treatise "On the Problems of the Soul," where the relation of soul to cosmos is examined at considerable length, especially in its last section, IV.4.18–IV.8. Graeser—*Plotinus and the Stoics* (Leiden: E. J. Brill, 1972), 68—emphasizes this connection between sympathy and cosmology in Plotinus.

3. The restriction of sympathy to the physical cosmos is pointed out clearly in my article, "Sympathy in Plotinus," *International Philosophical Quarterly* 24 (1984), 395–406, especially in opposition to K. Keilung, *Über die Sympathie bei Plotin* (Dissertation: Jena, 1916), who misconstrues the two aspects of sympathy: the harmony of the physical cosmos and the various types of perception or influence based on it. Keilung seems to take these latter as establishing a connection between the sensible and intelligible worlds, but in fact they only spell out the cosmic relation between the heavens and the earth.
4. In my article, "Sympathy in Plotinus," there is a preliminary attempt to articulate the connection between consciousness and sympathy, especially in terms of reconciling unity and individuality (403–406), but the intricacy of this connection becomes even clearer in terms of the structure of unity discerned in my book, *Plotinus: The Experience of Unity* (New York: Peter Lang, 1988). That structure presents a combination of vertical and horizontal dimensions that explains how sympathy is rooted in the transcendent world soul and how it is manifest on the same horizontal level in different ways, both for nature in general and human experience in particular.
5. Graeser, *Plotinus and the Stoics*, indicates the blending of Stoic and Platonic elements in the Neoplatonic use of sympathy in three areas (69–72): cosmic sympathy and friendship (*Laws* 903b), the providential governance of the universe (*Phaedrus* 246b and *Timaeus* 30–31), and the influence of the heavens on the earth, more eminently Stoic.
6. Graeser, *Plotinus and the Stoics*, supports the idea that Plotinus is attacking the atomists from a Stoic point of view, but denies the possibility that there is also an implicit attack on the Stoics themselves in terms of soul as source of sympathy (77). It should be noted that sympathy is used to translate two Greek words: *sympatheia* and *homopatheia*, both of which have a similar meaning and function.
7. Both Bréhier, *Plotin "Ennéades"* (Paris: Société d'édition *Les Belles Lettres*, 1924–1938) IV, 179–188, and Igal, *Plotino: "Enéadas" I–II, III–IV* (Madrid: Editorial Gredos, 1982, 1985) III–IV, 281–283, point out that IV.7 uses the method of the *Phaedo* and the *Phaedrus* in showing the soul to be a transcendent substance, starting from Plato's ontological dualism. Later, in IV.2, Plotinus recapitulates the argument of this treatise and introduces a new method based on *Timaeus* 35a1–4, yielding a four-fold division: the primary divisible and indivisible, and the secondary divisible and indivisible. In the context of this argument against the Epicureans, however, other aspects of the *Timaeus*—the elements and the demiurge—are more clearly the background. P. Friedländer, *Plato: An Introduction* (Princeton University Press, 1969), 246–260, discusses these aspects of the *Timaeus* in relation to modern atomic physics. His comments concerning the parallels between the two in method and in the structures utilized can serve also as background for what Plotinus is attempting, given that there is a similar divergence in

vocabulary and imagery between Plotinus and modern culture that obscures such parallels at the surface level.

8. Igal (III–IV, 282) mentions three factors that should be kept in mind to understand Plotinus' purpose here: (1) it is a division of the four degrees of Being, thus the One and matter are excluded from consideration; (2) the criterion used in this fourfold scale is the degree of quantitative division; and (3) the formula of *Timaeus* 35a1–4, 'the indivisible and divisible,' is taken as the equivalent of *Parmenides* 155e5, 'one and multiple.'
9. It provides a parallel to the discussion of quality and soul in IV.2[4].1, with certain nuances added. The dependency of the qualities on the bodies is more explicit, with no affection existing by itself nor known except in a body. The soul, on the other hand, is numerically one throughout the body and only appears to be divided because the body itself is made up of parts, to all of which the same soul is present. He writes:

> Similarly someone would reasonably inquire in this case, how the soul is given magnitude accidentally. For it is obviously not in the way a quality, like sweetness or color, is distributed through the whole body, that the soul is so distributed. These qualities are affections of bodies, so that the whole passive object has the affection and no affection exists by itself, since it is known only as belonging to a body. It follows necessarily from this that it is of such a size, and the white of one part is not sympathetic [*homopathes*] to the white of another. In the case of whiteness, it is the same in species, the white of one part relative to the white of another, but in the case of soul, it is the same in number, whether it is possessed by the foot or the hand, as perceptions make clear. In general, then, it appears that for qualities the same thing can be divided, but that in the case of the soul the same thing cannot be divided, even though it is said to be divided, since it is everywhere. (VI.4.1, 16–18)

10. The meaning of this passage becomes clear if the barely visible parallel structure is recognized. Thus, if being became a form, it would be the form of a particular, *genomenon toude*, and belong accidentally to the other, *kata symbebekos allou*, but being remains separate and thus is neither: *ou genomenon ekeinou* and *oud' au allou*. The translation has been thoroughly revised and corresponds to that in my article, "Plotinus and the Platonic Parmenides," *International Philosophical Quarterly* 32 (1992), 441–455.
11. The manuscript tradition is in disagreement whether *symparathein* (BxUCz) or *sympathein* (w) is present in line 20, but 'keeps pace with' hardly sheds light on this convoluted passage. It either amounts to sympathy or connotes a vague relationship between soul and body that scarcely merits the intricate distinctions Plotinus has been making.

12. The topic of perception, so briefly mentioned in this passage, receives ample investigation in the last part of this treatise on the soul, IV.5[29], to be treated in the next section.
13. J. M. Rist, *Plotinus: The Road to Reality* (Cambridge, 1967), 199–212, presents a discussion of prayer in Plotinus, tracing out sources in Plato and the Stoics, with a distinction between the vulgar petitions of the many and the silent prayer of the purified soul in its ascent to the One featured in V.1[10].6, V.8[31].9, and III.5[50].6. In these passages prayer is directed to Intellect or the One, and not to the world soul or the divine souls of the stars and planets. This section is also significant in E. de Keyser, *La signification de l'art dans les Ennéades de Plotin* (Louvain, 1955) in articulating the difference between religious and secular art—the imitation of transcendent forms and not mere sense objects.
14. E. de Keyser, *La signification de l'art*, points out the shift of this image in Plotinus from the more rigid movement of the classical chorus to the mime of the individual dancer, a change reflecting the art of his own day (23).
15. When writing "Sympathy in Plotinus," I saw more congruity between my own position and that of D. Rodier—"The Problem of Ordered Chaos in Whitehead and Plotinus," *The Significance of Neoplatonism*, ed. R. Baine Harris (Norfolk, VA: International Society for Neoplatonic Studies, 1976), 301–317—with his distinction between predictive and operative sympathy. Rodier sees divination as a sign of predictive sympathy, indicating only the external relation between parts of the universe as forming one organic whole, while prayer, magic and, in general, perception are based on an operative sympathy localized to specific parts of the universe and internalized in an agent. In describing their common dynamism, however, their congruence is much more thorough, making it very difficult for him to maintain any real difference between them. It is much easier to see them as diverse manifestations of the same cosmic sympathy, with Plotinus' real aim the grounding of the human soul's independence within the concatenation of cosmic causes.
16. Graeser, *Plotinus and the Stoics*, 77—following G. H. Clark, "Plotinus' Theory of Sensation," *Philosophical Review* 51 (1942), 357–382—is even stronger in his denial of a medium between object and organ, since the organ already functions as medium between object and soul. H. J. Blumenthal, *Plotinus' Psychology* (The Hague: Martinus Nijhoff, 1971), admits in his brief summary of the argument in IV.5 that for some of Plotinus' opponents a medium is necessary (78)—stating only later that the necessity of sympathy for all perception dispenses with a medium (137), with a disparaging remark about R. E. Witt, "Plotinus and Posidonius," *Classical Quarterly* 24 (1930), for suggesting (205) that air is the medium, though not the instrument, of vision. Witt in this instance has hit upon the right solution, but unfortunately his comment was too brief to overcome the tide of opposition.

17. This is discussed In *Plotinus: The Experience of Unity*, Chapter 2, 67–72, and shows the conjunction of the two terms in explaining perception. In IV.4.23, Plotinus argues that the distance between the knower and sensible object and the presence of organs are necessary for sensation to take place. In that context, however, the argument moved internally, from the fact of sensation to the reason why the soul needs such information, either as a necessary consequence of its nature or for the purpose of maintaining its presence in the body (IV.4.24). Neither of these is sufficient for the presence of sensation, and Plotinus moved further back to find its root in the disposition of the soul to look (IV.4.25).
18. Armstrong appends a note to this passage, in which he admits Plotinus' logic in terms of the priority of sympathy as the basis of perception, but notes a logical lapse in another area (IV, 315). He claims that Plotinus' distinction between the Hypostasis Soul and the world soul and individual souls in IV.3[27].1–5 leaves the possibility open that other souls, like the world soul, could produce a distinct universe, still having some sympathetic relation to this one. A more careful examination of IV.3.1–5, as shown in *Plotinus: The Experience of Unity*, indicates, however, that the world soul is not such because it is soul of this world, but rather is world soul because all after the Hypostasis Soul must be united within it (23–30). This consistent structure of unity would not allow for Armstrong's alternative and, conversely, his alternative would have disastrous results, if applied with similarly logical rigor. Thus, could not one also posit additional Hypostases Souls, all equally members of the Intelligible world and equally capable of producing world souls and individual souls? And in a similar way, also in the case of Intellect in relation to the One? The logic of Plotinus' structure seems therefore to be a little more tightly drawn than Armstrong suspects at this point.
19. Thus, 12,12–32 seems to fit better after 5,21, with some minor adjustments, as noted by Igal (I–II, 385 & 393: n30, n31, n68, n71).

PLOTINUS, NATURE, AND THE SCIENTIFIC SPIRIT

Michael F. Wagner

...Those on whom
Delusion cast its gloomy pall of doubt,
Upborn now on the wings that genius lends.
May penetrate the mansions of the gods
And scale the heights of heaven...
Admitted to the banquet of the gods,
We contemplate the polities of heaven;
And spelling out the secrets of the earth,
Discern the changeless order of the world
And the aeons of its history.[1]

Science has a privileged status in our culture as discerner and arbiter of human knowledge regarding the natural cosmos. In this regard, modern science is the intellectual progeny of ancient philosophers' attempts to discern the elements (*stoicheiai*), principles (*archai*), and causes (*aitiai*) of our cosmos. At the same time, however, ancient philosophers were deeply concerned with issues that today are not normally considered pertinent to science—e.g. with the relationship between human history and conduct, on the one hand, and the inexorable order of natural causality and metaphysical Being, on the other. In their struggles to discern order and law amid the evident diversity and complexity of our cosmos, the ancients grappled also with such issues as contrariety among its sensible appearances, apparent irregularities in its celestial movements, incommensurability and the continuum, the nature of movement and change, and its place within metaphysical reality more generally. Perhaps it is a mark of intellectual progress that scientists no longer burden themselves with most such issues. At the same time, however, the foregoing indicates that piecing together the history of scientific thought often requires recognizing scientific outlooks and concerns amid issues, even worldviews, which might strike contemporary readers as generally nonscientific.

The diverse doctrines, hypotheses, and methods generated by the fertile minds of ancient philosophers constituted a vital step in humanity's quest for scientific understanding. To some among the ancient philosophers themselves, however, this diversity called into serious question whether intellectual progress was being made or could be made at all. Chief among them were the Pyrrhonian Skeptics, whose critiques of so-called dogmatic philosophy were compiled and elaborated by Sextus Empiricus (*fl. c.* 200 A.D.). Plotinus, who began teaching in Rome approximately forty years after Sextus' standard flourishing date, has been portrayed as a (perhaps unwitting) collaborator with the Pyrrhonian abandonment of the Greek scientific spirit. Leon Robin, for example, casts Plotinus as chief villain in his exposition of the "Decline of Greek Thought", wherein he alleges that in late antiquity "the natural rationality of the old Greek [scientific] spirit yielded more and more to the invasion of Oriental superstitions."[2] Robin's assessment may be more extreme and pejorative in tone than most scholars'; but the overall image of Plotinus' *Enneads* which it conveys is by no means uncommon—even among Plotinus scholars.

In this essay I shall examine features of Plotinus' Neoplatonism which, far from aiding and abetting Pyrrhonism, seek to save Greek rational or scientific philosophy from its Pyrrhonian attackers. Perhaps most important in this regard is Plotinus' insistence that our cosmos is rational and its rationality is universal, pervasive, and irrevocable; that the *natural* cosmos (the order of Becoming investigated by natural science) is one and the same with the *observable* cosmos (the objects of human sense experience); and that the metaphysical principles which underlie our cosmos and are responsible for its rationality are immune to the Pyrrhonian critique, and so provide an epistemically sound foundation for human investigation of our cosmos. I am not interested here in how particular details of Plotinus' conception of our cosmos might have influenced subsequent thinkers so much as in that conception's place within a philosophical framework which makes rational science epistemically possible. I will, of course, consider specific texts from Plotinus' *Enneads* to piece together *a* textually viable account of his conception of the natural cosmos and the metaphysical grounds for a scientific understanding of it. But first I shall note some pertinent features of Modern scientific thought, focusing specifically on Galileo Galilei's views on the relationship between science, observation, and metaphysical principles.

1. Science, Observation, and Metaphysics

A chief goal of science is to discern the causes of (all) natural processes and things, the principles (or laws) which order and determine them, and the fundamental substances which underlie or comprise them; and it presumes that, in doing so, it is thereby explaining the same processes and objects which we observe daily by means of our senses. Now, Plotinus identifies the *causes* of nature with its governing or ordering *principles*; and he identifies both of these in turn with the metaphysical grounds for nature's existence—*i.e.* with its *substance*. The first identification yields his doctrine of *vertical causality*, according to which the cause (or sufficient reason) for a given process or existent is not to be found horizontally—on its same level of Being—but in a higher level of Being to which it stands as an image to its archetype, as an expression of law to the law expressed, as an instantiation of principle to the principle it instances, or the like. The second identification yields Plotinus' doctrine of *hypostasis* (or of *the hypostases*), according to which the metaphysical principles and true (vertical) causes of our cosmos are also ontologically the most fundamental (or real) of all existents; indeed, they comprise the existential ground (substance) of all 'lower' existents, including especially our cosmos. Finally, Plotinus maintains that the natural (or natured) cosmos effected, enunciated, (il)luminated, or temporally instanced by the hypostases just *is* the world of Becoming we observe in sense experience.

Galileo, in contrast, favors material atomism's account of our cosmos' existential ground (substance), and he accepts horizontal causality (i.e. real causal relations among substances within the natural cosmos itself). Despite departing from classical Neoplatonism's identification of nature's causes, its determining principles and its existential ground, Galileo nevertheless insists upon the importance of metaphysical understanding to establishing a scientific conception of our cosmos and even to observing scientifically its sensible manifestations or appearances. To this extent, at least, Galileo echoes basic themes Plotinus develops in his *Enneads* where he argues for the natural-*cum*-sensible cosmos' utter (existential) dependency on metaphysical principles of absolute order (unity), intelligibility (or **rational** order), and life (or **temporalized** intelligible order).

Galileo's *Dialogue Concerning The Two Chief World Systems* is a testament to the view that scientific theory and scientific observation depend upon metaphysics to legitimate them. Galileo attempts in his *Dialogue*, first, to undermine Aristotelian support for the Ptolemaic cosmological system and, second, to establish the Copernican system's superiority over the Ptolemaic. His efforts in pursuing this end rest upon, at times even explicitly employ, at least three methodological principles:

(i) Legitimate science presupposes an understanding of principles which metaphysically inform the natural cosmos and govern its movements and processes.

(ii) These principles are inherently rational, in themselves and as they inform our cosmos or determine its movements and processes.

(iii) Observation is pertinent to scientific deliberation just insofar as it also presupposes these principles (is itself rational). The rationality of an observation or method of observation is, in particular, a prerequisite for using it to confirm a scientific theory based on observable appearances or phenomena implied (or 'predicted') by it.

The first two of these principles are especially crucial to Galileo's critique of Aristotelianism, which he summarizes by admonishing Aristotle for "trying to accommodate the architecture to the building instead of modeling the building after the precepts of architecture."[3] The 'building' in this case is our cosmos; and Galileo is insisting that a legitimately scientific conception or model of our cosmos must conform to the 'precepts of architecture.' These precepts, Galileo believes, are mathematical (more precisely, geometric); and so they also are absolutely rational and deductive in their relationships and implications. These precepts are *sine qua non* for any adequate scientific theory. Indeed, the methodological principles stated above, and the Neopythagorean character of Galileo's conception of the metaphysical principles or precepts they mention, are never debated in Galileo's *Dialogue*. They are treated as prerequisites for any legitimate scientific deliberation and debate to occur at all; any scientific model or theory which does not conform to them is necessarily mistaken, and so lies beyond the pale of further rational or scientific discussion.

For Plotinus, the principles informing nature's architecture are his hypostases (the One, Intellect, and Soul). Whether this commits Plotinus to a fundamentally different conception of those principles from Galileo's Neopythagorean conception of them lies beyond the scope of this essay.[4]

More importantly, Galileo is especially concerned in his understanding and use of methodological principles (i) and (ii) that science's conception of our cosmos should not be grounded instead on sensory appearances—most especially, not on pre- or *un*scientific observations of nature. In this regard, Galileo echoes Plotinus' insistence that metaphysical principles—the preconditions or grounds for natural order—cannot be abstracted from sensory appearances. Plotinus cautions that when attempting to grasp the (metaphysical) nature and order of Being itself, we must not allow ourselves to stray back into the sensible cosmos; we must steadfastly attend to the principles which define and govern that (vertical) order itself (VI.5.2, 19–23). In like fashion, Galileo admonishes Aristotle partly for not attending adequately to metaphysics apart from or *prior to* his scientific speculations, and especially for the resulting subordination of his conception of our cosmos and the principles informing it to terrestrial appearances.

Galileo focuses on two Aristotelian doctrines in demonstrating Aristotle's error:

(a) The Earth is the center of celestial motion and the physical referent of all terrestrial motion (i.e. earth and water naturally move towards it, and air and fire naturally move away from it).

(b) All motions of complex bodies (i.e. bodies composed of more than one of the four elements) are complex motions which result from the natural and simple motions of the elements composing them. (E.g. the motion of a body composed partly of air, whose natural motion is away from the Earth, and partly of earth, whose natural motion is towards the Earth, is determined by which of these two opposed elements predominate in the mixture.)[5]

Doctrine (a) illustrates the dependency of Aristotelian principles upon terrestrial observation, which surely does suggest that the Earth is the center of our cosmos and that moving objects incline towards or away from it. Of course, the Copernican system shares the Ptolemaic belief that a physical body is at the center of our cosmos; whereas the geometric principles of nature do not entail that any physical body must occupy the center of the cosmos. Below I shall say a bit about Galileo's rationale for favoring the Copernican system over the Ptolemaic. For now, the point is that whether there is a physical body at the center of our cosmos (and if so, which one) should not be inferred directly from terrestrial appearances (and likewise for Aristotle's conception of 'natural' motion); but, Galileo intimates, Aristotle did precisely this.

Nevertheless, doctrine (a) *might* be true, since the desideratum to conform cosmology to geometry does not rule it out. The same cannot be said for doctrine (b), however, thus negating any support that the Ptolemaic system may hope to derive from Aristotelian science. Aristotelian mixed motion is straightforwardly irrational, hence scientifically inadmissible, since it implies that real motions of natural bodies may be (indeed, oftentimes are) resultants from simple motions which are opposed to one another—as in the case of a body composed partly of air and partly of earth; and such an implication, Galileo apparently feels, is as irrational as supposing that a square and a circle can be combined into a real shape of some sort. Moreover, the Aristotelian response, which differentiates our cosmos into two parts and argues that its terrestrial (sublunary) part need not conform to the rational rigors of "mathematical demonstration,"[6] thereby further compromises reason and the (geometric) principles of 'architecture' for the sake of Aristotle's metaphysically inadequate conception of the 'building.'

Galileo's insistence that legitimate science *presupposes* rational (and geometric) principles which therefore are not directly or commonsensically inferred from terrestrial (sensory) appearances, however, does not entail for him that observation and sensory appearances are utterly irrelevant to science—and nor that scientific theory is irrelevant to what we do or can observe. Galileo (like Aristotle, and also Plotinus) holds that the cosmos modeled and investigated by science is in fact the same cosmos as the one we experience daily through our senses in our terrestrial context. Moreover, Galileo's ultimate aim is not just to undermine Aristotelian support for the Ptolemaic system but to argue for the Copernican system's superiority over the Ptolemaic; and, considered apart from its Aristotelian affiliations, the Ptolemaic system *per se* is as geometric and rational as the Copernican. Some sort of nondeductive principles of rational choice (e.g. elegance or simplicity) might argue in favor of the Copernican; but Galileo does not develop such an approach. He appeals to observation but, as methodological principle (iii) indicates, not observation *simpliciter*. Precisely where and how observation fits into scientific deliberation for Galileo is itself a matter of ongoing debate among Galileo scholars. In rough and general terms, however, it seems that Galileo distinguishes what might be termed *scientific observation* from nonscientific observation; and, though perhaps not dismissing the latter altogether (i.e. he seems interested in 'saving' as much of appearances as possible), he seems to maintain that the former is at least more germane to scientific deliberation than the latter.

Perhaps the best known observational evidence offered by Galileo to support Copernicus are his observations of Sun Spots through the telescope. Galileo notes how it

> ...came about that, continuing to make very careful observations for many, many months, and noting with consummate accuracy the various [Sun] spots at different times of the year, we found the results to accord exactly with the [Copernican system's] predictions.[7]

This suggests that observation pertains to scientific deliberation when it confirms a theory's predictions or implications; but prediction and confirmation seem to be only part of the story. Galileo seems, in particular, to be equally concerned with the rationality of a given observation or appearance. Thus, for example, he commends Aristarchus and Copernicus for remaining "confident of that which *reason* told them must be so" in light of *certain of* their observations, despite also recognizing that their conception of our cosmos conflicted with other observations or appearances.[8] Clearly, not all observations or appearances are equally pertinent to scientific deliberation and, e.g. to theory confirmation. Thus, Galileo seems as intent in the above passage on emphasizing the "very careful observations [and]... consummate accuracy" of his work with Sun Spots as he is on noting its conformity with predictions he derived from his Copernican geometrics. Similarly, he also seems convinced that a heliocentric system (whether Copernicus' or Aristarchus') is simply *more rational* than a terracentric system, and so the explanatory light it sheds even on certain *pre*telescopic observations imbues them with a scientific significance which outweighs potentially falsifying or disconfirming observations. Indeed, Galileo goes so far as to suggest that certain recalcitrant appearances of Mars and Venus are not merely (mathematically) imprecise but in fact are *mistaken* (though he does offer some explanation for why they occur).[9] Observation, or at least *scientific* observation, must somehow share in the rational strictures which Galileo demands *a priori* of scientific theory itself. Although he wishes to account for or 'save' as much of appearances as possible, Galileo seems to hold that since the rationally informed cosmos of scientific theory is the same as the cosmos of sensory observation, the latter confirms, manifests, or the like, the former only insofar as it also is informed by those same rational principles.

Ancient science has been faulted for allegedly lacking an experimental method—for not methodically submitting theory to observational confirmation, or for not amending or refining theory in light of methodical observation. I shall not enter into this controversy here. In Plotinus' case, it surely seems that experimentalism is not an **obvious** feature of his *Enneads*—though it also is the case that the *Enneads* have never been thoroughly investigated for this possibility. It suffices for here, however, that Plotinus' insistence that we must not "stray forgetfully back into the sensible realm" when seeking to understand the metaphysical order of his hypostases does not mean (nor entail) that we must (or even can) ignore the sensible cosmos altogether when we do 'descend' from the metaphysical order into the natural order to discern precisely *how* those principles in fact inform or function in our cosmos. Plotinus insists at length that although our cosmos is not itself a hypostasis, it nevertheless is genuinely and utterly an image of that order. Consequently, a Plotinian conception or model of our cosmos which does not conform it to the metaphysical principles of the hypostases must be incorrect, and *everything* in our cosmos—*including what is observable*—must be explicable in terms of those principles (as a descent from them); and Plotinus' own conception of our cosmos and its processes relies very much on sensory appearances or observed phenomena to discern how or in what way(s) our cosmos conforms to that vertical order. In this regard, of course, we have seen Galileo suggesting that certain appearances may simply be, if not mistaken *tout courte*, at least scientifically mistaken, as it were. But even this seems an echo of Plotinus' view that although our cosmos is genuinely and utterly an image of the hypostases, some of its appearances or observable aspects may manifest and reveal its order, rationality, and metaphysical aetiology more perspicuously than others (as we shall see later).

This section has identified several thematic aspects of Galileo's conception of science, observation and their (subordinate) relations to metaphysics. One additional aspect not highlighted thus far is Galileo's insistence that the principles of nature's architecture are, in Plotinian terms, omnipresent. Nature's precepts, Galileo insists, do not hold just for its celestial movements nor just for its simplest, most elemental constituents; they hold equally everywhere throughout our cosmos—for so-called sublunary as well as for celestial bodies, for 'complex' as well as for 'simple' (elemental) bodies, and for every movement of every one of these bodies and/or elemental substances. Plotinus' doctrine that the sensible cosmos is genuinely and utterly an image of the hypostases likewise implies that its order and rationality is ubiquitous and irrevocable—that our cosmos, *in toto* and throughout all of its parts and processes, is an image of the hypostases. To see how this and preceding themes are developed by Plotinus, and especially to see his own conception of nature, I now turn to several key treatises in his *Enneads*.

2. Plotinus' Metaphysic of Nature

Of Plotinus' three hypostases (One, Intellect, and Soul), the second of these (Intellect) is initially the most germane to the issues addressed in section 1 inasmuch as it is the vertical cause in virtue of which our cosmos is informed with rationality or intelligibility. My primary text for elaborating this point will be *Ennead* III.2, the first installment in Plotinus' two-part treatise on Providence. Among other things, Plotinus argues in this (half)treatise that Intellect is archetypally *cosmos*—the metaphysical prototype for what it is to be a cosmos, or for anything else's being truly a cosmos. He also argues that our cosmos truly *is a cosmos*, and it is a cosmos solely because it is an image of Intellect—i.e. because its relationship to its archetype (Intellect) is grounded in the principles of vertical causality. Plotinus' understanding of Intellect (or *Being*) establishes the 'precepts' to which any sensible, material, or otherwise existing object or system of objects must conform if it is to be investigated or explained rationally (i.e. as a cosmos); and he maintains that our cosmos (or *Becoming*) is irrevocably such an object or system of objects.

Plotinus begins *Ennead* III.2 by contrasting two approaches to understanding the cause or source of our cosmos' substance and structure (*ousian kai systasin*). On the one hand, the materialist (e.g. Epicurean) approach simply rejects the supposition that these have a cause, maintaining instead that they are fortuitous matters of chance (III.2.1, 1–2). The Gnostic approach, on the other hand, postulates a process of divine deliberation and foreknowing which precedes and causes the coming to be of our cosmos (III.2.1, 18). Plotinus' own approach will agree with the Gnostics, *pace* the materialists, that our cosmos is caused and that its cause (his Intellect) is metaphysically *prior to* it. However, Plotinus disagrees with the Gnostics' conception of this prioricity, especially denying that Intellect is a deliberative agent and our cosmos is an outcome of consciously foreknowing deliberations on its part. Rather, Intellect's prioricity over our cosmos is to be explicated in terms of its eternally, immutably perfect nature, by virtue of which it simply *is* "the true and first cosmos" or "the archetypal cosmos" and to which our cosmos is metaphysically related as an image that is "forever coming into existence" (*hypostantos aei*) in conformity with it (III.2.1, 26).

Plotinus maintains, it seems, that materialism requires denying the real existence of *meta*physical causes, and this leaves materialism without sufficient grounds for understanding putatively systemic or rational features of our cosmos, forcing them to view those features as inexplicable—as matters of mere chance. Given Plotinus' later insistence on the ubiquitous rationality of our cosmos **despite** putative appearances (or certain aspects of appearances) to the contrary, he may also be concerned that if such notions as 'system' and 'rational' are not grounded objectively—in an archetypal or *meta*physical reality—but are abstractions from whatever it is about our cosmos which happens to strike us that way, then we would have no grounds for investigating the rest of our cosmos (or other features of our cosmos) to discern whether, **despite** (perhaps) appearances to the contrary, they might not also *in fact* be systemic or rational in the same way. At the very least, his insistence on the everlasting ('forever') conformity of our cosmos to its archetype indicates a conscious concern that such abstractions would leave us with no grounds for supposing that the way(s) in which our cosmos is (or seems) systemic and rational now (or insofar as we have noticed this) is at all pertinent to its future (or continuing) condition and processes. In short, the materialist may strive to understand our cosmos and its processes systematically, but he will have no grounds (Plotinus believes) for universalizing that understanding—or at least his grounds will be no more objective than dumb luck or chance.

Plotinus says very little about materialism in the remainder of the treatise. His focus, rather, is on the Gnostic approach and its understanding of our cosmos as a deliberated outcome. Plotinus maintains that our cosmos *doubly* is not a deliberative outcome: first, in that Intellect does not (nor need it) deliberate on what a cosmos must be (or must 'be like') and, second, in that our cosmos' relation to Intellect is not like that between an outcome and a prior process of thinking or deliberating towards that outcome. Insofar as our cosmos is an outcome at all, it is an outcome entailed by, or generated and sustained according to, the *metaphysical* principles in virtue of which metaphysical reality itself is *eternally* and *immutably* ordered (and for Plotinus, of course, also *hierarchically* ordered).

Regarding his thesis that Intellect just **is** archetypally **cosmos** (and so need not deliberate on this), Plotinus explains that it is the archetypal cosmos because it

> ...does not stand apart from itself and is not weakened by division and is not incomplete even in its parts, since each part is not cut off from the whole; but the whole life of it and the whole intellect lives and thinks (*noousa*) all together in one, and makes the part the whole and all bound in friendship with itself, since one part is not separated from another and has not become merely other, estranged from the rest; and, therefore, one does not wrong another, even if they are opposites. And since it is everywhere one and complete at every point it stays still and knows no alteration; for it does not make as one thing acting upon another.[10]

This last clause ("for it does not make...") alludes to Intellect's eternal *contemplation* as the metaphysical process whose principles generate and sustain eternally Plotinus' vertical order of true causality, and also to Plotinus' difficult doctrine that Intellect is distinct from our cosmos as (one of) its metaphysical cause(s) but it is not thereby substantively *separate from* our cosmos. More important for now, however, are the features of Intellect which Plotinus believes render it the archetypal cosmos. These features are characterized in this passage in both negative and positive terms, as they bear both upon Intellect as a whole and upon its parts and also upon its parts' relations both to Intellect itself and to one another.

In negative terms, (a) Intellect does not stand apart from Itself; (b) Intellect is not weakened by division; (c) Intellect is not incomplete nor subject to change in any way; (d) each of its parts is not cut off from the whole, nor separated from any other part; and (e) one part is not merely 'other,' nor 'estranged' from the rest (of the parts), and nor does it wrong any other part (even when they are 'opposites'). Rather, in positive terms, (a*) the whole Intellect lives, or is wholly alive; (b*) Intellect and its life thinks "all [of its parts] together in one"; (c*) it is everywhere one and complete at every point; (d*) each of its parts is made the whole of Intellect; and (e*) all of its parts are bound together in friendship with Intellect. Implicit in this litany of Intellect's archetypal features is a presumption that a cosmos is a whole composed of parts; hence, if Intellect is to be the archetypal cosmos, it also must in some sense be (or be capable of being understood as) a whole composed of parts. The foregoing negative and affirmative characterizations indicate the unique, or at least distinctive, nature of Intellect as a whole, of its parts, and of their relationships. They focus especially on the distinctive nature of (i)

Intellect's life, (ii) its composition, and (iii) its *telos*. In so doing, they sound themes found elsewhere in the *Enneads* where Plotinus is not so intent on understanding Intellect in whole/part terms.

Plotinus maintains in the above passage (i) that the nature of its life is such that Intellect is not distinct from itself and nor are its parts separated or cut off from one another nor from it; rather, its life is *self-contained* (it is identical with Intellect's 'self,' or is a feature of Intellect just *qua* Intellect) and it is *interpenetrating* (it equally is a feature of Intellect as a whole and of each and every one of its parts). Hence, Intellect is not weakened in any way by its division (or, Plotinus may intend, Intellect is not weakened by any *real* division within itself); rather, (ii) its mode of division, composition or containment is by *omnipresence* to itself and to all of its parts as it "thinks all together in [any] one," and so is truly *one* or *unitary* in both its life and its composition. (iii) Intellect thus fully and irrevocably (or *immutably*) realizes its *telos*, as both it and every one of its parts are *perfect(ed)* just by virtue of the nature of its life and unity. Hence, Intellect can never be incomplete, and nor can its parts be in any real opposition with one another or with the whole. Howsoever we are to distinguish Intellect's parts (including even any contraries or 'opposites' among its parts), they are bound both to one another and to Intellect itself in perfect accord, conformity, or 'friendship.' Regarding its life, composition and *telos*, then, insofar as Intellect is (understood as) a whole composed of parts, it is so archetypally inasmuch as

(i) the whole and every one of its parts are productive or causative ('living') by virtue of the very nature of Intellect and in the manner or sense entailed by that nature (viz. by thought or intellection [*noēsis*]);
(ii) each part is the whole and the whole is each (and every) part, and so also each part is every other part and, indeed, is all of the whole's parts; and
(iii) the whole and all of its parts are eternally and immutably complete or actual, both in themselves and in all of their (internal) relationships to one another and to the whole.

In Plotinus' Neoplatonism, (i) reflects Intellect's status as a (vertically) causative principle; (ii) reflects its status as a (first) declination from Plotinus' absolutely first principle (the One); and (iii) reflects its metaphysical credentials as an hypostasis.

Our own cosmos departs from Intellect on all three scores. However, Plotinus' initial account in III.2 of the features of our cosmos which preclude its being the archetypal cosmos touch most fully and explicitly on (ii)—its mode of composition. This seems appropriate since it is Intellect's status as a (first-) declination from the One's absolute simplicity which makes it possible to understand it as a whole composed of parts—hence, as a metaphysical archetype of *cosmos*. Accordingly, contrasting our cosmos with Intellect with respect to (ii) should most sharply define its *non*archetypal nature, or why it is that our cosmos is not itself a cosmos archetypally. Plotinus claims, regarding our own cosmos, that

> ...it is many and divided into a multiplicity, and one part stands away from another and is alien to it, and there is not only friendship but also enmity because of the separation, and in their deficiency one part is of necessity at war with another. For the part is not self-sufficient, but in being preserved is at war with the other by which it is preserved.[11]

Significantly, this passage refers to our cosmos as a whole only initially, asserting—in contrast especially to (b)'s assertion that insofar as Intellect is a whole it cannot be "weakened by [a real] division" into its putative parts—that our cosmos (really) *is many* and (really) *is divided into a multiplicity*. The remainder of this passage deals primarily with this real multiplicity of its parts, contrasting them especially with Intellect's parts in terms of the negative characterizations observed in (d) and (e). Unlike Intellect's, our cosmos' parts *are* separated from (they really do 'stand away' from) one another, and they are not merely 'other' (or different) but each *is* estranged from (it is in fact 'alien' to) the other parts; and whereas each of Intellect's parts is complete and perfect (since each is 'made the whole' by Intellect's omnipresent and interpenetrating life), each of our cosmos' parts is by itself deficient (since each is really separated from and alien to the other parts). Finally, this deficiency in our cosmos' parts is characterized also in terms of each not being self-sufficient but dependent upon other parts for its preservation.

Paradoxically, it might seem that Intellect's parts should depend utterly upon one another (since each is irrevocably related internally to every other one), yet in fact each is by itself eternally complete or actual; likewise, it might seem that our cosmos' parts should not depend upon one another at all (since each is really separate from, and so is related only externally to, the rest), yet in fact each is incapable of preserving itself—indeed, each achieves its *telos*, or is preserved at all, only by virtue of other parts. But whereas the seemingly paradoxical condition of Intellect's parts attests to their immutable perfection and to that of their interrelationships, the paradoxical condition of our cosmos' parts attests to their metaphysical deficiency—to their temporal, interactive, or warlike character. In sharp contrast with Intellect's archetypal nature, we find regarding our own cosmos that

(i′) productivity or causality (metaphysical life) is not attributed to it at all;

(ii′) Plotinus emphasizes the real multiplicity and separateness of its parts, alluding to their relationship to (and so their composition into) a whole only indirectly—by reference to each part's inherent lack of sufficiency or completion; and so

(iii′) regarding their *telos*, our cosmos' parts are said to relate 'of necessity' to one another in such a way that one depends upon another for its preservation, and it does so in a warlike way (presumably, their real separateness makes any relations they might have violent, e.g. so that one part's preservation occurs at another's expense).

As noted, Plotinus' account in III.2 of how our cosmos departs from Intellect's archetypical nature says very little about our cosmos as a whole. He does not contrast our cosmos, for example, with respect to his earlier assertions that [a] Intellect does not stand apart from itself, and [c] Intellect is not incomplete nor subject to change. Moreover, although that account contrasts our cosmos mainly with respect to negative claims made earlier regarding what is **not** the case for Intellect, it does harken back to (e*) in saying that "there is not **only friendship**..." and in suggesting that, howsoever it is that the parts of our cosmos are in fact related to the whole (or to one another within the whole), this relationship preserves at least some of them at a given time—*albeit* somehow at the expense of other parts. It thus seems to be a positive characteristic of our cosmos that its parts are bound together in some sense, though not in complete friendship with one another. Whether this precludes their being bound together in (complete) friendship with our cosmos as a whole is unclear; but the enmity caveat regarding any friendship among our cosmos' parts does suggest that at least (b*) and (c*) would have to be modified if applied to our cosmos—i.e. the parts of our cosmos cannot be all together **at the same time** and, likewise, oneness or completion cannot be realized throughout every point (or part) of our cosmos **at the same time**. That caveat also seems to deny (d*) of our cosmos altogether; surely no part of our cosmos could be 'made the whole' cosmos if any given part's very preservation is only at the expense of other parts of that whole.

Perhaps more significantly, there is very good reason for Plotinus' saying so little about our cosmos as a whole in his initial account of its nonarchetypal character. Having stated features of Intellect by virtue of which it *is* the archetypal cosmos and features of our cosmos by virtue of which it is *not* archetypal, Plotinus immediately alludes back to an earlier claim that our cosmos is from Intellect (*para noū*) in such a way that Intellect's providence (*prōnoia*) connotes the metaphysical fact that our cosmos conforms with (*kata*) Intellect as an image conforms to its archetypal cause (see III.2.1, 20–22). Plotinus declares that our cosmos is not an outcome or end result of some divine reasoning (*logismoi*); rather, it exists (1) just by virtue of Intellect possessing the power to produce another without having to **try** to produce it (*aneu...zētein*) (III.2.2, 12–13) and, in particular, (2) just by virtue of Intellect "giving something of itself to matter"—viz. a *logos* whose source is Intellect itself, or its nondeliberative power (III.2.2, 16–19). Our cosmos is forever coming into existence *as a cosmos*, Plotinus argues, by virtue of a logos which molds, organizes and controls it on behalf of Intellect and which Intellect produces simply because it is in its nature (causative power) to do so. This logos continually produces out of the aforementioned multiplicity, diversity and (putative) enmity of our cosmos' parts a harmony and "singular ordering" of its parts into a whole (III.2.2, 30–31). *Only insofar as we view our cosmos from this perspective* can we understand it as a whole and appreciate how it is that our cosmos is indeed *a cosmos*.

Plotinus does not elaborate at this point on the notion that Intellect gives a logos of itself to matter. We shall see later that this logos is Nature, and that Intellect's production of it by a giving of itself is to be explicated in terms of eternal contemplation. Instead, Plotinus now emphasizes two important implications of this notion. First, it allows him to maintain that Intellect remains archetypal or pure (so, metaphysically distinct from our cosmos) without suggesting that Intellect produces and governs our cosmos as an outside, deliberative agent might seek to mold and order it—say, as a terrestrial artist might plan and then work purposively to fashion a work of art.[12] Our cosmos may be construed as a "coming together" of Intellect and Necessity, Plotinus indicates, in the sense that through its logos Intellect "descends towards irrationality" (*alogian*) while remaining wholly itself and undefiled, and able to govern and control matter or Necessity (III.2.2, 33–37). Second, this eternal (or at least everlasting) mixing of Intellect with Necessity does not denote an actual mixing of opposed metaphysical elements or principles but connotes the metaphysical fact that our cosmos both is not *archetypally* a cosmos—i.e. it is an image of Intellect as descending *towards* irrationality, matter, or Necessity—and yet it is still truly *a cosmos*.

Plotinus argues regarding our cosmos that although only Intellect's logos (its presence within our cosmos) is strictly speaking an intelligible thing (*noētos*), this does not imply that our cosmos as such is not truly a cosmos—or, that it is ***a**-cosmos*. The world of Becoming can be construed as a sort of mixture in the sense that metaphysically it lies between inchoate, irrational matter, Necessity, or Non-Being and rationality, law, or Being itself; but in this mixture Intellect's logos (now referred to as a soul) presides utterly—with complete and sole authority—over the very *substance* of our cosmos, so that Intellect itself may be said to direct our cosmos by a "kind of presence" (*parousia*) (see III.2.2, 36–42). Because of this presiding presence of Intellect in the very substance and fabric of our cosmos, moreover, our cosmos is itself an in-its-own-way likeness or manifestation of Intellect's better (i.e. archetypal) nature (III.2.3, 5–6). More precisely, the world of Becoming is not a concatenation of chance concurrences, nor is it really an irrational realm upon which we (or Intellect) have sought arbitrarily to superimpose an order or structure of some sort; rather, our cosmos is in fact

> ...a whole, all beautiful and self-sufficient and friends with itself and with its parts, both the more important and the lesser, which are all equally well adapted to it.[13]

When considering our cosmos as a whole, from the perspective of its metaphysical aetiology instead of the diversity and separateness of its parts, Plotinus' highly negative characterization of that separateness and the related enmity among its parts gives way to a highly positive statement of its overarching self-sufficiency, its order (beauty), and its *bona fide* friendship with itself and with each and every one of its parts (and *vice versa*).

To this extent at least, our cosmos, like Intellect, does *not* "stand apart from itself" [a]—although Plotinus is yet to indicate whether our cosmos also is 'alive' otherwise than just in having Intellect's logos present in it [a*]; it is complete [c]—although it cannot be "one and complete" at every point (at least not concurrently), except perhaps insofar as Intellect's logos is ubiquitously one and complete in it [c*]; its parts are *not* "cut off" from our cosmos as a whole [d], even though they are diverse and separate from one another and so cannot each be made the whole—although here, also, Intellect's logos may be an ubiquitous whole to or in each and every part which it makes and binds together **into** a whole [d*]; and, of course, despite its parts being estranged from one another and wronging one another when our cosmos is viewed part-by-part [e], these same parts in fact are utterly in friendship with the cosmos as a whole—and to some degree, or in some sense, with one another within (or from the perspective of) that whole [e*]. Our cosmos thus contrasts sharply with Intellect in that it **is** "weakened by division" [b] and in that howsoever Intellect's logos in fact "binds" its parts into a unity and friendship, this cannot be in a "life [which] thinks all together in one" *simpliciter* or archetypally; but on all other points characteristic of Intellect [(a), and (c)–(d)], our cosmos is unlike but also **like** Intellect.

In line with Plotinus' caution regarding the sense in which our cosmos is a mixture of Intellect and Necessity, those features of our cosmos which demonstrate its nonarchetypal nature (e.g. that it truly is many and divided and its parts are, or appear to be, at war with one another) and those features which render it truly a cosmos nevertheless (e.g. its unity and sufficiency, order and friendship, when viewed as a whole) are indeed distinguishable from one another but they do not denote (really) distinct parts or elements which somehow combine to form one cosmos, or which derive somehow from distinct and opposing metaphysical principles.[14] The warfare we observe among our cosmos' parts, for example, is not something distinct from its (and their) friendship; rather, the putative warfare is in fact *a type of* friendship inasmuch as the objects and warlike processes comprising our cosmos are in fact governed and ordered into a single harmonious whole by Intellect's logos—or, inasmuch as this warfare is in fact Intellect's archetypal friendship adapted to or descended towards multiplicity and matter by way of its logos.

To discern the friendship which is in fact present in—which does truly characterize—our cosmos, we need not look at something other than its many, warring parts; rather, we need only to look more discerningly at "the parts in relation to the whole, to see if they are harmonious and in concord with it; and when one considers the whole one must not look at a few little parts" (III.2.3, 11–13). Plotinus believes that when a person does this, moreover, she will recognize that the parts are indeed harmonious and in concord with the whole. When thus viewed in light of its metaphysical aetiology—or the resulting presence (and operation) of Intellect's logos within it—our cosmos (i*) may as such be still metaphysically dead but at least Intellect's life is present within it in the form of Nature (a logos of Intellect); and so,

(ii*) though really separate (from one another) and a multiplicity, its parts are in fact friends with our cosmos as a whole—and even with one another, inasmuch as they do compose a single, harmonious whole by virtue of that presence; and

(iii*) our cosmos as a whole and all of its parts, though incomplete when compared with the archetypal perfection of Intellect's *telos*, are fully well adapted to one another and do constitute a fully ordered, utterly unified whole or system—*albeit* one which is continuously evolving or moving and is never finished or completed.

Though still not an archetypal cosmos, our cosmos is thus much more like Intellect than Plotinus' initial part-by-part account, summarized earlier in (i')–(iii'), suggested.

We can reach the same result from considering the fact that Plotinus' Intellect also is the archetype of rationality: Our cosmos truly *is* a cosmos by virtue of the archetypal cosmos (Intellect) informing it with its own rationality through the ubiquitous presence of its logos (Nature). Plotinus' negative [(a)–(e)] and positive [(a*)–(e*)] characterizations of Intellect's nature suggest, in other words, Plotinus' conception of rationality. They suggest, for example, that in an archetypally rational system the principles defining its nature (its *meta*principles, if you will) define the system without remainder (the system as a whole, including all of its parts, is derivable from them), and they thereby also define each and every one of its parts (the principles interpenetrate the system). Moreover, the nature and contents of such a system cannot change (they are immutable); and nothing is missing or lacking from the system which is necessary for its completion, or which would render it more faithful to or fully derived from its principles. Finally, every part of the system is related to every other part; these relationships are also defined or entailed by the system's principles; and they are unalterable (immutable) and such that every part may be derived from every other part as well as from (or within) the whole.

Since Becoming differs from the archetypal cosmos most evidently in the nature of its parts, we should expect it likewise to depart from archetypal rationality particularly with respect to its parts. Although we may be able to discern *a posteriori* that any given part, process or relationship within our cosmos conforms to its systemic principles, for example, we cannot deduce each and every one of them from the principles by themselves and certainly not from one another; and although the nature or principles of the system (of our cosmos) as a whole cannot change, its contents (parts) and their relationships to one another certainly do change. Likewise, though perhaps nothing is missing from our cosmos as such, its deficiencies relative to some aspects of an archetypally rational system do render it forever incomplete inasmuch as its faithfulness to or conformity with its principles may continually be tested as hitherto unobserved contents and relationships emerge, or inasmuch as our understanding of precisely how its contents conform to its principles admits continually of reformulation or refinement. Indeed, inasmuch as Becoming's systemic principles do not define (or entail *a priori*) the system, or at least not each and every one of its contents, it is not wholly unreasonable to question whether Becoming is in fact a rational system at all—as opposed, say, to a lucky conglomeration of disparate parts; its rationality is not evident, or at least it is not self-evident or immediately evident, to every rational person.

In the final section of this essay, which addresses Plotinus' response to Pyrrhonian Skepticism, we shall see that Plotinus' notion of archetypal rationality suggests that an archetypally rational system would in effect be (perhaps among other things) a system of necessary truth. This suggests, in turn, that the task he sets for natural philosophers (scientists) is to discern how our cosmos as a whole and all of its parts in fact are governed by, are manifestations of, or are explicable in terms of a system of archetypal (necessary) truth. Plotinus' conception of the *meta*principles defining Intellect's nature (and so archetypal rationality and truth), moreover, is based on the five most-high types (the *megista genera*) of Plato: Being, Same, Difference, Motion, and Rest. Before discussing those principles, however, and some details of Plotinus' conception of our cosmos as an image of the archetypal cosmos they define, I return to Plotinus' notion that our cosmos is "forever coming into existence" in conformity with Intellect, relying especially on *Ennead* III.8 for further elaboration.

Ennead III.8 is first in a four-treatise sequence that continues with *Enneads* V.8 and V.5, and concludes with *Ennead* II.9. The middle two treatises focus on Intellect, the second of these especially emphasizing that Intellect is a true, archetypal unity. For, although Intellect is a descent from the One—its unity falls short of the One's absolute, unqualified unity—it nevertheless is (as seen in *Ennead* III.2) utterly self-contained, self-sufficient, eternally one ("in friendship") with itself and its parts, and the like. The final treatise in this sequence is a more sustained attack on Gnosticism. Here, however, I am most interested in the two main conclusions Plotinus draws in *Ennead* III.8. One is that the One is the first principle and source of all Being and life (both archetypal and sensible). The other conclusion is that the entire vertical order (down to its lowest levels) is bound together and proceeds by contemplation, where 'proceeds by' does not connote a temporal or deliberative process but denotes a metaphysical ordering explained by the nature of contemplation—an eternally self-focused act which entails, however, a phantasm or image whose substance is defined by the contemplated object. Together these conclusions guarantee in turn that the *meta*principles defining Intellect's nature—its archetypal principles of rationality and of *cosmos*—are themselves grounded in the utterly first principle of all reality (the One) while also informing every level of reality which derives in turn from Intellect. Since our cosmos is itself ineluctably an image or (by-)product of this metaphysically causative order, moreover, its rationality—though not archetypal—is irrevocable, ubiquitous and 'forever' nonetheless.

The argument of *Ennead* III.8 begins with Plotinus postulating or "playing with" the paradox (*paradoxon*) that all activities in the natural cosmos—including the natural processes and movements of plants and the Earth, and also the actions of animate and rational beings—are in fact "serious efforts at contemplation" (III.8.1, 14). He does not tell us why this postulate is (or at least appears to be) a paradox. Perhaps he has in mind the Aristotelian view that contemplation is paradigmatically a *non*productive activity.[15] Or he may be foreshadowing a crucial point to emerge later—viz. that since (archetypal) contemplation characterizes the activity of Being, his own metaphysics implies that the activity of *Becoming* is in fact an image of (or an effort to act like) *Being*. In any case, Plotinus begins to resolve or explain this seeming paradox by introducing Nature as "a logos which produces another logos, an offspring of itself which gives something to the substrate while itself remaining unmoved" (III.8.2, 28–30). This response to the paradox will justify invoking contemplation as the archetypal act at which even natural processes and actions are efforts because the power to produce another, or to give something to another, while remaining unmoved (or unmoving) is paradigmatically a characteristic of contemplation (III.8.23, 16–17). I shall discuss how such an act could be the archetype of Becoming as I proceed; but first I wish to emphasize a refinement introduced here to the notion of Intellect's logos seen in *Ennead* III.2. In particular, Plotinus here asserts a *double* logos: first, a logos which he identifies with Nature itself and, second, the logos which is finally given to matter—now identified as an *offspring of* Intellect's logos (Nature).

I begin with Plotinus' further claim that this offspring of Nature is the final logos because it is "dead and unable to produce another" logos; it produces *visible form* or shape instead (III.8.2, 30–34). This additional claim seems meant to distinguish, for example, between the process or activity of a tree growing and the visible or sensible form(s) in which this process manifests itself to human sense experience—say, as we observe the tree altering in size as it grows. Strictly speaking, Nature's offspring would be the tree's *growth*—the tree's growth *process* or *activity* as this transpires in the natural world. The observable alterations in the tree's size is the way in which that natural process manifests itself to our sense experience and is an *image* of the tree's growth, just as the process of growth itself is an image, manifestation, or offspring of the logos Nature. In producing its own visible form—i.e. in manifesting itself to our sense experience—Nature'slogos (e.g. the tree's growth-process) is dead since (we shall see later) a true or living logos always produces another living or productive logos as its image; but Nature's logos does not do so. It produces visible form, which is not a *logos* (it is not a metaphysical or intelligible phenomenon, as it were) but a *sensory* or experiential phenomenon. By itself, however, this threatens a vicious regress: If every living logos must produce another living logos, whereas Nature produces a dead logos, then Nature would seem to be a dead logos—and so on, for however far up the vertical order Plotinus' notion of *logos* would extend. To avoid this regress, I note (as we shall see later) that when viewed in its descending mode, once the vertical order proceeds below archetypal life, 'alive' and 'dead' are no longer absolute or all-or-nothing characteristics. Rather, as the vertical order descends from (or beyond) *archetypal* life, its life then becomes increasingly weak and diffuse. In these terms, it may be more accurate to say that Nature's life is so weak—is so far removed from archetypal life—that its offspring is more dead than alive, or has become effectively dead instead of alive.

In claiming that Nature's offspring produces its own visible form, moreover, Plotinus is **not** alluding to any physical processes (e.g. to any purported physical causes of sensory appearances), but to the vertical (metaphysical) causes of sensible Becoming's Being—for example, the intelligibility of the observed alterations in a tree's size in fact *being a process of growth*. Plotinus' model for this sort of (vertically) causal account of sensory appearances is the way in which, as he sees it, a geometer has lines comprising visible shapes directly "fall from" her activity of geometric contemplation—as opposed to her using physical instruments to draw lines, say, in the dirt (III.8.4, 9–11). Plotinus maintains that this is the true (complete, or sufficient) account of the line-image shapes which manifest themselves to the geometer while she is contemplating and, indeed, that all occurrences of visible (or sensible) forms are to be explained similarly—in terms of the vertical causes of their Being, with Nature being the metaphysical agent of the contemplation which produces sensible form when this is *sensed* rather than imagined by some person. Of course, one point of disanalogy between Nature and Plotinus' contemplative geometer is that what immediately 'falls from' Nature's (attempt at) contemplation is not sensible form as such but real activities, natural processes, or 'Becomings'; and it may be that the ways in which these processes in turn manifest themselves to us as sensible form(s) admit of descriptions which—despite the sufficiency of Nature's contemplative agency—refer also to physical processes or causes of our sensations, or sensory experiences, of them. Nonetheless, the key point to Plotinus' analogy remains, that the true cause(s) which (sufficiently) explain sensible form(s) is not another sensible or observable thing (or things) but is that which defines it as the sensible manifestation of some Being (-in-Becoming)—*e.g.* of tree-growth, or of triangularity.

Plotinus maintains that the sensible lines—the phantasms of lines—imagined or internally sensed by the geometer are direct products of her (attempts at) contemplating Being (say, triangularity). Analogously, the observed alterations in a tree's visible size are in fact *nothing other than* the tree's growth-process, which surely is a direct result of Nature's (attempt at) contemplating, say, the Being of *treeness.* Now, it may be that when explaining why or how it is that we do not (externally) sense just the tree's growth-process as such but certain sensible forms (e.g. sequences of shapes and sizes), we postulate that (external) sensation occurs only when Nature produces other processes (e.g. in our sensory organs) alongside or "in sympathy with" the external tree's growth-process. But while this postulate regarding Nature's *modus operandi* might explain why internally sensed phantasms are manifestations of our own (attempted) contemplations whereas externally sensed phantasms are manifestations of another's (viz. Nature's) contemplations, it is not *necessary*—much less sufficient—even for explaining the sensible form itself. As objects of (external) sense, the observed alterations in the tree's size just *are* the tree's growth-process; they are not in fact real objects distinct or apart from that process, and so they do not require any cause(s) other than the (vertical) cause of that process (in the logos Nature) to explain them—even though, unlike the geometer case, those (externally) sensible forms remain distinguish*able* from Nature's direct product in Becoming (the growth-process as such).

Plotinus' approach to sensible form is symptomatic of his views on causality generally. While for many philosophers individual observable things are causes *par excellence*, for Plotinus they are metaphysically ineffective or causatively impotent.[16] The real causal order is not horizontal, or determined e.g. by generalization *from* (repeated) concurrences or sequences of sensible objects. The cause of any thing or process is that which governs, orders, or unifies it. For Plotinus this will be that which defines or gives it substance and Being; and this is a metaphysical or vertical matter, not a physical or horizontal one. As seen from *Ennead* III.2, insofar as the diverse things and processes comprising our cosmos are viewed on their own terms—as a mere multiplicity, or a collection of discrete parts or sensible objects—it seems more a place of fragmentation, warfare, even irrationality, than of rational governance, order and unity. In fact, however, our cosmos is *not* really fragmented, irrational, and the like, because the true causes of its rationality, order, and the like—indeed of its parts themselves—are not to be found amid its observable multiplicity but in the intelligible (*non*sensible) power of Nature, or only insofar as we can refer sensible objects to intelligible principles which inform Nature's power. *All* things and processes in Becoming are in fact offspring (effects) of that power; and, Plotinus contends, this fact becomes increasingly evident when instead of viewing the diverse parts of our cosmos on their own terms, we consider the sensible cosmos as a single whole and strive to discern how within that whole its parts in fact behave in an harmonious and ordered way, or conform to a system of governance enacted by Nature to inform and order that whole.[17]

Of course, we have seen that in *Ennead* III.8 Plotinus postulates an intermediate logos (or logoi) between Nature and sensible things or forms—viz. Becomings themselves. The world of Becoming has two distinguishable (though not distinct, nor separable) aspects or, as it were, sides: processes of or activities in Becoming as such, which are still images of Being (as expressed, say, in "this temporal process *is* one of *tree-growth*"); and their sensible appearances or forms (e.g. the many diverse sizes observed of the tree as it grows), which strictly speaking are no longer images of Being—though, unlike pure matter, they at least are images of images of Being. The fact that strictly speaking Becomings themselves are the (final) images of Being which result from Nature's attempts to contemplate Being indicates that Being itself, though static in that its substance is eternal and unchanging, is *dynamic* in that processes, activities, or life (in the terrestrial sense) *are* genuinely and (at the level of our cosmos) appropriately manifestations of it. The (meta)principles defining Intellect's nature establish it as concurrently archetypal Motion and archetypal Rest (its substance or reality *is a motion—albeit* one that is eternally at rest) and the existence of Becoming is explained by Nature's inability to contemplate Being in its archetypal condition of (eternal) Rest but only in its aspect of Motion, or only as the principle or archetype of motion.[18] Plotinus thus understands Becoming itself as a sort of Being: The Aristotelian conception of horizontal causality as a web of efficient causes actualizing the potentialities of diverse (sensible) substances gives way to a conception of causality even within our cosmos as a (final) effort at contemplation, or as a (lowest) type of vertical causality. Sensible substance no longer need be capable of the metaphysical feat of jumping from potentiality to actuality; rather, Plotinus considers processes or instances of Becoming to be fully actual and real already—*albeit* owing to Nature's capacity for metaphysical contemplation.

More important, Plotinus' reconception of Becoming discerns intelligibility within the sensible cosmos itself. In our tree example, the differing sensible forms observable through time (its visible size at one moment, succeeded by another visibly taller size at a later moment, and so forth) abstract from what in fact is a single, real, *continuous* process—its *tree-growth* (or *-growingness*, if you will). Accordingly, philosophers of nature should not model our cosmos on its diverse sensible forms and whatever patterns or regularities they may discern among them; rather, to understand our cosmos (indeed, also to explain whatever patterns or regularities they do observe among its sensible forms) natural philosophers should focus on its processes, activities, or instances of Becoming as such—as themselves intelligible realities (*albeit* intelligible realities which we may first notice sensorially, or as sensible realities)—and conceive them to be parts of a single, rational system informed throughout and for all time by immutable principles of Being as these manifest themselves under conditions of Becoming (i.e. space and time).

In terms of the Platonic tradition, this allows Plotinus, on the one hand, to accept Plato's formula that Becoming is the 'moving image of eternity' without invoking a metaphysical principle outside the vertical order of his hypostases to account for how an image of eternity could be moving. On the other hand, Nature's inability to preserve (or contemplate) motion in its archetypal condition of eternal rest allows Plotinus to maintain a trace of Plato's metaphysical dualism. We have seen Plotinus insist in *Ennead* III.8 that, unlike the archetypal cosmos (Intellect), the vertical causality operative in our cosmos is inherently only an *attempt at* contemplation. As a result of Nature's unceasing effort to attain what Intellect has (or is) eternally, its offspring (our cosmos) departs so significantly from what is above (vertically prior to) it that it may be considered a distinct sort of reality altogether—e.g. a world of Becoming instead of a world of Being. Thus Plotinus speaks at times as if there were, on the one hand, *a* sensible world and, on the other hand, *an* intelligible world, even though in fact there is just the single vertical order and its various levels of reality—the sensible world being just its lowest level, a final image or manifestation of its substance and its principles.

In *Ennead* III.8 Plotinus expresses this obeisance to Platonic dualism by alleging that when the vertical order reaches our cosmos of Becoming, it finds itself entering the world of *participation in* Being and exiting the world of Being as such (see III.8.5, 12–13). Various scholars have noted, of course, that Plotinus' notion of participation differs markedly from Plato's notion. In terms of our current discussion, the notion seems meant to indicate that the sensible cosmos, in addition to being metaphysically dead (impotent, or not genuinely causative), is also inherently *partial* and *incomplete* as an image of Being. In *Ennead* II.1, for example, Plotinus refers to body as forever hastening and flowing (II.1.1, 8); and in *Ennead* III.7, he says, concerning celestial motion, that

> ...it, too, hastens towards what is going to be, and does not want to stand still, as it draws being to itself in doing one thing after another and moving in a circle in a sort of aspiration to substance...[so that it continuously] hastens in this way to everlasting existence by means of what is going to be.[19]

In its attempt to mimic the *telos* of the archetypal cosmos, Becoming behaves as if there were "restless energy" present in it forcing it onwards and "pursuing and destroying countless forms" in its pursuit and hastening (see VI.4.27, 23–25). In contrast, Being as such is eternally whole, complete, self-contained, settled, and quiet. It is not the existence of Becoming or motion as such within our cosmos but the never-settled, forever-restless and -aspiring character of that motion which differentiates it from the archetypal cosmos. Indeed, our cosmos *is* a partial image of (a participant in) Being only because, as noted earlier, (archetypal) motion is itself 'part' of Being—*albeit* along with archetypal Rest. Plotinus thus argues in *Ennead* VI.2 that the Platonic genus of Motion is in fact another name for Being, whose quietude consists in its being eternally at rest in that archetypal motion (VI.2.7, 8 & 15; also see III.7.3).

I shall not analyze in detail Plotinus' argument in *Ennead* VI.2 for his contention that the five Platonic genera—Being, Same, Difference, Motion, and Rest—in fact *all* denote the same metaphysical cause (Intellect), nor precisely how conceptually distinguishing them as *meta*principles of Intellect articulates and explains its (causative) nature. For now, the key point is just that (archetypal) Motion *is* a 'part' of Being, and so our cosmos is a *partial* image of Being just by virtue of its motion or Becomingness.[20] It also is significant, however, that when Plotinus portrays motion in our cosmos as sharply different from (or only participatory in) Intellect's Motion-in-Rest, he typically alludes to manifestations of Becoming in *sensible form*(s)—e.g. the circularity of celestial movements and, in general, Becoming's seeming pursuit and destruction of countless (sensible) forms. For, classical Platonism's sharp dualism begins to dissolve as soon as we consider motions or processes as such, apart from or *prior to* their manifestation to us as sequences of sensible form. Thus, a growing tree may seem to be "pursuing and destroying countless forms" (observable sizes); yet, even regarding the observable tree, we can intellectually consider "simply the motion" (as Plotinus puts it in Ennead VI.1)—e.g. the tree-growth as such—which, far from being pursued and destroyed by the tree, allows us to make sense of its seemingly countless changes of sensible form while itself just *being* (and continuously *remaining*) an image of some motion-in-Being (e.g. an instance, or moving image, of tree-growth). Similarly, for an example given in the *Enneads* themselves, we can consider a person's activity of walking, as we observe it, as a continual changing of place; but we also can consider it as—from its outset and continuously throughout its existence—simply an instance of *walking* (see VI.1.16, 4–17).

Nonetheless, the fact that motion in our cosmos is **not** Intellect's archetypal Motion-in-Rest entails that even when viewed as intelligible and simple (or unifying) processes of Becoming, motion in our cosmos possesses a sort of aspiring and incompleteness which is not found in Intellect's motion even though it derives from it. For, Plotinus tells us, when considered apart from its eternal condition at Rest in archetypal Being, archetypal Motion itself entails repetition or "once again" (*to palin*) and a striving towards difference and succession (VI.1.16, 5–8). Walking, for example, is a matter of moving in a certain way towards someplace different from one's current location. Accordingly, even if walking as such is not really a matter of pursuing and destroying the countless sensible forms in which it manifests itself to our sense experience (e.g. the numerous observable locations or slices of sensible space a person traverses), it nevertheless is a sort of instance of Being which (at the level of Becoming) can exist only so long as its *telos* (the location toward which one is walking) lies outside it. Paradoxically, as soon as an instance of walking-in-Becoming completes itself (attains its *telos*), it no longer *is* an instance of *walking* (see VI.3.23, 11–12).

Another upshot of Plotinus' conception of Becoming seems to be that even when considered intelligibly, as an image (or images) of (part of) Being, motion in our cosmos must be **in**—or perhaps, it must be generative **of**—*space and time*; and this is so, once again, because of the nature of motion itself when it is not eternally at-Rest in Intellect. Once again, Plotinus does not conceive of Becoming as resulting from Being compromising with another metaphysically real principle that lies outside of or opposes Being. Becoming's source is wholly vertical inasmuch as Being itself "enters" our cosmos through its logos (Nature), and

> ...shakes, drives, rouses, and thrusts those that partake in it so that they neither rest nor remain in their own identity in order that they may be caught in that restlessness and turbulence that is only an image of Life [or Motion]. (VI.3.23, 1–5)

Of course, Nature could not "shake, drive, rouse, and thrust" the partial images of Being comprising our cosmos in the manner of an Aristotelian efficient cause—by virtue of itself shaking and thrusting about and somehow imparting, or actualizing a potential for, this among natural things. Plotinus has argued in *Ennead* III.8 that Nature's causality is properly understood as contemplation (or, at least, as an attempt at contemplation) because it "produces another while itself remaining unmoved [and unmoving]"—to which Plotinus immediately adds that Nature thereby produces Becoming itself, but in such a way that it *oversees* it (*epistatōn*) and truly remains a logos of Being instead of itself becoming an activity (*praxis*) in Becoming (III.8.3, 4–5). Since Nature causes Becoming without itself being in Becoming, it must, Plotinus maintains, be a type of soul. More precisely, he argues, Nature must be a soul because the 'living' power in virtue of which it produces its offspring is not just one aspect or part of its Being but comprises its entire essence: "For it, producing is what it is, and its productive power is identical with what it is" (III.8.3, 18). Nature cannot be identical with the hypostasis Soul, however, but must be a lower soul since it is itself an offspring of a prior soul (III.8.4, 15). Plotinus' reasons for these points rest, moreover, on his use of contemplation as the means by which anything real is grounded in, or is metaphysically caused by, the principles defining his vertical order of the hypostases.

The cause of each level of reality after the One coming into existence as an image of a prior or higher level is contemplation, and is explained by the nature of contemplation. In particular, it is explained by the fact that contemplation is inherently productive because it includes the power to produce an image of its object as a by-product, or offspring, of the very act of contemplating that object. Any deficiency in such an image's Being is not to be explained by any principle or cause outside the act of contemplation itself but by a deficiency in the *clarity* and *completeness* of a given contemplative act. Plotinus argues that the 'dead' nature of Nature's offspring, for example, is due to the fact that Nature's contemplation is "somewhat blurred" and "a weak [or blurred] contemplation produces a weak object," i.e. offspring (III.8.4, 28–30). The blurred and weak character of Nature's contemplation also accounts for Becoming's partiality and incompleteness as an image of Being. The hypostasis Soul, in contrast, is "always filled and illuminated by the higher realm" of Intellect itself—by Being in its eternality and entirety (III.8.5, 10–13). Hence, Nature cannot be the hypostasis Soul (nor *vice versa*); it must be a secondary soul, a descent from the hypostasis soul. To be sure, hypostasis Soul's contemplation is also deficient and weak in relation to Intellect's (archetypal) contemplation; but its weakness is *not* a matter of obscurity, partiality, or blurredness. The weakness of its contemplation is seen, rather, in its need to utter and expound its object in order to learn it (III.8.6, 22–24). Unlike Intellect's offspring, Soul's are more than by-products of its contemplative activity. While the nature of contemplative activity always entails the production of offspring, in Soul's case this production also is the necessary means by which it 'learns' the object of its contemplation. This need to learn its object by expounding it in images gives Soul its essence as making-power; but it also is responsible for Soul's offspring having an obscured, blurred or partial contemplation of Being. In other words, the hypostasis Soul does 'learn' its object utterly and with complete clarity—even if not with Intellect's interpenetrating immediacy, or through the self-identification which characterizes Intellect's contemplative activity; but in Soul's 'learning by expounding' lie the seeds of Becoming and of the obscuring or blurring of archetypal Being that leads ultimately to sensible form.

How does weakness of any sort arise in reality's contemplative activity in the first place? Plotinus argues that "what is produced [by contemplation] must always be of the same kind (*homogenes*) as its producer but weaker through losing integrity (*exitēlon*) as it descends [from the contemplator, or from its act]" (III.8.5, 23–24). Plotinus' insistence that a product of contemplation will be 'of the same kind' as its producer further buttresses his view that a lower level of reality is not the result of a higher reality somehow compromising with an opposing principle or with some real, independent substrate; rather, a lower reality is a lower, deficient manifestation of the level of reality immediately higher than it.[21] This principle, that a lower level must lose something of its producer's integrity also explains why its own contemplative activity must be weaker than its producer's contemplation. This principle applies already to the hypostasis Soul, inasmuch as Soul is itself the by-product of Intellect's contemplation. Just as Nature is a type of soul since it is a by-product of Soul's contemplative activity, so too must the hypostasis Soul in fact be a kind of Intellect, Plotinus argues, but one which has lost some of its integrity in that it inherently "sees another" (III.8.6, 26). This inherent 'seeing' of its object as 'another' (or, Soul's need to expound its object in order to 'learn' it) differentiates Soul from archetypal Intellect, and once again yields the above result that, for Soul, its making is its essence—i.e. defines it as Soul, even though it also is a kind of Intellect.

Plotinus' notion of an image's loss in integrity relative to its metaphysical producer ultimately denotes a loss in *unity*. This becomes evident when he turns next in *Ennead* III.8 to Intellect as now the archetypal contemplator—just as in *Ennead* III.2 it was the archetypal cosmos. In discussing that treatise, recall, I noted that the One could not itself be the archetypal cosmos because 'cosmos' connotes a *system* of some sort, and so a whole composed of parts. A primary feature of Plotinus' description of Intellect in *Ennead* III.2.1, however, was that Intellect's parts are not separated from one another, nor from Intellect as a whole, but are effectively *one* within the unity of Intellect's thought and with Intellect itself. In other Plotinian terms, Intellect is metaphysically but one remove from Absolute Unity because even the fundamental duality in its nature (between its Motion, Activity, or Life, and the object or *telos* of that Motion) does not denote a real distinction in Intellect. Intellect's Motion and its object are not really distinct from one another—nor from Intellect itself, the ground or 'agent' of this Motion—because Intellect's archetypal Motion is archetypal contemplation, and archetypal contemplation is not a motion directed by an agent towards a distinct object; rather, in archetypal contemplation the contemplator, the act of contemplation, and the contemplated object are in fact one and the same.[22]

In *Ennead* III.8, Plotinus expresses this by describing Intellect as nothing but "living contemplation" (*theōria zōsa*) (III.8.8, 11). It is essentially living since it is a (first) descent from Absolute Unity just by virtue of its Motion, along with the implied (at least logical) difference between motion and its object. It also is essentially contemplative since its Motion is eternally at Rest in Intellect and is eternally the Same as Intellect, and as its object. Likewise, Intellect is also primal (archetypal) Life (III.8.8, 18):

> If, then, the truest life is life by thought (*noēsei*) and is the same as the truest thought, then the truest thought lives; and contemplation, and the object of contemplation at this level, is living and life, and the two together are one.[23]

Plotinus thus solidifies Intellect's credentials as the archetypal cosmos by identifying it as a first descent from Absolute Unity or, viewed the other way around, by recognizing that the only metaphysical principle which could be higher than Being (Intellect) is the One.

Plotinus argues in *Ennead* III.8 that in contemplating itself, since it is utterly and truly a unity, Intellect could contemplate only Unity itself as the archetype or source of its substance and essence.[24] Accordingly, Intellect is "first in the order of outgoing" (III.8.9, 34) from the primal substance of all reality; but there must therefore exist a yet higher, absolutely first principle which is the source, power, or cause of the outgoing and of Intellect's archetypal Life within that order (III.8.10, 1–4). Since Intellect's own archetype could only be Absolute Unity—or, since the primal substance of all reality and the (absolutely first) cause even of Intellect are one and the same, viz. Absolute Unity—Plotinus concludes *Ennead* III.8 by insisting that any thing *is* or can *be* just insofar as it is in some way *one* (III.8.11, 19–28). Nothing is intelligible, explicable, alive, or at all real except insofar as it is some sort of Unity (or is a descent from Unity); and, insofar as any thing is causative, it must be a cause or source of unification. The ultimate primacy of unity (and unification) to real substance (and causality) is even more fundamental than the five Platonic *meta*principles defining Intellect's nature and than the principles of intelligibility, rationality, or *cosmos* immanent in Intellect. Indeed, these subsequent principles and *meta*principles depend upon it (Unity) for their own validity or truth, and so it is also *sine qua non* above all the others for any adequate conception of reality—hence, for any adequate conception of our cosmos, or for any scientific explication of our cosmos and its processes. I now turn to final remarks on Plotinus' own conception of our cosmos and, especially, of Nature.

In his *Phaedo*, Plato posits as the "causes of (things in the world of) generation and corruption" what come to be known as his Forms—suggestingthat something in the world of Becoming is beautiful, for example, just insofar as it partakes in Absolute Beauty. In *Timaeus*, however, he adds a "receptacle of random powers" to account for the nature or process of Becoming by which things in our cosmos pursue and partake in form.[25] In contrast, Aristotle posits that things *are* by Nature, which he conceives distributively—as that aspect of his primary substances or hylomorphic individuals which is the "source of being moved and of being at rest in that [substance or individual] to which it properly belongs."[26] In *prima facie* contrast both to Plato and to Aristotle, Plotinus posits Absolute Unity as the utterly first principle of all (real) things, and Living Unity or Primal Life (Intellect) as a derivatively-first principle for things which are not utterly-*one* but which are *one* nevertheless.[27]

In effect, however, Plotinus incorporates elements both of Plato's and of Aristotle's views in his metaphysic of Nature. Like Plato, Plotinus maintains that the archetypal cause of our cosmos is eternal Being or Form (though as he conceives of this, of course), and that Being as such must be prior to and devoid of all Becoming. Unlike Plato, however, Becomingness is not explained by a receptacle or some similar principle or substrate, but by Being itself descending to the (metaphysical) level of sensible Becoming. Like Aristotle, Plotinus maintains that the proximate cause of motion and its forms in Becoming is Nature, which is both internal to our cosmos and a logos of Being. Nature—which, unlike Aristotle, Plotinus conceives nondistributively, as *a soul*—has this dual-facing status by virtue of its being *unifying power* (*dynamis*).[28] As seen earlier, it is the proximate cause of Becoming by virtue of the "once again" character implicit in the nature of its causative activity, owing to the "somewhat obscured and partial" character of its (attempt at) contemplation; yet it thereby also effects Becoming's participation in Being by virtue of the unifying effects of this activity, owing to Plotinus' principle that something *is* just insofar as it is *one* (or is *unified*) in some way.

Partaking in Being by virtue of inner, unifying power seems especially characteristic of life, or of living things; and so we might say that Becoming, as effected by Nature and despite its own causatively impotent (or metaphysically dead) status, is a system of life or of living things. Thus, in *Ennead* I.7 Plotinus maintains that all things in our cosmos—including putatively soulless things (*apsycha*)—partake in Unity, and so also in Being, because Form (or Being) is an image of the Good (i.e. the One) (I.7.2); and in *Ennead* IV.4 he argues that our cosmos is universally alive (or living throughout)—everything within it living according to its own appropriate (sort of) life—so that even things which may not seem to be self-moving or animate must possess their own "hidden life" as the proximate cause of their motion (see IV.4.36). In *Ennead* VI.9.1 Plotinus argues that even *continuous magnitudes*—the movements of celestial or terrestrial bodies through space—*are* just in virtue of a unity which those magnitudes possess as effects of some soul or power. Earlier, of course, we saw Plotinus distinguishing between the logos Nature itself, Nature's logoi, and those logoi's sensible forms. That the various processes and activities in the world of Becoming, when considered by themselves (prior to their sensible forms), are logoi of a single soul (Nature) is ultimately confirmed by the fact that they *all* are explicable as manifestations of one (metaphysical) thing—viz. unifying power. Nevertheless, that something multiple or composite in Becoming may be unified (and so given Being) from within Becoming itself seems most evident in the case of organically alive things; and so Plotinus' conception of our cosmos relies heavily on notions associated with (organic) life, including when he has in mind such diverse natural processes as a person's walking, the celestial movements of heavenly bodies, the burning of a fire, the flowing of a river, or the falling of rocks in an avalanche.

This coalescence in Plotinus' thought of inanimate and animate processes, and their common dependency on Nature's unifying power, is the main theme of *Ennead* IV.4. In this treatise, Plotinus sometimes refers to Nature as "the soul of the all," and sometimes as "the giver of order" (*to kosmoun*) or as a "divine craftsman." The first title is perhaps most apt insofar as it emphasizes that Nature is not an agent which operates from outside our cosmos but is "the life of our cosmos that possesses leadership within itself." The latter two sorts of descriptions are also helpful, however, since they emphasize that Nature's unifying power operates not only in things which we would normally consider to be alive or animate but *wherever* discernible order (*taxis*) exists to demonstrate the presence of unity amid what otherwise may seem just a sensible multiplicity—as, for example, the ordered circularity discernible in a celestial body's continuous change in its observable position. By discernible order, of course, I do not intend order which necessarily someone has discerned or actually observed. Plotinus maintains that our cosmos is *in fact* rational throughout because—despite its diversity, Becomingness, and its countless multiplicity of sensible forms—every real thing or process within it in fact *is* ordered in some way. Our cosmos as a whole and *everything* within it is effected and 'crafted' by the unifying power of Nature: *all* processes in Becoming are vertical effects (manifestations, logoi) of one master (*hēgemonoun*), because Nature is a soul and "a soul is a unity and its artisanship is [always] one" (see IV.4.10, 1–16). Thus, our cosmos is a vertical effect of a living unity and a logos of Living Unity (IV.4.11, 1).[29]

In my examples of Becoming, I have focused thus far on individual motions, activities or processes within our cosmos. *Ennead* IV.4.10 emphasizes the important fact, however, that Nature's primary function is to be the soul, or unifying power, of our cosmos as a whole. Indeed, Nature's presence within individual things or processes derives from that primary function, denoting (part of) the means by which it unifies our cosmos as a single whole. In *Ennead* IV.4 Plotinus proffers a variety of conceptions for how Nature promulgates its primary governorship over the entirety of our cosmos. He tells us, for example, that Nature flows into all things, dominating them and conducting them into a single, circumscribed whole (see IV.4.10, 25 & IV.4.11, 1–4); that diversity springs from a logos, and therefore is always guided in its 'difference' and sequentiality by a logos (see IV.4.12, 37ff); that our cosmos is a sympathetic whole because of Nature, and it thereby is itself a living unity (see IV.4.32, 14), wherein all things are established as to their physical conditions, positions, and structures as are the parts of a single living thing (see IV.4.33, 26–33); and that because of Nature all things in our cosmos are entwined into a unity (see IV.4.38, 18). Similarly, Plotinus says elsewhere that the divine logos (Nature) composes what is *one* cosmos from the *many* parts as it orders them into a single whole (I.6.2, 19–20); that the soul of our cosmos "runs over its surface" ordering all things (II.9.7, 29); that our cosmos is a weaving together of all things (III.2.15, 2); that it possesses a soul which binds it together and "brings it entirely under the rule of reason" (see IV.3.9, 43ff & IV.3.10, 11ff); and that the author of all (natural) things is a soul which has breathed life into them all—which has shaped and ordered the heavens and still conducts the heavens in their harmonious movements, and which likewise gives to *all* (natural) things law and motion and life (see V.1.2).

Implicit in the foregoing paraphrases are thus two dimensions to Nature's operation or function. There is Nature's distributive ubiquity—the immanence or presence of its unifying power within every thing and process in our cosmos. Soul as such is "power streaming into life" (VI.7.31, 3), and Nature is that power as operative in Becoming in such a way that every individual (real) thing in our cosmos is a living unity. This dimension to Nature's operation is most evident, I have noted, in those sorts of things which we would normally consider to be living or animate. A plant or an animal is doubly a multiplicity: first, in that it is composed of parts and, second, in that it and its parts move through space and change through time. In both respects, however, such an organism is ordered and patterned into a single whole because both its (organic) parts and its (or their) movements and processes spring from a single active unity within the organism—a productive logos, binding power, or soul (see VI.2.5). Indeed, my earlier discussion of *Ennead* III.8 implied that things in our cosmos are (at least when viewed *sub specie naturalis*) in fact nothing but (ordered patterns of) movements, processes, or Becomings. Insofar as a given process (e.g. a tree's growth) does not exhaust the reality of a thing in Becoming (e.g. the tree), we may distinguish the thing itself (the tree) from that process (its growth). In reality, however, it seems that for Plotinus the reality—indeed, the *substance*—of things in Becoming is comprised of, or is exhausted by, patterns or sets of Becomings which manifest Nature's unifying power in a certain rationally discernible way (or, perhaps, as operative at a certain unificative point within our cosmos). Second, there also is Nature's own *primary* unity as essentially the soul or unifying power of our cosmos as a whole. Thus, we saw in *Ennead* III.2 that it is our cosmos in its entirety, not any individual thing(s) or process(es) within it, that is most clearly and fully an image of the archetypal cosmos.[30] Indeed, Plotinus argued there that it is only in relation to our cosmos as a whole, or to one another as ordered into a single cosmos, that individual processes and their seeming interactions or interdependencies become rationally explicable and 'friendly.' In this dimension to its operation, Nature is a single, undistributed logos or soul—effecting and governing our cosmos as one entirety, wherein individual things and processes are in fact comparable to the diverse parts, or organs and processes, comprising a single living organism.

These two dimensions to Nature's operation are not opposed to one another. Indeed, I have argued that its concurrent presence in diverse individual things and processes, ordering and unifying (or subordering and subunifying) them, derives from its primary status as *the* one (and only) unifying power present in our cosmos. Just as ordering and thereby unifying various parts and processes of a plant or an animal would contribute to its soul's governance of the plant or the animal as a whole, so too does Nature's (sub)ordering and (sub)unification of individual things and processes in Becoming contribute to its operation as the soul of our cosmos as a (single) whole. Plotinus brings these two dimensions together in *Enneads* II.2.3 and VI.7.7 by arguing that as Nature "runs through" our cosmos effecting, ordering, and governing it, there occurs an "effective separation of [its] powers" wherein its single unifying power manifests itself in various ways in various parts of the cosmos. Thus its distributive ubiquity is in fact (at least part of) the way in which Nature promulgates its primary, undistributed function of ordering and unifying our cosmos as one, single whole.

Plotinus' explication in *Enneads* II.2.3 and VI.7.7 of Nature's distributive ubiquity (as I have termed it) in terms of an "effective separation of powers" implicit (it seems) in its undistributed or primary unificative power might seem to compromise the latter's primacy. Lest Nature as a single soul become something like Aristotle's form of the outermost sphere or a power located (like, on one reading, Anaximander's Indefinite substance) at the cosmogenic center of our cosmos from whence various powers radiate or separate, it might seem necessary that this "separation of powers" denote a distribution or descent of Nature itself, wherein its purportedly singular power in fact becomes many diverse and discreet (sorts of) powers. Nor would it suffice for preserving Nature's primal unity to characterize this counterfactually—e.g. by arguing that even though its power does distribute itself in a certain way, it could have distributed itself differently (indeed, in any number of possible ways which might be consistent with effecting *a* cosmos). This would not suffice because Nature is a *reality* or an *actuality* for Plotinus. Indeed, Nature is *more real*, or is *higher in* the order of reality, than the world of Becoming and than the various ways in which its power might manifest or separate its self within various parts of our cosmos. The appropriately Plotinian resolution to this conundrum lies, I think, midway between adopting a merely counterfactual account of the primacy of Nature's primal power of unification and denying that Plotinus' separation-of-powers explication of Nature's ubiquitous (self-)distribution denotes a *real* or *actual* (vertical) process. In particular, Plotinus intends, I think, that Nature itself and its primal power *are* in reality already *ubiquitous*—i.e. are present completely (or nondistributively) at every point or within every part of our cosmos.[31] At the same time, Nature's primal unity and power is surely not *absolutely* or *utterly* primal (since the One alone is). Consequently, my notion of Nature's distributive ubiquity and Plotinus' explication of this as a separation of powers denote the fact that at each point or within each part of our cosmos Nature (in fact, or in actuality) *utilizes* its primal power, or *manifests* a 'part' of its primal self, in the manner most appropriate to or effective in that part of our cosmos.

The importance of this way of conceiving Nature is perhaps most evident when we recognize that in addition to unifying various parts of our cosmos individually or distributively and to unifying our cosmos as a whole, Plotinus intends Nature also to unify or order observable *interactions* between or among diverse parts of our cosmos. Indeed, we saw in *Ennead* III.2 that our cosmos' rationality, beauty, or friendship is most evident when we recognize the harmony and rationality which in fact obtains among seemingly warring parts of it. Whether in the case of a fire consuming wood, a lion attacking an antelope, or boulders bouncing off one another during their head-long descent down a mountain—each and every putative interaction among things within our cosmos is in fact a rationally orchestrated, lawfully ordered manifestation of Nature's unifying power. (I'm ignoring, of course, the issue of free will in human behavior.) To suppose that real conflict or warfare exists in such cases would be at least as absurd as supposing that my body is at war with food as it consumes it for nourishment, or that my hands are in conflict with one another when I bring them together in a clapping motion and they bounce off one another after impact. For, while 'consumes' and 'bounces off' may still suggest conflict in some sense, what these terms in fact denote in these examples are lawful sequences of observable events or complex processes of (sensible) Becoming which transpire in a quietly ordered fashion as themselves in reality just parts of the rationally orchestrated cosmic drama being effected in its entirety by Nature. Our cosmos, and the things and processes which comprise it, as further testimony to its nonarchetypal nature, are constrained by principles of contrariety—for example, such that two bodies cannot occupy the same place at the same time, or that the same organic material cannot be both part of an antelope and also part of a lion at the same time. But these principles do not denote any real warfare or actual contrarieties among various parts of our cosmos. What was once part of an antelope now *becomes* part of a lion, for instance; and this is itself simply *a* natural process—or, *a* manifestation of Nature's unifying power as *fully* present throughout our cosmos, including wherever a seeming *inter*action might occur.

A final point of emphasis regarding Plotinus' conception of Nature: Although Plotinus maintains that Nature is a soul and that souls differ from (sensible) bodies in not possessing size, mass, quantity or position, he does not conceive of Nature and the world of Becoming as two separate *substances*. Instead, we have seen that as the vertical order descends from the One and Intellect towards Becoming, each lower level of reality is the same *in substance* as its immediately prior level but weaker or less unified in that substance. The world of Becoming, in particular, just *is* Nature manifesting itself first in Becoming as such and then to our sense experience—therein 'acquiring' size, mass, place, etc. Of course, it then is our cosmos and is no longer Nature as such, inasmuch as 'Nature' denotes the unifying power which is metaphysically prior to and causative of our cosmos. Nevertheless, Nature does not become a separate substance from our cosmos but is "present within it" as that living unity or productive power which in fact is manifesting *itself* at the level of Becoming and sensible form(s). All reality and substance in fact is a descent or outflow from the One, and Nature is prior to our cosmos in the order of that descent or in its reality as a manifestation of that one primal substance; but, for this very reason, it thereby is not itself a (metaphysically primal) substance which somehow constitutes a separate substance from another putative (metaphysically primal) substance which somehow constitutes our cosmos.

This last point is pertinent especially to seeing Plotinus' Neoplatonism and its conception of Nature as a response to Pyrrhonism—my final topic in this essay.

3. Plotinus, Pyrrhonism, and 'Scientific Spirit'

Far from supporting the notion that Plotinus' preoccupation with metaphysics implies a disinterest in this-world, or a rejection of its rationality or of the legitimacy and value of scientific investigation of it, the textual discussions in section 2 of this essay have demonstrated a concerted effort in the *Enneads* with saving our cosmos from the irrationality of matter and from intellectually unwarranted conceptions of it. I have, of course, dealt with a very small and select body of texts from Plotinus' *Enneads* and have barely scratched the surface even of those texts. Nevertheless, we have seen a Plotinus who is hardly willing to abandon our cosmos to Gnostic deprecation or to Pyrrhonian indifference. Plotinus' ascent to Intellect in *Ennead* III.2 and to Intellect and the One in *Ennead* III.8, for example, are clearly meant to establish Becoming's pedigree as a *bona fide* image of Being that is all-beautiful, harmonious, *etc.* Together with *Ennead* IV.4 and other texts I have mentioned, moreover, that ascent also prepares the ground for science itself, among other things, by identifying unifying power as the essence of Nature, by conceiving of Becoming itself as an intelligible and rational object for human investigation, and by suggesting as guiding concepts for discerning and studying Nature's lawful effects in Becoming such notions as order, harmony, pattern, and the like.

That Plotinus' rational beatification of our cosmos is a response to Gnosticism is, of course, explicit in the *Enneads* themselves. That it also responds to Pyrrhonism is not explicit. Indeed, Plotinus never mentions Pyrrhonism by name, much less individual Pyrrhonists, in the *Enneads*. I shall rely upon Sextus Empiricus' *Outlines of Pyrrhonism* to sketch the main elements of Pyrrhonism's challenge to "Greek rationality" before articulating how Plotinus' Neoplatonism responds to that challenge.

Ancient Skepticism took two principal forms: Academic Skepticism, and Pyrrhonian Skepticism. The former tradition—as enunciated by Cicero, for example[32]—argues that the true natures of things are obscured and hidden from us by sensory appearances and that, as a result, a wise person ought never to assent to anything as *true* but instead should accept and act upon what *seems-true* just in (or from) appearances themselves (what they also term the "probable" or "truth-like"). In this way, Academics hoped to maintain that the goal of the wise person is still truth, or the true natures of things; but this goal is unattainable by any human being. Only truth's likenesses (i.e. appearances) are within our reach; and so, we must be content with the "probability" which lies within our reach, even while striving for our real *telos*—truth itself. Pyrrhonism is a more radical Skepticism whose goal is *quietude*—an utter surcease of the desire to attain truth. A Pyrrhonist will not assent to, nor even just "accept," *any* theory about the true natures of things whereas an Academic, though he would never "assent to" (commit himself to the truth of) any such theory, may accept a theory if it seems-true at the time or resonates with the probability of sensory appearances.[33]

Both Academics and Pyrrhonists thus live by appearances alone, but they do so for different reasons and in different ways. An Academic lives by appearances because they are truth-likenesses or seemings-of-truth, and he tries to discern in them reason to accept provisionally various of the ideas, beliefs and theories he encounters while vigorously pursuing the forever-elusive truth which lies just beyond his reach—on the other side of appearances. A Pyrrhonist, in contrast, lives by appearances, not because they are (allegedly) truth-likenesses, nor because he believes instead that they themselves must somehow be the truth. He lives by appearances, rather, simply because they are all that lie within our grasp; he has no use for the philosophers' notion of 'truth' at all, and so disregards it altogether. In Sextus' terms, it is simply the case that appearances are the only things that are "evident" to us. Whether they also are all there is to reality, and so are themselves the truth about it, or whether they are images or likenesses of further reality (and ones which may or may not perspicuously manifest it to us), is of no concern to the Pyrrhonist. Rather, the Pyrrhonist intends to live a solely practical life, thinking and acting in terms of appearances alone and not utilizing or appealing to them in any way whatsoever to speculative ends—unlike the Academic.[34] Sextus' writings, for example, while they do articulate the Pyrrhonian viewpoint, seem more fundamentally meant to lead Pyrrhonists away from pursuing philosophy's traditional end (truth) and towards quietude and perhaps also to serve as a prophylactic for any Pyrrhonist who backslides into searching for truth.

Sextus' *Outlines of Pyrrhonism*, like all of his writings, is long and complex. I shall focus on two of its main features: Its analysis of what Sextus terms *Dogmatic* philosophy, and its attempt (which accounts for its length and complexity) to lead Pyrrhonists towards quietude by establishing an "equipoise" among all Dogmatic beliefs and arguments. For, only after speculation has thusly annihilated or at least paralyzed itself can the Pyrrhonist be free to live his practical life amid the "evident" appearances of sense.

As Sextus sees it, *all* philosophy, not just Pyrrhonism, is *in fact* a search for quietude (*ataraxia*). More precisely, philosophy arises from a recognition of some apparent puzzle or anomaly (*anōmalias*) that disturbs (or disquiets) us, and its goal is to restore quietude by resolving the anomaly.[35] Traditional philosophy, however, has sought to restore quietude by distinguishing between truth and falsehood and supposing that the way to resolve apparent anomalies is to find the truth, and so has come to suppose even that truth is itself the *telos* of philosophy. But an apparent anomaly *is* anomalous in appearances, and so traditional philosophy is forced to suppose that the truth is not to be found in appearances themselves.[36] It thus is forced to go outside appearances—and so, Sextus maintains, outside what is "evident to us"—and to postulate *non*evident things (*adēla*) which philosophers express in propositions or conceive in thoughts that Sextus terms *intelligibles* (*noēta* or *nooumena*), and which contrast with appearances (*phainomena*). Sextus calls these traditional philosophers Dogmatists, and he defines Dogmatism as "assenting to a non-evident proposition" or as "assenting to certain of the non-evident things sought by science."[37] As Sextus defines the term, Dogmatism does not mean, say, close-mindedness or assenting to something without argument or reasons. On Sextus' definition, even Academic Skeptics, who insist upon continually examining and reexamining the available evidence and its "probability," are Dogmatists insofar as they search for *non*evident things or choose (provisionally) to accept nonevident propositions. Any philosopher who pursues quietude by seeking truth in nonevident propositions or things is a Dogmatist; and, Sextus believes, anyone who seeks the truth *must* do so in nonevident propositions since, as noted, appearances *are* anomalous and so cannot themselves be truth.

Central to Sextus' understanding of Dogmatism is his notion of nonevident propositions, or of propositions which postulate nonevident things. To get some idea of what Sextus has in mind by '*non*evident things,' it is interesting to note that the philosophical tradition least discussed by him is Platonism. Sextus' paradigm of Dogmatic philosophy seems, instead, to be materialism—especially Atomism and Stoicism, and also Aristotelianism. Thus, Sextus offers as prime examples of Dogmatism Anaxagoras' attempt to resolve the anomaly that snow seems to be a form of water which, however, seems unique among forms of water in that it appears to be white by positing "Snow is frozen water; water is black; therefore, snow is black";[38] and Democritus' attempt to resolve the anomaly that honey tastes sweet to some people and bitter to others by postulating that in reality honey is neither sweet nor bitter but instead is composed of (tasteless) atoms and void.[39] In both of these examples, the Dogmatic move is to postulate a real or true material world which underlies appearances and resolves apparent anomalies just by itself not being anomalous. Thus, in Anaxagoras' material hypokeimenon snow shares with all other forms of water that it is really black—it only appears to be white; and in Democritus' material hypokeimenon all things are really tasteless—they only appear to be sweet, bitter, or whatever. Sextus' arguments in his *Outlines* range over all areas of Dogmatic philosophy, not just natural science; and they attack a wide range of Dogmatic philosophers, not just Atomists and Pluralists. Throughout his arguments, however, *material hypokeimena* remain his paradigms of nonevident things; by *non*evident propositions or thoughts ('intelligibles') Sextus consistently has in mind propositions or thoughts whose objects lie outside the propositions or thoughts themselves and which—like Anaxagoras' black snow and Democritus' atoms—exist beyond appearances as such. This understanding of intelligibles is also the basis for Sextus' method of equipoise.

The bulk of Sextus' *Outlines* is occupied with his strategy of leading Pyrrhonists to quietude by establishing an equipoise (*isostheneias*) among all Dogmatic intelligibles, thereby annihilating or at least paralyzing speculation's desire to reach the truth.[40] Establishing this equipoise will not resolve the apparent anomalies which give rise to speculation, of course; but, strictly speaking, Dogmatic philosophy does not resolve them either. The apparent anomalies remain anomalies in appearances for the Dogmatist who 'resolves' them by seeking refuge from them in his nonanomalous (by postulation) realm of nonevident hypokeimena. The Pyrrhonist differs from the Dogmatist on this score, however, precisely because he recognizes that the Dogmatist's 'resolution' of the anomalies of appearances is bogus—that it does not really resolve them at all. More precisely, Sextus' equipoise method demonstrates the bogus character of the Dogmatist's response to the riddles of appearances by showing that Dogmatism cannot lead to quietude. His method does this by showing that every Dogmatic intelligible has Dogmatic competitors which contradict it, and that any argument a Dogmatist might give for assenting to his intelligible has competitors which argue against that intelligible and in favor of opposing intelligibles.

The basis for Sextus' method is the fact, as he sees it, that the conflicting intelligibles of the Dogmatists are by themselves all of equal worth since they all are equally nonevident propositions, or thoughts about nonevident things.[41] For this reason, it is incumbent upon the Dogmatist to base his intelligibles upon arguments which seek to prove them and to disprove his competitors' intelligibles. The Dogmatist, Sextus argues, cannot apprehend the objects postulated in his intelligibles just by the act of conception itself (*to noein*); he must implicitly add to the act of conceiving an intelligible an assumption of the existence (*tēn hyparchin*) of its postulated object(s).[42] For, as noted earlier, the objects postulated in intelligibles are external to the intelligibles themselves; and thought "does not make contact with external objects and receive presentations by means of itself but by means of the senses, and the senses do not apprehend the external real objects [postulated in intelligibles] but only, if at all, their own affections [*i.e.* appearances]."[43] Since the Dogmatist's postulated objects are not "evident" within the act of conceiving intelligibles itself (nor in sensory appearances), their assumed existence must be made to rest upon arguments which would justify his assenting to them. But the arguments mobilized by Dogmatists in attempting to prove their intelligibles (and to disprove their competitors') can all be shown in turn to be by themselves of equal worth in their logic (validity) and in their relevance (or lack thereof) to appearances (what is "evident"), and so they also stand in need of their own proof—and so on, and so on, *ad infinitum*.[44]

Not only can traditional philosophy never lead us to the truth (or, at least, never to recognition of the truth), and so return us to a condition of quietude; it cannot even demonstrate that one intelligible is stronger than another. All of the Dogmatist intelligibles are equally provable, and equally refutable.

The Pyrrhonian attack on the Greek scientific spirit has speculative quietude or scientific indifference as its goal, and its focus is the Dogmatic character (the Pyrrhonists believe) of all traditional Greek philosophy. In light of this, it is crucial to recognize that, although Plotinus' Neoplatonism seeks to resolve the apparent puzzles and anomalies of sensible Becoming by finding reality or truth, it is *not a form of Dogmatism*. For one thing, Plotinus' philosophy denies the presumption that apparent anomalies in fact *are* anomalies in appearances, and so also the Dogmatist's approach to 'resolving' them by postulating a realm of hypokeimena beyond all appearances wherein lies the truth. In thus rejecting the Dogmatic program of finding truth in such hypokeimena, moreover, Plotinus also rejects the nonevident intelligibles of the Dogmatists. Truth *is* to be found in, or by means of, intelligibles for Plotinus; but the so-called 'intelligibles' of the Dogmatists are not genuine intelligibles to begin with.

Plotinus maintains, we have seen, that our cosmos as a whole and every part of it is ordered and unified by Nature, and our cosmos is not separate in substance from Nature but it and its parts are in fact manifestations of Nature itself. The world of Becoming is, as a result, thoroughly rational; and this is in fact the very same world as that which appears to us in sense experience, or which we also discern in sensible form(s). Plotinus' Nature, in other words, is not a hypokeimenon, or 'underlie,' for appearances at all.[45] Sensible form (or appearances) is just a final manifestation of the one real substance which extends or proceeds from the One all the way to the level of sense experience. To be sure, the consequent rationality of sensible Becoming is not always *self*-evident in the "evident" world of sensory appearances. At times, it may become evident only after much careful study and scientific investigation informed by an understanding of how the principles of rationality or *cosmos* operate and manifest themselves to us, ultimately in sensible form(s). Apparent anomalies are thus not really anomalies in appearances, but are appearances whose (nonanomalous) rationality might not be readily discernible insofar as it is not self-evident in appearances. But to say that the sensible cosmos' thorough rationality is not self-evident is not to say that it must therefore be *non*evident, or that it therefore can be a feature only of a realm of hypokeimena which lies outside all appearances.

Recalling the anomalies of snow's whiteness and of honey's taste, for example, the Plotinian idea would seem to be that these are not to be 'resolved' by postulating an underlying matter in which snow is not white and honey is not really sweet nor bitter; instead, they are genuinely to be resolved by understanding the various ways in which Nature appropriately and rationally manifests itself, or operates, in the diverse parts and amid the complex circumstances or conditions found in our cosmos. For example, whiteness *is* the appropriate visible form for water to take under certain conditions, and sweetness (or bitterness) is the appropriate flavor for honey in certain circumstances (which include conditions in the person tasting it). As St. Augustine tells the Academic Skeptic in his *Contra Academicos*, regarding whether we can apprehend "evident truth" in appearances: "Perhaps it cannot be apprehended by you or other fools, but why can it not be apprehended by a wise person?" (Book III, 21). The context of Augustine's remark is somewhat different from our present discussion; but its upshot is the same: That appearances in the world of sensible Becoming appear anomalous or irrational to someone who does not understand how Nature operates within it (or manifests itself by means of it) does not mean that they really are anomalous, or that they would be so even for one who does understand this.[46]

An important element in Plotinus' metaphysical system which I have ignored almost completely in this essay is his theory of the intelligibles (or Forms). I shall not attempt to detail that theory here either;[47] I only will indicate in programmatic terms how Plotinus does conceive of intelligibles as postulates of Intellectual activity, yet of a sort which sharply contrasts with how Sextus and his Dogmatists conceive them. Recall that for Sextus and his Dogmatists, intelligibles are propositions or thoughts which postulate hypokeimena—i.e. objects that exist apart from their Intellectual conception (as well as beyond all sensory appearances)—and so they are nonevident and require a separate assumption, and so also proof, of their existence before we can assent to them. For Plotinus, in contrast, the objects of genuinely Intellectual acts or conceptions are far from nonevident. In fact, they are archetypically *self*-evident.[48] A genuine Intellectual object (or intelligible) exists solely by virtue of (and so "within") its Intellectual conception; it is an object of Intellectual *contemplation* wherein the contemplative act and its object are one. Since genuine Intellectual activity, in other words, is contemplation and since the contemplative object is already present within the activity of contemplation itself, there is no other outside or external object whose existence is merely a postulate of Intellect. Knowing *external* objects, or knowing objects externally, is the goal (and need) of sense experience, not Intellection. Consequently, genuinely Intellectual conceptions must always be true and can never be false. Likewise, such notions as deliberation, plausible belief, assent, persuasion, hesitation, doubt, possible error, and the like, are simply out of place when discussing Intellect and its activity or mode of conceiving intelligibles.[49] And so once again, no separate justification or proof is needed to establish the existence of the objects of genuine Intellectual activity; any putative object whose existence is not self-evident in its very conception (and so also true by its very conception) simply is *not* an object of genuinely Intellectual activity—and this is especially the case with material hypokeimena.

I realize that the foregoing gives an idea of what Plotinus' intelligibles *are not* more than of what they *are*. Nevertheless, it does indicate further how Plotinus' Neoplatonism is a non-Dogmatic response to Pyrrhonism. In doing so, however, it focuses on Plotinus' hypostasis Intellect as the archetype, source or metaphysical agent of all Intellectual activity. How does this relate to the conceptions or thoughts of individual philosophers (or scientists)—the living targets of Sextus' attacks? It would, of course, be appropriate here to discuss Plotinus' views regarding our souls' relationship with Intellect—regarding the intellects-in-us and their relationship to archetypal Intellect. Roughly, since Intellect eternally "fills and illumines" Soul (see III.8.5, 10), and since our souls (as well as Nature) are offspring of Soul, insofar as we engage in genuinely Intellectual activities our conceptions will be one and the same with Intellect's and with those that inform Nature's operations.[50] Once again, however, this only points towards the outlines of the theory, and it also raises the further question of how we are to *recognize* when we are engaging in genuine Intellectual activities. Inasmuch as Plotinus' main concern is to distance his own intelligibles from those characterized by Sextus, however, I can only presume that he intends genuine Intellection "in us" to share the same features as those noted earlier regarding archetypal intellection—e.g. that since the objects of genuine Intellectual activity must already be present within the activity itself, their conception must be self-evident, and so they *must* be true and *cannot* be erroneous or false.

In closing, this section has contrasted Plotinus' intelligibles with those postulated by Sextus and his Dogmatists: First, they are not hypokeimena which underlie appearances and which are tailored to provide a refuge in our cosmos from the anomalies of appearances.[51] Indeed, Plotinus rejects the presumption that appearances really *are* anomalous, or irrational; he conceives sensible Becoming to be in fact a final manifestation of intelligibility or rationality itself. Second, in their pure form at least—that is, as objects of genuine Intellectual activity or as prior to the objects of sense experience which manifest them—Plotinus' intelligibles are self-evident and so, it would seem, are true *necessarily*. No Pyrrhonian equipoise of competing (genuine) intelligibles is possible: During genuine Intellectual activity only *one* set of intelligibles is even *possible* (viz. those which are true *necessarily*, and so whose denial or 'opposing conception' must be *false* necessarily). Insofar as a conception (or its object) is merely possible, postulated, or putatively factual (contingent), it cannot be a genuinely Intellectual activity nor an intelligible.

I still have not articulated fully or precisely the nature and character of the items comprising the (one, self-evident, necessarily true) set of intelligibles which Plotinus believes is conceived by genuine Intellectual activity (i.e. archetypal contemplation, and its images in the soul of the cosmos and in human souls); nor have I discussed Plotinus' grounds for adopting the Platonic *megista genera* as *meta*principles defining Intellect's nature, its consequent contents (the intelligibles, or Forms), and any vertical effects (logoi and images) of it. Moreover, as I alluded when discussing archetypal rationality and our cosmos in section 2, the foregoing leaves the Plotinian natural philosopher (scientist) the formidable task of discerning precisely *how* each and every appearance, sensible form, or sense-observable Becoming (including seeming-anomalies) in fact *is* explicable as an instance of those intelligibles. My concern in this section, however, has been with Plotinus' historical context and, in particular, with Skepticism in its classical form(s). In that regard, moreover, Plotinus is clearly no friend of Pyrrhonism, even unwittingly. Plotinus' well-known insistence that *true quietude* can be found only in Intellect (and the One) can now be seen as—far from an abandonment of rationality and its (scientific) applications in understanding our cosmos—potentially a profound source of renewal for the so-called scientific spirit of the Ancient Greeks as they sought to understand the phenomena and puzzles of our cosmos.

The University of San Diego

NOTES

1. From Edmund Halley's ode to Isaac Newton (translated by Leon J. Richardson) in *Sir Isaac Newton's Mathematical Principles*, translated by Andrew Motte and revised by Florian Cajori (Berkeley: University of California Press, 1934, 1962).

2. Leon Robin, *Greek Thought and the Origins of the Scientific Spirit* (New York: Russell & Russell, 1928, 1967), 361.
3. Galileo Galilei, *Dialogue Concerning the Two Chief World Systems*, translated by Stillman Drake (Berkeley: University of California Press, 1967), 16.
4. For an elaboration of pertinent aspects of Plotinus' philosophy, see my "Realism and the Foundations of Science in Plotinus," *Ancient Philosophy* 5 (1985), 269–292.
5. Galileo, 15 & 412.
6. Galileo, 14.
7. Galileo, 335. Alexandre Koyré argues that the Platonic (or Neopythagorean) approach adopted by Galileo severs scientific theory from the observable cosmos and, as a result, rests upon a "basic contradiction: it requires a total conversion, a radical substitution, of a mathematical, Platonic world for the world of empirical reality...while at the same time it renders this total substitution impossible, since instead of explaining empirical reality it does away with it, because instead of saving the phenomena it creates, between empirical and ideal realities, a fatal chasm of unexplained facts": *Galileo Studies*, translated by John Mepham (Atlantic Heights, NJ: Humanities Press, 1978), 155. In contrast, see William A. Wallace, "Galileo and Reasoning *Ex Suppositione*," *Prelude to Galileo*; ed., W. A. Wallace (Dordrecht, Holland: D. Reidel Publishing Co., 1981), 129–159. As Ernst Cassirer also sees it, Galileo represents the last stage of development in the Renaissance conception of the relationship between mathematics and empirical reality, concerning the beginnings of which Cassirer remarks that "So long as definite *criteria* of experience were not created through the medium of mathematics and through the other new intellectual means furnished by it, the empiricism of the Renaissance lacked objective standards of value and any principle of selection among the teeming phenomena"; but, after a transitional stage whereon Koyré's assessment might be *apropos*, in Galileo "the empirical is no longer to be resolved in the ideal, therewith stripped of its specific character. On the contrary, the ideal can only be genuinely fulfilled in the empirical, where it is tested and justified"—*The Individual and the Cosmos in Renaissance Philosophy*, translated by Mario Domandi (New York: Harper & Row, 1963), 151 & 172.
8. Galileo, 335.
9. Galileo, 336.
10. A. H. Armstrong translation (Loeb Classical Library): *Ennead* III.2.1, 28–37.
11. Armstrong translation: *Ennead* III.2.2, 2–8.
12. Dominic O'Meara maintains that Plotinus rejects Plato's notion of a (or the) divine, cosmic craftsperson (or *demiurge*) because (1) "the world must derive from one ultimate source"; (2) "soul, and only soul, is the proximate cause of the world"; and (3) "[h]e accepts the Aristotelian claim that natural

processes are far superior to human craft" in that (3a) "nature does not need to calculate and deliberate; it does not toil over its work" and (3b) it "does not work on matter, as it were, 'with its hands' or with instruments...[but it] produces without moving"—*Plotinus: An Introduction to the Enneads* (Oxford & New York: Oxford University Press, 1993), 70–76. These points are important, and accurate. However, they do not entail a wholesale rejection of Plato's notion. Plato himself surely recognized that this conceit is but an image, even a metaphor, for his *divine, meta*physical demiurge; and O'Meara is correct to point out various respects in which Plotinus' use of that conceit must denote a reality, or feature of reality, which differs from its human model even more so than Plato's does. As we shall see below, however, Plotinus **does use** the notion in his own discussions of our cosmos' archetype and vertical cause(s)—and so he hardly could be *rejecting* it—since it *does* convey quite well certain features of our cosmos' metaphysical aetiology and archetype. Perhaps among other things, it conveys the intelligence inherent in that vertical order; its unfailing reliability, if you will; and the fact that it yields a product which is not some amorphous, unintelligible mess-of-matter but which is shaped, ordered, (well-)formed, and the like. For, central to Plato's classic notion of a craftsperson or artisan is that she possesses *art*—i.e. a set of (intelligible, cognitively discernible) *principles* and *standards*—and she is eminently accomplished at crafting products which conform to those principles and standards. At least in *these* regards, Plotinus does *not* consider craft-activity inferior to natural activity but a feature of it—or, perhaps, a *precondition* for it (see section 1 of this essay).

13. Armstrong translation: *Ennead* III.2.3, 7–9.
14. Thus, in *Ennead* I.8.4, Plotinus also argues that "bodies" may be said to "partake in matter" insofar as they are considered to be deprived of life, to destroy one another because of their (purportedly) disorderly motions, and to hinder Soul's operation and so to evade substance (*ousian*) as they continually flow or move. But insofar as we thus conceive of bodies as partaking in matter, we are not thereby attributing to them a (material) *substance* of their own; rather, we are conceiving of them as *evading* or *departing from* substance. Thus, in *Ennead* II4.12 & 14, Plotinus argues further that matter, considered absolutely or by itself, *seems* to be a hypokeimenon—a substrate for sensible qualities. So considered, however, matter does not even possess size, nor even corporeality (*sōmatotēs*). Instead, its distinctive nature (*idiotēs*) is purely *relational* and is not really "absolute" at all; it becomes purely "other than"—a privation or taking away of qualifications and delimitations from reality. In short, something is *material* just insofar as it departs from, or is deprived of, substance or Being.
15. See, for example, *De Anima* III.7, 431a15 & 431b3.

16. In *Ennead* II.3.13, Plotinus explicitly interrelates the degree to which something is lifeless (or dead) and the degree to which it is impotent and passive.
17. Indeed, Plotinus argues in *Ennead* II.9.16 that the first step in our ascent toward recognizing the real substance and causes of our cosmos lies in recognizing order and proportion within it.
18. Thus, in *Ennead* I.4.3, 34–41, Plotinus distinguishes *levels* or *grades* of life (rather than distinct sorts of life), where the True, Real or perfect life is that of the intelligible world and where the various sorts of life we commonly distinguish in our cosmos are in fact various incomplete grades or traces of that archetypal Life.
19. Armstrong translation: *Ennead* III.7.4, 29–33.
20. Dominic O'Meara argues that Plotinus' solution to the Platonic problem of the "relation between intelligible and sensible reality" revolves around effecting a "reversal" in the way in which we conceive that relation. Whereas Plato (at least until his *Parmenides*) conceived the relation from the perspective of (sensible) particulars—as one wherein, in his most common vocabulary for this, particulars participate in intelligibles (Beings, or Forms)—Plotinus conceives the relation from the perspective of intelligibles, i.e. as one wherein intelligible reality is present in sensible reality (or particulars) and, more precisely, as one whereby sensible reality has intelligible reality present in it by virtue of its being *causally dependent* upon that higher reality. It seems, then, that on this approach Plotinus is seen to resolve the Platonic problem (1) by considering the Platonic expression for the problematic relation—'x participates in *F*'—to be reducible to (or, perhaps, to be replaced by) the metaphysically more perspicuous expression '*x* is causally dependent (vertically) upon *F*'—perhaps by way of first reducing it to, or replacing it with, '*F* is present in *x*'; and then (2) by explicating '*x* is causally dependent upon *F*' in context with explicating the procession (or "derivation," O'Meara acutely prefers) of all reality from the One, down to its limit (sensible matter)—see *Plotinus: An Introduction*..., 22–27. This approach is ingenious, fruitful and, I think, right-headed. At the same time, however, there is something to be said for Plotinus' continued use of the Platonic participation-relation to connote features of the relationship which are not connoted (at least not evidently, or explicitly) by the presence-, or the causal dependency-, relation. Most especially, a key feature of Plotinus' understanding of Platonic participation that there ***is*** a sense in which Becoming possesses (manifests, exhibits, or is metaphysically related to) part of Being, and so may be perspicuously said to *part*icipate in Being. In the opening section of his *Parmenides*, of course, Plato worries about the fact that (in Greek) 'participates in' suggests or connotes 'has a part of', and so also that Being must somehow be comprised of 'parts' which are distributed or apportioned among sensible things—as a (physical) sail may be viewed as comprised of spatially extended parts (contiguous portions of

sail-cloth) which may be distributed over various objects were it draped over them. Plotinus, of course, would reject *this* depiction of Being as much as Plato did. But although Being does not come in parts which are distributed among sensible things as surface-portions of sail-cloth might cover various objects (i.e. one part uniquely covering, relating to, or exclusively possessed by each object), it is nevertheless true *of all sensible things* that each and every one of them possesses a *part of Being's nature*—most especially, we have just seen, that part of its nature (and so of its contents, the Forms) defined by Motion (and *sans* its—and their —Rest). Thus, '*x* participates in *F*' means, or at least entails, '*x* is *F*-in-Becoming' or '*x* is *F*'s Motion [*sans* its Rest]'. To be sure, this does not invalidate the approach I abstracted above from O'Meara's discussion. For one thing, Becoming participates in Being in this way (or sense) only *because* Soul seeks to 'learn' Being by expounding it, and so by means of (*dia*) a logos whose sequential (or sequencing) activity necessarily expounds it *sans* its Rest. For another, the possibility of two numerically distinct (sensible) particulars participating in the same intelligible—i.e. how it could be the case that *x* is *F*-in-Becoming and *y* is *F*-in-Becoming, where *x* is not (identical with) *y*—can, likewise, be *explained* in Plotinian terms only by understanding the natures and operations of the items comprising his metaphysical system of vertical causes (or derivations from the One towards sensible matter). The point, however, is that—as I argued previously regarding Plotinus' use of Plato's *demiurge* notion—his use of the Platonic 'participation' vocabulary should not be reduced, replaced, or dismissed too quickly; it expresses, or at least entails, important features of Becoming's relation to (archetypal) Being which are not obviously, or at least explicitly, conveyed by O'Meara's other expressions for that relation—even if those features' explanation(s) require other, metaphysically more perspicuous terms.

21. Similarly, Plotinus argues in *Ennead* I.8.6 that the Good (i.e. the One) just *is* substance (*ousia*) or the archetype of substance, and that the contrary to universal substance (as all "flows from" the One) is not another *type* of substance but *non*substance. Thus, Plotinus indicates in *Ennead* II.9.3, 10–13, that secondary (incomplete) life exists just so long as primal Life exists, since secondary things always exist just from the higher things themselves; and in *Ennead* III.3.7, he uses the image of things in our cosmos existing by "flowering from" their principles (*archai*).
22. Accordingly, Plotinus maintains that Intellect is defined by its own intellectual activity (*noēsis*), so that the "two" are in reality truly one (VI.7.41, 18–21).
23. Armstrong translation: *Ennead* III.8.8, 27–29.
24. See, for example, III.8.8, 31; III.8.9, 1–7; and VI.7.15 & 16.
25. See *Phaedo* 96–101, and *Timaeus* 49–53.
26. *Physics* II.1, 192b.

27. See, for example, IV.2.2; V.3.15, 13–15; V.3.17; V.6.3; VI.2.5; VI.7.17; and VI.9.1 & 2.
28. More generally, Plotinus argues that Soul is responsible for all order inasmuch as it is a power second in the order of real activity only to Intellect (IV.4.16, 18–20); for, Soul is that which took power into life from that higher life (i.e. Intellect's) which streamed into it (VI.7.31, 1–4).
29. Indeed, Plotinus argues, what Soul most essentially gives to our cosmos through its logos (Nature) is one, single life (see, e.g. IV.4.32 & VI.5.12).
30. Similarly, in *Ennead* II.1.3, 1–4, Plotinus argues that our cosmos shares in immortality (archetypal self-preservation) by virtue of the fact that, although it is always flowing, it flows only within itself and never "out of" or "away from" itself.
31. Although Soul does not itself possess size or mass, Plotinus argues, it must nevertheless be *present* wherever there is any size or mass (see IV.2.1, 70, & VI.5.9). Moreover, wherever Soul is present, it is *fully* present (or is present in its entirety or full self-identity). In this regard—and contrary to what some recent commentators on Plotinus suggest—Plotinus *contrasts* Soul's ubiquity with sweetness, whiteness, and the like in *Ennead* VI.4.1, rather than comparing it with them.
32. See Cicero's *Prior Academics*, especially chapters xxxi–xxxiii, xxxix, and xlviii.
33. Sextus Empiricus, *Outlines of Pyrrhonism* (Loeb Classical Library edition), I.vii, Iix, and Ixi.
34. Sextuas, *Outlines* I.xi.
35. Sextus, *Outlines* I.vi & I.xii, 29.
36. In *Outlines* I.xxix, Sextus attempts to diffuse possible objections to his acceptance of apparent anomalies as really anomalies in appearances by claiming that this is not a *dogma* but simply a *fact* (*pragma*) that everyone recognizes. Of course, by saying it is not a dogma, Sextus means that the Pyrrhonist restricts his belief in the reality of the anomaly to appearances and does not commit himself on whether any underlying causes or material substrates of the anomalous appearances are also anomalous (see *Outlines* I.xiv, 94). It is important to keep in mind the nature of Dogmatism as understood by Sextus whenever discussing his own Pyrrhonian concepts and claims, lest one be led into seeing inconsistencies in Sextus' philosophy that do not exist. Thus, David Sedley, for example, argues that it "is clear from Sextus' usage that *epoche* for the Pyrrhonist is no longer suspension of assent, since despite his '*epoche* about all things' he does assent to appearances, over which he has no control": "The Motivation of Greek Skepticism," *The Skeptical Tradition*, ed., Myles Burnyeat (Berkeley: University of California Press, 1983), 9–29; 19.
37. Sextus, *Outlines* I.vii, 14 & I.viii.
38. Sextus, *Outlines* I.xii, 33.

39. Sextus, *Outlines* I.xxx. Sextus' understanding of the "nonevident things of Dogmatism" is further emphasized in *Outlines* I.xxxii, where he argues that the principal difference between Pyrrhonism's non-Dogmatic reliance on appearances and Protagoras' philosophy that humans are the measures of all things is that Protagoras dogmatically held that the explanations (logoi) of appearances still *subsist in matter* (*hypokeisthai en tēi hylēi*). (Hence, again, we must avoid the sort of common interpretative mistake mentioned above in n36.)
40. Sextus, *Outlines* I.iv, I.ix, and I.xix, 190.
41. See Sextus, *Outlines* II.i, 7–9.
42. Sextus, *Outlines* II.i, 4 & 9.
43. Sextus, *Outlines* II.vii, 72 (R. G. Bury translation: Loeb Classical Library).
44. See Sextus, *Outlines* I.xiv, 115–117 & 122; I.xv, 172–177; and II.v, 34–41.
45. Indeed, Plotinus does not posit a real hypokeimenon to the sensible cosmos at all. Observable 'material' bodies may be *provisionally* conceived as mixtures of soul and matter; 'matter' does not denote a real substrate for Plotinus, however, but the darkening of Soul's illumination as it descends (see I.8.14).
46. Plotinus likewise argues in *Ennead* I.4.8, 10—when discussing pleasure and pain—that things do not look (or appear) in the same way to a good (or wise) person as they do to others.
47. For example, I have emphasized Plotinus' doctrine that the object of Intellect's activity is in fact just Intellect itself since in its archetypal activity (contemplation) Intellect "turns towards" the One as its archetypal source. How, then, can Plotinus also conceive Intellect's activity to have a number of objects—intelligible*s*, Being*s*, or Form*s*? In *Ennead* VI.2.19 & 20, Plotinus addresses this question by distinguishing two phases of Intellect. In its first phase, Intellect's Being or substance is conceived to be prior to all Forms or shares of Intellect (*pro pantōn hōs eidōn kai merōn*). In its second phase, Intellect is conceived to be the supplier and leader (*chorēgos*) of these items. Forms are "shares" of Intellect because, like Intellect, each contains the cause of its reality within itself (VI.7.2, 26); indeed, they may be conceived as just various Intellectual powers, or powers of Intellect (VI.2.21, 7; V.9.6). Elsewhere, Plotinus depicts Intellect's second phase as a matter of it "overflowing" with Forms—shares or powers of itself—or "unrolling" itself, because of the superabundant power of its Life (III.8.8, 34–38 & VI.2.21, 58). This second phase provides a foundation in Being for the variety and order of Soul's operation as it manifests itself—through its offspring—in the world of Becoming.
48. Thus Plotinus, like the Pyrrhonist, does not "assent" to nonevident things. Unlike the Pyrrhonist, however, Plotinus maintains that both speculative *and* practical wisdom (*sophia kai phronēsis*) consist in contemplating what lies within Intellect—its archetypal unity and overflowing power (I.2.6, 13). For,

even when judging appearances or sensory impressions, our reason—which formulates every judgment—contemplates Forms, since reasoning is essentially an Intellectual activity (see I.1.9, 19–22). Indeed, even *praxis* is in fact an "attempt at contemplation," we have seen in *Ennead* III.8.

49. See, for example, I.4.9, 28–30; III.5.7, 50–54; III.7.4, 1–13; IV.3.18; V.1.4; V.3.1, 5 & 6; and V.5.1 & 2.

50. Thus, Plotinus insists that sciences are *logoi* of Intellect present in our souls, by virtue of Intellect itself—the cause of all science—being present in the soul (VI.9.5, 10–13). For, all rationality—whether scientific or just "common judgment" on appearances—comes from Intellect (see III.6.2, 32); and this is so, not just for thought (*to noein*) "simply and absolutely considered," but for individual persons (see II.5.7, 50–54). How this conception of all "true thoughts" leads Plotinus to the self-transcendence of intellectually active souls and their resulting union with archetypal Intellect as the true agent of their intellections is articulated, for example, in *Ennead* IV.4.2. As for Nature, Plotinus argues that the diversity and order manifest in its product (our cosmos) is explained by the fact that Nature—itself a logos of Soul—contains within its unifying, productive power a model or pattern (*paradeigma*) constituted from logoi of Being, to which Nature is subservient in its operations (IV.4.12). The basis for Plotinus' notion that a logos of Soul (e.g. Nature) will contain its own set of Being's logoi is the two phases of Intellect noted earlier. Plotinus postulates that Intellect in its unfolded phase *is* the Form (*eidos*) of Soul, while in its primal phase Intellect *gives* Form to Soul by giving it logoi of itself (V.9.3, 31–39). In these terms, then, the hypostasis Soul just is the outflow from Intellect, and this outflow itself contains a complete set of logoi or shares (Forms) of Being—hence, so too do any images of Soul (e.g. Nature), which 'learn' them through their own intellectual acts. Finally, in our cosmos, Form (*eidos*) denotes that which composes and "brings bodies to unity" (see I.6.2)—or what completes them by giving them an identity and actuality (see VI.7.3). Hence, what in Soul are intellectual acts (*noēmata*)—Forms as logoi of Being—"in matter" are additional logoi—viz. of Nature's unifying power as subservient to the pattern of Form(s) from Intellect (see II.3.17 & VI.5.8).

51. I have argued in this essay that the bottom of Plotinus' vertical order contains natural processes, activities or Becomings manifesting themselves to sense experience in various sensible forms. However, when viewed as composing a horizontal order in abstraction from their vertical aetiology, we commonly conceive these processes to coalesce around "centers of passivity and sources of production" within our cosmos (VI.3.4, 36); and we conceive these centers in turn to be nothing but individuals or "thises" which are not "predicable of any other" but instead are themselves the proper subjects for all the predicates we apply to the sensible cosmos (thus, see VI.3.5). We commonly designate these "thises" or proper subjects by proper names (e.g. 'Socrates') or, insofar as we do consider them as images of Being (or partakers in Form),

by sortal terms (e.g. 'human'). As a result, we also can denote the Forms which "illuminate matter" through Nature with sortal names—for example, conceiving one of them to be the Form of Humanity (*anthrōpou eidos*) (VI.3.10, 18). But our common notions of proper subjects do not in reality designate independent or "underlying thises" (*hypokeimena*); and nor do these sortal discriminations really denote separate Beings, independent essences, or the like. Instead, the former are abstractions from observably close-ordered or tightly-unified processes or segments of Becoming as effected by Nature; and the latter reflect systematic or structural relations among objects and images of intellectual activity entailed by the metaprinciples defining Intellect's nature—i.e. Being, Same, Difference, Motion and Rest (see, for example, IV.3.5; IV.4.12; VI.6.5; and VI.7.9).

Index *Propria*

Index *Locorum* (*Enneads*)

Ennead I

Ennead II

Ennead III

Ennead IV

Ennead V

Ennead VI